D1651862

GOLDEN MULTITUDES

THE MACMILLAN COMPANY
NEW YORK · BOSTON · CHICAGO
DALLAS · ATLANTA · SAN FRANCISCO

MACMILLAN AND CO., LIMITED
LONDON · BOMBAY · CALCUTTA
MADRAS · MELBOURNE

**THE MACMILLAN COMPANY
OF CANADA, LIMITED**
TORONTO

Golden Multitudes

THE STORY OF BEST SELLERS
IN THE UNITED STATES

by Frank Luther Mott

1947

NEW YORK · THE MACMILLAN COMPANY

TO
FREDERICK AND
CATHERINE MIDDLEBUSH

The more and less came in with cap and knee;
Met him in boroughs, cities, villages;
Attended him on bridges, stood in lanes,
Laid gifts before him, proffered him their oaths,
Gave him their heirs, as pages followed him
Even at the heels in golden multitudes.

Shakespeare's Henry IV, First Part

PREFACE

ALTHOUGH best sellers have been a matter of interest to the curious for more than a half-century past, no comprehensive study of them has been attempted, except for a few lists which begin with the 1870's. This study, then, is in the nature of a pioneer expedition, and has the weaknesses and vulnerability of such ventures.

It is now six years since active work on the "canon" of best sellers on which this book is based was begun. A lifetime interest in popular reading had resulted in the publication of an extensive history of American magazines, of which two volumes still remain to be written, and a single-volume history of American newspapers. Many suggestive items and articles about highly popular books had been noted in the yellowing pages of the old newspaper and magazine files; as they accumulated, they seemed not merely to invite but to demand further investigation of such questions as what books had established themselves as best sellers throughout our country, and when, and how, and perhaps why. Moreover, it seemed that the historical surveys of the magazine and the newspaper called for similar treatment of the book sold in great quantities, in order to fill in the picture of popular reading. It might be called "completing the circle" except that one can entertain no idea of completeness in regard to this total task.

The fascination of the materials has heartened the writer throughout the years of digging, sifting and classifying data. And the encouragement given by the hundreds of persons who have furnished information, often at the expense of much time and effort, is beyond thanks. The generous response of publishers and their staffs to a barrage of inquiries which sometimes must have seemed nothing less than persecution has been extraordinary. Of the scores of publishers queried, only two seemed to wish to draw a veil over their connection with best sellers; their aloofness was not unbearable, since when the direct way to necessary information was barred more devious paths were often found.

I wish to record here my heartfelt thanks not only to my many patient correspondents in publishers' offices, but also to the librarians who, after the custom of their guild, have been so invariably and intelligently helpful in connection with this study. The only reason I do not print their names here is that there are so many of them.

Two names I must set down, however: that of Arthur J. Levin, who was my research assistant at the State University of Iowa when this work was begun, and that of my wife, Vera Ingram Mott, whose help on proofs and index was invaluable.

FRANK LUTHER MOTT

School of Journalism,
University of Missouri

CONTENTS

GOLDEN MULTITUDES

I. "VOX POP"

It is rare that the public sentiment decides immorally or unwisely, and the individual who differs from it ought to distrust and examine well his own opinion.

Thomas Jefferson to William Findley

WHEN Harriet Beecher Stowe was a very old lady, she sat in her garden one summer evening, a frail, bent figure in the fading light. To the man who approached her there she seemed to have something of that remoteness which often surrounds the aged.

The man himself was by no means young, but he was robust and florid of face; his white hair was uncovered, for he held his cap in his hand. He was a retired sea captain. He made little apologetic noises to attract Mrs. Stowe's attention, and then repeated a ceremonious, rehearsed speech. He said that many years ago he was one of millions who read *Uncle Tom's Cabin,* and that he had made a little pilgrimage here this evening in order to shake the hand that had written those famous pages.

Mrs. Stowe put out her hand—the smooth soft hand of an old lady—but as the captain, bowing, was about to take it in his, she drew it back.

"No," she said, "this hand did not write *Uncle Tom's Cabin.*"

"What!" shouted the captain in his surprise. "You didn't write it?"

"No," replied Mrs. Stowe gently.

"Why—why, who did, then?"

"God wrote it," said the old lady simply; "I merely wrote his dictation."

"Amen!" ejaculated the captain devoutly; and, bowing again, he turned and walked thoughtfully away.

Now, this idea of Mrs. Stowe's about the Lord's dictation, though not wholly an afterthought, had grown and flowered in the sunshine of the immense popular favor accorded the book. That she had felt a religious rapture in writing certain passages there can be little doubt; but it was the enormous success of the work that convinced her that God had been holding her hand while she wrote of Tom and Topsy and Legree and Little Eva. If she had found no publisher willing to print her story, the importance of writing it would never have been magnified; if it had sold only a few hundred copies, God would never have been credited with an assist. But it sold in unheard-of quantities and affected the minds and feelings of millions of readers; therefore it seemed to the little white-haired old lady in the garden to have been God's own handiwork.

This was not a strange or a new reaction. It sprang from the oldest of the democratic concepts—that of the essential rightness of the popular verdict, the divinity of the popular decision. *Vox populi vox dei,* ran the old tag; and if the popular acclaim which greeted *Uncle Tom* was thus the very voice of God, could it not be said further that the author had produced the book under divine guidance? Not that Mrs. Stowe reasoned it thus, but her feeling about the matter was within the pattern of this essentially democratic theology.

Your sincere and convinced democrat, your true glorifier of *demos,* must indeed hold some such opinion. If it is true that God made so many of the common people because He loved them, does it not follow that He also had a hand in the production of the mountainous literature of the common people—Scott, Cooper, and Dickens, *Uncle Tom's Cabin, Ben-Hur,* and *Gone With the Wind?*

But whatever far-fetched theology may be implicit in these attitudes, the "convinced democrat" has freely expressed, from time to time, certain ideas about the importance of popular literature. He believes that the people, conservators of primitive and essential truth, may be depended upon to take to their heart the really great books; therefore, that books long popular must be great books. He perceives a richness, a variety, a profusion, and an amplitude in popular literature that takes the individual reader out of his narrow routines and brings him into an awareness of humanity at large. He thinks that such a literature has far more to tell the sociologist, the historian, the philologer, and even the philosopher and the artist, than the more precious compositions for the few. In short, he is convinced that popular literature—the newspaper, the magazine, the best seller—has a special and paramount importance because it is popular.

But what shocking doctrine this is for the esthetician! He is not interested in the popular audience, nor much concerned with any audience save that of the elect. Professional literary critics, many of them interested chiefly in esthetic values, have had a difficult time with best sellers. Watching one book after another come to the top in the competition of sales, they have usually formed the exasperated conclusion that the great popular audience seldom or never recognizes first-class literature, has no conception of good taste, and never agrees with their own judgments. "The public is just a great baby!" exclaimed Ruskin in *Sesame and Lilies.*

Vox pop, indeed! There have been many to scoff at the idea. Alexander Hamilton, in a speech before the Constitutional Convention, referred to the old maxim, but declared that "it is not true to fact. The people are turbulent and changing; they seldom judge or determine right." And peppery General Sherman, writing a letter to his wife from the battlefield, deplored the interference of the people in public policy and exclaimed in disgust: "Vox populi vox humbug!"

Consistent with this attitude is the repugnance which some authors have expressed (was the taste of sour grapes fresh on their lips?) for the very idea of producing a best seller. A leading American publisher wrote in the *Atlantic Monthly* back in the days of Harold Bell Wright that "one of our best critics, himself the author of many books well known to lovers of the best literature," had recently declared: "I should consider myself disgraced if I had written a book which in these days had sold a hundred thousand copies." * Miss Queenie D. Leavis, fellow of Girton College, Cambridge, wrote a monograph a few years ago which was devoted to the reprobation of what she called "lowbrow" literature. Though the book as a whole was unusually snobbish, certain of its attitudes were by no means singular. " 'Best seller,' " said Miss Leavis, "is an almost entirely derogatory epithet among the cultivated." Apparently it is so regarded by certain of the uncultivated, too, for the author quoted a letter from a popular author whom she classified as belonging to a lower class of "middle-brows," though she charitably preserved his anonymity: "Personally, I object very strongly to being called a 'best seller,' as though my novels owed their success to some trick of pleasing the popular mind." † Not only do such words as "popular," "successful," and "best seller" fail to establish credit at the shop of the "highbrow" critic, but they are definitely intended as terms of disparagement. P. A. Sorokin, in his voluminous work *Social and Cultural Dynamics,* writes: "I rarely trouble myself with reading a best seller: its being such is a sufficient evidence of its commonplace character." That is only a little more philosophical than the famous remark of Richard Monckton Milnes anent the extraordinary vogue of Macaulay's *History of England:* "Macaulay's success has been enormous; indeed, such as to convince one his book cannot be worth much."

This is the Platonic doctrine of *demos* versus excellence. All spitefulness and snobbishness aside, why should not the censor of taste grow contemptuous of books on the best seller lists? Even such an over-all, long-time list as that which provides the basis for our present study of American best sellers begins with Wigglesworth's doggerel *Day of Doom,* includes among its eighteenth-century offerings a good deal of false religiosity and such sentimental seduction-formula stories as *Charlotte Temple* and *The Coquette,* gives us Weems' *Washington* but not Irving's, and foists upon us Maria Monk's sensational and fraudulent *Awful Disclosures.* Later Mrs. Southworth, Mary Jane Holmes, and Augusta J. Evans appear repeatedly, followed by E. P. Roe, H. Rider Haggard, and Marie Corelli. In the first two decades of the twentieth century, Harold Bell Wright and Gene Stratton-Porter were leaders, and we also pick up *Three Weeks* and *The Sheik,* along with *Pollyanna* and *Tarzan.* More recently "westerns" and detective stories have crowded in.

* George P. Brett, "Book Publishing and Its Present Tendencies," in *Atlantic Monthly,* vol. CI, pp. 454-62 (April, 1913).

† Q[ueenie] D. Leavis, *Fiction and the Reading Public* (London, 1932), p. 72. The remark about "best seller" as an epithet is on p. 34.

In such books the literary critic has little more than a curious interest. But there are others. Upon a re-examination of the over-all best seller list we find not only the "low-brow" successes but many admitted masterpieces. Most of the first-rank American and English authors appear at least once. Shakespeare is on the list, and so are Burns, Byron, Tennyson, and Browning; Poe, Longfellow, and Whitman; *Robinson Crusoe* and *Pilgrim's Progress;* Franklin's *Autobiography* and the *Federalist* papers; Emerson's *Essays, Moby-Dick, Walden,* and many another classic.

We must guard against two misconceptions: (a) that there is, at a given time, only one best seller public; and (b) that anybody can describe, or conceive of, such a thing as a typical best seller.

The year 1888, to cite but one example, saw the publication of five books on our list: A. C. Gunter's cheap and melodramatic *Mr. Barnes of New York,* Edward Bellamy's sociological and provocative *Looking Backwards,* Marie Corelli's pseudo-psychological *Romance of Two Worlds,* Mrs. Ward's controversial *Robert Elsmere,* and Hall Caine's sombrely sensational story *The Deemster.* Now it is conceivable that some widely-ranging readers should go through this whole list of five disparate books, or that a large group should read both Marie Corelli and Hall Caine or both Mrs. Ward and Edward Bellamy; but we seem to discern here at least three fairly distinct best seller publics at work. Such things happen so often that we must conclude that books which appeal to readers of dull esthetic sensibility may become best sellers without crowding out those which are intended for a more discriminating audience.

It follows that there is no such thing as a typical best seller. There may be a typical "low-brow" best seller for a given period, or a typical fictional best seller for another period; but the idea of a general type for the popular book is clearly a fallacy. It is as wrong in its application to best sellers as it is in the fields of newspapers and magazines: variety, a dominant characteristic of all popular literature, makes limitation to a single type impossible. The idea of the typical best seller seems to spring from the tendency of the literary critic to lump all books that seem to him beneath notice, except for the odd phenomenon of their popularity, into one group and label them "the best sellers." This is, statistically, a mistake.

That a long-time, over-all list of best sellers has an advantage over the more ephemeral monthly lists in the inclusion of classics is obvious. A book whose popularity withstands the years commonly becomes a classic. As Samuel Johnson said in his life of Addison, "About things on which the public thinks long it commonly attains to think right."

Though the lines are hard to draw, it may be said fairly that about half the books on our best seller list have sufficient value to enable them to hold more or less assured places, at present, in the history of English and American literature. Our measure of assurance on such a point declines, of course, with the recency of a book's publication. Let us check our canon of best sellers against the lists of "best books." Some years ago Asa Don Dickinson, using more than fifty "authoritative lists," compiled a catalogue of "one thousand best books" in all literatures, ancient and modern. Sixty per cent of our best sellers to 1905 are found in Dickinson's lists.*

The long and the short of it seems to be that some best sellers are great books, while many others are good books according to ordinary literary standards. Still others—perhaps thirty per cent—fall pretty definitely outside the literary pale. Literary values alone do not determine best sellers, of course; and there is clearly a great variation from case to case in the extent to which that element is influential in book sales.

But popular reading furnishes subject matter for important and fascinating studies. Especially is the thoughtful observer of the workings of a democratic society concerned with the mass impact of so much reading matter upon the public. Only the cynic and the heedless can disregard popular literature. Here the sociologist finds material for his inquiries into the mores, the social historian sees the sign-posts of the development of a people, and students of government observe popular movements at work. As the best sellers are passed in review in the ensuing pages, readers may note their reflection of historical incidents and the development of American society, as well as the reappearance in them of such unifying elements as religion, sensation, self-help, good narration, and so on. These things bind our whole story together.

Nor can the literary critic be oblivious to the implications and problems involved in a survey of best sellers. A profound respect for people in mass, or for the wide stream of life, is by no means inconsistent with an appreciation of lone genius, or of the highest development of ideas. Indeed the two must go along together, and discrimination is a part of the study of masses. If a writer tries to describe a crowd, he will provide many details which are distinctively crowd details; but he will point up the whole with faces, voices, costumes, bits of color which are conspicuously individual. The study of people begins for all of us with a knowledge of persons, but we cannot know persons thoroughly without an understanding of people. A knowledge of popular taste, or tastes, is likewise essential to the study of masterpieces; nor is there any inconsistency in respectful attention to popular trends, on the one hand, and honor for what we esteem as best, on the other. Without either, the study of literature is incomplete.

After all, *vox populi*, if something less than *vox dei*, is at least a voice to which we must hearken.

* Asa Don Dickinson, *One Thousand Best Books* (New York, 1924). Our best seller list numbers 233 books before 1905, including 140 on the Dickinson lists. Few books published after 1905 are in those lists; but if we take it up to 1924, when Dickinson's book was published, we have 142 out of 259, or 55 per cent. One is forced to be more dubious about the books of the last twenty years.

II. WHAT IS A BEST SELLER?

A book, and, hence, any article of merchandise, whose sales are among the highest of its class.

Webster's New International Dictionary

IF YOU are willing to accept on faith the canon of best sellers on which this book is based, you may skip this chapter, which is uninteresting; but if you wish to know the principles that have governed the making of the list, you will have to read on through thick and thin.

Like many another superlative, the term "best seller" has steadily declined in its emphasis and significance. When it first came into use about 1910, it meant a book that was well ahead of its contemporaries in sales figures; now it often serves to indicate merely that a book is doing well. In publishers' publicity designed for the trade, the term has an exciting quality; but most of us, inured to the enthusiasms of promotion, accept Webster's recording of popular usage and speak of a book as a best seller if its "sales are among the highest."

But the highest in sales where and when? And for how long? The Colossal Department Store's best seller among Saturday's book bargains? Or the world's biggest seller in a round hundred years?

A single bookstore may have a best seller on a single day, or for a week or a month, without anyone getting excited about it. That particular title may be doing merely a little better than its fellows. Nothing spectacular—just a good item which, for that moment and in that spot, is actually a best seller. But let the enterprising reporters of the book trade check with a hundred bookshops in thirty cities scattered over the country and take those reports and use them as the basis for a list of leaders, and then national best sellers begin to emerge. That is what happened when, in 1895, the *Bookman* began its lists of "Books in Demand" in various cities. Later yearly summaries were added, and eventually the initial computations were put on a weekly basis.

But is a weekly, or even a yearly, leader necessarily entitled to the accolade "best seller"? Not a few of the yearly leaders since 1895 have fallen far below the half-million figure in total sales. In a dull year the top book may sell fewer copies than those which occupied second and third place the preceding year. Or it may not be a dull year at all, but a year lacking an outstanding pace-setter. Shall we, then, insist on the limitations of the calendar and declare that we must have one best seller, or ten or twenty best sellers, every twelve months, regardless of total sales? *

After all, it is the total sale that makes any long-time, over-all selling record; mere leadership for a year may make no more than a "better seller" among the

* Even P. A. Sorokin, who condemns best sellers for their "primitive and elementary

books of a decade. In most cases, a popular book's total sales do not fall neatly within a calendar year; and thus our yearly lists, valuable though they are, do not tell the whole story or the most important story.

When we place the whole calculation of best sellers on the basis of total sales, we get a different set of problems and a different picture. Strictly speaking, there is only one all-time best seller—the Bible—and all others are only "better sellers" or "good sellers." But bibles, manuals, textbooks, and so on, belong to distinct categories of their own and must have separate study; they must be omitted from lists of books devoted to general reading. When we take them out of our list, we still have the whole of popular literature—the area in which our inquiries are to be made.

But the compilation of a list of all-time big sellers presents many difficulties. How many copies shall we require a book to sell before it wins a place on such a list? When Edward Weeks made up his over-all best seller list for the period from 1875 to 1934, he set the figure at half a million.* This was, on the whole, a very satisfactory figure for the period he studied, but it is too high for the years before 1875 and too low for the 1930's and 1940's. It is obvious that we must have a scale adjustable by decades, according to the growth of population. It is unreasonable to require the same minimum sales for a best seller in 1800, when the population of the United States was 5,300,000, that we require in 1900, when it was 76,000,000. (Literacy records are not adequate enough to justify their use throughout the list.)

We have set the sales figure required to make a book a best seller at one per cent of the total population of continental United States for the decade in which the book was published. This gives a slight advantage to books published late in the decade, since census data for the eighties, for example, were gathered in 1880 and yet we must keep the same measurement through 1889 before raising it abruptly in 1890. But it is a usable method, and probably as fair as any that can be devised. We must have an arbitrary figure; and the one fixed upon serves our purpose, which is to screen out from ten to twenty-five of the highest-selling books of each decade. The screen provided works very well: though the number of best sellers is naturally low in the Colonial Period, after the 1780's it falls below ten in only four decades and rises above twenty-five in only three.

Compiled on such a principle, our list contains 324 titles. It is set forth chronologically, with the sale required for each decade, and with dates, authors, titles, and original publishers, in Appendix A. Total sales are not given in this list. In most cases exact figures are completely and hopelessly nonexistent. Estimates were made of the sales of many hundreds of books in connection with the

---

character," admits a "qualification": he thinks "the span of time" over which "the cultural value" is spread may limit his conclusions—though he is plainly unaware of the full importance of that limitation. See *Social and Cultural Dynamics* (New York, 1941), vol. IV, p. 273.

* Edward Weeks, *This Trade of Writing* (Boston, 1935).

studies on which this canon was built, and many of those estimates are given on the ensuing pages. But in the compilation of the lists the inquiry was not how many copies, precisely, were sold, but were enough copies of the book sold in the United States to reach the minimum set up for best sellers in the decade in which it was published? If the data procurable indicated an affirmative answer, the book was placed in the main list (Appendix A); if not, it was either discarded or relegated to a list of "better sellers" (Appendix B). This secondary list contains the dates, authors, and titles of books which have not, so far as the compiler has been able to determine, topped the hurdle set up for best sellers, but which have come close to it.

However, to satisfy the impatience of those readers who must have some definite facts about top best sellers immediately, we shall here interpolate a list of the books which have enjoyed sales of over two million copies each in the United States. Here are the twenty-one books of general reading which occupy a kind of best seller heaven of their own, arranged alphabetically by titles:

Alice in Wonderland, Carroll
Ben-Hur, Wallace
Christmas Carol, Dickens
Gone With the Wind, Mitchell
How to Win Friends and Influence People, Carnegie
In His Steps, Sheldon
Ishmael and sequel *Self-Raised,* Southworth
Ivanhoe, Scott
Last of the Mohicans, Cooper
Little Women, Alcott

Mother Goose
One World, Willkie
Plays, Shakespeare
The Robe, Douglas
Robinson Crusoe, Defoe
See Here, Private Hargrove, Hargrove
Story of the Bible, Hurlbut
Tom Sawyer, Twain
Treasure Island, Stevenson
A Tree Grows in Brooklyn, Smith
Uncle Tom's Cabin, Stowe

Sources of data on which the lists are based are widely scattered. Newspaper and magazine files and historical and biographical literature yield occasional notes and leads. Contemporary catalogues and later bibliographies are invaluable.* Given the number of editions of a given title and their dates, we have a good start; we know a good deal about common sizes of editions of the various presses in successive periods. Problems vary from period to period. In Colonial times importers' sales were important; and for them we have the booklists in newspaper advertising as a chief aid. In the nineteenth century, as the regular

---

* Invaluable for books before 1800 is Charles Evans' *American Bibliography.* Almost as helpful for many items is Joseph Sabin's *Dictionary of Books Relating to America.* Trübner's *Bibliographical Guide to American Literature, 1817-1857* occasionally affords help. Constantly useful are O. A. Roorbach's *Bibliotheca Americana, 1820-1861;* James Kelly's *American Catalogue, 1861-1871; American Catalogue, 1876-1910; United States Catalogue of Books in Print, 1912,* and its *Supplements;* and the *Cumulative Book Index* since 1898. Of course, the catalogue of the Library of Congress is helpful always.

publishing houses grew up, helps multiply. Publishers proud of their achievements made their boasts. The spectacular work of the pirate printers of Scott and Dickens was often the subject of comment in the periodicals. Advertisers sometimes gave actual figures of sales. John P. Jewett & Company gave such data on the titlepages of successive editions of *Uncle Tom's Cabin*.

But the trumpet-blowing of a jubilant publisher does not have the same degree of reliability as the financial statement of a bank. One has to guard against loose and easy statements. We all have a way of making big things bigger by talking about them. What an easy word "million" has become! Most of us are "millionaires," not in the sense of riches, but in our free and unthinking use of big figures. The investigator in the field of best sellers learns to distrust the statement that a book "must have sold a million copies."

And records are often faulty, or non-existent, even for books published in the last forty or fifty years. Moreover, some books have passed through the hands of several firms, complicating an investigator's problem. And hundreds of publishing companies have sunk beneath the waters of oblivion in the century and a half of active American book publishing, and usually they have carried their records with them down to Davy Jones's locker. A few contemporary publishers add to our embarrassments by citing a "rule of the house" which requires sales figures to be kept a close secret; in such cases we must base our estimates on statements of their less inhibited authors, reports currently accepted in "the trade," unofficial figures which employes are sometimes willing to furnish, and so on.

But persistent searching, the unremitting help of interested contributors of information, and the kindness of custodians of source materials have made a best seller canon possible. It is made up largely by means of estimates based on data drawn from a great variety of sources.

Six observations must now be made by way of explaining the list.

First. It omits all bibles, prayer-books, hymnals, almanacs, cookbooks, "doctorbooks," textbooks, dictionaries, and manuals. These are important, and a chapter will be devoted to them at the end of this book; but they have no place in a general reading list.

Second. Although it is a list of American best sellers, more than a third of its titles are by English authors. French and German writers contribute a number of books, and a few other nationalities are represented. But sales, which make a best seller, are American sales; distribution abroad, even of American books, is not included in our totals.

Third. The date given each book is that of its first American publication. This date fixes the minimum of sales necessary to make the book a best seller, since our requirement is based on decade population figures. It is obviously impossible to divide total sales by years or even by decades, and so later sales must be thrown back to the date of first publication. If it is objected that a book of late-blossoming popularity gains an unfair advantage by its dating in an earlier decade when the minimum was lower, we can only reply that no other method seems practicable, and that probably less than a score of books have got into the list by benefit of this "throwing back" method. Usually a prophet has not been without honor in his own generation, or his book without acclaim in the decade of its publication; and many works now called classics were popular books when first issued.

But what if they were not? We must get rid of the idea that best sellers are only sensational ephemerae. Some of them are, of course, but some grew to be best sellers by the accretions of many years. Anyone who wishes to study the "quickies" alone can easily pick them out and concentrate upon them; but the long-term augmentative best sellers must be studied too. A *Ben-Hur*, starting slowly, but riding high among best sellers for nearly a quarter of a century; a book like Emerson's *Essays*, a moderate *succès d'estime* when first issued, but built up to best seller stature by publication in many low-priced editions after its emergence from copyright; a *Leaves of Grass*, which its author labored for many years to popularize, taking its place as a best seller only through multiple editions after his death—these, and phenomena like them, are also full of significance and interest. The fundamental point, which we must not forget, is that a book becomes a best seller by selling better than other books. Rapidity of sales is a subject of importance,* but it must not be allowed to obscure the fact that a book read by millions over a hundred-year period is also a major phenomenon of popular culture.

Fourth. It will be observed that the sales of some books have benefited by their use for study or supplementary reading in the schools. Doubtless such use has sometimes reduced these works to the level of mere textbooks; but it is not always so, and many of us can remember classes in literature with deep pleasure. Most readers make their first acquaintance with Shakespeare in the schools, but it would be more than finical to distinguish between copies read out of the classroom and in it, at school and at home. The point is that Shakespeare was read—as one reads literature, let us hope, rather than as one studies a textbook in mathematics or geology.

Fifth. Fond inquirers after the books of Oliver Optic, Nick Carter, G. A. Henty, Laura Jean Libbey, "The Duchess," and such prolific writers may be disappointed when they look for those charmed names in vain. Or the books serializing the adventures of Elsie Dinsmore, Rollo and Jonas, Frank and Dick Merriwell, the Rover Boys, Tom Swift, and Nancy Drew. Many popular series have run to amazing totals, but single titles in such catalogues usually fall far short of the totals necessary to put them on our best seller list. Even Horatio Alger, Jr., the sales of whose 120 or more books are said to have run well into

---

* There is doubtless some difference in the quality of a readership concentrated in time (hundreds of thousands reading a book in the same month) and that of a readership dispersed over a long term. It is analogous to the question of whether propaganda is more effective in a brief but powerful barrage or in long-continued repetition.

the millions, is represented on the list only by *Ragged Dick*. Nor is Peter Parley, with his 170 books,* on the list at all.

Sixth. And what about the little books or pamphlets the contents of which would ordinarily fill only twenty or thirty fair-sized pages? We cannot call them "books" in the usual sense and place them side by side with other works of full size, even though they are commonly published separately. And so we reluctantly omit such children's classics as *Goody Two-Shoes* and *Little Black Sambo;* famous poems like *Elegy in a Country Churchyard* and *The Rime of the Ancient Mariner;* such widely distributed public papers as Washington's *Farewell Address* and Webster's 1850 speech; stories like Hale's *The Man Without a Country,* Mrs. Andrews' *The Perfect Tribute,* and van Dyke's *The Story of the Other Wise Man;* pieces like Hubbard's *A Message to Garcia* and Edwards' *Aeneas Africanus;* such religious essays as Drummond's *The Greatest Thing in the World* and Knight's *The Song of Our Syrian Guest;* and such humorous ephemerae as *Josh Billings' Allminax* and Chic Sale's *The Specialist.* The line is not always easy to draw; but the distinction must somehow be made between pamphlets and fascicles on the one hand and regular books, whatever the binding or format, on the other.

III. RELIGION AND SENSATION IN COLONIAL TIMES

> Cast over therefore once every day the number of thy dayes, by subtracting those that are past (as being vanished like yesternights dream) contracting them that are to come (sith the one half must be slept out, the rest made uncomfortable by the *troubles* of the *world,* thine own sicknesse, and the death of friends) counting only the present day thine; which spend as if thou wert to spend no more.
>
> Bayly's "Practice of Piety"

THOUGH a press was set up in Cambridge, Massachusetts, as early as 1638, it published few books designed for general reading. Its output for the first twenty-five years consisted chiefly of almanacs, catechisms, single sermons, and three editions of *The Whole Booke of Psalmes,* known as "The Bay Psalm Book." That many books which were not manuals were sold by importers and read by the Colonists in the seventeenth century we know, and some of these eventually appear on our best seller list under later dates which indicate their first publication by American printers. But the first press was so busy supplying needed almanacs, catechisms, and hymnals, and printing religious books "in the Indian language" that it did not get around to publishing more general books that might become best sellers until the 1660's.

* Many were textbooks, and they doubtless account for a large part of the seven-million distribution Goodrich claimed before his death.

When they came, they were, of course, religious in character. Of the first twenty best sellers, twelve were designed primarily to inculcate piety and teach doctrine.

In these days we can understand that religion may be transcendently important in the life of a given individual, but it is more difficult for us to comprehend how fully it can enter into and form the life of a whole people. That is what it did in early Colonial society. Piety was not a mere Sunday garment; it was of the texture of the life of the folk. Nor was theology a mere system of abstruse theories; it was intimate and deeply personal, and nobody could quite escape it.

The first American best seller was the Rev. Michael Wigglesworth's extraordinary exposition of Calvinistic theology in doggerel verse entitled *The Day of Doom.* There is nothing to indicate that it was written for children, though Cotton Mather, who preached Wigglesworth's funeral sermon, expressed therein the hope that it "may find our Children till the *Day* itself arrive." Doubtless what Mather had in mind was the fact that for many years before its author's death (as for a hundred years afterward) children were required to learn this versified statement of the savage Calvinistic dogma along with their catechisms. This phase of New England education is horrible to contemplate, for the sickly parson of Malden spared no ultimate cruelty in his sulphurous picture of the hatefulness of an angry God.

Yet after all, despite its frightful doctrine and its street-ballad form, the poem does have imaginative sweep and a firm sincerity. Thus suddenly cometh on the awful Day:

> For at midnight breaks forth a light
>   which turns the night to day,
> And speedily an hideous cry
>   doth all the world dismay.
> Sinners awake, their hearts do ache,
>   trembling their loins surpriseth;
> Amazed with fear by what they hear,
>   each one of them ariseth.
>
> They rush from beds with giddy heads,
>   and to their windows run,
> Viewing this light, which shines more bright
>   than doth the noon-day Sun.
> Straightway appears (they see't with tears)
>   the Son of God most dread,
> Who with his Train comes on amain
>   to judge both Quick and Dead.
>
> Before his face the Heav'ns give place,
>   the skies are rent asunder,
> With mighty voice and hideous noise,
>   more terrible than Thunder.
> His brightness damps Heav'n's glorious Lamps
>   and makes them hide their heads;
> As if afraid and quite dismay'd
>   they quit their wonted steads.

And soon the trump is sounded, the dead rise from their graves, the living are hunted out of their hiding places and dragged, shrieking, before the awful throne; then the tremendous court scene of the Last Judgment is described vividly and unflinchingly. The sheep are separated from the goats, and after a brief explanation of the dogma of election and grace, the Lord seats the elect on thrones to help him judge the others. The throngs of reprobates approach in separate herds—the hypocrites, the "Civil honest Men," those whose "true intent was to repent" but who had not found time to do so, those who were misled by men of learning, those who lived among disbelievers and dared not profess Christ, those who relied merely upon God's mercy, those who plead that it was not their fault that they were predestined to hell, and "a number numberless of Blind Heathen." Here is where the author gets in all his exposition of doctrine, for each group pleads its case and then the Lord refutes each before he condemns it to the infernal concourse.

And at last appears the most pitiful crowd of all—the babes who had died in infancy and who were reprobates solely by the doctrine of original sin. They plead:

> If for our own transgressi-on,
>   or disobedience,
> We here did stand at thy left hand,
>   just were the recompense;
> But Adam's guilt our souls hath spilt,
>   his fault is charg'd upon us;
> And that alone hath overthrown
>   and utterly undone us.

And there sits Adam on his throne, one of the elect, while the babes point to him and say "Not we, but he, ate of the tree." The Lord thereupon explains patiently to them this knotty point of the Calvinistic creed; yet when he comes to pronounce sentence, he suddenly and surprisingly relents a little—but just a little—for he concludes:

> . . . therefore in bliss
>   you may not hope to dwell;
> But unto you I shall allow
>   the easiest room in Hell.

Then the fire is lighted, the sulphurous fumes ascend and the caitiffs are dragged away to the pit, all the great multitudes of them. The Judge grows impatient:

> But get away without delay,
>   Christ pities not your cry;
> Depart to Hell, there may you yell
>   and roar Eternally.

The last stanzas, describing the felicity of the saints, are not enough to stop our ears to the cries of the damned.

It is easy to see why the Rev. Mr. Wigglesworth's opus was so popular.

Its content was a theological doctrine not only universally accepted in that time and place but of the highest importance to its readers. Its presentation had an emotional drive, a vividness of imagery, and a compelling narrative movement all combined in great effectiveness. Here were verses far more sensational than the ballads about murders and hangings that were sold on the street, and Wigglesworth's influence over generations of New Englanders came largely from his shocking sensationalism.

The Day of Doom was first published, probably in 1662, in an edition of 1,800 copies, nearly all of which were sold within a year. This would be about three per cent of the population of New England—a phenomenal distribution in so short a time. Later editions reached a growing public, and the bibliographer Charles Evans declares that Wigglesworth's masterpiece was "more popular throughout New England for a century than any other book, with the exception of the Bible." Wigglesworth wrote other popular books, notably an essay which did not fall far below best seller rank called *Meat out of the Eater*— a "meditation" on the "Necessity, End, and Usefulness of Affliction."

Another piece of religious doggerel was extremely popular in New England in the eighteenth century. It was called *The History of the Holy Jesus;* * the titlepage continues, "A pleasant and profitable Companion for Children; composed on Purpose for their Use. By a Lover of their precious Souls." The first eight editions of this little juvenile, though issued by various Boston printers, apparently used the same set of rude wood-cuts, which suggests a system of borrowing as a trade courtesy. Some of the pictures are curiously inept, as that of the full-rigged ship to illustrate the incident of Jesus on the Sea of Gallilee; it was doubtless picked up from some other publication. Others look as though the engraver had used a jack-knife. As to the verses, they have neither skill nor imagination; they merely put the leading events of Jesus' life into indifferent rhyme. The book's popularity must have been due to its novel presentation of standard religious matter, its pictures, and its cheapness. There were other rhymed theological works for children, too, as the younger Benjamin Harris' *The Holy Bible in Verse* (1717).

Sermons ranked high in the output of the Colonial press—higher for many years than any other single department of letters. If proof were necessary to show the primacy of Religion with a capital R in the lives of those early New Englanders, the amazing fact that two collections of sermons were American best sellers at the beginning of the eighteenth century † should be amply convincing, for even such sermons as are easy to hear are commonly hard to read. These two collections were Baxter's *A Call to the Unconverted* and Russell's *Seven Sermons*.

---

* This book was anonymous, and is not to be confused with William Smith's doctrinal prose book for adults of the same title.

† A little later collections of sermons by John Tillotson and Ebenezer Erskine came close to the top rank in popularity.

Richard Baxter was a famous English preacher and a voluminous writer. His greatest book is an English classic—*The Saint's Everlasting Rest*. This and the *Call* were both best sellers in England; but *Saint's Rest*, which was well ahead of the other in the mother country, was almost passed by in the new world in favor of the more evangelical book. *A Call to the Unconverted*, though sometimes verbose, is as clear and lucid an argument to "turn and live" as could well be marshaled—sometimes eloquent, and always utterly sincere and earnest. Four Boston editions of the volume were issued within a period of thirty years, besides two Cambridge editions of a translation into the Indian language by John Eliot. The Rev. Edmund Calamy, writing of this book, said: "Mr. *Eliot* translated it into the *Indian* language; and Mr. *Cotton Mather*, in his life [of Eliot] gives an account of an *Indian* prince, who was so well affected with this book that he sat reading it with tears in his eyes till he died." It is clear that this is a death-bed story, and reference to Mather's *Magnalia* reassures us that the chief was already on such a bed before he began reading the well named and effective *Call*.

The other collection, by an obscure English parson named Robert Russell, is inferior to the *Call* in clarity and vigor. But it was a smaller book, more publishable and more merchantable in early Colonial days, and it outran the more modest record of Baxter's volume. The *Seven Sermons*, moreover, emphasized the morbidly awful subject of "the unforgivable sin." Russell carried to an extreme the universal technique of the homiletics of those times in dividing and subdividing his topics. He pursued the trembling sinner from Firstly through Sixthly, to the Use and the Application. He passed easily from exhortation to imprecation:

No sooner is this dreadful sentence past but away you must be gone, away you shall be hurled by the Devils, with the rest of your damned crew, down into the lake that burns with fire and brimstone, and never have ease nor end.

Somewhat less rigorous and harsh were the two most popular devotional essayists of the Colonial period—John Flavel and James Hervey. The "painful and eminent" Flavel, a notably original English homilist, had an amazing following in America for a hundred and fifty years. Tedious and heavy he seems today, but he won his great audience by what then seemed a clever application of theology to the vocations of common life. His first and greatest success was *Husbandry Spiritualized*, in which the work of the farmer was made to illustrate religious doctrine. This book was first published in America in 1709, though imported copies had been in the bookshops for twenty or thirty years before that. Flavel's *Works* appear in the lists of titles advertised by Colonial booksellers probably more often than any others except those of Dr. Watts, and they continued popular well into the nineteenth century.

Flavel's books were staple long before Hervey's appeared, but the latter's *Meditations and Contemplations* certainly equaled in popularity any single work of his predecessor. "This book," declared an American publisher of it in

1794, "has been more read since it was first published than any other in the English language, excepting the Holy Bible." The first American edition of Hervey's masterpiece, by William Bradford, of Philadelphia, in 1750, contained "Meditations Among the Tombs," "Reflections on a Flower Garden," and "A Descant Upon Creation" in the first volume; and "Contemplations on the Night," "Contemplations on the Starry Heavens," and "A Winter Piece" in the second.

These titles indicate that Hervey was by way of being a nature-lover, and he did indeed fill many pages with descriptions of nature mingled with pious observations. But Hervey's was by no means a romantic attitude toward nature: the gardens which he depicts are of the formal kind, his sunsets are conventional, and his graveyards well cared for. Nature is always properly behaved and on show in Hervey's pages, where the commonplace is dressed up in an inflated style. One other book of Hervey's, though not a best seller, was widely read and discussed in the eighteenth century—*A Dialogue Between Theron and Aspasio*. A discussion of the Calvinistic doctrine of imputed righteousness, it drew replies from John Wesley, Robert Sandeman, and Joseph Bellamy, with rejoinders, and so on, to the extent of a considerable literature. Sandeman's reply was itself almost a best seller.

What a difference between Hervey's essays and those of Francis Bacon! It must be admitted that Hervey was far more popular than Bacon in eighteenth-century America. But Bacon's *Essays* were durable: they were popular in England before John Smith and his companions made the first English settlement in the new world, some of them were published by the elder William Bradford three years after he set up the first press in Philadelphia, and they have been reprinted and read and quoted ever since. They owe their place on the best seller list, however, to their later popularity. In the cheap-publishing "revolution" of the 1880's, for example, John B. Alden offered a paper-bound edition in his Elzevir Library at fifteen cents, and a little later cloth-bound editions at twenty-five cents were common. Truly, this is a book for the ages. The *Essays* are scarcely dated; even their style wears well. As their author said in his "Epistle Dedicatory" to the third edition, they "come home to men's business and bosoms."

Bradford's first American edition of the *Essays* was a curious book. They were included in what a modern publisher might call an "Essay Omnibus." It was edited by Daniel Leeds, the almanac maker of Philadelphia, and entitled *The Temple of Wisdom*. It included much fantastic mysticism, an essay on "the arts and sciences" by Jacob Boehme, some of the *Divine Poems* of Francis Quarles, and *Essaies and Religious Meditations of Sir Francis Bacon, Knight*. It was not the best possible introduction to the illustrious American career of Bacon's *Essays*.

Two guides to holy living are also among the best sellers of this period. They are the first of a long train of books, many of them very popular, which advise their readers on the details of every-day life; but these first are devoted wholly to religion.

The Practice of Piety, masterpiece of Lewis Bayly, Bishop of Bangor, is an extraordinary book. It went through more than seventy editions in England, and was translated into many foreign languages, including Eliot's abridgment for the Massachusetts Indians. It had a wide influence and was imitated in many briefer compilations. It was often published in form and binding similar to that of the Bible, and many readers regarded it as having equal authority.

The book is composed mainly of meditations and prayers for the various parts of the day and for all occasions. A meditation, be it understood, is an edifying line of thought. We have here meditations and prayers for the morning, for the day, for the evening, for the Sabbath, "on going to bed," for fasting, for holy feasting, "on taking Physick," as well as "Seven sanctified thoughts, and so many spiritual sighs fit for a sick man that is like to die," and "the last speech of a godly man dying." It is a ready-made coat of piety, or a whole closet-full of them for all occasions.

It would all seem rather silly and futile but for the real fire and imagination, the tremendous emotional drive, and the deadly reiteration, in some of these pages. Let us take some quotations from the second chapter, "Meditations of the misery of a man not reconciled to God." "O Wretched Man!" it begins, "where shall I begin to describe thine endless Misery? Who art condemned as soon as *conceived*, and adjudged to *Eternal Death* before thou wast born to a temporal Life?" Follows a concise and clear exposition of the doctrine of original sin, to show the unconverted reader just where he stands at the beginning; then an outline of the chapter, for Bishop Bayly was, like all preachers of his day, a great divider and subdivider. By that method, however, comes his terrible cogency; each point is a blow that cannot be countered, until the sinful reader is utterly confused and confounded.

First, then, the author invites us to "take a view of those Miseries which accompany thy body, according to the four ages of thy Life," and he begins with infancy:

What wast thou, being an *Infant*, but a *Brute* having the Shape of a Man? Was not thy Body conceived in the *Heat of Lust*, the *Secret of Shame*, and *Stain of Original Sin*? And thus wast thou cast naked upon the Earth, all embru'd in the *Blood of Filthiness* . . . so that thy Mother was ashamed to let thee know the manner thereof: what cause then hast thou to boast thy Birth, which was a *cursed Pain* to thy Mother, and to thyself the Entrance into a troublesome Life? . . .

But the infant reprobate survives and reaches youth, though "what is Youth but an untamed *Beast*? all whose actions are rash and rude, not capable of good Counsel when it is given, but *Ape-like* delighting in nothing but Toyes." Therefore the youth is "kept under the rod"—and the author, having for years been in charge of a boys' school and having gained some reputation for violence, should know. This passage ends with the declaration that the youth's state of servile bondage to his elders is "not worthy the description," and passes on to manhood:

> What is Man's Estate but a Sea, wherein (as Waves) one *Trouble* ariseth on the neck of another, the latter worse than the former . . . Now *Adversity* on the left hand frets thee; anon *Prosperity* on the right hand flatters thee: over thy Head *God's Vengeance* due to thy Sin is ready to fall upon thee; and under thy feet *Hell's Mouth* is ready to swallow thee up. And in this miserable Estate whither wilt thou go for Rest and Comfort? The *House* is full of Cares, the *Field* full of Toil, the *Country* of Rudeness, the *City* of Factions, the *Court* of Envy, the *Church* of Sects, the *Sea* of Pirates, the *Land* of Robbers . . .

It is this piling up of details in series, of which short quotations can give only a partial notion, that enables the author to achieve his favorite effect of knocking the reprobate out with a dizzying volley of sockdolagers. But he does not allow his victim to throw in the sponge until the time comes; let us look upon him now in old age. This meditation is worth quoting entire:

> What is *Old Age* but the Receptacle of all *Maladies?* For if thy Lot be to draw thy Days to a long date, in comes old bald-headed *Age,* stooping under *Dotage,* with his wrinkled Face, rotten teeth, and stinking Breath, *testy* with Choler, *dimm'd* with blindness, *wither'd* with dryness, *absurded* with deafness, *overwhelm'd* with sickness, and *bowed* down altogether with weakness, having no use of any Sense but of the sense of pain: which so wracketh every member of his Body, that it never easeth him of Grief till he hath thrown him down to his *Grave.*

But the miseries of his old age are but a foretaste of what is in store for the sinner: now he must die:

> After that the *Aged Man* has conflicted with long Sickness, and, having endured the brunt of *Pain,* should now expect some Ease, in comes *Death* (Nature's *Slaughter-Man,* God's *Curse,* and Hell's *Purveyor*) and looks the Old Man grim and black in the face . . . And, as thinking that the Old Man will not dispatch to go with him fast enough, Lord, how many darts of Calamities doth he shoot through him, Stitches, Aches, Cramps, Fevers, Obstructions, Rheums, Flegmes, Collick, Stone, Wind? &c. O what a ghastly sight it is to see him in his Bed, when *Death* has given him his mortal *Wound!* . . .

Now follows a description of the reprobate with the death-rattle in his throat which is scarcely less than revolting. The soul, knowing that she must now come forth from the body, is beside herself with fear, for she sees the devils lying in wait for her to carry her away. She looks everywhere frantically for help; she appeals to those parts which had been her fleshly support—the feet, hands, eyes, ears, tongue—addressing an impassioned speech to each, but all in vain. "O *Tongue,*" she cries, "who was wont to brag it out with the *bravest,* where are now thy big and daring words?" But after the long-drawn agony, the soul is dragged off to the bottomless lake burning endlessly with fire and brimstone, while "the loathsome *Carcase* is laid in the grave." And finally we come to a picturesque but sometimes subtle description of the infernal goal of the reprobate—

> into which *bottomless* Lake after that thou art once plung'd, thou shalt ever be falling down, and never meet a *bottom;* thou shalt always weep for pain of the *Fire,* and yet gnash thy teeth for the extremity of *Cold* . . . There thy lascivious *Eyes* shall be afflicted with

sights of ghastly Spirits; thy curious *Ears* shall be affrighted with the hideous noise of howling Devils and the gnashing teeth of damned Reprobates; thy dainty *Nose* shall be cloyed with the noisome stench of Sulphur; thy delicate *Taste* shall be pained with intolerable Hunger; thy drunken *Throat* shall be parched with unquenchable *Thirst* . . .

In contrast with all this lurid sensationalism, the meditations of the man reconciled to God, which follow, are tame indeed.

Bayly is too melodramatic and perfervid, whether in imprecation or in the day-by-day meditations; but it is easy to see what an impression his vivid passages might make. The other best seller in this field is far calmer, shorter, and more commonplace. Samuel Hardy's *Guide to Heaven* is concerned chiefly, as its titlepage indicates, with "Good Counsel how to close savingly with Christ; Some Short but Serious Questions to ask our Hearts every Morning and Evening; and especially Rules for the strict and due Observation of the Lords-Day."

John Bunyan, a young rowdy with a special talent for profanity, was married about 1648 to a respectable young woman of religious family. John was a penniless tinker; his bride, no better provided in money or household goods, brought to him as her sole portion two books, left her by her father. One of them was Bishop Bayly's *Practice of Piety*. In these books they often read together, as Bunyan tells us in his autobiographical *Grace Abounding*, adding that "they did beget within me some desires to religion." How much influence the powerful and tumultuous Bayly had upon him Bunyan himself probably did not know; but one can scarcely doubt that his frequent readings in *The Practice of Piety* had no inconsiderable part in bringing on those spiritual anxieties, those "sinkings" and dreads and terrifying dreams, which are detailed in *Grace Abounding*. Thus Bayly had his part, though indirectly, in *The Pilgrim's Progress*.

Of the first dozen best sellers in our list, Bacon's *Essays* and *Pilgrim's Progress* are the only great classics. Not that Bunyan's masterpiece was so recognized at first; for more than half a century it was regarded as mere popular reading (a best seller, forsooth!) and sneered at by fine judges like Mr. Addison, the critic, and Mrs. Montagu, the bluestocking. But at long last the critics also took it up; they named the virtues that its humbler readers had only felt, and enthroned it. By that time it had sold hundreds of thousands of copies.

Three years after its first publication in England, *Pilgrim's Progress* was reprinted in the new world, by Samuel Green, "upon assignment of Samuel Sewall and to be sold by John Usher, of Boston"; and Bunyan himself tells us with no unbecoming pride that it was received in America with "much loving countenance." Since then edition after edition has come from the press. Library of Congress cards record more than 120 American publications of the book; but there have been many more, some priced at ten and twenty cents. In 1928 the New York Public Library made an exhibition, in honor of the tercentenary of Bunyan's birth, of the more than five hundred editions in its own collection, including translations into forty languages.

The simplicity and picturesque narrative of the work have made it long a favorite with children. It pleased the boy Ben Franklin so much that he began a long career of book-buying by putting his pennies into the purchase of the remainder of Bunyan's works in small volumes. Isaiah Thomas was the first in America to bring out an edition abridged for children, deleting the long theological dialogues between Christian and Hopeful, which were by 1798 no longer required reading for the little ones, and which both children and adults will skip today. Children invented games based on the story. In the first chapter of *Little Women,* Mrs. March says to the girls:

"Do you remember how you used to play Pilgrim's Progress when you were little things? Nothing delighted you more than to have me tie my piece-bags on your backs for burdens, give you hats and sticks, and rolls of paper, and let you travel through the house from the cellar, which was the City of Destruction, up, up to the house-top, where you had all the lovely things you could collect to make a Celestial City."

"What fun it was, especially going by the lions, fighting Apollyon, and passing through the Valley where the hobgoblins were," said Jo.

"I liked the place where the bundles fell off and tumbled down the stairs," said Meg.

Today *Pilgrim's Progress* is still read, abridged editions of it are for sale in the ten-cent stores, its imagery and language have passed into the general cultural stock of the people. Its greatness is in its universality: we all grow weary under our burdens, but we must all drag through the Slough of Despond, climb the Hill of Difficulty, fight with Apollyon and Giant Despair, and pass through the dread Valley, to see, dimly, the Delectable Mountains afar.

Pilgrim's Progress attracted its great audience partly through the interest in adventure and conflict. These elements are also the essential stuff in two accounts of Indian captivities which were very widely read in Colonial America. "Captivities" were popular in America for two hundred years. They were nearly always sensational narratives, with their brutal massacres, tortures, and abductions. In the early ones, there was much religion, for the incidents were presented as examples of the workings of divine providence, and were liberally besprinkled with texts.

Mrs. Mary Rowlandson has the distinction of being the first American author to write a prose best seller. No copy of the first edition of her book has been preserved, but here is the titlepage of the second edition, issued in the same year as the first:

The Soveraignty and Goodness of GOD, Together With the Faithfulness of His Promises Displayed; Being a Narrative Of the Captivity and Restauration of Mrs. Mary Rowlandson. Commended by her, to all that desires to know the Lords doings to, and dealings with Her. Especially to her dear Children and Relations. The second Addition, Corrected and amended. Written by Her own Hand for Her private Use, and now made Publick at the earnest Desire of some Friends, and for the benefit of the Afflicted. . . . Cambridge, Printed by Samuel Green, 1682.

There are unforgettable things in Mrs. Rowlandson's narrative. The unrelenting realism with which this parson's wife tells of the barbarous slaughter of her friends and neighbors by "those merciless Heathen," the starvation-hunger which the narrator suffered, the skilful needlework by which she earned a little kindness from her captors, her abstention from tobacco because she had (by the grace of God) conquered her early liking for a pipe—these things help to make a convincing and intimate story. The writer of the preface of the *Captivity and Restoration* had much to say of "this Gentlewomans modesty" even though she came before the public on the printed page; it would have been a pity if such considerations had restrained her.

Almost as generally read in the Colonies was the Rev. John Williams' *Redeemed Captive,* published twenty-five years later. It lacks the sinewy narrative and toughmindedness of its predecessor; but here again the massacre is impressive, and the sufferings of the narrator on long forced marches to the North are memorable. A chief element in Williams' book is the account of his resistance to the efforts of the French-Canadian Jesuits to convert him.

One other sensational adventure book remains to the best seller list of the earliest period—Jonathan Dickinson's graphic narrative entitled, in its first edition, *Gods Protecting Providence Man's Surest Help and Defence in the times of the greatest difficulty and most Imminent danger; evidenced in the Remarkable Deliverance of divers Persons,* etc. Since the words "Remarkable Deliverance" are displayed in large type on the first titlepage, it would seem as though they might be accepted as the short title for the book; but the definitive and scholarly recent edition edited by Professor and Mrs. Andrews * calls the work *Jonathan Dickinson's Journal; or, God's Protecting Providence.* That is probably the most satisfactory solution of the problem posed by the bewildering lot of titles given the book in its various reprints.

The preface of this book, like its titlepage, is loaded with piety, with its numbered "special providences" and its deathbed story of Robert Barrow, the Quaker missionary. But once we are launched on the narrative, neither texts nor preaching impede our course. The story is in the form of a diary, and is often dramatic and always full of interest.

Dickinson, a Quaker merchant with connections in both Jamaica and Philadelphia, was returning from the West Indies with his wife and baby, a kinsman, ten Negro slaves, one Indian girl, and Barrow the missionary when their ship went down in a storm off the coast of Florida. The Dickinson party and nine sailors reached the shore, where they were set upon by a horde of naked Indians, who "came down to us in a Furious manner, having a dismall aspect and foaming at the mouth." The defenseless travelers, just escaped from an angry sea, were seized and bound. The men were placed in a sitting posture on the ground, the Indian chief in the midst; and behind each man bent a savage, his knees at his captive's shoulders, flourishing a great knife with one hand and laying hold of his victim's head with the other. Thus they paused, waiting the word of

* New Haven: printed for the Yale University Press. Edited by Evangeline Walker Andrews and Charles McLean Andrews. 1945.

the chief. But that word never came, though the scene held and all were "like men amazed the space of a Quarter of an Hour."

This seemed, as well it might, a miracle in their behalf. But all the prisoners were stripped before they were released, and all the food they had saved was taken. A cold rain set in, the kinsman and the old Quaker were ill, and the ship's master had a broken leg. Nevertheless, the party managed to make its way in seven weeks to St. Augustine, repeatedly robbed and harried by the Indians, seized and threatened and then released. It became very cold. The efforts to preserve the life of the child make a harrowing recital. Five of the party perished during the travel of the last day and night before the remainder reached St. Augustine, naked, emaciated, and half-frozen.

Dickinson thought these Indians were cannibals, and he and his party were paralyzed with fear whenever they saw a big fire built by the savages. It was soon perceived that the Indians were under the influence of the Spanish and hated the English, and Dickinson tried to disguise his nationality by various clever dodges. Yet he did find some traces of English influence among the Indians, as in this instance:

At which time I heard a saying that came from one of the chief Indians, thus "English Son of a Bitch" which words startled me, for I do believe they had some of our nation in their possession.

Dickinson's book was originally published by Reinier Jansen, a second-rate printer whom the Philadelphia Quakers had put in charge of a press they had set up after the elder William Bradford had tired of his battles with them and moved to New York. It was the first order of business for Jansen in his new job; the Quakers ascribed much importance to it because Barrows was one of their most admired characters, and his sufferings while carrying the testimony of the Friends afar made required reading for all the sect. It was immediately reprinted in London, where it went through seven editions in the eighteenth century. It was translated into Dutch and German. In America there were four Philadelphia editions, and local printers reissued it in several Colonies and eventually as far west as Ohio. It was doubtless sold as a chapbook by the peddlers.

The fact is, it was one of the best adventure stories of its times. It compares favorably with Mrs. Rowlandson's well known narrative and is much better than that of John Williams; but, unlike those books, it has been wholly neglected by historians of early American literature.

Before we leave this group of early American best sellers, we must note that twelve of the first twenty were by English authors. This fact should serve to remind us of two important considerations. First, the American Colonists were chiefly Englishmen pioneering on a new English frontier. Even though some of them were refugees, England was "home" to them. Bayly and Bunyan were their own national writers. In the second place, the religious feelings which are dominant in these best sellers were characteristic not of American society alone, but of the English people of this era. *Pilgrim's Progress* grew out of the religious experience of a large proportion of the English people in the seventeenth century.

It is too easy to think of New England piety as something apart—a localized phenomenon. Religion was extremely important in the other Colonies, too: all of them were English. For years the Quakers ruled the press in Philadelphia much as the Puritans controlled that of Boston. At least one of William Penn's books became a best seller not only among the Quakers but among the deeply pious outside the Society of Friends—that masterpiece of faith and reason entitled *No Cross, No Crown*. Sold in English editions, frequently reprinted in both Philadelphia and Boston, it is still a religious classic.

IV. A NOTE ON BOOK PUBLISHING IN THE AMERICAN COLONIES

> Here dwelt a Printer, and, I find,
> That he can both print books and bind;
> He wants not paper, ink, nor skill;
> He's owner of a paper-mill:
> The paper-mill is here, hard by,
> And makes good paper frequently.
> > *From John Holme's reference to*
> > *William Bradford in his "The*
> > *Flourishing State of Pennsylvania"*

THE first books published in the American Colonies were issued from the Cambridge printing office which had been set up as an adjunct of Harvard College. Five of our first six best sellers came from this shop, which was, for a quarter of a century or more, the only printing establishment in the Colonies. It carried on until 1692.

It was a firmly controlled press—an integral part of the New England theocracy. As has just been observed, the earliest Philadelphia presses were conducted under stern Quaker eyes. And the "royal," or official, printers in each of the Colonies were more or less under censorship.

But despite controls exerted or attempted, the Colonial printers, booksellers, and importers managed to give the readers of the new land about what they wanted. Often the printer was a bookseller, and nearly all booksellers were importers; so the three functions were not infrequently combined in one man's activities. The booksellers were much more numerous than the master printers; and through their importations they furnished an important tie with the mother country. A perusal of the lists of titles of imported books which they published in their newspaper advertisements shows a more catholic taste among readers than we usually suspect: Boston shops did not limit their stocks to Puritan literature nor Philadelphia stores to Quaker books. Novels, scandalous memoirs, plays, and joke-books were prominent in the offerings of most Colonial book-shops, whether in New England, the Middle Colonies, or the South.

If the printer was not a bookseller himself he would usually work closely with his town's bookshops. Printers would place specific booksellers' names in their imprints, thus beginning the now almost universal distinction between the printer and the publisher (or distributor) of a book; for example, the first American edition of *Pilgrim's Progress* was "printed by Samuel Green," but was "to be sold by John Usher," a Boston bookseller. These printers and booksellers were local men, intimately acquainted with their home communities, and knew what their public wanted. Much of their work was cooperative: together they would supply the hawkers who sold cheap books through the countryside, and together they would plan and execute the subscription books—a very common device for taking the risk out of a project by a pre-publication guarantee.

But there were no specialists whose facilities were wholly devoted to the mak-ing and distribution of books, as are those of the men in the modern book indus-try. When a master printer equipped himself with type and a press, he expected to turn out all possible kinds of printed matter—commercial forms, broadsides, a newspaper, pamphlets, almanacs, laws, primers, sermons, small books, and possibly a magazine. The output was slow at first; but if the printer's business grew and he was able to add more type, a second press, and a couple more journeymen, it poured forth with more speed and profusion. Thus a successful printer in a big town might print a considerable number of small books in a year, and possibly one or two large "books of price."

And as printing spread into the new towns and villages of the interior, small-scale book publishing went with it. The little one-press shop, with only one "hand" besides the proprietor, would set up a book during the dull midsummer days, print an edition of a few hundred, and have it ready for the Christmas trade. Such work played a real part in the production of best sellers, for the books chosen for reprinting were often those which had a growing popularity.

Though no great publishing houses could develop in this non-specializing, diffused economy, some of the printers in the big seaport towns became notable as printers of books.

Boston was the most bookish town of all. Samuel Green, the greatest printer of the Cambridge press, was the founder of a large family of good printers, who scattered throughout the Colonies. His son Bartholomew, of Boston, printed the first edition of *The Redeemed Captive* and (with John Allen) the first American issue of Russell's *Seven Sermons*. John Foster, first Boston printer, performed a similar service for Hardy's *Guide to Heaven*. Thomas Fleet pub-lished the first American *Mother Goose*. John Boyle and the Drapers were fairly active in book production, as were the Fowles, Daniel and Zechariah.

Philadelphia became the second Colonial town to establish printing when William Bradford set up a press there in 1685, but his difficulties with the

Quakers combined with an offer of New York's official printing to take him to the little town on Manhattan and to make him the father of New York's great publishing business. Reinier Jansen, who printed the Quaker adventure story, *God's Protecting Providence,* followed Bradford in Philadelphia; but Andrew Bradford, son of William, was a greater Philadelphia printer of books, and Benjamin Franklin a greater yet. Robert Aitken was an enterprising publisher; he issued the first English-language Bible to be produced in America. Robert Bell, printer and book auctioneer, was a shrewd picker of best sellers and has a notable list of first American editions to his credit.

Among famous New York publishers of books before the Revolution were James Parker, Franklin's protégé; Hugh Gaine, the Revolutionary turncoat; and James Rivington, son of a famous English publisher.

In the latter part of the eighteenth century, a few outstanding publishers are found among the general printers—Isaiah Thomas, of Worcester, Massachusetts, who, with his partner Ebenezer Andrews, also had a printing house in Boston; Hugh Gaine, who always seemed to land on his feet and begin making money after any misfortune; Franklin & Hall, of Philadelphia, the senior partner now retired; Christopher Sower, the great German printer of Germantown, Pennsylvania; and others, such as T. & J. Swords in New York, Manning & Loring in Boston, Hudson & Goodwin in Hartford, and so on.

But all this time the little printers were busy, too. To take but one example, Dr. Watts's *Divine and Moral Songs for the Use of Children* was printed, in the eighteenth century, not only in Boston, New York and Philadelphia, but also in Charleston, South Carolina; Hartford and Norwich, Connecticut; Newport, Rhode Island; Rutland and Bennington, Vermont; Dover and Keene, New Hampshire; and Worcester, Springfield, Charlestown, Newburyport, Haverhill, and Leominster, Massachusetts.

Population was sparse, illiteracy percentages were high, and few could afford luxuries; but it is clear that the people generally had a high regard for books. Prices in the middle of the century had a common range of two to eight shillings, depending on size; but such a noble tome as Cotton Mather's *Magnalia* (imported) sold for twenty shillings. Though these prices do not seem inordinately high, books were harder for a poor man to own than they are today. An eighteenth century best seller obviously could not be the creation of a quick mass enthusiasm or sudden fad; it had to grow slowly through a decade or a century. Yet it was then, as now, the creature of popular taste and the result of popular approval.

V. FOR CHILDHOOD AND YOUTH

I in the burying-place may see
  Graves shorter there than I;
From Death's arrest no age is free;
  Young children, too, may die.

My God, may such an awful sight
  Awakening be to me!
O that by early grace I might
  For death prepared to be!
  "New England Primer"

CHILDREN all have a hard time. To learn how to live in a strange world is probably more difficult for the babe than any undertaking he may have to engage in later, when his faculties are developed. The little one has to struggle not only against such evils as colic, kisses, and castoria, but also against all the perversities of arrogant parenthood.

Even the Spartan custom of exposing infants alone outdoors for a few nights to see if they were tough enough to live was not worse than some more modern customs. The child in the typical New England Colonial home had almost as hard a lot. The doctrine was that the youngster was full of original sin. To cast out the old Adam from his soul required much use of the rod from the tenderest age, a daily program which allowed no time for idle play, and religious teachings which placed so much emphasis on hell-fire and early deathbeds that many children were frightened into nervous convulsions. The Puritans were a great people, and our country is indebted to them for many good things; but when we consider the way they treated their children, we feel an inclination to agree with the wit who said that it would have been better if Plymouth Rock had landed on the Pilgrims.

The first book for children published in America was the Rev. John Cotton's catechism, *Milk for Babes, Drawn out of the Breast of Both Testaments, Chiefly for the Nourishment of Boston Babes*. Ten other catechisms were published by American presses before the end of the seventeenth century. The little ones had to learn the catechism, with its hair-splitting, logic-chopping theology, so that early death—and great numbers of them did succumb to early deaths—would have no terrors.

This spectre of imminent death was continually held before the child. Every night he prayed:

  If I should die before I wake
  I pray the Lord my soul to take.

That prayer, as well as the lines which preface this chapter, and many other pieces designed to frighten small readers, were printed in the *New England*

Primer, most popular of all Colonial textbooks. Collections of the deathbed scenes of children were common. Widely circulated over many years, though probably not quite a best seller in the Colonies, was *A Token for Children,* by that popular English divine, James Janeway. Its subtitle ran: "Being an exact Account of the Conversion, Holy and Exemplary Lives, and Joyful Deaths of Several Young Children."

One of the most popular little juveniles of eighteenth century America was *A Token for Youth; or, Comfort to Children.* Its longer subtitle reads: "Being the Life and Christian Experience of the Wonderful Workings of the Spirit of God on Carteret Rede, from her Infancy to her Last Moments, as it was faithfully taken from her own Mouth, by her Mother." When poor little Carteret was four years old, she was asked what was her "greatest enemy," and dutifully replied, "Sin." But very evidently her greatest obsession was death. One evening she cried for something her mother "tho't not fit to give her, fearing it would make her sick." Mrs. Rede asked her if she was ready to die.

> She immediately answer'd Yes, if the Lord will take away Sin from me, then I shall go to Heaven, for I would not die in my Sins; for if I should, God hath said that such shall depart to the Devil and his Angels; The Lord knows all we do and say, and our very Thoughts; his presence is everywhere; I must meditate upon God in the Night watches . . .

Carteret "took great delight" in reading the Bible before she was five. She died at the age of six, after having said a great many pious but unhappy things. Two months before she closed her eyes upon her painful and distorted world,

> As she was going to Bed, she said the Devil does sometimes tell me he will appear to me, that makes me so afraid; she said also that I have dream'd that the Devil was pulling me into Hell, but God kept me and held me fast.

It is a pleasure to turn anywhere away from this cabinet of perversions. There might be better books to turn to than the *Divine and Moral Songs, Attempted in Easy Language, for the Use of Children,* by Isaac Watts, D. D., for Dr. Watts, too, often reminds the children of early death and gaping hell:

> 'Tis dang'rous to offend a God,
>   Whose pow'r and vengeance none can tell;
> One stroke of his almighty rod
>   Will send young sinners quick to Hell.

The repugnance of the Puritan mind to pleasure is admirably illustrated in Watts's verses. The doctor had a feeling for beauty, but he always sternly subdued that inclination, making it serve only incidentally to teach lessons about duty and worship. Not one of these little songs echoes to laughter, or lends itself to the games and play which are so necessary to the child's orientation. Every one of them seeks to enjoin a task, correct a fault.

The *Divine and Moral Songs for Children,* published in tiny books with crude little woodcuts, were popular in America for a hundred and fifty years. They were easy to reprint, and many scores of printers issued editions. The

Stone collection of the *Songs* in the library of the American Antiquarian
Society exhibits two hundred and forty editions, English and American. Still
remembered are a few of the pieces that got into the readers and copybooks;
they are the ones which are less "divine" and more "moral," as:

> Let dogs delight to bark and bite,
>   For God hath made them so;
> Let bears and lions growl and fight,
>   For 'tis their nature to.
>
> But Children, you should never let
>   Such angry passions rise;
> Your little hands were never made
>   To tear each other's eyes.

The remainder is more pious. Similar is a stanza in Song XVII:

> Birds in their little nests agree;
>   And 'tis a shameful sight
> When children of one family
>   Fall out, and chide, and fight.

The best known of all is this one:

> How doth the little busy bee
>   Improve each shining hour,
> And gather honey all the day
>   From ev'ry op'ning flower.
>
> How skilfully she builds her cell!
>   How neat she spreads her wax,
> And labors hard to store it well
>   With the sweet food she makes!
>
> In works of labor or of skill,
>   I would be busy, too,
> For Satan finds some mischief still
>   For idle hands to do.
>
> In books, or work, or healthful play,
>   Let my first years be past,
> That I may give for ev'ry day
>   Some good accounts at last.

The undeniable fact that *Mother Goose* seems as out of place in this pious
literature as a gypsy dancer in the pulpit of Old South has led many to question whether Thomas Fleet actually did publish *Mother Goose's Melodies for
Children* in Boston as early as 1719. No copy of this edition is known to be
extant—which is not strange, as the books that children like are commonly
worn out with loving use—but we have a record of the volume by a bibliophile
whose veracity we have no cause to impeach.* In fact, there seems little sound
reason to doubt that saucy Tom Fleet launched a small edition of *Mother
Goose* in the very teeth of the Puritan gale. We should not forget that not quite
everybody was pious in the New England of the "theocracy." Tom Fleet dis-

* See *The Colophon*, Autumn, 1935, for the detailed story of this literary incident.

liked the clergy; his newspaper was the brightest in New England; he was an active printer and a wit. It was just like him to print the *Mother Goose* rhymes, and thus become the first of the long line of American publishers of the nonsense verse which is dearest to the hearts of little children.

There used to be a tale about Fleet's mother-in-law, whose name was Vergoose, being the original "Mother Goose." Possibly she was, for some of the rhymes seem to refer to Boston neighbors of the Fleets and Vergooses. That there was a French "La Mère l'Oye," who told fairy stories a half century earlier, seems not especially pertinent.

Mother Goose never became really popular in America in the eighteenth century. The oldest extant copy is one of the Thomas edition of 1785 in the American Antiquarian Society library. The popularity of the rhymes seems to have started with the Munroe & Francis edition of 1827,* to grow and grow with the passing years. Few books have surpassed it in sales in modern times. One recent edition, *The Tall Book of Mother Goose,* with Rojankovsky's pictures, sold over 325,000 copies in about two years.

Few books, aside from manuals and schoolbooks, had a steadier sale through the eighteenth and nineteenth centuries in America than *Aesop's Fables.* Imported English editions in both Latin and English, but especially the English texts of Croxall and Draper, were common before the Revolution; and it is probable that American editions appeared in Boston before the middle of the eighteenth century. Isaiah Thomas tells us that when his old master Daniel Fowle started a paper in Portsmouth, he wanted some little picture to place between the words *New-Hampshire* and *Gazette* in order to "dress up" the paper's frontpage name-plate; but the only thing in the shop that would serve his purpose was a set of type-metal cuts that had been used for an abridgment of Croxall's *Aesop.* So he inserted the one of the crow and the fox; when that was worn down, he put in the one of Jupiter and the peacock; and so on for years. Fowle had been in the printing and publishing business in Boston in the forties, and started his Portsmouth paper in 1756; when the double-duty cuts were first used in Boston nobody knows.

The pictures were quite as important as the stories in the Aesop books. Badly drawn and badly cut, they were nevertheless interesting; and there was always one for each and every fable. Grownups probably considered the "Applications" by Dr. Croxall, which appeared in many American editions, important; but we may be allowed to doubt whether the children bothered to read them at all. They were often longer than the fables which they "ap-

---

* Oliver Goldsmith is thought to have had something to do with John Newbery's London edition of *Mother Goose,* which largely set the standard form of the rhymes in English. Goldsmith is also believed to have been the author of *Little Goody Two-Shoes,* which should have been included in our list of best sellers had we not resolved to omit pamphlets. *Goody Two-Shoes* (1771) was perhaps no slenderer than Fleet's *Mother Goose* (1719), but enough enlarged and augmented versions of the latter have been published to require its inclusion in our list.

plied," extremely preachy, and mostly tiresome; yet Croxall's views of the manners and politics of his times are now and then in a good vein of satire.

Indeed, old Croxall's notes, if put together differently, might have made one of those behavior books of which our eighteenth-century forebears were so fond. Eighteenth century? We shall do wrong to speak of such guides to the principles of living as confined to any one period. They dot the entire list of best sellers—from *Practice of Piety* to *How to Win Friends and Influence People*. Dale Carnegie is a child of the twentieth century, as Bishop Bayly was of the seventeenth, but the voice of the earnest personal adviser is much the same.

The earliest of these behavior books were wholly devoted to telling their readers how to live the religious life; but by the middle of the eighteenth century, there were many which gave more attention to what might be called secular manners. There was, for example, *A Father's Legacy to His Daughters,* by Dr. John Gregory, famous physician and professor of physics in the University of Edinburgh. The Introduction begins:

MY DEAR GIRLS, you had the misfortune to be deprived of your mother, at a time of life when you were insensible of your loss, and could receive little benefit, either from her instruction, or her example. Before this comes to your hands, you will likewise have lost your father.

The legacy which this father leaves his daughters, therefore, is a little book of advice and admonition. It begins with a section on religion, liberal for the times, and goes on to discuss female delicacy, amusements, friendship, love, and marriage. Though quaintly sentimental, the little book contains a deal of sound sense. Dr. Gregory had been affected by the new educational ideas of his times. "I do not want to *make* you any thing: I want to know what Nature has made you, and to perfect you on her plan."

The ideas of the period of "sensibility" are pervasive in the *Legacy*. "When a girl ceases to blush, she has lost the most powerful charm of beauty," says the good doctor. A girl should not fall in love; that is man's prerogative. "A man of taste and delicacy marries a woman because he loves her more than any other. A woman of equal taste and delicacy marries him because she esteems him, and because he gives her that preference." * If, despite all, she loves him, "let me to advise you never to discover to him the full extent of your love; no, not although you marry him. That sufficiently shows your preference, which is all he is entitled to know. If he has delicacy, he will ask for no stronger proof of your affection."

The *Legacy* was vastly admired both in Great Britain and the American Colonies. Indeed, it continued to be reprinted in the United States well into the middle of the nineteenth century. Helpful as these fatherly admonitions

---

* Compare Mr. B.'s declaration of his love for Pamela, in which he asserts "true love" on his part, but asks only "preference" on hers.

may have been to the girls, we are happy to know that Dr. Gregory also left them good legacies in pounds sterling.

Published about the same time, and even more popular in America, was Lord Chesterfield's *Letters to His Son*. Gregory, often published in little twelvemos of forty or fifty pages, is very slight in comparison with Chesterfield's four volumes. The two works are, indeed, not comparable: Chesterfield's *Letters* are full and ripe and well phrased, fresh and quotable even today. They had their great American circulation in abridged editions, necessitated by both their bulk and the questionable nature of some of this father's advice on relations with women. But the abridgement of the Rev. George Gregory (no relative of the Gregory of the *Legacy*) and his American follower, the equally Rev. Jedidiah Morse, was singularly judicious; they did not squeeze all the juice out of the *Letters*, and their version found a place in thousands of home libraries under the title *The Elements of a Polite Education*.

The illegitimate son to whom the letters were written, as part of his father's effort to make him "a perfect gentleman," died while still a young man. Not until then did Lord Chesterfield learn that he had a daughter-in-law and two grandsons; but, whatever his feelings may have been in regard to his son's secret marriage, he made due provision for the widow and a generous settlement upon the two grandsons. It was this widow who, after Lord Chesterfield's death, defied his family and published the letters despite court actions and threats of reprisals. Whatever her motives were, Mrs. Stanhope did a service to literature.

Commonly ascribed to Lord Chesterfield is another best seller among behavior books. The titlepage as it appeared in what is probably the first American edition ran:

The Family Companion; or the Oeconomy of Human Life, on the perusal of which, and following the instructions laid down therein, all persons may be healthy, wealthy and wise, even from the Crowned Head to the meanest subject. Every man will be here instructed in the true methods of attaining happiness and wisdom in whatever situation in human life the Almighty has been pleased to place him. Containing the sentiments of an ancient Bramin and translated from an Indian manuscript found among the archives deposited in the Grand Temple, in the Province of Lasa, in the County of Thibet. Transmitted in a letter from an English gentleman now residing at Pekin in China to a noble Earl in England. Boston: Printed and sold by D. Fowle in Queen Street. 1751.

The most popular literary hoax of its times, the *Oeconomy of Human Life* is composed of precepts, maxims, and aphorisms arranged under many heads, such as Modesty, Emulation, Prudence, Love, Woman, Husband, Father, Temperance, and so on. The sayings seem to be more or less imitations of those in the wisdom literature of the Old Testament, and the compendium doubtless gained in authority from its resemblance to the Book of Proverbs.

The wise continueth to live from his first period; the fool is always beginning.
Labor not after riches first, and think thou wilt afterwards enjoy them. He who neglecteth the present moment throweth away all that he hath. As the arrow passeth through

the heart, while the warrior knew not that it was coming; so shall his life be taken away, before he knoweth that he hath it.

Robert Dodsley, the famous London bookseller and writer, probably collaborated with Chesterfield in this curious work. Indeed he may have written the whole of Part I. In the year after its first London publication, it was reprinted by Fowle in Boston, by Franklin and Hall in Philadelphia, and by Parker in New York. Sabin lists forty separate editions of it in America before the year 1800.

The appetite that readers must have had for dissertations upon manners in the late seventeen hundreds! Or was it not, rather than an appetite that anyone had for them, a stubborn determination on the part of parents that their children should read and study these codes of politeness, morals, and thrift? From "Poor Richard" to Mrs. Piozzi's "Letter to a Gentleman Newly Married," from John Cotton's *Vision of Marriage* to Hannah More's *Essays*, youth of both sexes were instructed on how to be good, thrifty, elegant, sentimental, and happy. Very often two or three of these little works were bound together, undoubtedly for birthday and holiday gifts. The young ladies seem to have been more frequently the objects of parental solicitude, and love and marriage the most popular topics. Gregory's *Legacy* was premier in a field which included such items as Lady Pennington's *Unfortunate Mother's Advice to Her Daughters*, Swift's *Letter to a Young Lady Newly Married*, Moore's *Fables for the Female Sex*, Witherspoon's *Letters on Marriage*, Fordyce's *Sermons to Young Women*, and Halifax's *Address to a Daughter*. And the magazines and newspapers printed serially not only these works, but also many others, often in the form of the periodical essay.

We need have little doubt that the young people read these things, and were influenced by them. They yielded to parental persuasion; but they must have read the behavior books as a duty, and then turned eagerly, and often clandestinely, to current fiction. There they found, indeed, the same problems of manners discussed, but more entertainingly.

This brings up a difficult question in the study of best sellers: what novels are to be considered as juveniles? The behavior books were apparently designed for young people of, say, seventeen to twenty, who also undoubtedly read *Pamela* and *Clarissa*. Even small children read these two novels, and also *Grandison* and Fielding's *Tom Jones* and *Joseph Andrews*, in little abridgments prepared for juveniles. These books are usually classed as adult fiction, despite the didactic purpose so evident in some of them. Defoe surely wrote *Robinson Crusoe* for adults, but it is generally thought of as a juvenile classic. We shall have to be arbitrary; *Robinson Crusoe*, *Gulliver's Travels*, and *Arabian Nights* we shall consider as children's books.

Little can here be said of *Robinson Crusoe* that is not common knowledge. One of the most familiar characters in world literature, our shipwrecked hero is known chiefly through abridgments of Defoe. But Defoe himself abridged Defoe, and the story is of a kind which well withstands the pruning knife. Its religious phases, including Crusoe's conversion, have often been deleted from popular editions in later years.

Robinson Crusoe was widely read in America for years before any printer on this side of the Atlantic issued his own edition. William Byrd, of Virginia, referred to Crusoe in a journal he kept in 1728; and the title is found in many booksellers' lists of imported books by midcentury. The first known American edition, however, is the tiny volume of 1774 entitled *The Wonderful Life and Surprizing Adventures of Robinson Crusoe, Who Lived Twenty-Eight Years on an Uninhabited Island Which He Afterward Colonized.* This abridgment was for sale "by Hugh Gaine at his Book-Store in Hanover-Square [New York], where may be had a great variety of Little Books for Young Masters and Misses."

Robinson Crusoe has been translated into nearly all living languages and dialects, including Esperanto; it has been put into Braille, of course, and later on records for the "talking books"; it was published in the "toy-book" form, with tiny woodcuts, for eighteenth-century children; and it is found today in large-type child's books, with large colored pictures, in the dime stores. In Isaiah Thomas' toy-book *Crusoe* appears this advertisement: "If you learn this book well and good, you can buy a larger and more complete History of Mr. Crusoe at your friend the Bookseller's in Worcester, near the Court House."

Defoe's masterpiece was essentially journalistic. Written for the popular audience, based on the actual experiences of a Scotch sailor, Alexander Selkirk, by a practiced popular writer, it is in the best journalistic tradition. In the words of Professor Trent, the narrative is "one of the most uninvolved and human stories ever written." It was a best seller from the start. It has the distinction of having been the first story used as a newspaper serial, appearing in *Heathcot's Intelligence,* of London, in the same year (1719) that it appeared in book form.* Here is one book whose reasons for extraordinary popularity seem clear. *Robinson Crusoe* became a best seller because of its pure adventure theme, given a simple, vivid form which compels the reader to share the hero's planning, fears, and successes. Did ever reader fail to put himself imaginatively in Crusoe's place? Or to admire the man's cleverness, his handiness, his self-possessed good sense? This was, and is, a good book for young America; it teaches while it pleases—something the wise saws and adages of the behavior books could not do.

Such was Dean Swift's plain intention, too, in *Gulliver's Travels.* He chose the form of satire, which is certainly not for children; consequently the teachings of his book are disregarded by little readers in favor of the fable. And since it has never been tremendously popular among adults, and not a

---

* And Defoe's *Religious Courtship,* itself almost a best seller, was the first serial in an American newspaper, appearing in Keimer's *Pennsylvania Gazette* in 1728.

little of the satire is topical and dated, the splenetic Dean's teachings—except for those of a general character inherent in the story's theme—tend to drop out and disappear. This process has been aided by expurgators, editors, and abridgers.

What has saved it for immortality is the convincing, straightforward narrative of fantastic adventure, based on a philosophical concept of fundamental importance. That the children who have been the book's chief readers find this concept amusing rather than profound at the time of reading is probably unimportant. For them it is a good story of giants and pygmies, with marvelous pictures. It was no more in the movie version.

This combination of fairy-story interest and pictures was what also made the success of *The Arabian Nights' Entertainment,* more properly called *The Thousand Nights and a Night.* Here was a matter demanding abridgment, not only because some of the stories were too free in their treatment of sex for general circulation, but also because of the large number of tales in any one of the several variant manuscripts under this title. Burton filled ten large volumes with his translation of one manuscript, and six more with tales from others. As a matter of fact, the average collection by American publishers is likely to contain only a few tales—the seven voyages of Sinbad, Aladdin and his lamp, Ali Baba and the forty thieves, the enchanted horse, the magic carpet, and perhaps "The Sleeper Awakened."

We have now come a long way from *A Token for Youth.* It is the difference between Puritanism and a more sophisticated urban society, the beginning of the eighteenth century in America and its end. There are indeed lessons in the *Thousand and One Nights,* but the tales are mainly escapist fantasy; they are, as the title proclaims, *Entertainment.* The magic carpet is "of the essence"; American childish fancy, with the aid of the Arabian rawi, or storyteller, had come into its own.

VI. SEDUCTION AND TEARS

For while she reads romance, the fair one
Fails not to think herself the heroine;
For every glance, or smile, or grace,
She finds resemblance in her face,
Expects the world to fall before her,
And every fop she meets adore her.
Thus Harriett reads, and reading really
Believes herself a young Pamela; *
The high-wrought whim, the tender strain
Elate her mind and turn her brain:
Before her glass, with smiling grace,
She views the wonders of her face;
There stands in admiration moveless
And hopes a Grandison, or Lovelace.
John Trumbull's "Progress of Dulness,"
Part III.

Probably nobody ever reads *Pamela* any more. In basic problems and general movements, there is much in the eighteenth century that is very close to our own times; but those codes of behavior, details of living, and more superficial forms of thought that form the weft of an eighteenth-century novel are largely outside the interests of the modern reader. Thus even *Robinson Crusoe* must be abridged to find a public today. And nobody reads *Pamela* but students of social and literary history.

But in the latter half of the eighteenth century, everyone with any pretension to literary interests had read *Pamela*. It was the center of a great controversy—what was called in France "la querelle de Pamela." Many readers cried over the heroine's sufferings; others laughed at the whole performance. The Danish dramatist Holberg observed that the world was divided into *Pamelists* and *Antipamelists*. The story of the pretty serving-maid's clever and determined fight to preserve her virtue became the great best seller of its times.

That this book belongs to the behavior literature designed for youth is fully apparent; it might, properly enough, have been discussed along with Gregory's *Legacy to His Daughters* in our last chapter. It does not need the author's specific declaration that it is intended for "the minds of youth of both sexes" to apprise us of its purpose: the pen of Pamela, who knows her own "place" so perfectly, drips with observations about what is proper in all situations. She is concerned not only with the proprieties of poor but honest folk, of servant-girls, farmers, and footmen; but also with the proper behavior of curates, the landed gentry, and the nobility. Religion and morality are parts

* Here pronounce it *Pameely*, not only for the sake of the rhyme, but because this was, and is, a common pronunciation.

of the code, and the preservation of what is known technically as female virtue is the central theme of the novel.

Letter-writing, which provides the form of *Pamela,* was in itself regarded as a polite accomplishment. The origin of Richardson's first novel is well known. Two booksellers (one of them the Charles Rivington whose son was later a famous Tory journalist and bookseller in New York) had asked Samuel Richardson, a successful printer, to prepare a book of letters for the guidance of middle-class people who might wish to improve themselves in the epistolary art. Richardson had sometimes done hackwork for the booksellers, who were the real publishers of the time in London. He suggested that the letters might have more appeal if they were not empty forms, as in other manuals of the kind,* but were related to a series of incidents. His booksellers approved, but the author soon found the story running away with him. He thereupon laid aside for the moment the *Letters Written to and for Particular Friends, on the Most Important Occasions,* and gave himself up to the story which had unexpectedly developed itself. He kept the epistolary form, and made much of it; indeed Pamela's letters, purloined by Mr. B., did much to soften that villain-hero's heart. Richardson must have worked day and night on the story, buoyed up by the praise of his wife and a young lady who lived in their home; he said later that he finished the two-volume work in two months.

Closely allied with the publishing business as he was, Richardson knew all about good promotion and effective publicity. The book was a success upon its publication late in 1740. A correspondent of Horace Walpole says that he wrote, doubtless in 1741: "The late singular novel is the universal and only theme—Pamela is like snow, she covers everything with her whiteness." A new fan was soon in the shops on which were painted pictures representing "the principal adventures of her life, in servitude, love, and marriage." A clergyman recommended the book from the pulpit—an unprecedented thing, and perhaps a piece of promotion arranged by the author. The great Alexander Pope praised the novel highly. It was soon dramatized, and David Garrick appeared in the play; an opera founded on one of the dramatic versions followed. A *Pamela Versified* came out in the *Scots Magazine.* The novel was praised by imitation, and several pseudo-Pamelas appeared. James Highmore painted twelve pictures illustrating Pamela's adventures, and engravings were made and sold for two guineas the set. Finally the ultimate London popularity was signalized by the exhibition of waxworks at sixpence per admission, representing the virtuous serving-maid's career from her first going into service to her marriage.

Meantime *Pamela* had gone on to new triumphs abroad. It became a best

---

* If manuals were included in our best seller list, we should have to list William Bradford's *Secretary's Guide* (1698) and the English John Hill's *The Young Secretary's Guide* (Boston, 1708). Richardson's *Letters* are much like the latter.

seller in France, and was later popular in Holland, Germany, and Italy. There were many Continental dramatic versions, from Goldoni's famous *Pamela Nubile* to a curious melodrama in which the heroine is kidnaped by pirates and is later found to be the daughter of the Viceroy of the West Indies.

Though imported editions had been in American bookstores for two or three years before, it was not until 1744 that the book was published in the Colonies. Franklin published it in Philadelphia in that year, Parker in New York, and Harrison in Boston; it is barely possible that two of these (or even all three) were identical except for the imprint. Franklin advertised it in his *Pennsylvania Gazette* as follows:

> Just Published,
> And to be SOLD by the Printer hereof.
> *PAMELA: or VIRTUE rewarded.*
> *In a Series of FAMILIAR LETTERS from a beautiful young Damsel, to her Parents.*
> *Now first Published, in order to cultivate the*
> *Principles of Virtue and Religion in the Minds*
> *of the* Youth *of both Sexes.*
> *A Narrative which has its Foundation in* Truth *and* Nature; *and at the same time that it agreeably entertains, by a Variety of* curious *and* affecting INCIDENTS, *is entirely divested of all those Images, which, in too many Pieces, calculated for Amusement only, tend to* inflame *the Minds they should instruct.* Price 6s.

Herbert Ross Brown * has gathered together many American comments on *Pamela* from the magazines and journals of the latter part of the eighteenth century; the most hysterical of all is one in which Richardson is compared to Jesus Christ, and not unfavorably. "I know no moderation in my love of Richardson," the critic added convincingly. But the most interesting evidence of Pamelism in America is found in the native seduction stories in epistolary form—of which more anon.

If some believed Richardson perfect and *Pamela* divine, there were many who thought both author and heroine merely silly. That would doubtless be the verdict of the modern popular audience, if one could be obtained for such a book. A modern heroine would, at the very least, have addressed one of her many letters to the police; she would certainly not have fainted to escape a rapist. But Pamela is modern in one way at least: she knows the Facts of Life. She is only fifteen, but she is not ignorant of what a young girl ought, perhaps, to know. She is, moreover, clever, shrewd, and persistent. She aims at selling her *petit capital* for the highest price—an honorable marriage—and to do so she uses her beauty and charm for all they are worth. This is putting it baldly, but not much more baldly than Richardson puts it. After all, it is not wholly incredible that a tender child with Pamela's backgrounds should have such aims, and should succeed in them. Nor is it quite inconsistent that the girl who later tells Mrs. Jewks that she talks "like a vile London prostitute"

* *The Sentimental Novel in America, 1789-1860* (Durham, N.C., 1940).

should be so embarrassed when her master offers her some of his late mother's clothes, including

four pair of white stockings, three pair of fine silk ones, and two pair of rich stays. I was quite astonished and unable to speak for awhile [writes Pamela]; but yet I was inwardly ashamed to take the stockings, for Mrs. Jervis was not there: if she had, it would have been nothing. I believe I received them very awkwardly; for he smiled at my awkwardness, and said, "Don't blush, Pamela; dost think I don't know pretty maids should wear stockings?"

I was so confounded at these words, you might have beat me down with a feather. For you must think there was no answer to be made to this: so, like a fool, I was ready to cry, and went away curtseying and blushing, I am sure, up to the ears.

Never mind, Pamela; you did it all quite perfectly! Everything according to the code.

But sarcasm is the wrong note for *Pamela*, as Henry Fielding discovered. Perhaps the right note is that of the little folk story which Sir John Lubbock recounts. A blacksmith in an English village was accustomed, in idle times, to lean upon his anvil and read aloud from favorite books to his cronies who frequented the smithy. Thus he began *Pamela* and went on from day to day, to the neglect of his business but the growing interest of his auditors. So great did the excitement of all become as the story approached its climax, that they would take no adjournment for meals or business; and when the marriage was assured, the whole group rushed out of the smithy, made for the church, and rang peal after triumphant peal on the church bells.

Clarissa, which appeared seven years after *Pamela*, was a better book, as most critics agree; but it was never so generally read as its predecessor. It did become, however, over a series of years, an American best seller, largely by virtue of abridgments. After all, it was a very long novel—eight volumes in twelvemo. Granted that Richardson needed this length in order to develop all the attitudes and counter-attitudes and cross-influences in perfecting his plot, the general reader was likely to find the result tedious.

The tragic *Clarissa* and the "low" *Pamela* must be thought of together by anyone who searches for the roots of the American sentimental novel. And doubtless *Sir Charles Grandison*, too, though it apparently fell short of the best seller level. Different as they are, the three are of a piece—alike in so many ways that we need have no hesitation in assigning much the same reasons for the popularity of all three—the behavior, or self-improvement, theme, with religious and moral didacticism; long-drawn-out suspense before the climaxes; a certain spiciness, or sensation in sex incidents; a method of sketchy characterization, part caricature, part lively commonplace, which has always pleased the general reader. *Pamela* had one additional attraction— its partisanship for the humble classes in their struggle with the rich. It must also be remembered that these new and "singular" novels of Richardson's were far truer—more convincing and realistic—than the interminable old romances which had hitherto been accepted as the pattern for full-length fiction.

The first popular American novel had, in the main, the Richardsonian basis of appeal. It may be called American though it was first published in England and its author was English born.

Charlotte, a Tale of Truth, was issued in London early in 1791; but not until it was published in Philadelphia three years later did it catch the popular fancy. Its early scenes are laid in England; but the seducer is an English lieutenant bound for the American war, and he takes the heroine to New York, where the final tragic episodes occur. The author was Mrs. Susanna Rowson, who was born in Portsmouth, England, and was brought to America by her father, Lieutenant Haswell, an officer assigned to the revenue service in Massachusetts. During the Revolution the family returned to England, where Miss Haswell married and began her career as a novelist. She had written three or four novels, including *Charlotte,* before financial reverses drove the Rowsons to the theatre to make a living. Mr. Rowson was an orchestra leader, and his wife was "an agreeable singer and performer in the musical afterpieces." In 1793, their company made an American tour. It was when she was appearing on the stage of the New Theatre in Philadelphia, that Mrs. Rowson made arrangements for the American issue of her little books, scarcely more than novelettes, by Mathew Carey, then just beginning his great career as a publisher. It became Carey's first notable success, and one of his greatest.

Thus *Charlotte,* often entitled *Charlotte Temple,* was started on its long life as a popular sentimental story. It had an amazing success. Eighteen years after its initial publication, Carey was able to write to Mrs. Rowson:

It may afford you great gratification to know that the sales of *Charlotte Temple* exceed those of any of the most celebrated novels that ever appeared in England. I think the number disposed of must far exceed 50,000 copies; & the sale still continues.

So it did for the next hundred years, during which over two hundred editions of the little book were issued in the United States, according to the bibliographer R. W. G. Vail. Scores of country printers put out editions for the local trade and for the chapbook peddlers, frequently with poor typography and worse presswork.

Though the book was written without distinction and interrupted by occasional pages of motherly preaching, the sorrows of the young Charlotte nevertheless won the sympathy of hundreds of thousands of readers. Who shall say how many tubfuls of tears were shed over this lachrymose romance? Mrs. Rowson herself had great respect for tears: "Forever honored be the sacred drop of humanity!" she exclaims in a chapter called "Reflections."

Doubtless the subtitle, "A Tale of Truth," helped to gain acceptance for the story. It is supposed to have been based on an episode in the life of Colonel John Montresor, called Montraville in the book. Montresor was a kinsman of the author; he was an engineer in the British army and saw some service in the American war. The heroine was thought to have been Charlotte Stanley;

and on the stone over Charlotte Stanley's grave in Trinity churchyard, New York, "Temple" was substituted for "Stanley" in later years by some admirer of Mrs. Rowson's romance.

Another story by this author-actress which narrowly missed becoming a best seller was *The Fille de Chambre*. Mrs. Rowson completed her career with one more phase: she became mistress of a highly successful school for girls, which she conducted for more than twenty years. She died in Boston in 1824, famous and respected.

A better novel, though less popular, was Mrs. Hannah Foster's *The Coquette; or The History of Eliza Wharton*, which appeared in Boston in 1797. It was much more Richardsonian than *Charlotte*—epistolary in form, introducing a seducer whom readers compared to Lovelace, featuring a midnight elopement like Clarissa's, and using the master's technique of repeating incidents from differing points of view. The letter-writing is at times quite as brilliant as Richardson's, but the action is much less striking.

"Founded on Fact," declared the titlepage. That Eliza Wharton was the simulacrum of Elizabeth Whitman, a Hartford belle who "came to a bad end," there is none to dispute; but though it has often been alleged, it has never been proved, that the wicked Major Sanford was Pierrepont Edwards, eleventh son of Jonathan Edwards. Pierrepont doubtless had too big a dose of Calvinism as a child, and later the orthodox shook their heads at his libertarianism. Yet he was elected to the Continental Congress and was in latter life a noted politician and judge.

Mrs. Foster, the author, was the wife of a Massachusetts clergyman. Her husband was a cousin of Elizabeth Whitman, whose story was thus family talk. Mrs. Foster's writings were varied, including *Our Boarding School*, a behavior book; but none of her other work gained such fame as *The Coquette*.

Another novel which achieved a considerable popularity in America in the latter part of the eighteenth century, and much more in the nineteenth, was *The Vicar of Wakefield*. First issued in the Colonies six years after its original publication in London, it had at least nine different editions in various American cities before 1800. It got a slow start in England, but at length became very popular there and on the Continent, as well as in America. "It found entry into every castle and hamlet in Europe," wrote Thackeray many years later. It was especially popular in Germany, where men like Goethe and Herder praised it often. Goethe once wrote: "The influence which Goldsmith and Sterne exercised upon me, just at the chief point in my development, cannot be estimated."

How Goldsmith would have enjoyed such acclaim! And how prodigally he would have dispensed the fortune which a best seller should properly bring into an author's pockets! Goldsmith was born to poverty; he had no more of a head for business than good Doctor Primrose himself, or son Moses— those two easy marks in a hoss-trade. If one character in a best seller could laugh at one in another, how David Harum must have laughed, across a hundred and twenty-five years, at the gullible Vicar!

How the manuscript of Goldsmith's novel finally went to the publisher has been related by several contemporary authors—and always imperfectly, it seems. The story most nearly correct, it is generally admitted, is the one that Boswell vouches for. He is quoting Dr. Johnson:

> I received one morning a message from poor Goldsmith that he was in great distress, and as it was not in his power to come to me, begging that I would come to him as soon as possible. I sent him a guinea, and promised to come to him directly. I accordingly went as soon as I was drest, and found that his landlady had arrested him for his rent, at which he was in a violent passion. I perceived that he had already changed my guinea, and had got a bottle of Madeira and a glass before him. I put the cork into the bottle, desiring he would be calm, and began to talk to him of the means by which he might be extricated. He then told me that he had a novel ready for the press, which he produced to me. I looked into it, and saw its merit; told the landlady I should soon return, and having gone to a bookseller, sold it for sixty pounds. I brought Goldsmith the money, and he discharged his rent, not without rating his landlady in a high tone for having used him so ill.

And yet an inscribed copy of the first edition of *The Vicar of Wakefield* has sold for $6,600—some twenty times what Goldsmith received for the entire copyright. Such are the ironies of authorship.

Goldsmith's story, though its central incident is a seduction, differs markedly from Richardson's novels and their American echoes. Its humor and its portrayal of rustic customs have given it a longer life; it can be read today with real amusement. Its comment on good manners is not merely aphoristic, but satirical in method; the reader has no trouble in making modern applications.

These novels centering upon seduction, manners, and religion were by no means the only fiction read in eighteenth-century America. *Rasselas, The Adventures of a Guinea, Don Quixote, The Sorrows of Werther, Tom Jones, Gil Blas, Roderick Random,* and two or three of Mrs. Radcliffe's gothic romances were almost popular enough to be accounted best sellers.

Laurence Sterne's *Life and Opinions of Tristram Shandy* must be placed on the list, less by reason of its eighteenth-century readership, than because of its later popularity. In 1774 James Humphrey, of Philadelphia, published a five-volume edition of Sterne's *Works;* but the sentimental prebendary of York was known to American readers chiefly through a volume of selections entitled *The Beauties of Sterne,* from which all the naughty passages had been deleted. This little book was imported by many booksellers from London and reprinted several times in Philadelphia and Boston. Later admirers of *Tristram Shandy* made something of a cult of their enthusiasm, and Shandeans still read their favorite book in modern editions and find in its whimsy and eccentricities an inexhaustible pleasure.

A curious collection of legends of "Dr. Faustus" and his necromancies was undoubtedly an over-all best seller in America throughout a century and a half. It circulated in various forms. Seventeenth century bookstores had the

English translation of the Spies version, picturesquely entitled *The History of the Damnable Life and the Deserved Death of Dr. John Faustus*. Later forms were subject to editing by American printer-publishers, and titles were toned down. Isaiah Thomas called it, in his edition, *The Surprising Life and Death of Dr. John Faustus, D.D.* Commoner was *The Famous History of Dr. Faustus*, or just "the Faust book." It was staple in the peddler's pack far into the nineteenth century.

Finally, though their fictional content was usually small, the English essay periodicals must be mentioned here. They were bound up or reprinted in volumes, and in that form were to be found in all the bookstores. Most popular were *The Spectator*, *The Adventurer*, *The Rambler*, *The World*, *The Tatler*, and *The Guardian*. Few imported volumes were advertised more frequently than *The Spectator*, though it did not, so far as we know, have an American edition until 1803. After that, a number of American issues appeared, usually in three or more small volumes. Selections from the papers became common and maintained their popularity for many years, and the Sir Roger de Coverley essays have long been used in schools.

VII. THE PENSIVE POETS

> The pensive poets painful vigils keep,
> Sleepless themselves, to give their readers sleep.
> *Pope's "Dunciad," I*

In the *Massachusetts Gazette and Boston Weekly News-Letter* for January 31, 1771, appears an advertisement for the sale of "A Great Variety of Books at Public Vendue." A number of titles are listed; and the catalogue ends with three "lots" in which the remaining books are placed, as follows: "72 doz. Proof Catechisms, 7 doz. small Histories, and 20 Groce of Verses." If this seems a contemptuous assignment of the Muse to the tail of the catalogue, it should also be considered that "20 Groce" made a very large "lot." It would be interesting to know the titles and authors of these poetical efforts, but we can be sure there was much of Watts and Pope.

It is possible, if you set yourself to it, to devise a theory accounting for the popularity of as dull a poet as Isaac Watts. In the first place, he brought his wares to two good markets—juvenile poetry and hymnody. There had been but little even passable verse for children before Dr. Watts, and some of his little poems soon became memory pieces. The churches which had so long endured dull and harsh hymnody were ripe for something "that arises a degree above Mr. Sternhold," to use our author's own expression. His successes in these fields made the name of Dr. Watts familiar throughout England and her Colonies, and probably better known in early New England than that of any other poet; thus his later lyrics were bound to have a good hearing. In the second place, what seems insufferable dullness today once seemed matter of lively interest. Such things are comparative. In contrast with many contemporary devotional writers, Watts was—occasionally, at least—exciting; in fact, he thought it necessary to explain in the preface of his *Horae Lyricae* why he sometimes attempted the innocent entertainment of youth:

> Young gentlemen and ladies, whose genius and education have given them a relish of oratory and verse, may be tempted to seek satisfaction among the dangerous diversions of the stage, and impure sonnets, if no provision of a safer kind be made to please them. While I have attempted to gratify innocent fancy in this respect, I have not forgotten to allure the heart to virtue, and to raise it to a disdain of brutal pleasures.

True enough, for even the more lively pieces have all a moral end. Religious meditations, moral counsel, and reminders of death and mortality, are on every page.

> Lie still, my Plutarch, then and sleep,
> And my good Seneca may keep
> Your volumes closed for ever too,
> I have no further use for you:
> For when I feel my virtue fail,
> And my ambitious thoughts prevail,
> I'll take a turn among the tombs,
> And see whereto all glory comes:
> There the vile foot of every clown
> Tramples the sons of Honor down:
> Beggars with awful ashes sport
> And tread the Caesars in the dirt.

Thus Watts earns himself a place, perhaps, among the "graveyard poets," of whom there were many in the eighteenth century.

All these things together contributed to the popularity of Watts's volume of lyrics, for a best seller is seldom made by one cause alone. As to the popularity itself there is no doubt. "The poetry of Watts took the religious world of dissent by storm," says the *Dictionary of National Biography*. But in America the reputation of the little doctor of divinity (he was scarcely over five feet tall, and slender withal) was more than sectarian; it was widely diffused and lasted for a hundred and fifty years or more. Benjamin Franklin was the first American publisher of *Horae Lyricae*, but he was followed by scores of others.

Another "graveyard poet" was the Rev. Edward Young, LL.D. His *Poem on the Last Day* was popular in America for many years, but it was the *Night Thoughts on Life, Death, and Immortality* that made him a best seller. This long and doleful series of meditations in blank verse had a great success in England, throughout Europe, and in America. The Germans admired it, and Herder's praises increased Young's audience in that country. Diderot and Lamartine helped to make it popular in France, where Letourneur's translation had a wide distribution. It is said that Robespierre kept it under his pillow during the nights when the excitements of the Revolution made him wakeful; it is still a good book to go to sleep on. Though Evans records only seven editions of it before 1800, there are more than a score of nineteenth-century printings of the *Night Thoughts* in the Library of Congress. "For many a year," wrote Donald G. Mitchell, "a copy of Young's mournful, magniloquent poem, bound in morocco and gilt-edged, was reckoned one of the most acceptable gifts to a person in affliction."

A chief quality of *Night Thoughts* is its quotability. In other words, the poet occasionally displays an ability to fashion impressive and memorable lines.

> Be wise today; 'tis madness to defer;
> Next day the fatal precedent will plead;
> Thus on, till wisdom is pushed out of life.
> Procrastination is the thief of time . . .

Here again are the aphorisms, the good advice to youth, the instructive reflections, which form so large a part of the popular literature of the aspiring eighteenth century—sententious, proverbial, with all the sound of ripe wisdom. Here too is plenty of sermonizing at length.

But of course nothing could compare in sententious wisdom—or quotability—with Pope's *Essay on Man*. That the prosperity of the proverb is always in the mouths of the folk is obvious; perhaps the liking of the popular audience for wise sayings in literature has not been so well recognized. At any rate, the general reader was delighted with what seemed to him the transcendent gems of wisdom in the *Essay on Man*. Gems they are indeed, but often more of wit than of wisdom.

There can be no doubt that Pope's 400-line masterpiece was the most popular poem of the eighteenth century. Professor Wilson, writing in *Blackwood's* a hundred years after its first publication, said it was "in every house where there were books in England." Kant admired it; Voltaire called it the most useful and sublime didactic poem ever written in any language.

First published in America by William Bradford the younger, of Philadelphia, in 1747, it was frequently reprinted, not only in such other large towns as New York, Boston, Richmond, and Hartford, but in scores of country printshops—Bennington, Vermont (1785); New London, Connecticut (1791); Wrentham, Massachusetts (1795); Hallowell, Maine (1811); Canandaigua, New York (1814), to name but a few. It got into the schools, of course. Though it cannot be said to be popular in modern times, it is not forgotten, like Young's *Night Thoughts;* an edition of it in the Little Blue Books about 1920 sold over fifty thousand copies.

Byron's pious hope that Pope might one day be recognized as "the national poet of mankind" will never be fulfilled: so much is clear, but it is also clear that he will always have his admirers on both sides of the Atlantic. Unlike Doctors Watts and Young, he is usually readable. It may be that the philosophy underlying the *Essay on Man* is really not greatly superior to that of another much later best seller named *Pollyanna*; but Pope's justification of the ways of Providence is far more convincing at the moment of reading than the later opus, by reason of its eloquence and lofty expression:

> All nature is but art unknown to thee;
> All chance, direction which thou canst not see;
> All discord, harmony not understood;
> All partial evil, universal good:
> And, spite of pride, in erring reason's spite,
> One truth is clear, Whatever is, is right.

In 1777, in the midst of the American Revolution, Robert Bell, of Philadelphia, published three long English poems all of which were destined to become American best sellers—Young's *Night Thoughts*, Milton's *Paradise Lost*, and Thomson's *The Seasons*. *Paradise Lost* was, however, a popular offering in American bookshops long before that.

Originally published by the London bookseller Samuel Simmons in 1667, Milton's great poem had a slow sale in England for its first fifteen or twenty years. The author's contract with Simmons provided for a royalty of five pounds down and then five pounds for each of three editions of 1,300 copies each as they might be called for and sold. The third of these editions was not published until 1678; thus it is evident that it took at least eleven years (more likely fourteen) to sell 3,900 copies. Doubtless some copies made their way to the new world; certainly some did after Jacob Tonson took over the copyright in 1683. By the middle of the eighteenth century *Paradise Lost* was staple in the bookstores; and it was one of the five titles which appeared most often in booksellers' advertisements of importations in 1760-1775, where it was commonly listed as *Paradise Lost and Regained*. It was Robert Bell, of Philadelphia, who published the first American edition, in two volumes containing *Paradise Lost, Paradise Regained, Samson Agonistes,* and the life of Bishop Newton. In the course of time editions multiplied, and no private library was considered complete without Milton's stately numbers.

Remarkably popular in the latter half of the eighteenth century was Thomson's *The Seasons*. Jamie Thomson, a young Scotsman, came down to London to seek a literary fortune about 1725. He had his *Winter* in his pocket, but when he applied to the bookseller-publishers of London he found that nobody wanted to risk printing a didactic work in blank verse by an unknown youth of twenty-five. And at last, when one of them was persuaded to risk it, paying the author three guineas, the verses lay neglected on the counter. Enter Thomas Whately, a young Londoner of literary tastes and acquaintance (later famous for a book on gardening), who happened to pick up the slender volume in the bookstore; and, says Thomson's biographer,

finding something which delighted him, perused the whole, not without growing astonishment, that the poem should be unknown, and the author obscure.

In the ecstasy of his admiration, he went from coffee-house to coffee-house, pointing out its beauties, and calling upon all men of taste, to exert themselves in rescuing from obscurity one of the greatest geniuses that ever appeared. This had a very happy effect; for, in a short time, the impression was bought up.

Thus one of the greatest literary successes of its times gained its initial impetus. Other editions were issued; Thomson was spurred by his sudden popularity to the production of poems on the other three seasons, and his book became, and long remained, a best seller in both England and America.

Thomson was one of the "pensive poets," and he has long stretches of religious and moral disquisition which tend to "give their readers sleep"; but he also has something else—something comparatively new in the poetry of the time. In the midst of passages which were thought by many to have grandeur and fine moral feeling, but now seem so much turgid, ineffectual, and trite rhetoric, the reader comes upon a true and honest little vignette, like the one about the redbreast in the winter storm:

> Half-afraid, he first
> Against the window beats; then, brisk, alights
> On the warm hearth; then, hopping o'er the floor,
> Eyes all the smiling family askance,
> And pecks, and starts, and wonders where he is—
> Till, more familiar grown, the table-crumbs
> Attract his slender feet.

This is worth reams of apostrophes to the sun and views of the wonders of a torrid zone which the poet had never seen. Not that Thomson did not occasionally strike off a fine line in the more ambitious passages: some twenty verses above the quotation just given, we are told of the winter clouds:

> Heavy they roll their fleecy world along,
> And the sky saddens with the gathered storm.

But we can be sure that the great popular audience, though impressed by the purple passages, found their real delight in those homelier bits about the robin, the sheep-washing, and rustic festivals.*

This homely and realistic note reached a far greater development in another poem of great popularity—Cowper's *The Task*. Cowper is a "pensive poet" in the sense that he is thoughtful; but he is not often mournful, and no reader need go to sleep over him. Few readers, however, will take Cowper from the shelves today unless they have somewhat old-fashioned tastes and a catholic feeling for—well, for Cowper. But how lively, how satisfying readers of 1800

* There was doubtless much the same type of appeal in *The Deserted Village* and *Elegy Written in a Country Churchyard*. Both of these poems were often published separately in America, but their brevity forbids their inclusion in a list of best-selling books.

must have found him! He is inexhaustibly quotable. Let us take something from Book IV, "The Winter Evening":

> Hark! 'Tis the twanging horn! O'er yonder bridge,
> That with its wearisome but needful length
> Bestrides the wintry flood, in which the moon
> Sees her unwrinkled face reflected bright,
> He comes, the herald of a noisy world,
> With spattered boots, strapped waist, and frozen locks,
> News from all nations lumbering at his back. . . .
> He whistles as he goes, light-hearted wretch,
> Cold, and yet cheerful: messenger of grief
> Perhaps to thousands, and of joy to some,
> To him indifferent whether grief or joy.
> Houses in ashes, and the fall of stocks,
> Births, deaths, and marriages, epistles wet
> With tears that trickled down the writer's cheeks
> Fast as the periods from his fluent quill,
> Or charged with amorous sighs of absent swains
> Or nymphs responsive, equally affect
> His horse and him, unconscious of them all. . . .
>   Now stir the fire, and close the shutters fast,
> Let fall the curtains, wheel the sofa round,
> And while the bubbling and loud hissing urn
> Throws up a steamy column, and the cups
> That cheer but not inebriate, wait on each,
> So let us welcome peaceful evening in.

Its religious tone and severe Calvinistic morality doubtless had much to do with the popularity of *The Task*. Goldwin Smith once declared: "As *Paradise Lost* is to militant Puritanism, so is *The Task* to its author's time. To its character as the poem of a sect it no doubt owed and still owes much of its popularity."

In general, the literary critics were lukewarm toward Cowper, or worse; but the common people loved him. In America he was promptly republished, and editions multiplied. It was not a professional literary critic, but a shrewd judge of most matters, who wrote to the poet:

The relish for the reading of poetry had long since left me, but there is something so new in the manner, so easy and yet so correct in the language, so clear in the expression, yet concise, and so just in the sentences, that I have read the whole with great pleasure, and some of the pieces more than once.

The name signed to the letter was that of Benjamin Franklin; the criticism was worthy of his acute mind.

"Is not *The Task* a glorious poem?" wrote young Robert Burns to his friend and accomplished correspondent, Mrs. Dunlop. Burns published his own immortal first volume the year after *The Task* appeared; both represent that "something so new" of Franklin's phrase. There are vast differences, to be sure, between the two poets—in singing quality, in Calvinistic fervor, and in poetic genius—but both turned away from the classical school simply because truth and nature appealed to both.

The story of the "Kilmarnock Burns" is familiar to all bibliophiles. The romantic young Scotch farmer had got into trouble over a girl—or two or three girls—and besides, his farming was a failure. In this crisis, a friend told him of a job as bookkeeper to be had in faraway Jamaica; but the catch in this solution of all his difficulties was that the passage-money thither amounted to nine guineas, and Burns could not raise half of that. Then the landlord from whom he rented his humble farm made a suggestion for which the world is still grateful. These poems, he said—these songs you have been writing down and reading to us when you should have been plowing or reaping—why don't you get them printed? Authors make money out of books. But, objected Bobby Burns, who would publish them? That is easy, replied this best of landlords; we'll get up a list of purchasers in advance, and then Printer Wilson, over at Kilmarnock, will do the job. So it was worked out: some 350 copies were subscribed for, some 600 were printed, and the author made altogether about twenty pounds profit—more than twice enough to take him to Jamaica. But the book had made him suddenly famous, and his new friends besought him to come to Edinburgh instead of burying himself in the West Indies. Which he did.

Some years ago a single worn copy of the "Kilmarnock Burns" sold for more than sixty times Burns's profit on the whole edition.

A second issue of these *Poems, Chiefly in the Scottish Dialect* appeared in Edinburgh the year following the Kilmarnock success, and the next year editions were produced in both Philadelphia and New York. Since that time there have been probably as many as two hundred American editions of Burns's *Poems*—"selected" and "complete." One standard publisher—the Thomas Y. Crowell Company—has published over a quarter of a million copies of its edition of Burns since 1881; its earlier records have been destroyed by fire. Burns has been one of the most popular of all poets in the United States.

And why should Burns not be popular in America? He is the true democratic poet—spokesman for the man who is a man for a' that. His poetry, as Carlyle said, "is redolent of natural life and hardy natural men." Thoroughly Scottish, it is also thoroughly American. And yet it was not merely the social and political ideology of Burns that made him one of the most popular American poets, but his sentiment and tunefulness as well.

Thus, in our survey of the poets who were most popular in America in the eighteenth century, we have passed from the purely "pensive" writers, occupied with religious and moral generalities, to those who saw man and nature more distinctly in the clear light of common life. But all were part of their times; all spoke to the hearts, the hopes, the minds of their great audiences.

Not one of them was an American poet, though we shall find, in the next chapter, a native American writer of political satire in verse whose work reached best seller heights of popularity.

VIII. POLITICS AND LITERATURE IN THE REVOLUTIONARY ERA

> Each leather-apron'd dunce, grown wise,
> Presents his forward face t' advise,
> And tatter'd legislators meet
> From every workshop through the street.
> His goose the tailor finds new use in,
> To patch and turn the Constitution;
> The blacksmith comes with sledge and **grate**
> To iron-bind the wheels of state;
> The quack forbears his patients' souse,
> To purge the Council and the House;
> The tinker quits his moulds and doxies,
> To cast assembly-men and proxies.
> *"M'Fingal," Canto III*

THREE tracts for the times reached best-sellerdom in the decade which preceded the Declaration of Independence. They were John Dickinson's *Letters from a Farmer in Pennsylvania,* Thomas Paine's *Common Sense,* and John Trumbull's *M'Fingal.*

Dickinson was a Philadelphia lawyer of ability. In a country without professional literary men, the clergy and bar furnished most of the writers; but to establish a philosophical mood for his discussion of burning political questions, Dickinson set himself forth as a gentleman-farmer:

I am a Farmer, settled after a variety of fortunes, near the banks of the river *Delaware,* in the province of *Pennsylvania.* I received a liberal education, and have been engaged in the busy scenes of life: But am now convinced, that a man may be as happy without bustle, as with it. My farm is small, my servants are few, and good; I have a little money at interest; I wish for no more: my employment in my own affairs is easy; and with a contented and grateful mind, I am compleating the number of days allotted to me by divine goodness.

On the whole, however, Dickinson does little with the farmer masquerade, and the reader is soon aware that the *Letters* are written by a man learned in the law and skillful in reasoning. Though unalterably opposed to the Parliamentary pretensions to a taxing power over the Colonies, Dickinson disapproves of anything savoring of disloyalty or rebellion. "The prosperity of these Colonies is founded in their dependence on Great-Britain," he writes; and again:

We have an excellent Prince, in whose good dispositions toward us we may confide. We have a generous, sensible, and humane nation, to whom we may apply. They may be deceived: they may, by artful men, be provoked to anger against us; but I cannot yet believe they can be cruel or unjust; or that their anger will be implacable. Let us behave like dutiful children, who have received unmerited blows from a beloved parent. Let us complain to our parents; but let our complaints speak, at the same time, the language of affliction and veneration.

The twelve *Farmer's Letters* were first printed in the *Pennsylvania Chronicle*, of Philadelphia; and each was immediately reprinted, as soon as it appeared, in nearly all the other newspapers in the Colonies. When the last one was published, they were brought out in book form in Boston, Philadelphia, and New York, and perhaps in paper or board covers in other towns. The statement quoted in Sabin that thirty editions were published in six months may have been an exaggeration; but it seems likely that nearly everybody in America who could read pored over and digested the Farmer's arguments.

Franklin arranged for editions in London; the *Letters* were issued in Dublin, with Franklin's introduction; they were translated into French, and published in Amsterdam. Burke and Voltaire praised them. In America, town-meetings and grand juries commended the Farmer; songs were written in his honor; his likeness was engraved and printed for sale at a shilling, or "glazed and framed" at five shillings; the College of New Jersey made him a Doctor of Laws. In the lists of toasts at patriotic meetings in the late sixties and seventies—those lists which begin "The King; The Queen" and run on to a score or more—"The Farmer" was sure to appear not too late in the enumeration.

Paine's *Common Sense* was very different from the *Farmer's Letters*. Nearly eight years had passed; the situation had changed; the British had fired upon the patriots at Lexington; something different was needed now. Besides, Thomas Paine was a man of a temper far different from that of John Dickinson. Here was no appeasement; here was open defiance of England, her king—"the royal brute of Britain,"—and her armed forces. The main thesis of the pamphlet * was the logic of independence:

> Small islands not capable of protecting themselves are the proper objects for kingdoms to take under their care, but there is something very absurd in supposing a continent to be perpetually governed by an island. In no instance hath nature made the satellite larger than the planet, and as England and America, with respect to each other, reverse the common order of nature, it is evident they belong to different systems: England to Europe, America to itself.

Impetuous, often badly reasoned, *Common Sense* was nevertheless a powerful appeal to popular sagacity. It was well titled; it bypassed the technical questions of law and loyalty, and struck squarely upon the common-sense solution of independence. It was a strong reagent, precipitating revolution.

It produced a greater popular sensation than anything else that had issued from the American press since the beginning of printing on this side of the

* Commonly called a pamphlet, and often published in about sixty octavo pages, with paper covers, it has also been issued as a little book of over a hundred pages and often between boards. It runs to about 22,000 words.

Atlantic. George Washington, writing to Joseph Reed two or three months after the publication of the tract, said, "By private letters which I have lately received from Virginia, I find *Common Sense* is working a powerful change there in the minds of men." Benjamin Franklin spoke of the "prodigious effects" of Paine's essay. More than any other writing, it prepared the way for the Declaration of Independence.

It was published by Robert Bell, of Philadelphia, who had once employed the author as a clerk in his shop. It appeared within the first few weeks of 1776, and was very soon reprinted in the leading cities and towns. Within a year probably 150,000 copies had been sold; reckoned on the basis of increased population, that would represent a distribution today of close to eight million copies.

One other work by Paine is on the best seller list—*The Age of Reason*. This book was written in the midst of his own participation in the excitements of the French Revolution, and the proofs of Part I were corrected while Paine was daily expecting to be wheeled off to the guillotine. In it the author attacks established religion as another form of tyranny. He writes with the same vigor, the same headlong fervor and lapses of taste that were so characteristic of *Common Sense*. The worst of it is in the silly and ignorant criticism of Old Testament literature. The book stirred theologians to wrath; but it was really not for them, for it had no theological scholarship. *The Age of Reason* found its audience almost immediately among strong, individualistic, simple thinkers who resented any kind of intellectual or emotional dictatorship. America was full of such men; the frontier provided an environment which fostered their idiosyncrasies. O. B. Frothingham, the Unitarian clergyman, once pointed out that *The Age of Reason* "went everywhere, into holes and corners, among backwoodsmen and pioneers." It still holds this type of audience, and is the joy of the free-thinker, the weapon of the local "atheist." "It has done as much," wrote Paine's leading biographer, "to modify human belief as any book ever written."

Paine was, of course, not an atheist, but a deist. Yet he brought down upon himself such a storm of abuse as has seldom fallen upon any writer. He died the victim of this vilification, and under revolting circumstances. Nor did his detractors abandon him in death; his name is still anathema in many places. When, some years after his death, William Cobbett stole into New Rochelle, New York, at night, dug up Paine's coffin, and carried it off to England, in order eventually to hold a fitting funeral, and erect a monument over his bones, so many difficulties were put in his way that he himself died before he completed his project. Today nobody knows where Paine is buried, or if he was ever re-buried. Byron wrote:

> In digging up your bones, Tom Paine,
>   Will Cobbett has done well;
> You visit him on earth again,
>   He'll visit you in hell.

The vindictive poet evidently had no thought of making a third at that meeting.

Philadelphia saw the appearance in the same month of the two important revolutionary tracts, *Common Sense* and the first part of John Trumbull's *M'Fingal.* Trumbull was already well known as a satirist in verse, chiefly through *The Progress of Dulness,* a satire on educational methods which is still pertinent and amusing today. He had gained some local notoriety about twenty years earlier by his precocity. He had learned to read at the age of two, and soon had read and memorized Watts's *Lyrics.* Before he was four he had read the entire Bible, and by the time he was five he was writing verse. He then took up the study of Latin, and at the age of seven he passed the entrance examinations at Yale College. His parents had sense enough not to send him to Yale at once, though he did enter at thirteen. Afterward he was teacher, littérateur, and law student under John Adams of Boston.

It was inevitable that a briefless lawyer with a genius for lively couplets should sooner or later try to catch the issues and personalities of the exciting 1770's in his net of verse. There is no doubt that the urging of Silas Deane, probably that of John Adams, and possibly that of Washington himself, had some part in the planning and the publishing of *M'Fingal.* It is certain that the poem imitated *Hudibras,* and Churchill's *The Ghost* even more. But all this should not make us forget that the brilliant, ambitious, scholarly Trumbull was himself moved to write a verse satire which is a masterpiece in its kind and which was for many years regarded as the greatest American poem.

It is never read now, save by students and antiquaries, so a thumb-nail résumé is necessary. Squire M'Fingal is a powerful speaker at town-meetings, the more effective (and funny) because of his boasted gift of second sight. A meeting is called to discuss the issues forced upon the people by the events at Lexington and Concord, at which the Patriot Honorius makes a strong address arraigning Britain and British policy, and describing the long-suffering loyalty of the Americans:

> So once Egyptians at the Nile
> Ador'd their guardian Crocodile,
> Who heard them first with kindest ear,
> And ate them to reward their pray'r;
> And could he talk, as kings can do,
> Had made them gracious speeches, too.

At length, the Tories break in with boos, and M'Fingal makes his speech, defending kingship and the Tory leaders in New England by name, but going so far as to make himself ridiculous. He threatens the rebels:

> And who believes you will not run?
> You're cowards, every mother's son!

A hot debate ensues, and the chief occurrences of the past months are reviewed with some passion. Finally the meeting breaks up in disorder; and while a general fight threatens within, the meeting-house is suddenly attacked by a mob from without. As everyone rushes outdoors, the moderator, who has been hiding under a bench,

> Peeped up his head to view the fray,
> Beheld the wranglers run away,
> And, left alone, with solemn face,
> Adjourn'd them without time or place.

Thus ends the first part. In the remaining half, Trumbull planned to have the mob tar and feather the Squire, and then to have him, hiding in a turnip-bin in his own cellar, be seized by an access of that second sight for which he was famous, and prophesy the course of the war and America's triumph. But since the poet was not himself a prophet, he thought it best to await events before finishing his satire. In the meantime, Deane went ahead and secured the publication of the first part by the Bradfords, father and son, in Philadelphia.

There were only two American editions of this first part alone, and one in London, so it may be surmised that the poem was not highly important as a morale-builder during the course of the Revolution. But when, in 1782, Trumbull was able to complete the work as planned, it went like hot cakes. Lacking copyright protection, it was immediately brought out by two pirate publishers, and thereafter by many others. Trumbull later wrote: "Among more than thirty different impressions, one only, at any subsequent time, was published with the permission, or even the knowledge, of the writer; and the poem remained the property of newsmongers, hawkers, pedlars, and petty chapmen." Trumbull's complaints had much to do with the enactment of the first American copyright law, that of Connecticut; but in the other states he had no redress. Eventually nearly everybody in the country read the poem. Quotations from it, which were very common, came to be called "macfingalisms": perhaps the most famous of them all was this couplet:

> No man e'er felt the halter draw
> With good opinion of the law.

Or the Squire's sarcastic question, "What has posterity done for us?" In the fifty years between the publication of the complete poem and Trumbull's death —a barren half-century in American poetry, to be sure—M'Fingal became the American poetic classic. In 1829 the anthologist Samuel Kettell pointed out the fact that for many years Trumbull's masterpiece had enjoyed "a greater celebrity than any other American poem." *

These were years in which the people lived and breathed politics. Just as "matter of religion" was dominant for the first hundred years and more of

---

* Quoted in John Cowie's *John Trumbull, Connecticut Wit* (Chapel Hill, 1936), where material about *M'Fingal's* popularity may be found in abundance.

American reading, so "matter of politics" ranked above other topics in popular thinking for some seventy-five years after the Stamp Act. The only reason there are no more political books on the best seller list for this period is that the newspaper, the short pamphlet, and the stump-speech were in most respects better adapted to political argument than the bound volume. But of the popular craze for politics there need be no doubt. A witty writer in the *New York Journal* in 1787, when the debate on the new Constitution was at its height, described political discussion on the streets; two men could scarcely meet without one crying out, "Hello, damme, Jack, what are you, boy? Federal or Anti-Federal?" A modern historian complains that the political essays in the newspapers, such as those of *The Federalist,* were "heavily written and too long for the average reader of the day." By no means. Heavy-and-long was all right for the earnest and politically minded "average reader of the day." No student of the popular literature of the eighteenth century can believe that the heroic reader of that age was affrighted by length, weight, or fine type.

The thing is not now susceptible of proof, but most people at the time thought that the *Federalist* papers, written by Hamilton, Madison and Jay, and most of them published first in the *Independent Journal,* of New York, then reprinted widely in other papers, and finally brought out in book form, exerted an important influence in the contest over the adoption of the Constitution. The book continued to be reprinted through the nineteenth century; Ford's bibliography lists forty editions by 1865. Even in recent years it has had a number of new editions. Through a century and a half *The Federalist* has been recognized not only as a masterpiece of political writing, but as a leading authority in the interpretation of the great instrument which it discusses.

It is interesting to note how political controversies in foreign countries have called forth translations of this work. So it was in France in 1792-1795, in Germany in 1864, in Brazil in 1840, and in Argentina in 1868.

IX. SHAKESPEARE: AMERICAN BEST SELLER

> Monopolizing Britain! boast no more
> His genius to your narrow bounds confin'd;
> Shakespeare's bold spirit seeks our western shore,
> A gen'ral blessing for the world design'd,
> And, emulous to form the rising age,
> The noblest Bard demands the noblest Stage.
>   *Peter Markoe*

PETER MARKOE asked only that Britain should not "monopolize" Shakespeare; P. T. Barnum asked rather more than that. Having learned, on one of his trips to England, that Shakespeare's birthplace at Stratford-on-Avon was for sale, the great showman attempted to purchase it, with the intention of cutting it into sections, shipping them to New York, and setting them up again in his American Museum. But when news of the offer leaked out, all England was aroused, English funds were quickly raised, and the Shakespeare house was bought and dedicated as a national shrine. Later, as Barnum relates in his autobiographical best seller, he had better luck in another quarter. He bought from the Royal Zoo and brought to America, against the protests of the English newspapers, the London children, and (he maintains) Queen Victoria herself, the largest and mightiest quadruped known to exist upon the earth—none other than the great Jumbo himself. And Jumbo made a bigger hit for Barnum's show than Shakespeare's house could have been expected to make.

Absurd as some of the efforts to make Shakespeare a full-fledged Yankee may seem, they must be recognized as a phase of the militant nationalism of a period which lasted for many years after political independence was won. They must be understood as the highest possible tribute to the great dramatist. Shakespeare was adopted by America, and that in spite of his British origins. He was, in the language of a coarse Revolutionary broadside,

> Old Shakespeare, a poet who should not be spit on,
> Although he was born in an island called Britain.*

Shakespeare was little known in the Colonies before the middle of the eighteenth century. There is nothing strange about that, however; some four thousand copies of volumes containing his plays sufficed for all England in the seventeenth century, and the American outposts of English culture were slower than the motherland to develop a popular appreciation of any literary leader.

Betterton's interpretation of Shakespeare on the stage did much to advance his reputation in England; but in America, the stage itself was pretty generally taboo until about 1750. After that there was some Shakespeare in the theatres of Philadelphia, New York, and Williamsburg, Virginia. Meantime, some copies of Rowe's editions of the plays were brought over from England; we find imported *Hamlets* and *King Lears* advertised in the *Connecticut Courant* at eleven pence. By the time of the Revolution Shakespeare was fairly well known to most educated persons.

Apparently the first printing of Shakespeare in the new world was by Isaiah Thomas in 1786 in a little volume of Mother Goose rhymes. John Newbery, of London, had included in his Mother Goose, said to have been edited by Goldsmith, some of Shakespeare's most charming songs, such as "Where the bee sucks" and "When the daffodils begin to 'pear," and Thomas copied Newbery. The next year appeared a little book, or pamphlet, entitled *The Twins: or*

---

* Quoted in Esther Cloudman Dunn's *Shakespeare in America* (New York, 1939), p. 112. This book and Alfred Van Rensselaer Westfall's *American Shakespearean Criticism* (New York, 1939) are the two most comprehensive works on the subject of the reading, study, and acting of Shakespeare in America. A. H. Thorndike's British Academy lecture and Henry W. Simon's *The Reading of Shakespeare in American Schools and Colleges* (New York, 1932) are also valuable.

Which is Which? A farce in three acts, altered from Shakespeare's Comedy of Errors. One William Woods was the author, according to Evans, and it was published in Philadelphia for Thomas Dobson. No extant copy is known. Then in 1794, the year in which public plays were first allowed in Boston, a series of acting versions of some of Shakespeare's plays was printed in that city, doubtless for sale in the theatre. But the first complete Shakespeare was published in eight volumes in 1795 and 1796 by Bioren & Madan, of Philadelphia. Joseph Hopkinson, Philadelphia man of letters and prominent lawyer, the author of "Hail, Columbia," probably did what editing was necessary for this edition, using the Ayscough text.

This was a creditable edition, but it was probably less important in the development of a general audience than one which came out in Boston a few years later. In 1802 Munroe & Francis published the plays in monthly numbers—sixteen in all, at thirty-five cents each to subscribers and fifty cents to others. Illustrations were by the first important American engraver on wood, Dr. Alexander Anderson. This was a very popular edition. More than half the students in residence at Harvard were subscribers, including Edward Everett and Richard H. Dana. When a second edition was "called for," the type had to be entirely reset, for this was before the days of stereotyping. The publishers themselves did the presswork on a hand press; the senior partner was the editor, selecting text and notes. In 1810 a third edition was produced, from type again reset, and with the addition of two numbers including the *Poems.*

As the various editions came from the press, in paper-covered numbers or in seventeen-volume editions, the popularity of the great dramatist grew mightily upon the American stage. At the beginning, the theatre belonged to polite and fashionable society rather than to the rabble; and Shakespeare was for the educated, though dances and divertisements and after-pieces were thrown in to "lighten" the program. But as the theatre followed the frontier, it became more definitely popular, and *Richard III, Romeo and Juliet, Hamlet,* and *Othello* became standard offerings to a public which liked them largely because they were good shows and not merely because they were proper theatre.

It was partly the declamation in these plays that delighted people who loved oratory and were accustomed to applaud the rolling periods of their stumpspeakers. And it was also the spectacle and costuming, and the sensational blood-letting and play of passions. And there is no doubt that it was also partly the feeling that when you saw Shakespeare, you not only enjoyed a good show, but you were improving yourself. So it was on the frontier, and later in small-town opera houses, and even in the great metropolitan theatres where new Hamlets and new Desdemonas have so often created sensations.

Richard III in the old op'ry house! Perhaps it was your first play. Your father, who usually frowned on the tawdry shows that came to the village theatre, up over Brown's General Merchandise, yielded to your begging "Why can't **we** go, pa?" when he saw the announcement in the local paper that it was *The Tragedy of Richard III* that would be presented in the Opera House on such and such a night. Was not *Richard III* history? And was it not Shakespeare, too? And so he took you to the play, and you saw the crook-backed Richard, heard him plotting for the throne and tempestuously wooing Lady Anne. You wept over the young black-velveted princes in the Tower and their terrible fate, and you thrilled at the ghosts: "Let me sit heavy on thy soul tomorrow!" And that midnight soliloquy of Richard:

> Give me another horse! Bind up my wounds!
> Have mercy, Jesu!—Soft! I did but dream.
> O coward conscience, how thou dost afflict me!
> The lights burn blue. It is now dead midnight.
> Cold, fearful drops stand on my trembling flesh. . . .

The marching and counter-marching, the two orations of the leaders to their armies, and finally the tremendous excitement of the duel between Richard and Richmond. Your father had to explain to you that Richmond's sword really did not go through his adversary. It was a trick sword; this was only a stage-play. But it took the reappearance of Richard before the curtain to reassure you. . . . The experience was memorable; it was not, after all, such a bad way to make the acquaintance of Shakespeare.

On the reading side, the single-volume editions were great popularizers of Shakespeare. The first of these was issued by that distinguished editor, book-publisher, and lover of the theatre, Joseph T. Buckingham, of Boston. It was printed in very small type, with double-column pages and no notes. It was not very attractive, perhaps; but it was cheap, and it was the forerunner of the scores of other cheap, one-volume Shakespeares which made it possible for the humblest homes to have Shakespeare in blue and gold on the shelf beside *Pilgrim's Progress,* the Bible, and Tennyson or Longfellow.

Most of the single-volume editions came after 1850, however. Before that, the *Complete Works* in six to ten little volumes were popular. In 1839 Harpers bought the plates of the ten-volume Durell edition of 1817, from which seven editions had already been printed by three different publishers, and issued an edition of their own, which was followed by seven more printings, the last in 1868. Harpers also purchased the Borradaile (1825) plates of a two-volume set and issued editions for different booksellers with their imprints for some forty years.* In 1843, during a price-cutting contest among publishers, one of the Harper contributions was a set of Shakespeare in eight weekly parts at twenty-five cents each. The next year the Verplanck Shakespeare was issued in weekly parts, illustrated, at half that amount.

Even after the single-volume editions became so common, new and pretentious sets continued to be published with some regularity. This is not the place

---

* These statements are based on the studies of Henry N. Paul, leading collector of American Shakespeareana, as quoted by Westfall, *op. cit.*

to discuss the work of American editors, but it may be observed that American Shakespearean scholarship has for the past generation or two been of the highest importance in activity, volume, and authority.

The number of editions of Shakespeare continuously available in the United States is amazing. Leypoldt's *American Catalogue* for 1876 listed no less than sixty-five editions of the complete plays then in print. This computation regards the various bindings of a given offering as a single edition.

School readers also did much to bring Shakespeare home to the people, and to make some of the passages from his plays almost as familiar as verses from the Bible. The shrewd Dr. McGuffey, though he would never mention the names of the plays from which he took his extracts, caused many a schoolboy to declaim Antony's oration over Caesar, Hamlet's soliloquy, Cardinal Wolsey's reflections on fame in *Henry VIII,* and many another eloquent piece. The elocution books, with all their absurdities, taught the youth of the time to recite Shakespeare.

Then in the late eighties, the use of complete English classics in secondary schools and colleges became common, supplementing the study of literary history. Henry N. Hudson and William J. Rolfe edited single-play volumes for the schools with copious notes. By this time efforts were being made for uniformity in college entrance requirements, with the result that certain plays, as *Julius Caesar, The Merchant of Venice,* and *Midsummer Night's Dream,* were fixed even more firmly in the high school curricula.

Just what effect has the required reading of Shakespeare in the schools made upon the popular appreciation of the Bard of Avon? When the Harvard boys bought the paper-covered plays in 1796, they read them with zest. Shakespeare was not quite approved by their elders. But when he came to be not only approved but required, what was the effect? Opinions differ; probably no general answer is possible. For many youngsters, studying Shakespeare is an experience of some real esthetic value; for some it means little or nothing; in others it produces an active dislike. But the net result of the system in general probably promotes respect, if not love, for the poet.

At any rate, Shakespeare marches on. Clubs still study his works, as they have for a hundred years in this country. Both the commercial play-house and the little theatre still produce his plays, and a new production still excites interest. We still quote his lines, and many of us still read him occasionally for pleasure. The Pocket Books series published a volume of his tragedies in 1939 as one of their first issues; it has sold over 750,000 copies. The World Publishing Company's single-volume edition has sold more than 800,000 copies. Shakespeare is still a best seller in America.

X. FIRESIDE HISTORY AND BIOGRAPHY: EIGHTEENTH CENTURY STYLE

. . . and as the Evenings are grown long, and the Winter setting in, said Noel presumes he may inform his Customers, that he has provided a curious Parcel of books, both for Profit and Amusement at their Fire sides.

> Advertisement of Garrat Noel,
> bookseller, in New York Mercury,
> November 10, 1760

By the firesides of Colonial America, in the long winter evenings, our serious-minded forebears read many an extended and leisurely historical work. Rollin, Josephus, Voltaire, Plutarch, Robertson's and Buchanan's histories of Scotland, Hume's and Smollett's works on English history, Rapin's and Rider's ditto, Neal's *History of the Puritans,* and Fox's *Book of Martyrs* were favorites. Most of these histories were read from imported copies in many-volumed sets of small sextodecimos.

A religious age was especially interested in Flavius Josephus. His *Antiquities* could be studied as supplementary to the Scriptural narrative, and his smooth and lively style, in L'Estrange's or Whiston's translation, was easy to read. Its popularity continued throughout the nineteenth century, and the many cheap editions of Whiston brought it into multitudes of family libraries. Its sales were stimulated by the growth of Bible classes in Sunday Schools.

Another book of religious history widely read in Colonial America and later to be found on the shelves of Sunday School libraries was John Fox's *Acts and Monuments of the Church,* best known as the *Book of Martyrs.* The first edition of it was published in Latin, in Strasbourg, Germany, while Fox was a refugee on the Continent. Later it was enlarged in English by Fox and published in London, and still later edited and expanded by many hands. It was in many American bookstores and libraries in the eighteenth century, but the first American edition was the large quarto published in parts, for binding in two volumes, by William Durell, of New York, in 1794-1796. This was an elaborate project, with many large copperplate illustrations by James Scoles and Benjamin Tanner; and each of the forty parts sold for two shillings. Durell had recently published Josephus in a similar form. Many cheap editions of the *Book of Martyrs* came on the market in the next hundred years, most of them with woodcuts depicting the tortures and executions. Fox's veracity has often been questioned, but the worst accusation to be brought against his famous book is that it is sadistic in its appeal. Surely it was never a helpful, or even a safe, book for the Sunday School libraries.

The most popular imported historical work for a decade or more before the Revolution was William Robertson's *History of Scotland,* but it was not reprinted in America until 1811. The Protestant bias and lucid style of Robertson won him a large audience in this country. His *History of America* appeared on the eve of the Revolution and never won the audience it deserved on this side of the Atlantic, though parts of it appeared in American periodicals.

Second only to Robertson's *Scotland* in the field of historical writing was David Hume's *History of Great Britain,* which, in respect of style at least, was probably Robertson's model. Hume's *History* was reprinted in Philadelphia in 1795-1796, when Samuel Harrison Smith issued a six-volume edition in octavo for Robert Campbell, the bookseller. Its nearest competitor for American popularity in its field was Smollett's *History of England,* the first volumes of which were intended to rival, and the latter volumes to continue, Hume's superior work.

Late in the eighteenth century appeared two great best sellers in the field of American biography. Franklin's is the greatest autobiography in American literature, and Weems's *Life of Washington* possesses special interests, curious and otherwise, as an early essay in popular biography.

No American classic has had a stranger history than Franklin's famous book. Its piecemeal composition, the chances and mischances of its manuscript copies, its translations and publications in garbled texts, combine to furnish a fantastic tale which can be told here only in general outline.

In 1771 Franklin was sixty-five years old. He had known many famous and interesting people, and borne an important part in events of great importance. He was at the time, to all intents and purposes, the general agent of the American Colonies in England. That summer he spent two weeks in retirement at the home of his good friend, the Bishop of St. Asaph's, at Twyford; and there he began his memoirs, writing at that time a little more than a third of what we now have. But Franklin's vacation was short, his life was occupied with varied and weighty affairs, and not until thirteen years later did he resume work on his autobiography. Now he was residing at Passy, near Paris, as American Commissioner to France. This time he wrote about a fifth of the manuscript. Whereas the first part had been written informally, and mainly for the eyes of his son, he now wrote for the general public. Four years later he was back in Philadelphia, an old man of eighty-two, suffering with the gout. More painstakingly than before, he wrote most of the remainder of the work. The next year he wrote a few pages more, and in 1790 he died.

Thus the manuscript was in four parts—the first written at Twyford, the second at Passy, the third at Philadelphia in 1788, and the fourth at Philadelphia in 1789. Now Part I was in a chest of his papers which, having been shipped to Philadelphia, was broken open and partially looted during the war; and it finally came into the hands of a friendly Quaker merchant of Philadelphia who eventually restored it to the author—but not until some of his clerks (it has been asserted) made a copy of it. Do not forget this copy.

Then when Franklin had finished Parts I, II, and III, he had his grandson,

Benjamin Franklin Bache, later a famous Philadelphia editor, make two "fair copies" from his much interlined original; and these he sent to two close friends, one in England and one in France, for their criticism. It seems likely that Bache made many emendations in the course of the copying, probably with his grandfather's approval.* Then Franklin sat down and added Part IV to the original, which he bequeathed on his death to his other grandson, William Temple Franklin, an English resident.

Note that now there were at least four copies of the manuscript, or parts of it, scattered about the world. Grandson William Temple had the original in London, and promised a careful edition from it. The Quaker clerks' manuscript of Part I was presumably somewhere. A copy of the first three parts was in the hands of the Englishman Vaughn, and another in those of the Frenchman Le Veillard.

William Temple Franklin delayed his edition from year to year, but it was too much to expect that the memoirs would not get into print through some other owner of a manuscript. Indeed, the year after Benjamin Franklin's death, a little book entitled *Mémoires de la Vie Privée de Benjamin Franklin* appeared in Paris. Probably this came from the Quaker clerks' copy, for it comprised only Part I. It was badly enough translated, but it was soon badly translated back into English for the London press. And as though the comedy had not been carried far enough, the English translation of the French translation was now translated back into French again for a Paris edition of 1798.

So it went on. Various uses were made of all the more or less variant copies. William Temple Franklin borrowed le Veillard's "fair copy" and used it instead of the original for his edition, which appeared in 1818 and became the recognized text on which literally hundreds of editions in many languages were based. Half a century later John Bigelow, United States minister to France, got interested in the search for the original manuscript, which had disappeared from sight. An American newspaper man finally found it, and bought it for Bigelow for 25,000 francs; from it Bigelow published the edition which has been generally accepted since its appearance in 1868.

The new editor thought that William Temple Franklin had used the original manuscript, and was very severe on him for refining his grandfather's robust phrases; but Dr. Farrand's researches show that Bigelow and those who have followed his lead were wrong, and that the W. T. F. edition of 1818 represented the Le Veillard "fair copy" very closely. Thus the substitution of more elegant phrases for such expressions as "guzzlers of beer" and "Keimer stared like a pig poisoned" was Franklin old correcting Franklin, if not young, at least younger. Moreover, it also appears that Bigelow's edition was itself far from a faithful reproduction of the original manuscript. We are promised an accu-

* See Max Farrand's *Benjamin Franklin's Memoirs*, reprinted for private circulation from *The Huntington Library Bulletin*, No. 10, October, 1936. This is much the best account of the manuscripts and texts.

rate presentation of it by the Huntington Library, now the custodian of that manuscript, together with variorum readings from the other copies and editions. And, more to the point so far as popular reading is concerned, we are also promised an edition based on a text which is nearest the intention of the author, so far as scholarship can separate the true Franklin from his two grandsons and from the mess that friends and translators, editors and get-rich-quick publishers have made of him.

But despite all the injuries that it has suffered in publication, Franklin's *Autobiography* has long been both a classic and a favorite—"one of the most widely read books in the English language," as Max Farrand declared.

More simple is the story of the other American biography which was a best seller at the beginning of the nineteenth century—Parson Weems's *Life of George Washington; with Curious Anecdotes, Equally Honourable to Himself, and Exemplary to His Young Countrymen.* Weems had lost his pulpit, but had immediately found his true vocation in book-peddling. We have noted how the hawking of various books through the countryside helped to make best sellers out of them. But Mason Weems was no ordinary ragged chapman: he kept his character as a clergyman, and added those of author, compiler, and peddler. He possessed both dignity and shrewdness. Had not Washington himself written a testimonial for Weems's behavior book? That compilation was called *The Immortal Mentor; or, Man's Unerring Guide to a Healthy, Wealthy, and Happy Life,* and the first ex-president had testified that he had "perused it with singular satisfaction" and found it "invaluable." With such a recommendation in his pocket, the good parson could set out from his Virginia home in his gig with the books piled all around him, "drive like Jehu" (as a friend said he always did) from farmstead to farmstead, and return in the evening sold out.

Immediately after Washington's death, Weems wrote a pamphlet about the great man's life and character which sold so well that he enlarged it from edition to edition until it was in the form of the biography which made Weems famous. As the subtitle indicates, this is anecdotal biography. The illustrative stories are of the folk-tale sort; some critics have credited the author with inventing them, but it is more likely that he was part compiler, part inventor, and mostly embellisher. Here is the most famous of them:

When George was about six years old, he was made the wealthy owner of a *hatchet!* of which, like most little boys, he was immoderately fond; and was constantly going about chopping every thing which came in his way. One day, in the garden, where he often amused himself by hacking his mother's pea-sticks, he unluckily tried the edge of his hatchet on the body of a beautiful young English cherry-tree, which he barked so terribly, that I don't believe the tree ever got the better of it. The next morning, the old gentleman, finding out what had befallen his tree, which, by the by, was a great favourite, came into the house; and with much warmth asked for the mischievous author, declaring at the same time, that he would not have taken five guineas for his tree. Nobody would tell him anything about it. Presently George and his hatchet made their appearance. *"George,"* said his father, "do you know who killed that beautiful little cherry tree yonder in the garden?"

This was a *tough question;* and George staggered under it for a moment; but quickly recovered himself; and looking at his father, with the sweet face of youth brightened with the inexpressible charm of all-conquering truth, he bravely cried out, "I can't tell a lie, Pa; you know I can't tell a lie. I did cut it with my hatchet."—Run to my arms, you dearest boy, cried his father in transports, run to my arms; glad am I, George, that you killed my tree; for you have paid me for it a thousand fold. Such an act of heroism in my son is worth more than a thousand trees, though blossomed with silver, and their fruits of purest gold.

Much as he admired truth-telling on the part of George, the Rev. Mr. Weems veered from the strait and narrow when he named himself on his title-page "formerly rector of Mt. Vernon Parish." There was no such parish; and the nearest Weems had come to being Washington's rector was his delivery of a few sermons at the Pohick church, which the great man had once attended. So far as we know, Washington never heard Weems preach, though interested in him as a compiler and peddler of books. That interest, however, gives a kind of poetic justice to Weems's treatment of him in a book built chiefly of edifying fables and the rhetoric of the pulpit. The Weems *Life* fits well enough, indeed, into the category of behavior books approved by Washington.

"Washington outsells anything I have, no comparison," wrote Peddler Weems to Mathew Carey, his publisher. Nearly a score of the editions of the book were required before the death of the author, and more than fifty have appeared since. The story of the cherry tree got into *McGuffey's Third Reader*, and the one about the cabbages which spelled out George's name into the Fifth. And we are reminded on each recurrent February twenty-second that a little hatchet is inseparable from the memory of the first President.

Finally, the remarkable and long-continued popularity of Volney's *The Ruins* may be mentioned here. This was a series of "meditations" and visions by the French savant and publicist Constantin François Volney, conveying a philosophical view of the causes of the ruin of empires. Its thesis is that the basic disaster is the abandonment of natural religion, and thus the book becomes a tract for the deists.

This eloquent and provocative book was first published in Geneva in 1791; but when its author came to America four years later with the intention of making his home in the new land, one of the first things he did after paying his respects to President Washington was to arrange for the publication of an English translation of *Les Ruines* in Philadelphia under his own copyright. It was immediately successful, and the next year William A. Davis, of New York, issued the book for eleven different booksellers. These were the first of many editions. Among the translators were Thomas Jefferson and Joel Barlow. Cheap editions have been common for more than a hundred years, ranging as low as five cents in the Little Blue Book series.

XI. THE WIZARD OF THE NORTH
AND THE AMERICAN "GAME"

. . . when Time, that old ravager, has done his very worst, there will be enough left of Sir Walter to carry his name and fame to the remotest age.
Augustine Birrell, "Essays"

In the history of American best sellers, the novels of Jane Porter appear to be forerunners of those of Walter Scott. This sequence need not mislead us into any false notions about literary influences. Walter Scott was an early friend of the Porter sisters, and the success of *The Scottish Chiefs* in Edinburgh may have afforded one of the impulses that led him to finish *Waverley*, begun some years before; but there the connection appears to end. Scott knew many literary masters, being widely read; but he reacted chiefly to Scottish border minstrelsy and, in the case of the first third of *Waverley* especially, to Maria Edgeworth's Irish sketches in *Castle Rackrent*.

Jane Porter's two popular novels were best sellers in America for a long time. Their obvious shortcomings—in historical and local color, and in realism and truth in delineation of character and incident—have caused critics generally to underestimate them. The omnivorous and categorical Saintsbury, for example, dismisses them shortly as "rubbish." But thousands of humbler readers, oblivious of the dicta of that awful figure perched on his tripod with piles of books about him, the bearded and spectacled reader-judge, have clutched their *Scottish Chiefs* to their bosoms and scurried off to obscure corners to pore over their treasure with delight.

Thaddeus of Warsaw, Miss Porter's first success, was scarcely a historical novel. It dealt with the adventures of a member of the Sobieski family, first on Polish battlefields and later as a refugee in England. It was widely read in England and Scotland, in Poland, and in America. Kosciusko sent his portrait and a medal to the author, and she was made honorary member of various foreign societies.

Though *Thaddeus*, with its Polish patriot elements, represents some improvement over the current high-society romance of the turn of the century in England, it is not much better than those emotionally excessive romances. The great best-seller example of that class was *Children of the Abbey*, by Regina Maria Roche, in which the heroine weeps and faints through a series of irrational catastrophes, escapes all the traps that blackest-hearted villainy can contrive, refuses the offers of dukes and earls, and in the end lives happily ever after in the best circles. *Children of the Abbey* is a link between *Clarissa* and midcentury best sellers like *East Lynne* and *Lady Audley's Secret*.

Scottish Chiefs is better. It is distinguished by movement, many characters, intricate plotting, passion, and rhetoric. It is, of course, too full of sound and fury and high-flown fustian. One does not need the titlepage quotation from Ossian to realize Miss Porter's debt to that magniloquent poet, himself not far short of best-sellerdom in America. There are many passages like this:

Together they struck into the most impenetrable defiles of the mountains, and proceeded till, by the smoke, whitening with its ascending curls the black sides of the impending rocks, Wallace saw he was near the objects of his search. He sprung on a high cliff which projected over this mountain valley, and, blowing his bugle with a few notes of the well known *pibroch* of Lanerkshire, was answered by the reverberation of a thousand echoes.

At the loved sounds, which had not visited their ears since the Scottish standard was lowered to Edward, the hills seemed teeming with life. Men rushed from their fastnesses, and women with their babes eagerly followed, to see whence sprung a summons so dear to every Scottish heart. Wallace stood on the cliff like the newly aroused genius of his suffering country. His long plaid floated afar, and his glittering hair, streaming on the blast, seemed to mingle with the golden fires which shot from the heavens. Wallace raised his eyes: a clash as of the tumult of contending armies filled the sky, and flames and flashing steel and the horrid red of battle streamed from the clouds upon the hills.

Scotsmen! cried Wallace, waving the fatal sword, which blazed in the glare of these Northern Lights like a flaming brand, behold how the heavens cry aloud to you! I come in the name of all you hold dear, of your lives, your liberties, and of the wives of your bosoms, and the children now in their arms. The poignard of England is unsheathed: innocence, age, and infancy fall before it! With his sword, last night, did Hesselrigge, the English tyrant of Lanerk, murder my wife!

A shriek of horror burst from every mouth. "Vengeance, vengeance!" was the cry. . . .

Highfalutin, to be sure; but scarcely rubbish. In its context, it seems to have a certain romantic validity; at any rate, hosts of readers found it very compelling for nearly a hundred years after its first publication. It was in 1842 that an American committee sent to Miss Porter, in Edinburgh, "an elegant carved armchair, trimmed with crimson plush," to testify to "the admiring gratitude of the American people." John Harper, chairman of the committee, might well have donated this work of domestic art himself, since his firm had profited largely from reprinting Miss Porter's novels in America, without the formality of payment for same.

To the less discriminating public which admired *The Scottish Chiefs* was added the growing body of readers of taste when *Waverley* came along in 1814. Indeed, nearly everyone who could spell out a page read not only *Waverley*, but *Guy Mannering, Rob Roy, Ivanhoe,* and *Kenilworth,* which now came from the press at intervals of only a year or two, bearing on their titlepages the line "By the Author of *Waverley*." His desire for anonymity, which he held in common with many gentleman-writers, made the most popular author of his times "the great Unknown" for many years.

It was pointed out in connection with our discussion of the popularity of *Pamela* that part of Richardson's appeal was due to the fresh truth of his portrayals in comparison with those of the old romances. Scott himself, writing of Richardson, said: "It requires a reader to be in some degree acquainted with the huge folios of inanity over which our ancestors nodded themselves to sleep, ere he can estimate the delight they must have experienced over this return to truth and nature." Now compare this with the remarks which Scott makes 'about his own purposes in writing *Waverley,* in the introductory chapter of that novel. There he repudiates, in humorous but categorical terms, the fictional types which had been common in his own times—Gothic tales, German romance, stories of sensibility, and novels of high life. What he aimed at and what he achieved was a new "return to truth and nature." The success of the formula now was even greater than in the case of *Pamela,* and the boundless enthusiasm of the entire reading world greeted *Waverley* and its successors.

There were other reasons for Scott's popularity, of course. Americans took him to their hearts not only because of the fresh and novel truth in the delineation of his characters and incidents, but also because, like Burns, he was democratic enough to be interested in humble folk. The Scottish efforts against England, so prominent in *Waverley, Rob Roy,* and *Guy Mannering,* could not but remind them of their own recent struggle and triumph, different though the cases were. And then the historical content of the novels had a great appeal to readers who wished to improve themselves while they were being entertained; this element, and the author's method of occasional insertion of passages in the vein of what may be called commonplace philosophy, did much to take the curse off novel-reading for the serious-minded reader, and to make the more casual seeker after the pleasures of fiction feel that he too was being edified. It is true that critics decry a certain lack of depth in Scott; but when such a reader as Goethe could say, "He gives me much to think of," surely it is not strange if lesser minds have found him often wise and thoughtful. Another factor of his appeal was his romantic description of scenery. This is a type of writing that has few modern partisans; but Scott was often praised for it, he did it probably better than anyone before or since, and there was then a popular taste for it. Nor can we forget Scott's humor, which played upon characters not to distort them but to make them real to us in all their foibles. Finally, there was the genius of the man whom his admirers loved to call "the wizard of the North," the force of which was chiefly thrown, to use his own terms, upon the passions of his characters.

But whatever the reasons for it, the tremendous popular following of Scott in America was an important fact throughout at least the first third of the nineteenth century. "The victories of Napoleon were not so wide, nor his monuments so likely to endure," wrote W. B. O. Peabody in the *North American Review;* and Nathaniel Parker Willis thought it "a great privilege to live in the same age with the author of *Waverley.*" When Scott died in 1832, New York held a great mass meeting as a memorial to him.

But even at the time when the loved and admired master was making a supreme struggle to pay off the debts of the publishing concern in the collapse of which he was involved, Scott received very little, if anything, from the American publishers of his works. In default of international copyright, there was, of course, no legal obligation upon the American publishers of English books. And, ironically enough, this piratical publishing did much, through its wide and cheap distribution of the Waverley novels, to make Scott beloved in the new world by robbing him of proper American returns for his genius.

Scott's novels were the first top-flight immediate best sellers in the United States, except, perhaps, for Paine's *Common Sense*. Quick development of very large sales was unlikely, and often impossible, under the publishing system of the eighteenth century. But by the time of *Waverley*, the early method of distributing books through the cooperative effort of booksellers and printers was shifting to book-publishing by firms which, although they did their own printing and sometimes sold books at retail, centered their effort upon the specialized task of producing books to sell to bookstores in quantity. In other words, professional book-publishing had begun. Leaders among these firms about 1820 were Mathew Carey & Son, Moses Thomas, and Collins & Company, of Philadelphia; J. & J. Harper, C. S. Van Winkle, and Kirk & Mercein, of New York; Cummings & Hilliard, West & Richardson, Wells & Lilly, and Samuel T. Armstrong, of Boston; Beers & Howe, of New Haven; and O. D. Cooke, of Hartford. Names pretty much forgotten, except for the first and fourth.

These publishers issued books of many kinds, but chiefly textbooks and English reprints. At first there was no very warm competition among them; but about the time of *Waverley* and *Guy Mannering*—books to which there was an eager public response—they awoke to the fact that the first one of them to offer a sure-fire best seller to the bookstores would cash in on some quick profits. In 1817 Carey wrote to his London correspondent that American publishers * were "so very active" that it was imperative to forward books that would bear republication in America to him "by first and fastest sailing vessels" so he could beat everyone else in this lively marketing operation. To get the edge on his "very active" competition, Carey soon began to pay, through his English agent, certain sums up to seventy-five pounds to the publishers of the most desirable English books for "advance sheets" instead of waiting for regular publication in London or Edinburgh; and it may be presumed that Scott received something from Carey's payments. But as soon as a book thus issued from "advance sheets" appeared in the bookstores, the pirates seized it and got out their own editions; so that the advantage gained was small, and an American publisher could never afford to pay large sums for what was at best a short head-start.

This, then, was the game as it developed by 1820. The leading publishers employed agents in London and Edinburgh to get their hands on the chief books published in those cities as quickly as possible. The agents would buy "advance sheets" if they could; London and Edinburgh publishers considered this so much velvet, agreed to sell these particular sheets to nobody else, and

* Carey still spoke of them as "booksellers."

usually kept their promises. Competing agents sometimes bribed clerks in pub-lishing houses, however; failing that, they obtained the earliest copies possible through booksellers or reviewers. If a novel was published serially, like so many by Dickens, it was the last installment or two that the agents fought over.

Meanwhile, the New York, Philadelphia, and Boston publishers had their arrangements all made and waiting. When a ship expected to bring "copy" of a new book by one of the popular authors was sighted, a messenger rounded up the typesetters so they would be waiting, composing sticks in their hands, when the precious sheets were rushed to them from the waterside.* The "copy" was then divided into "takes" and distributed to the thirty or forty compositors, who took pride in their records for speed in typesetting. Work was then rushed day and night at top speed until the book was printed and bound. *Niles' Weekly Register* had an item on July 20, 1822, to the effect that a New York publisher put *The Fortunes of Nigel* into the hands of workmen at eight o'clock one Thursday morning, and it was for sale in the bookstores the fol-lowing Saturday morning. But the next year Carey & Son left that record far behind when they turned out *Quentin Durward* in twenty-eight hours. There is a tradition in the House of Harper that when they got *Peveril of the Peak,* one of the longest of Scott's novels, into their shop, all hands worked without rest, with lunches brought in and eaten standing, the proprietors sharing in the hurry and strain, until the three volumes were sent out to the bookshops in twenty-one hours from receipt of copy. Of course, competitors picked up these first American editions, reset and reprinted them, and tried to undersell to the bookstores; but the first edition commonly had the advantage of about three days' business. This, when dealing with a public which stormed the book-stores, eager for the latest from Scott or Dickens, meant the cream of the profits.

It would be hard to exaggerate this eagerness. John Hay, speaking at the unveiling of the bust of Scott in Westminster Abbey in 1897, said: "I have heard from my father—a pioneer of Kentucky—that in the early days of this century men would saddle their horses and ride from all the neighboring coun-ties to the principal post-town of the region when a new novel by the Author of *Waverley* was expected." Sometimes a first edition of three thousand copies or more was actually sold over the counters in one day, leaving late comers begging for more. The Scott madness, far from being confined to eastern cities, raged as well in the South, and in the pioneer districts of the West. Indeed, it is probable that Southern readers loved Scott more devotedly than the people of any other region outside of Scotland itself. "Few men," declared William E. Dodd, historian of the South, "ever had greater influence over the cotton planters than the beloved Scottish bard and novelist."

The publishing technique just described—which Carey sometimes called

* Earl L. Bradsher, in his *Mathew Carey* (New York, 1912) quotes a letter in which Carey complains to the Secretary of the Treasury about the clearance of books through customs delaying republication, to the advantage of a competitor (p. 86).

"the Game"—was employed, with appropriate variations, until well past the midcentury mark. After the Civil War, improvements in printing, transportation, and the customs of the booktrade brought in new methods, though pirating of new books by English authors ended only with the International Copyright agreement of 1891. Not all the books published by the rush methods of the "game" were top-bracket best sellers, since sales then, as now, were by no means accurately predictable; some were only "better sellers," and some comparative failures.

Yet this very competition had an exciting effect on the public, and it made immediate best sellers possible. Many of the hurry-scurry editions were ill printed from small type, and cheaply bound; but they were the editions that made Scott, Byron, Dickens, and Bulwer popular in America.

Carey and the Harpers in the 1820's usually bound a Scott novel in two volumes and sold it for $1.75, but keen competition brought cheaper methods and lower prices. By 1830 there were at least ten printing establishments in Philadelphia alone which engaged in the reprinting of Scott, and perhaps nearly as many in New York. Before 1840 Parker, of New York, was publishing the Waverley novels at twenty-five cents, and in 1841 Israel Post issued them in twenty-cent weekly numbers. After the cheap-book era of the early forties, prices for Scott were reasonable for two decades: there were cheap issues, but also such de luxe editions as Appleton's set of twelve volumes at eighty dollars in 1847. Ticknor & Fields published Scott in fifty small volumes in the late fifties, boasting a sale of 300,000 of the well made little books at seventy-five cents each by 1861. But in 1868 Appleton brought the novels out in twenty-six volumes at six dollars, and T. B. Peterson put them into twenty-five volumes at five dollars. By that time a flood of cheap importations from England was challenging American publishers. Then in the middle seventies a second outbreak of cheap-book publishing in America upset the trade and put hundreds of thousands of Scott's novels in cheap quarto form into the hands of the people at ten cents each. Since then Scott has usually been obtainable as low as twenty-five or thirty-five cents a volume.

Of all Scott's novels, *Ivanhoe* was and is the most popular. Anthony Trollope, in his life of Thackeray, spoke of it as "perhaps the most favourite novel in the English language." That was in 1879. Its use in the schools has given it an advantage in America; one school series alone (Macmillan's Pocket Classics) has sold over a million copies of it.

Scott's *Poems* are also in the best seller class; indeed both *The Lady of the Lake* and *Marmion* could be included independently. S. G. Goodrich wrote in his autobiography of the impression which these poems made on the youth of their time—partly, he says, because of the romance of their scenes and stories, and

partly also because of the pellucidity of the style and the easy flow of the versification. Everybody could read and comprehend them. One of my younger sisters committed the whole of *The Lady of the Lake* to memory, and was accustomed of an evening to sit at her sewing, while she recited it to an admiring circle of listeners. All young poets were inoculated with the octosyllabic verse, and newspapers, magazines, and even books teemed with imitations and variations inspired by the "Wizard Harp of the North."

In long-term popularity Sir Walter has an assured preëminence: no other novelist but Dickens has been republished so often by American publishers in multiple-volume editions, and no other novelist but Dickens has enjoyed so universal and enthusiastic a following in America for so long a time.

XII. IRVING AND COOPER

The Americans are a brave, industrious, and acute people; but they have hitherto given no indications of genius, and made no approaches to the heroic, either in their morality or character. They are but a recent offset indeed from England; and should make it their chief boast, for many generations to come, that they are sprung from the same race with Bacon and Shakespeare and Newton. . . . During the thirty or forty years of their independence, they have done absolutely nothing for the Sciences, for the Arts, for Literature, or even for the statesman-like studies of Politics or Political Economy. . . . In the four quarters of the globe, who reads an American book? or goes to an American play? or looks at an American picture or statue?

Sydney Smith in the "Edinburgh Review," January, 1820

ON OCTOBER 26, 1809, the following advertisement appeared in the *New York Evening Post*:

DISTRESSING

Left his lodgings some time since, and has not since been heard of, a small elderly gentleman, dressed in an old black coat and cocked hat, by the name of KNICKERBOCKER. As there are some reasons for believing he is not entirely in his right mind, and as great anxiety is entertained about him, any information concerning him left either at the Columbian Hotel, Mulberry street, or at the office of this paper, will be *thankfully* received.

P.S.—Printers of newspapers would be aiding the cause of humanity in giving an insertion to the above.

Nearly two weeks later a paragraph appeared in the same paper signed "A Traveller" which told of a person answering the description of the old gentleman advertised for having been seen resting by the side of the road "a little above Kingsbridge." After another interval, the landlord of the Columbian Hotel signed the following communication in the *Evening Post*:

Sir: You have been good enough to publish in your paper a paragraph about Mr. Diedrich Knickerbocker, who was missing so strangely from his lodgings some time since. Nothing satisfactory has been heard of the old gentleman since; but a *very curious kind of a written book* has been found in his room in his own handwriting. Now I wish you to notice him, if he is still alive, that if he does not return and pay off his bill, for board and lodging, I shall have to dispose of his Book, to satisfy me for the same.

Seth Handaside.

On December 6 New York papers carried a notice that *A History of New York* in two duodecimo volumes was "this day published by Inskep and Bradford" at three dollars. A few lines about the scope of the book, its "curious and interesting particulars never before published," and its "philosophical speculations and moral precepts," were followed by the statement that "This work was found in the chamber of Mr. Diedrich Knickerbocker, the old gentleman whose sudden and mysterious disappearance has been noticed. It is published to discharge certain debts he has left behind."

The Knickerbocker fable continued even through the book's titlepage and dedication to the New York Historical Society. The purchaser of an early copy—sobersided reader interested in historical works—must have read a page or two and muttered, "Well, this is a queer book!" Then another page or two, and exclaimed, "Why, the old fellow *must* have been daft!" But soon he must have reached the passage telling of the effect on the phlegmatic Hendryk Hudson when he first viewed the island of Mannhata:

> When the great navigator was first blessed with a view of this enchanting island, he was observed, for the first and only time in his life, to exhibit strong symptoms of astonishment and admiration. He is said to have turned to Master Juet, and uttered these remarkable words, while he pointed towards this paradise of the new world,—"See! there!" —and thereupon, as was always his way when uncommonly pleased, he did puff out such clouds of dense tobacco-smoke, that in one minute the vessel was out of sight of land.

Then our first reader of the first edition of the first humorous masterpiece of the new world must have uttered a great guffaw, slapped his thigh, and cried, "I've been sold! And by a right clever scribbler, I'll be bound!"

Our friend probably went about later, recommending the new history seriously to other gentlemen in an effort to fool them as he had been fooled. But the quality of the performance soon became known, and it was not long until New York literary circles were all laughing over it. All, indeed, but a few descendants of the city's first families who thought it unfitting to laugh at the peculiarities of their forebears.

The Knickerbocker *History of New York* was a great success. "It excited an interest in the metropolis," wrote the anecdotic Dr. John W. Francis, "never before roused up by any literary occurrence—scarcely, perhaps, by any public event." Though not perhaps an immediate best seller (that would have been scarcely possible for a three-dollar book by an American in 1809), it did have an extremely cordial reception both at home and abroad, and its sales grew with edition after edition. Carey & Lea became its publishers in 1829 and published a new printing every year or two until the middle forties, when the incursion of the very cheap reprints of English works apparently drove Irving's books out of the American market. But Putnam took them over in 1848, put them out in low-priced editions, and sold large quantities again both in sets and separate works. Many of the cheap publishers of the 1870's issued editions of Irving, his copyrights having expired.

When Sydney Smith asked his famous question, "Who reads an American book?" in the *Edinburgh Review* in 1820, he might have been reminded that

Edinburgh's most famous citizen, Walter Scott, had read Knickerbocker aloud to the delight of his family (it still reads well aloud) not many years before; and in that same year England's most famous publisher, John Murray, was bringing out a London edition of the Knickerbocker history along with the new *Sketch Book*. Indeed only a few months after it printed Sydney Smith's insulting query, the *Review* carried a laudatory notice of the *Sketch Book*, in which it remarked that "a few such works" would "go far to wipe off the reproach" of lack of taste and literary ability among Americans. Though smug and magisterial, this criticism had a certain justice.

The *Sketch Book* was not only written in England, but dealt chiefly with English scenes, customs, and characters. Only two sketches were distinctively American, though they were the two which have done the most to make the book an enduring classic—"Rip Van Winkle" and "The Legend of Sleepy Hollow."

The *Sketch Book of Geoffrey Crayon, Gent.* was published in seven separate parts, ranging from seventy to a hundred and twenty pages each, and issued at irregular intervals averaging about ten weeks. All except the last were published first in New York, and later in London. These issues were beautifully printed in large type on excellent paper, and sold for seventy-five cents each. The New York printer was C. S. Van Winkle, who apparently was not deterred by the liberties taken with his patronymic either in the *Sketch Book* or in the gossipy pages of the irrepressible Knickerbocker; or had he forgotten that worthy's reference to "the Van Winkles, of Haerlem, potent suckers of eggs, and noted for running of horses, and running up of scores at taverns"? But C. S. Van Winkle was, in this case, not the publisher; he was merely the excellent printer. As in the *History* venture, Irving took the whole financial risk; but since he was still in London, he delegated the distribution of the issues among booksellers to that most devoted of friends, Henry Brevoort, and later to his brother Ebenezer. Thus there was a simultaneous publication in New York, Boston, Philadelphia, and Baltimore.

Seventy-five cents for a pamphlet of as many pages was pretty steep for those days, when prices were so low that Commodore Decatur, offering Irving a Navy job at $2,400 a year, said that was enough to enable him to live in Washington "like a prince." In a letter to Brevoort, Irving wrote:

You observe that the public complain of the price of my work; this is the disadvantage of coming in competition with republished English works, for which the booksellers have not to pay anything to the authors. If the American public wish to have a literature of their own, they must consent to pay for the support of authors.

Very true; but the public always buys (a) what it likes and (b) what it can afford, without much regard for the welfare of authors. It liked the *Sketch Book*, bought up the first edition of two thousand copies of Part I in about three months, and went on buying the other issues and calling for more editions. The sales of this book had somewhat the same history as those of

"Knickerbocker," dropping in the forties, and rising when Putnam published it in 1857 at sixty cents in cloth binding and fifty cents in "paper boards."

From the time of his return to America in 1846 until his death thirteen years later, Irving was a highly popular national celebrity. A writer in the *Southern Quarterly Review* spoke of him in 1856 as "the most favorite American author at home and abroad." The popularity of his work in England and on the Continent (the *Sketch Book* was early translated into French and German) brought a glow of pride to the hearts of his American friends. No other American writer except Longfellow ever enjoyed so fully the sincere affection of his readers. That this affection was translated into dollars is evidenced by Henry Carey's assertion in his *Letters on International Copyright* (1853) that Irving's works had sold better than those of any other American author.

The *Sketch Book* made its way into the schools very early. It was firmly fixed in preparatory school curricula long before the universities got together on entrance requirements, and few school children are so unfortunate as to escape reading at least a part of it.

The schools have also done much to keep at least two of James Fenimore Cooper's novels alive—*The Last of the Mohicans* and *The Spy*. Teachers do not commonly emphasize the fact that Cooper was dismissed from Yale College when he was a boy of fifteen, though some of them have chuckled over the sententious remark of Professor Lounsbury, of Yale, in his book on Cooper:

We need not feel any distrust of his declaration, that little learning of any kind found its way into his head [while he was at Yale]. Least of all will he be inclined to doubt it whom extended experience in the classroom has taught to view with profoundest respect the infinite capability of the human mind to resist the introduction of knowledge.

Very schoolmasterish, and true enough so far as it goes.

Cooper entered the path of literature, as have many others, drawn by the desire of emulation. Reading one of the current English novels of high life aloud to his wife—probably, his daughter says, one of Mrs. Amelia Opie's tales— he flung it aside in disgust, and remarked that he could do better himself. Oddly enough, the poet Thomas Moore tells in his diary about reading Mrs. Opie's latest story aloud to *his* wife at about the same time,* and finding it so dull that he also stopped in the middle of it. But the experience did not move Moore to try the same game himself; while Cooper, dared by his wife to do his worst, forthwith produced *Precaution; or, Prevention Is Better Than Cure*. As an imitation, it was probably a success; many readers have also imitated Cooper and Moore in throwing *Precaution* away half-read. Cooper later wrote, in the preface to *The Pioneers*, that *Precaution* "was written because I

* See the Diary for February 18 and 20, 1819. Moore was reading Mrs. Opie's *New Tales;* Miss Cooper names no specific novel, and does little more than guess that it was by Mrs. Opie.

was told that I could not write a grave tale; so, to prove that the world did not know me, I wrote one that was so grave that nobody would read it; wherein I think that I had much the best of the argument."

Then Cooper goes on to say that he wrote *The Spy* "to see if I could not overcome this neglect of the reading world." And again he had the best of the argument, for the first small edition of the new book went off in a few weeks, and a second of three thousand and a third of five thousand were published within the year. The story was successfully staged within a few months of publication. It had been out only a little more than six months when a friend informed the English publisher Murray that Cooper had already received "near a thousand pounds" profits on it.[*] Small wonder that *The Spy* was hailed as the most successful book in American literature.

The Carey firm, quick to seize upon best sellers, took Cooper over in 1827 and continued to publish him for fifteen or twenty years. Cooper, like Irving, kept his own copyrights; but his printers were, from the first, his publishers—that is, they distributed his books.

In the cheap publishing era of the forties, Burgess, Stringer & Company (later Stringer & Townsend) were given a chance to exploit the Cooper novels and sold great quantities of them at twenty-five cents in paper-covered volumes; they later brought out a set of Cooper in thirty-three volumes, repeatedly reprinted, sometimes with F. O. C. Darley's illustrations. Putnams took over the Cooper books in 1849, issuing "revised" editions. As the copyright renewals began to expire in the sixties, many publishers put *The Spy*, the Leatherstocking tales, and *The Pilot* on their lists. Appletons issued a set with the Darley illustrations, paper bound, at seventy-five cents a volume in 1872; and a few years later, when the cheap "libraries" upset American publishing, Cooper's novels were sold very widely at twenty cents each. Street & Smith published them at ten cents for many years, up to 1920 at least. In the 1920's an abridged edition of *The Spy* was a Little Blue Book offering at five cents. Meanwhile Houghton, Mifflin & Company, G. P. Putnam's Sons, and other standard publishers continued to reprint the collected works steadily; and the many series designed for school use printed hundreds of thousands of copies of the chief Cooper titles.

Easy leader among the seven novels by Cooper which are on the best seller list is *The Last of the Mohicans*. It was the second of the Leatherstocking novels to be written, but it was more lively and adventurous than *The Pioneers*, its predecessor. Critics generally prefer *The Pathfinder* and *Deerslayer* for their more careful workmanship, but boys of several generations have delighted in the exploits of Hawkeye in *The Mohicans*. That novel has doubtless sold two million copies in America alone, and *The Spy*, which is next in

[*] Benjamin N. Coles, quoted in Spiller, Robert E., and Blackburn, Philip C., *A Descriptive Bibliography of the Works of James Fenimore Cooper* (New York, 1934).

order of popularity, over a million. *The Pathfinder* and *The Pilot* seem to be at the bottom of the list of the Cooper best sellers.

"There is no doubt that very various opinions are entertained by different persons as to the precise degree of Cooper's merit," observed a writer in the *North American Review* in 1831. So it has always been. Some have thought him superior to Scott, and the greatest romancer of his generation; some have found him coarse, slovenly, unconvincing, and—most damning of all—dull. Mark Twain, aroused by Lounsbury's statement that *Deerslayer* was "a work of art," replied by an indignant essay on "Fenimore Cooper's Literary Offenses," ending:

A work of art? It has no invention; it has no order, system, sequence, or result; it has no lifelikeness, no stir, no thrill, no seeming of reality; its characters are confusedly drawn, and by their acts and words they prove that they are not the sort of people the author claims that they are; its humor is pathetic; its pathos is funny; its conversations are—oh! indescribable; its love-scenes odious; its English a crime against the language. Counting these out, what is left is Art.

Much of Cooper is indeed irritating to any careful reader—shapeless and ragged. But what a great public, faithful to these books for some hundred years, saw in them, in the main, was the very spirit of high, clean, adventurous romance—romance of the Revolution in *The Spy*, romance of the sea in *The Pilot*, and romance of the forest, the Indian, and the pioneer in the Leatherstocking series. The ardent Americanism of these tales, their emphasis on right and justice, and the rather naive humor of occasional characterizations help further to explain the immense vogue of these novels.

Their popularity was by no means limited to the United States. All were promptly republished in England, and soon appropriated by piratical publishers. French translations were enthusiastically greeted, and generally read over many years. When America entered the first World War, one of the French leaders cried, "The spirit of Leatherstocking is awake!"—a phrase quite as well understood in France as in America. The Germans, Italians and Spanish also had their versions, often published at the same time as the American and English editions. Samuel F. B. Morse, a close friend of Cooper's, wrote in 1833:

I have visited, in Europe, many countries, and what I have asserted of the fame of Mr. Cooper I assert from personal knowledge. In every city of Europe that I visited the works of Cooper were conspicuously placed in the windows of every bookshop. They are published as soon as he produces them in thirty-four different places in Europe. They have been seen by American travelers in the languages of Turkey and Persia, in Constantinople, in Egypt, at Jerusalem, at Ispahan.

Cooper himself arranged simultaneous publication of some of his books in Philadelphia, London, Paris, and Berlin; but he soon gave the plan up, and Morse's story indicates the extent of piracies of his friend's books on the Continent.

And Cooper still sells in America. The wilderness has disappeared, the

Indians have gone the way that Chungachcook foresaw so clearly, styles in fiction have changed; but Leatherstocking still glides through the forest with his easy stride, and performs those amazing feats of marksmanship with his long rifle. And Harvey Birch is still the symbol of unselfish courage and devotion to country.

XIII. "THE GREAT REVOLUTION IN PUBLISHING"

We are friends of the people, and our motto is, "The greatest good to the greatest number."

The "New World," 1844

THE first great incident in the history of cheap publishing in the United States occurred in the years 1842-1845.

In July, 1839, two leading literary journalists of the time—Park Benjamin and Rufus Wilmot Griswold—had started, with the backing of the Wilson & Company printing firm, of New York, a new weekly periodical which they named *Brother Jonathan*. They called it a newspaper and used the large-page newspaper format in order to send it through the mails under cheap postage, but its news was subordinated from the first to its serial fiction. Its real purpose was to pirate the popular English novels of the day—the works of Dickens, Bulwer, Lever, Marryat, Ainsworth, James, Mrs. Gore, Miss Pardoe, and any others which might fall into their hands.

After six months of this, Benjamin and Griswold were apparently crowded out of the *Brother Jonathan*, probably because Benjamin H. Day, founder of the *New York Sun* and father of one-cent journalism in the United States, had bought into Wilson & Company. At any rate, the two ousted littérateurs soon persuaded Jonas Winchester, Horace Greeley's printer-partner on the *New-Yorker*, to start a new piratical weekly for them to edit. The *New-Yorker*, for which Benjamin and Griswold had worked, was on its uppers, and Greeley was thinking of starting a daily. Winchester was easily persuaded, and later became the central figure in the cheap-book crusade. The paper which the three men then founded, in June, 1840, was called the *New World*. It was very like the *Brother Jonathan* in appearance and content, and the aims of the two were identical. The *New World* had a quarto, or "library" edition for binding, as well as its folio edition, from the first; and the *Brother Jonathan* changed to quarto at the beginning of 1842.

But the serial publication of pirated fiction was not enough for these enterprising editors and printers. In July, 1841, the *New World* issued the first volume of Lever's *Charles O'Malley* as a "supplement" in the paper's regular size and format, selling it at fifty cents, and the *Brother Jonathan* immediately brought the same book out as an "extra" at twenty-five cents.

It was not until the beginning of 1842, however, that these papers began the more frequent issue of such "extras" and "supplements."

Up to this time Harper & Brothers and Carey & Hart and other American publishers specializing in foreign reprints had produced well printed cloth-bound volumes, of which, except in the cases of such highly popular authors as Scott, Bulwer, or Dickens, they could sell only small editions. This, with good standards of book-making, kept prices up from one to two dollars for a two-volume work. That was real money for those days, though much less than the usual English price of twenty-one shillings. The chief factor in the "revolution" which now came on apace was the new printing technology, utilizing rapid Napier and Hoe cylinder presses and paper produced by the fast Fourdrinier machines. This was what had made the cheap penny press possible in the preceding decade, and it was now turned to the uses of the cheap book.

For these "extras" were printed on newspaper presses, were unbound, and were sold by newsboys on the streets. Bulwer's *Zanoni* and *Eva,* Miss Pardoe's *Hungarian Tales,* and five other books were issued by *Brother Jonathan* at twenty-five cents before the *New World's* competition brought the price down to half of that (the American shilling). The *New World* issued *Zanoni* at a shilling, and thereafter always dated what it called "the great revolution in publishing" from that event. Shorter books came down to six and a quarter cents by 1843. Books of odd lengths were sometimes issued at 18¾ or 37½ cents.

Flimsy, bright-colored paper covers were eventually put on the "extras" sold in New York, but the tens of thousands mailed out of the city were left coverless in order that they might continue to look like newspapers and be carried under low postage rates. The *New World* "extras," in large quarto, commonly had twenty-four to forty-eight pages; but in 1843 the page size was reduced to large octavo with twice as many pages. The *Brother Jonathan* issues were a little smaller in page size, but thicker. At the height of the crusade, in the winter of 1842-1843, both papers issued their "extras" semimonthly with considerable regularity.

Continental authors soon came to be drawn upon steadily. Fredrika Bremer became popular in the "extras." Balzac, Hugo, de Kock, and Sue were the chief French authors to contribute involuntarily. *The Wandering Jew* made a great success in 1844-1845. Some American writers were represented—Cornelius Mathews by *Puffer Hopkins,* John Neal by *The Captain's Wife,* Walter Whitman by his justly forgotten temperance novelette *Frederick Evans,* and others. American writers received royalties, of course; and payments came to be made, in some cases, for advance sheets of foreign works. History and science were represented in the offerings.

How large were these editions? Not as large as one might perhaps think: a sale of five thousand was profitable, and it is doubtful if the biggest hits ever ran over thirty thousand. Thus no book was ever made a best seller solely by the sale of these "extras." But the revolution which the "extras" started had a profound and long-continued effect on the creation of best sellers.

In Boston, the *Notion* took up the new plan, and the *New York Mirror* and such regular newspapers as the *New York Sun* and the *Philadelphia Public Ledger* adopted it for a time. Israel Post, of New York, played a part in the "Books for the People" crusade by publishing Scott's *Works* and Thiers' *French Revolution* in twenty-cent volumes, issued weekly; J. S. Redfield published a pictorial Bible in twenty-five cent parts; and Curry & Company handled Dickens, Cooper, and the *American Encyclopaedia* in the same way. Post, Redfield, and Curry, however, did not print their books on newspaper presses.

Of course, all this was a sad business for the regular publishers. Benjamin addressed the readers of the *New World*: "You are not so green as to pay a dollar for what you can get for eighteen pence or a shilling [12½ cents]—not you!" Harper & Brothers were particularly indignant. Their fortune had been built largely on the foundation afforded by their Family Library of English reprints, sold at a dollar or more. To pirate English novels and sell them at a good price was accepted practice, but this undercutting of compatriots was too bad; it was stealing from the English author with one hand and from the American publisher with the other. The situation amused Benjamin vastly: he imagines an English writer taunting Harpers: "Ah, ha! you have caught it at last yourselves, have you? The robbers have been robbed; the filchers have had their pockets picked! . . . We like to see the pirates made to walk the plank!"

Harpers resolved to fight fire with fire, and began to publish in rapid succession popular English novels in brown paper covers at twenty-five cents; and when even this was ineffective, they reduced their price to half of that at retail, with a third off to the booksellers. This was real price-cutting, but *Brother Jonathan* laughed at them: "We welcome them to the field, hoping they may 'turn their money quick,' as did the bright lad who purchased apples at two for threepence and sold them at three for twopence." Other publishers joined the slashing fray, and the market was soon glutted. "Literature," observed *Jonathan* in April, 1843, "is now a drug. All the markets are overstocked."

This was the month in which the Postoffice Department, under what impulsion we can only guess, changed its policy toward the "extras" and began charging book postage on them. That was a body blow against novels in newspaper form; and though the publishers continued to issue them, their sales declined.

In January, 1844, *Brother Jonathan* sold out to the *New World*. The cheap books were no longer called "extras," and all were large octavo in size; but they still were printed on the rapid cylinder presses. Jonas Winchester sold the business in November, 1844, to his son Ebenezer and J. W. Judd, the latter taking over the cheap-book side of the firm's affairs. The *New World* became a folio again in 1845, but it was suspended in May of that year. The reason was that Congress had passed a new Postoffice Act, lowering rates for mailing books; and the publishers saw a bigger opportunity in their cheap-book business than in a story weekly. Their extensive list was now stabilized at twenty-five and fifty cents a volume; and for several years they continued, under the name of J. W. Judd & Company, to manufacture and distribute re-prints at these prices.

The effects of "the great revolution" were lasting. Harper's paper-covered novels continued for a time at lower prices than the *Family Library*, which was now re-established at fifty cents a volume. For about a decade fifty-cent books in cloth were very common; while such publishers as Harpers, Burgess & Stringer, Israel Post, and Zieber & Company, of New York, and Willis P. Hazard and Lea & Blanchard, of Philadelphia, often brought out small volumes at twenty-five cents. Publishing in parts was common, as was publication simultaneously in cloth and paper covers at, say, seventy-five and fifty cents. In England the cheap reprints, due to the same technological changes which were cheapening books in America, had worked a revolution in British pub-lishing. Many of these reprints were imported into the United States and helped to keep book prices low. At the same time newly published books were still expensive in England, and many high-priced books were issued in America. The whole publishing scene, with its great book auctions, book fairs, pirating, subscription sales, and wildcat book speculations, was con-fusing. It may be said with assurance, however, that never again after the "great revolution" were cheap books out of the picture.

XIV. DICKENS AND THE PIRATES

> I seriously believe that it is an essential part of the pleasure derived from the perusal of a popular English book [in America] that the author gets nothing for it. It is so dar-nation 'cute—so knowing in Jonathan to get his reading on those terms. He has the Englishman so regularly on the hip that his eye twinkles with slyness, cunning, and delight; and he chuckles over the humor of the page with an appreciation of it quite inconsistent with, and apart from, its honest purchase.
>
> *Dickens to Forster, 1842*

ONE day in 1835 the famous caricaturist Robert Seymour mentioned to his publishers his wish to do a series of English sporting pictures—hunting, fishing, riding, games, and so on. Chapman & Hall, young and aggressive publishers, said yes, by all means, and we'll issue them in monthly parts, and whom shall we get to do the text to go with the woodcuts? They agreed upon Charles Whitehead, but when that popular young writer was approached about the matter he hung back until the artist's patience was exhausted. Then Mr.

Hall remembered a little book with caricatures by Cruikshank and sketches by "Boz" which had recently appeared. We'll try "Boz," said Mr. Hall.

To "Boz" he went accordingly, finding the writer who used that flippant pen-name to be a personable young fellow of twenty-three, a reporter for the *Morning Chronicle,* named Charles Dickens. The young man was planning to marry his boss's daughter, and the fifteen guineas a month for twenty months offered him for this job seemed a providential wedding present. The bargain was promptly closed.

Dickens was not interested in hunting and fishing, however, and his sketches took a different turn from the original design. Seymour found himself, from the first, illustrating Dickens rather than drawing pictures for the young author to write around. On March 26, 1836, the following advertisement stretched across the top third of the last page of the London *Athenaeum:*

On the 31st of March will be published, to be continued Monthly, price One Shilling, the First Number of
THE POSTHUMOUS PAPERS
OF
THE PICKWICK CLUB
Containing a Faithful Record of the Perambulations, Perils, Travels, Adventures, and Sporting Transactions of the Corresponding Members
· EDITED BY BOZ
and Each Monthly Part Embellished by Four Illustrations
BY SEYMOUR

True to promise, the first number of *Pickwick* came out March 31 in a light green cover very much embellished by Seymour; and on April 12, true to a less public promise, Miss Hogarth, in bridal gown and veil, was married to Charles Dickens.

The wedding was a success, but not so the literary venture. The first number of *The Posthumous Papers of the Pickwick Club* sold only about four hundred copies. Then, before he had finished all of his pictures for the second number, Seymour committed suicide. The second number went to press with only three drawings; another artist did the illustrations for the third issue; and then Hablot K. Browne, who signed his pictures "Phiz," became the happy choice as illustrator of Number Four. Chapman & Hall, however, now seriously considered abandoning the whole venture, thus far unprofitable. They decided to try one more, and with the fifth number sales took a sudden spurt—and from then on to the end in the twentieth part, "Boz" and "Phiz" and Mr. Pickwick and Alfred Jingle and Sam Weller went on and up in a blaze of glory. "Pickwick Triumphant!" wrote Dickens in exultant round letters to his publisher friend John Macrone.

What caused this sudden upturn? Perhaps it was partly "Phiz"; but mostly it was Mr. Samivel Veller, to whom Dickens had given his entrance cue in the fourth number, and who so tickled the funny-bones of Londoners that soon they were fairly mobbing the bookstores. Surprised and delighted, Chapman

& Hall gave orders to their printers to keep the presses running, and soon the *Pickwick Papers* reached and maintained a circulation of some forty thousand for each number.

Now, every literary success in London was immediately reported on the other side of the Atlantic. Carey, Lea & Blanchard, of Philadelphia, had long employed agents in London who were to pick up such hits and hurry them across on the steamships which had so recently narrowed the ocean. Accordingly, this firm brought out, in November, 1836, the first Dickens book to be published in America—a small green volume with a paper label containing the first four numbers of *Pickwick,* in an edition of fifteen hundred copies to be sold at forty-five cents each. It was pirated, of course, though Carey later paid Dickens a royalty on it. But by the time the series was finished, in the autumn of 1837, other piratical American publishers were issuing the numbers and were ready to publish the complete book, quite without thought of royalties. Thus Dickens entered upon his career of unexampled and unrivalled popularity in the United States.

After *Pickwick* came *Oliver Twist* as a serial in *Bentley's Miscellany;* indeed all of Dickens' novels were published either in numbers or serially in magazines. The very first American appearance of the new story was in reprints of *Bentley's* by William and Jemima Walker, in New York. The Carey firm paid sixty pounds for advance sheets of the latter installments of *Oliver,* but this gave them only a slight head-start over rival publishers. The new book was even more popular in the United States than its predecessor; and just before it was finished, a leading American magazine, the *Knickerbocker,* declared that Dickens was "universally endenizened in the national heart" of the United States. "Dickens reigns supreme as the popular writer," wrote Longfellow to a friend abroad about this time.

For *The Life and Adventures of Nicholas Nickleby,* publication in numbers was again the method, Part One selling fifty thousand in London and probably more in the United States. Dickens' publishers refused to sell advance sheets of this book to American publishers, and there was a general scramble among the pirates.

Thinking to ease the strain of producing monthly parts on schedule, Dickens agreed to edit a weekly miscellany called *Master Humphrey's Clock* for Chapman & Hall. This had a fine initial sale; but as soon as it developed that it was to contain no serial novel by the editor, there was a prodigious slump. So Dickens re-nibbed his pen and went to work, and the *Clock* became merely a cover caption for *The Old Curiosity Shop* and later *Barnaby Rudge.* American pirated editions of *The Old Curiosity Shop* were for many years in two forms—one the bound-up parts, with the miscellany of the first few numbers of the *Clock* included; and the other the novel alone, those early sketches having been deleted. The former style was available certainly up to the time of the author's death in 1870.

It was early in 1842 that Dickens paid a visit to America. This was a tour on the grand scale. It lasted over four months, and it was filled with travel, sight-seeing, balls, dinners, and endless entertainment and adulation. All America idolized its favorite author, and the people showed their love for him in throngs. "I can give you no conception of my welcome here," Dickens wrote home.

There never was a king or emperor upon earth so cheered and followed by crowds and entertained in public by splendid balls and dinners and waited upon by public bodies and deputations of all kinds. If I go out in a carriage, the crowds surround it and escort me home; if I go to the theatre, the whole house, crowded to the roof, rises as one man, and the timbers ring again. You cannot imagine what it is. I have five great public dinners on hand at this moment, and invitations from every town and city in the States.

Had Dickens been wiser, he might have felt a danger to himself in all this; but he was just turned thirty, exuberant, and full of self-confidence. At first he enjoyed the lionizing, and wrote home about the "noble set of fellows" he met at Boston. "The women are very beautiful," he added. But it was not long before he tired of the ceaseless round of laudation and cheers and toasts; and in his revulsion he saw only the disagreeable features of American life. He began talking about American piracy of his novels at the banquets offered him; most of what he said was true, but one does not usually dine with a man in order to call him a thief. Young Dickens grew more tired and more homesick as he journeyed south and west. He loathed the tobacco-spitting, he loathed slavery, he loathed America. As Stephen Leacock points out in an admirable biography, Dickens was quite incapable of seeing the true meaning of the new nation pushing its frontiers westward, subduing the prairies and rivers, and building for the future. "I trust never to see the Mississippi again except in dreams and nightmares," he wrote incredibly.

The literary result of the unhappy visit came to print promptly under the title *American Notes for General Circulation.* Advance sheets, for which *Brother Jonathan* had bribed a London pressman, arrived on the steamer *Great Western* early Monday morning November 6, 1842, and the *Brother Jonathan* "extra," containing the entire book, was on sale in New York by that evening. *The New World* was not far behind, and Harpers and at least one publisher in Philadelphia were also prompt. By the end of the week fifty to sixty thousand copies of the *Notes* had been sold.* The hurricane of criticism provoked by the book helped to increase its sales, and the presses growled steadily on.

American publishing was now in the midst of that "revolution" described in the last chapter, and the Dickens novels were being issued, unbound but complete in quarto size, at twelve and a half cents, and sold on the streets like newspapers. When issued in parts, the installments sold for a penny each.

* Files of the papers which issued novel "extras" are valuable for the history of low-priced publishing in the early forties. For these figures, see *Brother Jonathan,* November 12, 1842 (Quarto Edition, Vol. III, p. 314).

In February, 1843, came the first number of *Martin Chuzzlewit*, published by the *New World* and *Brother Jonathan* at one cent as against the shilling charged for each of the seventeen numbers in England. The Harpers, now trading blows with the cheap-johns in earnest, also published *Martin* in penny numbers; and the story is told of how James Harper used to harangue the newsboys to arouse their enthusiasm before sending them out on the street with the new Dickens installment. Again there was loud complaint against the author's abuse of American people and customs; again the people bought the book, and again the presses ran on and on. Americans of that day were very much concerned over what foreign observers said of their institutions and their manners; and they wanted to read such comment, whether it was critical or laudatory, good humored or spiteful.

The *Christmas Carol*, published in London six days before Christmas of 1843, lost the seasonal advantage in America. It was serialized in the *New World* in February, and issued in a separate volume a little later by Carey & Hart. But it did not have a great immediate success. Paradoxical indeed is the comparative obscurity, at its first appearance, of the story which was, in the long run, to top the entire Dickens list and achieve a sale, in the United States alone, of over two million. English sales of the *Carol* were considered good, but the price (five shillings) was too high for the public at which the book was aimed, and Dickens was disappointed in the profits. The little book won high encomiums everywhere: Thackeray declared in *Fraser's* that it was "the work of the master of all the English humorists now alive." Christmas after Christmas—now a full hundred of them—it has had its tens of thousands of buyers. It is still full of emotional strength. Dickens said that he "wept and laughed and wept again, and excited himself in a most extraordinary manner in the composition; and thinking whereof, he walked about the black streets of London fifteen and twenty miles many a night when all sober folks had gone to bed." A hundred years after, it makes its readers laugh and cry again. Many of us make reading from the *Carol* as invariable a Christmas rite as lighting the candles on the tree.

Dombey and Son was published in parts, beginning in the fall of 1846. The "extras" were now history, and prices were a little higher; Wiley & Putnam sold the new novel in New York for an American shilling—twelve and a half cents—per part, while Lea & Blanchard issued it in Philadelphia at six cents a part. *David Copperfield* was handled similarly three years later. *Dombey* had been a popular offering; but it was now outdistanced by *Copperfield*, which eventually became the most popular of all Dickens' longer, twenty-part novels. Forty years after the first appearance of *Copperfield* it was still the most popular book in American public libraries.* Mr. Micawber, Uriah Heep, Aunt

* *Forum*, December, 1893 (vol. XVI, p. 508). In this study, popularity was measured by the number of times a book appeared on lists prepared by large public libraries to show what books were oftenest called for. Each list contained 150 titles.

Betsey Trotwood, Barkis, and Mr. Dick are a part of the culture of the English-speaking peoples, and by no means unknown in many other languages.

Bleak House was published in separate parts; the next four novels appeared serially in Dickens' periodicals, *Household Words* and *All the Year Round*. Beginning with *Bleak House*, the American publication of Dickens' books took on a somewhat different aspect.

The old Carey firm in Philadelphia, known throughout the publication of Dickens' early books as Lea & Blanchard, had been, in some respects, the preëminent Dickens publishers. As has been noted, they paid him small royalties on *Pickwick* and *Oliver Twist*. Their offer of a hundred pounds for advance sheets for *Nicholas Nickleby* was refused; they could not well risk more for the slight advantage which the sheets would give them over their competitors in the American market. But they were able to pay Dickens £112, 10s. as royalties on *The Old Curiosity Shop* and £107, 10s. on *Barnaby Rudge*. As the only American publishers who had paid royalties on these books, they thought they would now receive some consideration if they made a liberal offer for advance sheets; so they took the sum of the royalties they had paid on the last two books, doubled it, and proposed £440 for sheets of *Martin Chuzzlewit*. The refusal was emphatic, and thereafter Lea & Blanchard joined with other publishers in free piratical competition. Unlike the others, however, they stereotyped the pages of all Dickens' works regularly as they came out. In 1851 Isaac Lea retired, and the firm relinquished its Dickens business, selling its plates to T. B. Peterson & Co., of Philadelphia.

Harper & Brothers, of New York, now became the leading Dickens publishers. They had just started their *New Monthly Magazine,* and they used much of Dickens in it. In most cases they were able to make contracts for advance sheets. They paid four hundred pounds each for *Bleak House* and *Little Dorrit,* a thousand pounds each for *A Tale of Two Cities* and *Our Mutual Friend,* and twelve hundred and fifty pounds for *Great Expectations.* Shortly before Dickens' death they had contracted to pay two thousand pounds for advance sheets of *Edwin Drood.** The reason the Harpers were able to pay so much is found not solely in the increasing popularity of their author, but chiefly in what was called "courtesy of the trade" with regard to reprinted English works. In default of international copyright, reputable pub-

---

* The present writer has been unable to learn whether Harpers or any other publisher bought advance sheets of *Hard Times*. The figures given above are found in various places, especially in Forster's biography; but are gathered in R. Shelton MacKenzie's *Life of Charles Dickens* (Philadelphia, 1870), pp. 236-237. James T. Fields has written in detail of his personal relations with Dickens, but not of the business relations of Fields, Osgood & Company with the author. It seems impossible now to learn how much and for what this firm paid Dickens. We know that Dickens conveniently forgot an agreement with Fields, Osgood & Company when Harpers offered him a larger sum for *Edwin Drood*. Apparently both received early sheets, for Fields published the story serially in *Every Saturday* while the Harpers were printing it in their *Weekly*.

lishers now agreed that when any one of them contracted for advance sheets and published advertisements to that effect, the others would respect his priority. Sometimes the "courtesy" was disregarded; but, in the main, the system worked rather well. After the book thus protected had been out for a year or two, other publishers often brought out cheaper editions. Indeed, Harpers sold their stereotypes of the later Dickens works not long before the author's death to T. B. Peterson so that the Philadelphia firm, using them with the Carey plates, could bring out the complete works in cheap editions. Peterson, also by arrangement with Harpers, was the first American publisher of *A Tale of Two Cities* in book form; he brought it out in no less than twenty-five editions, ranging from fifty cents to five dollars in price.

Dickens visited America for the second time in the winter of 1867-1868. Twenty-five years of intense living had changed him from a youth to an old man. Now his broken health permitted only a minimum of entertaining, and he was not much interested in sight-seeing. What he was interested in was making money by his superlative readings of his own work; this he did to the tune of nearly a hundred thousand dollars net, after his agent was paid, all travel expenses and commissions were settled, and hasty and expensive discounts were taken for trading into pounds sterling. At the great farewell banquet given him at Delmonico's, he came as near to an apology for his earlier insults to America as was possible to him under the circumstances. But the old quarrel had been pretty much forgotten. "As for those old darts of offense which have rankled so long in the wounds of a few of us, he drew them out with a deft and tender hand," wrote Horace Greeley in a *Tribune* editorial on Dickens' farewell speech. "We do not know," he added, "that he was under obligation to do this, but we are glad that he has done it, for we would have him leave none but warm friends here."

Two years later the world's most popular author was dead. "If half the monarchs of Europe had been smitten down," wrote Donald G. Mitchell in *Hearth and Home,*

there would not have been so great a grief in the hearts of so many. He was so old a friend! He was so dear a friend! There is no living man who, in the last thirty years, has given such cheer and joy to so many millions as this great master whose living touch in any future story we shall wait for in vain.

During the first five years after the death of Dickens, the chief American publishers of his novels were Harper & Brothers, T. B. Peterson & Company, and D. Appleton & Company. The Harpers sold Dickens' works at 50 cents to $1, according to length, in paper covers, and at $1 to $1.50 in cloth. Peterson published the complete works with choice of paper covers at 25 cents and cloth at 50 cents or $1 a volume, and gave large discounts; in 1876 he advertised twenty different editions of Dickens in all sizes and bindings. Just before Dickens' death Appletons were advertising 25 volumes of Scott *and* 18 of Dickens, neat in green and gold, for $10; a little later they scattered their shots by selling Dickens in paper at 15 to 35 cents, in cloth at 75 cents, and in half-morocco at $7 a volume.

Then a cyclone struck the publishing industry and threatened for a time to wreck it completely. The cheap "libraries" of New York and Chicago publishers in the eighties will be described in a later chapter. They sold their millions at 10 and 20 cents a volume in double-column quarto form, before the producers of cloth-bound books more suitable for library shelves edged into the game. These cloth-bound books sold for 25 or 30 cents; and when they became popular, their publishers were able to do a big business in the merchandising of sets of such favorite authors as Dickens. Thus Belford, Clarke & Company, of Chicago, sold in the neighborhood of 40,000 sets of Dickens in the eighties at $4 to $5. John B. Alden, formerly of Chicago but now of New York, advertised in his catalogue of 1888 his 15-volume sets of Dickens. "Competition has become so sharp in certain lines," he said,

that it no longer pays to manufacture books for the absurd prices at which they sell. This is notably the case with the works of Charles Dickens. So I cease to manufacture, and have bought up a large lot of Dickens' Works which I can sell and make a little profit on at $4.50 a set.

P. F. Collier, of New York, using a different method for a better product, sold some 150,000 sets of Dickens in the thirty years beginning in 1879, through itinerant "book agents." Thousands of sets were distributed by a newspaper circulation-building plan in the late 1930's. Altogether it seems likely that at least 400,000 sets of Dickens have been sold to American buyers, and some old-timers in the book trade are sure that this figure is far too low. A few of the minor works of Dickens were sometimes omitted from these sets.

The reasons for Charles Dickens' overwhelming popularity are, after all, not far to seek. Not a little of it was due to the publishers, who, pirates and price-cutters though many of them were, gave Dickens such an audience as no other single author has ever had in any country. But primarily this popularity was, of course, a response to the genius of Dickens. It was as a humorist that he first caught the attention of readers; and humor was, save perhaps in the sole exception of *A Tale of Two Cities*, a chief phase of his appeal to American readers. But *Pickwick*, his leading comic work, though long first in the esteem of Britishers, has never held that top position on this side of the Atlantic. Pathos and sensationalism, along with comedy, were required to make the brew which Americans found so intoxicating in the Dickens novels they loved best. But there were other things added which made the drink stronger yet: a preoccupation with the fortunes of the lower and middle classes, with a disparagement of aristocracy; a reformer's burning sense of the injustices against childhood and against the poor and the weak generally; a flair for the rhetorical, and a love of fantasy and grotesquerie.

These things are all prominent in *A Christmas Carol*, at the top of the list in America; "A Ghost Story of Christmas," says the subtitle, emphasizing the sensation element. *Copperfield,* which comes second, has them all; Mr. Dick is not the only character in that book who supplies fantasy. *A Tale of Two Cities* is third; into this story Dickens put less humor than he was wont, and it might not rank so high in the scale of popularity were it not for the efforts of the schoolmasters. In *Oliver Twist,* fourth in the list, there is less of obvious fantasy, but more of sensationalism. One does not always realize the large part which crime and criminals play in Dickens. He was fascinated by the low dives and haunts of the "criminal classes" in London; and it is not strange that when in Cambridge, on his second visit to America, he asked to be taken to the Medical School and shown the very places in Dr. Webster's laboratory where that barbarous murderer had tried to dispose of the remains of Parkman. In *Pickwick Papers,* fifth in the list, the sensationalism is, of course, not very serious. Each of the five novels just named probably sold at least a million and a half in the United States, including copies in sets. Four others, and possibly more, are in the million class—*Nicholas Nickleby, The Old Curiosity Shop, Bleak House,* and *Hard Times.* If it seems strange that as poor a novel as *Our Mutual Friend* made the best seller list at all, it should be remembered that people once eagerly bought anything Dickens wrote, and later they bought complete sets of his work in almost incredible quantities. In all, sixteen books by Dickens are on our best seller list.

"No author was ever more popular in America than Dickens," observed a writer in *Putnam's Monthly* in 1856. He was then only a little past the meridian of his production, and his popularity went on increasing. Nor did his death stop the up-curve. Indeed, so far as sales are concerned, there were no doubt more volumes of Dickens sold in the eighties than in the sixties. Even as late as 1926, a study in the *International Book Review* showed Dickens far and away the best seller among standard authors.*

In his book on Dickens in the English Men of Letters series, published in 1882, A. W. Ward says:

He was the most popular novelist of his day; but should prose fiction, or even the full and florid species of it which has enjoyed so long-lived a favour, ever be out of season, the popularity of Dickens' works must experience an inevitable diminution.

Has that time arrived? A few years ago, a *Dickens Digest* met with much favor, and was used as a "dividend" by the Book of the Month Club. Many readers of judgment confessed that they found an abridged Dickens more enjoyable than the original. † Is this a sign of that "diminution" of which Professor Ward wrote? Perhaps it is; and yet many of us will see Pickwick diminished only over our pained protests—Pickwick, or Oliver, or Micawber, or Captain Cuttle, or Mrs. Gamp, or Little Nell, or Jo, or Pecksniff, or any of that

---

* Clarence E. Cason, "Dickens in America," *International Book Review,* September, 1926 (vol. IV. pp. 603-607).

† An abridged edition of *A Tale of Two Cities* has recently enjoyed a good sale in the dime stores. It is one of the Quick Reader Series.

great gallery of characters, comic, tragic, or satirical, which Dickens gave to the world of readers. Granted that the fat volumes in which these men and women and children live and move and have their being are over-written and sentimental, they are nevertheless full, even today, of the magic of the genius of Charles Dickens.

XV. HISTORY FOR THE MILLION, 1830-1870

Oratory and poetry are of little value unless they reach the highest perfection; but history, in whatever way it be executed, is always a source of pleasure.
Letter of Pliny the Younger

AMONG THE motivations of American best sellers, from the seventeenth century to the twentieth, one of the most prominent has been the desire for self-improvement. Indeed, it may be said that, by and large, there are only three classes of readers—those who seek improvement, those who seek entertainment, and those who seek both improvement and entertainment.

Improvement in the spiritual nature is what the many religious best sellers have aimed at. Improvement in manners has been the goal of all the behavior books published in America in the past three centuries, and it has also been an important motivation in many of the novels. The desire for improvement in esthetic appreciation has played a large part in the reading of poetry and the classics, in and out of the schools. And the bright lure of improvement in learning—getting "educated"—has drawn millions of readers to history and biography.

History came early into the best seller list, as has been pointed out in our review of eighteenth-century reading. But it was not until historical romance, especially that of the inspired Sir Walter, had demonstrated to the great masses of readers (with the help of cheap processes of printing) how fascinating the story of the past might be, that history really took a dominant place in popular reading. By 1830, Miss Porter's *Scottish Chiefs*, Irving's *History of New York*, Cooper's *The Spy* and *The Pilot*, Scott's Waverley series, Shakespeare's histories, and other best sellers dealing less prominently with the past, were showing the pleasures of history, or antiquarianism, or what have you, to the great popular audience.

Victor Hugo's magnificent medieval romance, *Notre-Dame de Paris*, was published by Carey, Lea & Blanchard in Philadelphia in 1834 and was later issued by the price-cutters at twenty-five cents. This was the Frederick Shobert translation with the title *The Hunchback of Notre-Dame*, which had made such a success in England under the Bentley imprint. In America the book came under the displeasure of moralists; whether because of this austere criticism or (more likely) because of the guide-book quality of many pages of the work, *The Hunchback* did not reach its greatest popularity in this country until

Les Misérables had made Hugo's a name to conjure with. In the cheap publishing era beginning in the middle seventies, the earlier masterpiece, with many pages about architecture deleted, sold by the hundreds of thousands; and Esmeralda and Quasimodo became characters well known to nearly all readers. A recent popularity has been based on the RKO picture starring Charles Laughton.

In *Les Misérables,* the historical element is subordinated to that of social reform, to be sure; yet two of the most admired passages in the novel are the description of the Battle of Waterloo and the story of the defense of a Paris barricade which occurred as a kind of postscript of the Revolution of 1830. *Les Misérables* was translated into nine languages before its initial publication, and its simultaneous appearance in Paris, London, Berlin, New York, Madrid, Brussels, St. Petersburg, and Turin in April, 1862, was a world literary event of the first magnitude.

It was scarcely an opportune time for the appearance of the book in America. One might think that an embattled nation would not have time for this French novel in five volumes: the Battle of Shiloh was fought three days after *Les Misérables* appeared in New York bookstores. On the other hand, perhaps the mood of the book was adapted to the times. At any rate, it was an immediate success; it sold at least fifty thousand copies before the end of the year 1862. *Les Misérables* made a sensation among literary folk. Opinion was divided, but everyone read it, and talked about it. "The book is everywhere," wrote Miss Sedgwick from her home in Lenox, Massachusetts. "It is plainly stamped with the broad seal of genius," said a reviewer in *De Bow's.* "It will do infinitely more harm than good," wrote E. P. Whipple in the *Atlantic Monthly,* and added: "The bigotries of virtue are better than the charities of vice." But the general public scrambled for it.

The book's first American publisher was well chosen to reach an immediate popular audience. He was George W. Carleton, of New York, specialist in low book prices. He brought *Les Misérables* out in five volumes, paper-covered at two and a half and cloth-bound at five dollars, and then followed with a single-volume edition at a dollar and a half. For these books he conducted one of the biggest advertising campaigns the American publishing business had ever known, spending, according to a fellow-publisher, ten thousand dollars.* Of course, other publishers took *Les Misérables* up without delay, but Carleton kept the lead for a long time. He deserved whatever he made out of it, for he had paid for advance sheets, he had advertised the book liberally, and he had made his price low enough. *Le Courrier des États-Unis* began printing the novel serially; when rebuked by the author for its piracy, the paper offered him a small royalty. "I'd rather you picked my pocket outright," replied Hugo.

But nothing could stop the pirates. A reprint of an English abridgment came out in 1862 and had a big sale. West & Johnson, of Richmond, brought out a

* J. C. Derby, *Fifty Years Among Authors, Books and Publishers* (New York, 1884) p. 240.

single-volume edition for the Confederacy early in 1863. Later, the cheap publishers of the seventies seized upon the book and sent the sales bounding. For forty years Street & Smith supplied their trade with the work in two volumes at ten cents each. Within its first half-century, *Les Misérables* reached a sale in America of at least a million copies. It was long a high-circulation library book and has enjoyed a popularity of prestige.

It is probable that Dumas has outstripped Hugo in American popularity. Each of Dumas' two most famous historical romances certainly has sold its million copies in this country. Both *The Three Musketeers* and *The Count of Monte Cristo* were published from their first American editions in the cheapest form as well as in library bindings. How many thousands of boy-readers have strained their young eyes to read of the adventures of D'Artagnan or Edward Dantes in twenty-cent editions! Not that these have been wholly or even chiefly boys' books; they have an appeal to all lovers of romantic adventure. We are told that Thomas A. Edison once pushed aside his laboratory paraphernalia to begin *Monte Cristo,* and then sat up all night to finish it. In recent years, the movies have renewed our interest in these books.

Doubtless *The Wandering Jew* is not properly a historical novel; but that marvelous compendium of melodramatic episodes brings in so much historical material in one way or another, that it may suitably be discussed here. Sue's sprawling but compelling romance, instinct throughout with hatred for the Jesuits, gained part of its American popularity from the anti-Catholic movement. Here is one book that should not be read in a de luxe edition, with its clear print on rich, white paper; the passion and terror of the strange work, its high-pitched unreality which, by mere force and mass, hypnotizes the reader into belief, is best interpreted by the double columns and the straining fine print on yellowed paper of one of Jonas Winchester's editions in six-cent parts.*

Most popular of English writers of historical romance after Scott was Bulwer-Lytton, and his most widely read work was *The Last Days of Pompeii.* Harpers published it from advance sheets in 1834 at about the same time it appeared in London, but scores of publishers have issued their editions of it since. It has appeared in de luxe editions at ten dollars and in paper covers at ten cents; the larger part of its circulation was in the twenty to thirty-five cent editions of the two decades following 1876. It was long popular on the stage. Though it is now the fashion to decry Bulwer, few readers of his masterpiece forget the story of the destruction of Pompeii, or the charm of the character of Nydia, the blind flower-girl. "Solemnly empty, imposingly unimportant," said William Dean Howells of Bulwer-Lytton; yet he devoted a chapter to Nydia in his *Heroines of Fiction.*

By a piece of sharp practice, advance sheets of *Rienzi,* Bulwer's story of medieval Italy, were sold to two competing American publishers—Harpers in

* Another Wandering Jew book, the Reverend George Croly's rhetorical *Salathiel,* was also widely published in American cheap editions.

New York and Carey & Hart in Philadelphia. The sheets for both firms arrived on the same boat. The Philadelphia publishers distributed theirs to twelve different printing houses; by nine o'clock the morning after they had received copy, printed sheets were in the hands of the binders, who already had their cases prepared. Abraham Hart then hired all the seats in the next stage for New York, filled the vehicle full of *Rienzi*, and got his books on sale in New York a full day before the Harper edition.

It may be that other novels by Bulwer-Lytton should be listed as best sellers; they were all widely popular. *Zanoni* and *The Last of the Barons* were published as "extras" of the literary newspapers, but *Harold* probably ranks next to *Rienzi* in total sales. *Eugene Aram* and *Paul Clifford* excited no little controversy—the former because of its alleged defense of crime, and the latter because of its prison reform thesis. Two other of Bulwer's novels of contemporary England had a special popularity—*Pelham* and *Kenelm Chillingly*. All his leading works were issued by the Harpers at twenty-five cents apiece in the forties, with one-half off to the trade, and continued at this price up to the war. The same firm put them at fifteen and twenty cents in the price-cutting contest of the seventies. In 1876 seven different publishers were offering Bulwer-Lytton's *Works* in sets varying in size from seven to forty-seven volumes and in price from DeWitt's paper-bound edition at two dollars and a half to Lippincott's de luxe set at $129.25.

How prolific these English romancers were! Bulwer's thirty-odd novels (to say nothing of his volumes of poetry and plays) are, of course, scarcely comparable in multitude to Mrs. Gore's seventy, G. P. R. James's eighty-seven, or Miss Pardoe's hundred separate publications. Charles Reade was industrious enough, but he produced only twenty novels.

Reade's masterpiece in the field of historical romance, *The Cloister and the Hearth*, was first published in America by the Harpers in 1855 from advance sheets. This was immediately followed by the edition of Carleton & Rudd, in the double-column form which Carleton had designed for his cheap books before he took in Rudd as a partner; it was in a single volume bound in green cloth, and sold for a dollar. The book found many admirers among the discerning, and has had a steady sale for years, both in the cheap editions and in better formats; but it never quite attained the popularity, alas, that was reached by two of the author's scandalous successes—*Griffith Gaunt* and *A Terrible Temptation*.

The *Atlantic Monthly*, which had come upon hard times after the Civil War, abandoned its policy of sticking to American authors in 1866 and bought *Griffith Gaunt* for serial publication at three pounds sterling per page. The story of bigamy and crime did not make a hit with *Atlantic* readers, and it failed to build circulation for the magazine. The pugnacious New York *Round Table* attacked the serial mercilessly, heading its diatribe "An Indecent Publication," calling the story "one of the worst novels that has appeared during this generation . . . an unpardonable insult to morality," and adding the claim that it had been "declined by some of the lowest sensational weekly papers of New York." Reade retorted upon his critics with his famous phrase "prurient prudes," wrote an angry reply to them for the *New York Times*, and brought suit for twenty-five thousand dollars damages against the *Round Table*. During the trial, the novel was introduced in evidence, and half of it was read to the jury by George Vanderhof, "the well known elocutionist." The jury found for the plaintiff, assessing the damages at the insulting figure of six cents. But Reade benefited by the publicity, for the newspapers were full of *Griffith Gaunt*. Augustin Daly made a play out of the book and showed it in New York; it won the distinction of a parody by Charles H. Webb, called *Liffith Lank*; and multiple editions sold like hot cakes. But the book was much more than a passing sensation; it ranks high in the list of Reade's novels.

Not so good was *A Terrible Temptation*, which *Every Saturday*, of Boston, printed from purchased proofs, but which *Harper's Weekly* vengefully published at the same time as an episode in its feud with the Boston paper. It was the London *Times* which took the author to task for *A Terrible Temptation*, the immorality in which seems to consist of a fairly spicy sketch of the wiles of a kept mistress early in the novel. In the dispute which ensued, Reade claimed that three American publishers had, among them, sold 370,000 copies of the novel. The usual American price was twenty-five cents. Reade considered that his American audience was three times the size of his English readership.*

Other Reade novels, such as *Put Yourself in His Place, Hard Cash, Foul Play, Never Too Late to Mend*, and *Peg Woffington*—most of them problem novels, but the last a good historical piece—may possibly have reached best seller figures; but the facts are hard to come at.

Indeed, there are scores of English historical romances which may be rated, comparatively, as "better sellers" in America. The multitudinous novels of G. P. R. James, some of which he is said to have dictated to a staff of stenographers, keeping two or three busy at once, after the fashion of the modern Erle Stanley Gardner, are a good example. James was popular in America for many years and was one of Harpers' most valued authors. His books sold chiefly in very cheap editions. Ainsworth's *Crichton, Old St. Paul's*, and other historical romances were also widely read on this side of the Atlantic. The works of Luise Mühlbach (Mrs. Mundt), based on European history, were published in both cloth and paper by Appleton in the seventies, and got into the cheap libraries in the next decade. Miss Pardoe's historical works were only a step removed from fiction. Agnes Strickland's *Lives of the Queens of England*, in abridgment, was long a popular history for girls.

These books, like most of those thus far discussed in this chapter, were popular by grace of literary piracy. The black flag floated over about half of the

* Malcolm Elwin, *Charles Reade* (London, 1931) contains much valuable material concerning the author's American connections.

American best sellers from 1800 to 1860. Must we think, then, of our publishing industry of those years as depraved and shameless?

By no means. During most of this period some of the leading American publishers, in default of an international copyright agreement, paid large sums to English authors for a priority in the American market which often afforded them no more than a slight advantage. For some years Charles Reade received from American publishers about the same amount on a new novel that the English serial rights brought him. Certainly not all American publishers were cynically contemptuous of the rights of English authors.

And something may be said, even at this late date, for the literary "free trade" of the pre-copyright years. It fostered cheap publication for the masses beyond anything that existed in England. Because of it, the works of Scott, Dickens, Bulwer, Reade, Collins, and Lever, and probably Thackeray, Eliot, and Trollope, have been sold in greater numbers in America than in England. By midcentury, cheap publication of reprints had become common in England; but new books were still issued at a guinea and a half in London, while New York publishers could bring them out at twenty-five and fifty cents when they still had the exciting advantage of being brand-new offerings. Cheaper publication increased gradually in England after 1860, but the new novel at a guinea and a half was common until the nineties.*

Three historical novels by American authors, besides those of Cooper, appear in the list of best sellers before the Civil War; and all of them are classics for youth. First was Robert Montgomery Bird's *Nick of the Woods,* the story of the bloody vengeance of a Kentucky pioneer who, as a boy, saw his home burned and his family butchered and thenceforward devoted his life to killing the "varmints." It was an antidote to the Leatherstocking Tales, and a forerunner of the dime-novel thriller. Boys read it with the avidity with which they were later to devour the less sincere literature of the another-redskin-bit-the-dust variety. It was published by Carey, Lea & Blanchard in 1837 and is said to have passed through more than twenty-five editions in this country, besides an unknown number in England. The year after its first appearance, Louisa Medina turned it into a melodrama which was to hold the boards for many years.

Much more popular was another boys' favorite, published only two years after *Nick of the Woods.* This was Judge Daniel P. Thompson's *The Green Mountain Boys,* issued first by E. P. Walton & Sons, of Montpelier, Vermont, in two volumes. The story was in some respects superior to Cooper, and was quite as full of adventuresome action. Beginning with the resistance of the Vermonters who occupied the "New Hampshire Grants," as they were called, against the claims of the "Yorkers," and carrying on into the Revolution, when their enemies were the redcoats, the story moves forward with vigor and a

* See Henry Curwen, *History of the Booksellers* (London, 1873) and Walter C. Phillips, *Dickens, Reade and Collins* (New York, 1919) for data on this general subject.

rough-and-ready directness. Ethan Allen is the hero, and a good one he is. *Green Mountain Boys* was an immediate success, was pirated in England and sold in shilling editions there, and was taken over in 1848 by the Bazin firm of publishers (the name varies) in Boston; by 1860 at least fifty American editions had been issued. In the seventies the cheap publishers picked it up, and it is probable that altogether the sales have not fallen far short of a million copies.

Another phenomenal best seller for youth—but this time in sacred rather than profane history—was Joseph Holt Ingraham's *The Prince of the House of David*. Ingraham was himself a remarkable character. He went to sea before the mast when he was little more than a boy; he took part in exciting scenes in connection with a South American revolution; he saw much of life and the world before he was of age. Then he settled down to study and a college course, supporting himself by writing novels and novelettes for the cheap weeklies on the sly. This reprehensible practice he continued even after he had reached the highly respectable position of professor of languages in Jefferson College in Mississippi. Even *Lafitte, the Pirate of the Gulf* was published anonymously, though it later bore its author's name and continued to be sold in paper covers for a hundred years. These stories resounded with action, luxuriated in florid description, and had much of the spirit then called Byronic. Longfellow, to whom *Lafitte* was dedicated, wrote to a friend that the stories of Ingraham were probably the worst novels ever written. Their author himself was eventually converted to somewhat the same opinion of these facile inventions, and at forty-six years of age, having produced eighty thrillers, he took orders in the Protestant Episcopal Church, and turned his back upon his past; he even tried to buy up the copyrights and stop the publication of his wild-oats literature.

But the writing urge was still strong, and he soon produced *The Prince of the House of David* and two other novels dealing with sacred history. *The Prince* was written very rapidly, according to its author's habit. It narrates the chief episodes in the life of Jesus in a series of letters from a young Jewess to her father in Egypt. It seems now to be no very remarkable performance; but it had a great religious appeal, and its rhetorical descriptions were much admired. The book was published in 1855 by Pudney & Russell, of New York, "with seven large splendid engravings," at a dollar and a quarter. When the copyright expired in the eighties, many cheap editions, including Street & Smith's at ten cents, came on the market. *The Prince of the House of David* was a "must" for the thousands of Sunday School libraries which sprang up in the nineties, and almost as compulsory in village libraries all over the country, while it was long recognized as a "suitable" gift for young misses.

The Rev. Mr. Ingraham had just returned from a trip to New York, where he had tried unsuccessfully to obtain large advance royalties on a novel about Paul the Apostle, as yet unwritten, when a pistol which he carried in his pocket was accidentally discharged as he was removing his coat in the vestry-room of his church, killing him instantly. When Carleton, the New York publisher, heard the news, he congratulated himself that he had not advanced the three thousand dollars which Ingraham had asked for.

The editor of the *Brother Jonathan* pointed out in 1842 that the historical romances which that paper and other journals of its class were publishing had made it possible to issue Thiers' *French Revolution* in six-cent parts for the popular audience. He was probably right. Though historical works had long been the favorite fare of many American readers and a few of them had become long-time best sellers, the romances probably stimulated the public taste for brilliantly written historical works.

If Prescott's *Conquest of Mexico* had been published at a low price, it would undoubtedly have made a tremendous hit. But its author cared far more for the praise of English and American critics and men of letters than for the acclaim of the multitude. He was a man of means, with a background of sound scholarly culture. He had the plates and engravings for his book made to his order, and Harper & Brothers paid him $7,500 for the right to print and sell five thousand fine three-volume sets at six dollars each. Even at that price, the book surprised everyone by selling four thousand copies within a month and six times that before Prescott's death in 1859. When it emerged from copyright restrictions in the eighties, it became more genuinely popular and sold hundreds of thousands of copies in cheap editions.

Perhaps the *Conquest of Mexico*, too, was historical romance, as later critics have sometimes said. Prescott was doubtless badly misled in the matter of Aztec ethnology; but in the main his narrative is said to be correct, and certainly his brilliant style and sense of the picturesque made the reading of his history a pleasant and sometimes exciting pastime.

What could be done by cheap publication of a brilliantly written historical work was well demonstrated when Macaulay's *History of England* appeared. The first two volumes came out in 1849; and though Harpers had paid £130 a volume for it (£650 for the whole work), the pirates picked it up at once, E. H. Butler & Company, of Philadelphia, selling it for fifteen cents a volume. When the third and fourth volumes appeared twelve years later, two hundred thousand copies were sold within a few months. Butler sold the four volumes in one for $1.12½ and Harpers priced it at twenty-five cents a volume. The Donohue printing house in Chicago manufactured, over a term of years, 120,000 five-volume sets of Macaulay's history for the cheap-book trade.

Here is an object lesson in piracy versus copyright, for the sale of Macaulay's history was some four times as great in America, where the freebooters took it over, as in England, where the copyright kept the price high. To be sure, the overemphasized Whig point of view was particularly pleasing in America; but the chief reason for the vastly increased sales in this country (the population of Great Britain and the United States being about equal) was the popularizing nature of literary piracy. It is due largely to its American sales that Macaulay's work long held the record as the most popular history outside the textbook field.

Bancroft's *United States,* long so highly regarded, enjoyed a sale which was dwarfish in comparison.

Two American biographies reached great popular audiences in the forties. The first was Jared Sparks' *Life of Washington,* published by F. Andrews, Boston, in 1839 as a supplementary volume in the author's edition of Washington's *Writings,* and then issued separately in an abridgment by the author. Twenty-four editions were published in the next decade, including one in six-cent numbers by Curry & Company, of New York. Eulogistic rather than critical, this book suited the temper of the times; and it was both more interesting and lower priced than Irving's biography of the fifties. Some five hundred lives of Washington have been published, and two of them—those by Weems and Sparks—have reached the over-all best seller list.

Napoleon and His Marshals, by Joel T. Headley, was the first American book published by Baker & Scribner. Issued in 1846 in two volumes, it had a phenomenal sale in the martial climate of the years following the Mexican war triumphs; and in 1861 Scribners published their fiftieth edition of it. Like J. S. C. Abbott's *Napoleon Bonaparte,* which made such a popular serial in *Harper's Magazine* in the fifties, Headley's book glorified its hero and held the reader by picturesque and occasionally lurid narrative. But Headley's biography was published more cheaply than Abbott's, and far surpassed it in book sales.

Headley had been educated for the ministry, but had resigned his first pastorate on account of his health, and thereafter devoted himself to journalism and authorship. He spent a year with Greeley as associate editor of the *Tribune,* and was editor for several years of the *Christian Parlor Magazine.* The year after the appearance of his book on Napoleon, Scribners published the most popular of his travel books, *The Sacred Mountains.* His *Washington and His Generals* was serialized by *Graham's Magazine,* which pitted Headley against Abbott in a losing race with *Harper's Magazine.* In book form, however, Headley's *Washington* probably did better than Abbott's *Napoleon,* though neither attained the best seller list.

Two American autobiographies may close our catalogue. *The Life of Mary Jemison* was the third narrative of an Indian captivity to reach bestsellerdom. Though the story was Mrs. Jemison's, the words were those of Dr. James Everett Seaver, who drew the aged woman's account of her life from her and put it into his own painstaking phrases. Few "captivities" tell us more about Indian life than this story of a woman who had lived with the Delawares for nearly seventy years, had married two Indian husbands (successively, to be sure), and in her old age was anxious to say nothing injurious about her Indian people. The publishing history of Dr. Seaver's book is interesting. It was published in 1824 by James D. Bemis, of Canandaigua, New York, famous pioneer bookseller, printer, and editor, in a small volume that sold for 37½ cents. It was picked up soon by English pirates, and there were at least four English editions within two or three decades. But its main circulation was in northern and western New York: there were editions at Buffalo, Rochester, Batavia, Utica, Auburn, and Westfield. Some of these were pamphlet abridgments, and others sizable books with addenda by local authorities on Indian lore. Of course, city publishers eventually took it up, but for half a century it was distinctively a New York state book.

The other autobiography also found its popularity outside the usual channels of publication. *The Life of P. T. Barnum, Written by Himself,* was first published by J. S. Redfield, of New York, in 1854. The great showman was at the height of his prestige. Exhibitor of General Tom Thumb, impresario of Jenny Lind, owner of the most popular show-place in the world—the American Museum in New York,—and proprietor of "Barnum's Great Asiatic Caravan, Museum and Menagerie," he had made his name as well known as any in America. His autobiography was written and published mainly for sale to the crowds that visited his museum and circus. He revised it from time to time; in 1869 it received a sweeping revision and a new title—*Struggles and Triumphs; or, Fifty Years' Recollections of P. T. Barnum.* It had other titles, too, and many forms; Barnum regarded it less as a literary work than as a money-making device. He claimed—modestly for Barnum—to have sold half a million copies. Why not? It was one of the first great success stories of the hustling, get-ahead new America. The first edition was properly dedicated "To the Universal Yankee Nation," and it was all written for the pushing, ambitious, pious but not-too-scrupulous, up-and-coming go-getter of the midcentury.

XVI. THE FERTILE VINEYARD

> Childhood is a most fertile part of the vineyard of the Lord. The seed which is planted there vegetates very soon, and the weeds which spring up are easily eradicated. It is in every respect an easy and pleasant spot to till; and the flowers and fruits which, with proper effort, will bloom and ripen there surpass all others in richness and beauty.
>
> *Closing sentences of "The Young Christian"*

WHEN we read how pleasant a garden is youth, in Jacob Abbott's *The Young Christian,* we realize that we have come a long way from the ideas of Bishop Bayly's *Practice of Piety.* The purposes of the two books are much the same; both are guidebooks to the Christian life. But the Calvinistic rigors of the older book have at length given place to the calm reasoning of fatherly Mr. Abbott, and the glow of the eternal bonfire has been displaced by a realistic background produced by a multitude of anecdotes of common life. To be sure, the pious severity of *The Young Christian* seems a bit shocking a hundred years after, as when the man who is tempted to row his boat out on the lake on Sunday evening (not for fishing—perish the thought!) is admonished, "Stop, Christian, stop!"—or when we are told of the midnight death-bed of poor Louisa, who appears to have been frightened to death because she could not repent properly. But there is also no little good common sense in the book, as to conversation, reading, keeping a journal, and so on.

The Rev. Jacob Abbott was one of the most prolific authors of his times. He was proprietor and master of the Mount Vernon School for Girls in Boston when he wrote *The Young Christian*, shortly before he was twenty-nine. Its success was remarkable and long continued, not only in America, but in Great Britain and her colonies, and in France, Germany, and Holland. The young man followed up this book with three others, to complete the *Young Christian Series* in four volumes at $1.75 each. His literary success caused him to move up to Farmington, Maine, and devote himself wholly to a writing career. The bibliography of his works includes over two hundred titles. Most famous of all are the "Rollo Books"—twenty-eight of them—vehicles for teaching children facts of travel, history, science, and morals. A narrative thread, with child characters, binds the facts together. The Rollo series, with its sequels, the Lucy and the Jonas series, numbered forty volumes, and sold a million and a quarter copies in twenty-five years; yet no single book of the forty had a large enough sale to put it on the best seller list. The same may be said of the "Peter Parley" books by S. G. Goodrich, written about the same time. Both authors made marvelous successes with many little books, all of them assured of excellent sales but none outstanding. The one exception was Abbott's *The Young Christian*, which sold at least a quarter of a million copies.

Jacob Abbott had a younger brother, John Stevens Cabot Abbott, who also became a Congregational minister, and who also gave up his pastorate for literature after a big success with his first book. The year after Jacob published *The Young Christian*, John wrote *The Mother at Home*. John's book was in the same style as Jacob's, but shorter; it used the same method of copious illustration by little stories, true and invented; it had the same brand of severe piety mixed with much common sense; and it sold in almost identically the same quantities. It was followed by a sequel—*The Child at Home*. One thing to be noted about the Abbott brothers is that although they seemed to know everything, their learning, after all, was rather superficial. They were surest, however, in theology, and it doubtless gave John a feeling of security to base his theories of child-training on "the body of divinity."

J. S. C. Abbott was the author of the famous "Napoleon romance" referred to in the last chapter and of *The Civil War in America*, one of several contemporary histories of the war whose large sales were not quite large enough to make them best sellers. The Abbott brothers, between them, did a long series of rather short, readable biographies of the chief figures in the history of the world which were uncritical to a degree, but which made history (or something like it) pleasant for thousands of schoolboys.

Two books of fairy tales came to be known to most American children— Hans Christian Andersen's and Grimms'. The first American collections of

Andersen's magical tales appeared in the late forties, in little books published in New York and Boston. Some of the later stories had their original publication in American magazines—the *Riverside* and *Scribner's Monthly*. Beloved as his name has been in so many childish hearts, Andersen was not fond of children; and he preferred some of his other work, now long forgotten, far above such classics as "The Constant Tin Soldier" and "The Ugly Duckling."

Still more popular in the United States were *Grimms' Fairy Tales*, first issued in Germany under the title *Kinder- und Hausmärchen,* in 1812 and 1815. The brothers Grimm attempted to preserve the domestic tales of the peasantry of Prussia and Hesse in narratives which became popular the world over. Crosby, Nichols, Lea & Company, of Boston, were the pioneer American publishers of the stories in 1861, using the title *Popular Tales and Household Stories*. The sales, in hundreds of cheap editions and some fine ones, have exceeded a million and a quarter in this country. The Book-of-the-Month Club recently distributed attractive editions of the Grimm and Andersen fairy tales as a "dividend," and some months later they gave a similar circulation to *Alice in Wonderland*.

Few will dispute that *Alice* is one of the greatest juvenile classics of all time. It is pleasant to remember that it was his love for the little daughters of his friend which inspired the gentle and whimsical Charles Dodgson, a bachelor thirty years of age, a clergyman, and an authority in the field of mathematics, to write the story now called *Alice in Wonderland*. He penned every page of it in charming italic lettering and illustrated it with his own sketches; that manuscript was sold in 1928 to Dr. A. S. W. Rosenbach, of Philadelphia and New York, for $75,250.

English as the little book is, it belongs in more than one way to America. Its first effective publication was in New York. It was brought out by Macmillan in London before that house was established in America; but Dodgson and John Tenniel, the illustrator, objected to the presswork on the book and the publishers recalled the few hundred copies that had already gone to the booksellers. Daniel Appleton, of New York, was in town; and it was agreed that he should take the ill-starred edition off the hands of the London publishers and distribute it in America, where presumably it would not embarrass author or artist. The original edition consisted of two thousand copies; Appleton took a thousand of them, in sheets, bound in his own titlepage, and sold them. Then he took nine hundred more—apparently all then available—putting in another titlepage not quite identical with his first one. The recalled London edition was dated 1865; the Appleton-Macmillan edition with two titlepages was dated 1866; and the second London edition, which was the first one effectively distributed there, was also dated 1866. What a bibliographical mess for the collector of first editions!

At any rate, the book was an American success from the start, many publishers issued editions of it, and grown-ups came to love it quite as much as the children did. Many of its phrases have attained a currency so general that their original source has been forgotten. The book belongs to that comparatively short list of best sellers whose sales are estimated at two million or more. The author, who spent his life as an Oxford tutor in mathematics, wearied of the immense popularity of this child of his youthful fancy; when Queen Victoria honored him by asking for an autographed copy of his book, he sent her his *Theory of Determinants*, respectfully inscribed. Later, Edward Bok hunted him down in Oxford and asked him to write a sequel to *Alice* for the *Ladies' Home Journal*; the unwillingly famous author pretended not to know who "Lewis Carroll" was, insisted that Mr. Bok had made a mistake in addressing him, and presented him also with a mathematical treatise by Charles L. Dodgson.

Alice was written for girls, but has perhaps found its most confirmed admirers among adults with wit enough to love nonsense. *Swiss Family Robinson* was and is for the family; but it is, above all, a boys' book, with a scoutish appeal long before anyone thought of the *Boy Scout Manual*. Johann Rudolph Wyss, professor of philosophy and librarian of the University of Berne, and author of the Swiss national anthem, published his *Der Schweizerische Robinson* in 1812-13. The next year it was translated into English and two editions of it (one in two volumes and one in four) were issued in London. Not until 1832 was it printed in America; then Harpers published it in two volumes, from what was called "the Seventh London Edition," as a number in their "Boys' and Girls' Library of Useful and Entertaining Knowledge." By the middle of the century it was procurable in one volume at seventy-five cents. Thenceforward it continued along the road of cheap publication, available to every boy with a quarter, providing enchanted afternoons and evenings of absorbed reading for literally millions of children. In short, it has sold at least a million copies in the United States, and is still an active title.

Another boys' book long popular is *Tom Brown's School Days*, also introduced by Harpers and also published cheaply by them and by others. Thomas Hughes, its author, had a long public career in England as an advanced Liberal, and he exerted some influence on American affairs, first as an abolitionist and later as a Socialist. His most famous book was designed primarily to show the influence of a great teacher in a boys' school—Dr. Thomas Arnold, father of Matthew Arnold.

Many boys found their favorite author in Jules Verne, whose *Twenty Thousand Leagues Under the Sea* and *Around the World in Eighty Days* exercised so much fascination upon so many minds that each of them reached the million mark in American sales. Published in the early seventies, these romances coincided with a pronounced interest in science on the part of the common people; and they also caught the impetus of the orgy of cheap publishing which distinguished that decade.

The authorities agree that Verne was French-born and had a normal French education and boyhood, and they supply convincing documentation of these facts. But Verne himself, incurable romanticist, loved to invent tales of the kind of boyhood he might have led for the journalists who interviewed him; and as a result it is hard to escape a certain amount of Verne mythology in looking into this author's origins. The most persistent story is that he was a Polish boy named Grünbaum who, with his brothers, escaped from conscription in the army of their native country to find their fortunes in France. It is one of those stories that seem better than the truth; doubtless that was the reason Verne invented it —that and the fact that he was something of a recluse, inclined to resent invasions of his privacy. Actually he was born in Nantes into a middle-class family, the son of a successful lawyer. Though himself marked for the law, his romantic interest in science caused him to make his place as the greatest science fictioneer of his times.

In 1889, when the story of Phileas Fogg's eighty-day world-girdling feat had been familiar to the American public for a decade and a half, one of the bright young men who were directing Mr. Pulitzer's *New York World* sent that paper's star gal-reporter on a trip to beat Phileas' record. Nellie Bly stopped over during her famous tour to visit Verne at his home in Amiens, and he wished her good luck. She got back to New York in a blaze of fireworks and glory and publicity after having shaved a little over seven days off the record of Verne's hero—and without taking advantage, as Phileas did, of the international date line to save a day.

Among midcentury boys' books by American authors, Richard Henry Dana's autobiographical *Two Years Before the Mast* holds the palm. Its simple and straightforward narrative of a common sailor's life at sea and its vivid but restrained description make it as readable today as when it first appeared in 1840. Dana had made the voyage he described for the sake of his health, and doubtless also for adventure. Though we call *Two Years Before the Mast* a boys' book, it was written for the general public, with the purpose of arousing interest in seamen's welfare—and also to make enough money for the young author to marry on. From the money angle the book was a disappointment. Harpers would not take it on a royalty basis, and paid only two hundred and fifty dollars for the copyright. They brought it out in their Family Library and it did well from the start. Moxon, the London publisher, put out an edition, and was courteous enough to send the author a sum larger than Harpers had paid for the American copyright. Several other English editions appeared, usually at a shilling. After the Harper rights expired, in 1868, the book got better circulation than before, and was reprinted by various publishers in great quantities. Paramount made a new movie of the famous story as late as 1945.

A mild success of the sixties was *Hans Brinker; or, The Silver Skates*, published by James O'Kane, of New York; but not until Mary Mapes Dodge, its author, had won wider recognition as editor of *St. Nicholas* was this engaging story of a little Dutch boy taken over by Scribners and started upon its greater popularity. And then, upon its emergence from copyright restrictions many years later, Hans took still another lease upon life. Indeed Mrs. Dodge's book has been a perennial favorite. The author got her idea for the story from reading Motley's *Rise of the Dutch Republic*; and though she was unable to visit Holland, she collected Dutch material for years before writing the book.

Like *Hans Brinker*, Louisa May Alcott's great successes were definitely designed for teen-age children. *Little Women*, the most popular girls' story in American literature, was written in response to repeated requests of Roberts Brothers, of Boston, for "a girls' book."

One cannot appreciate the history of *Little Women* without knowing something about the Alcott family. Of course, the reader of the book learns much about them, for the story keeps close to reality in both characters and incidents. But one should know also about the high-minded, improvident philosopher-father; about the education of the children by the father, and his encouragement of their self-expression; and about the family poverty. A. Bronson Alcott was amused when he was greeted on a lecture tour not as the founder of the Concord School of Philosophy but as "the grandfather of *Little Women*"; but his encouragement of his daughter's writing gave more than the obvious meaning to the latter appellation. The penury of the family was also a stimulus to Louisa's writing—too much of a stimulus, sometimes, for her health.

Miss Alcott's title for *Little Women*, when she first began to think about the story, was "The Pathetic Family." There was pathos in the family needs and in the frustration of brilliant minds and eager hearts, but the sympathetic reader of Louisa's journal finds himself moved most by the young author's brave attempt to pay her father's debts and provide for the pressing needs of the family by her pen. And so we rejoice in the fairy-tale denouement of her story. For August, 1868, occur these words in her journal: "Roberts Bros. made an offer for the story *Little Women*, but at the same time advised me to keep the copyright; so I shall." Seventeen years later, Miss Alcott wrote in, after this entry, a further comment: "An honest publisher and a lucky author, for the copyright made her fortune." Before her death she realized from her books, to say nothing of her magazine contributions, about two hundred thousand dollars, much of which she generously gave to the members of "The Pathetic Family," whom she loved so much.

A second part of *Little Women* was published some six months after the first. The book was translated into French, German, and Dutch, and had a wide circulation in Great Britain. Some two million copies have been sold in America. *Little Men*, published in 1871, had somewhat less than half the sale of *Little Women*.

Two big compilations for family reading, sold throughout the country by agents, must be mentioned here. The first was *The Wonders of the World, in Nature, Art, and Mind*—the most successful subscription book of the first half of the nineteenth century. It was illustrated by five hundred woodcut pictures and sold for two dollars and a half. It was issued by Robert Sears, a New York printer and publisher who put together many illustrated volumes, and supported the efforts of his traveling book-agents with liberal advertising.

A great success in the subscription field in the seventies and eighties was another family book, *The Royal Path of Life; or, Aims and Aids to Success and Happiness.* This was a series of little essays on such subjects as Life, Man and Woman, Mother, Children, Youth, Home, Family Worship, Ambition, Avarice, Gambling, Fame, and so on. The authors were a teacher and a preacher, Thomas L. Haines and Levi W. Yaggy. We should call them compilers rather than authors, for they did little more than put together tags and quotations: the whole has an effect of perfect triteness in the worst style of Victorian sentimental morality. There are half a dozen steel engravings, which may have had something to do with a sale said to have reached eight hundred thousand copies, mostly at two dollars and a half. There are many imprints, but apparently the authors were the publishers.

Finally, there was a best seller novelette of family life which may well be named here. It was a curious hit of the hard-times year of 1837, and made the reputation of Mrs. Hannah F. Lee. *Three Experiments of Living* was the intriguing title. In the story we are shown how Dr. and Mrs. Fulton lived first "within their means," then moved to a more fashionable neighborhood and lived "up to their means," and finally ruined themselves living "above their means"—despite the warnings of Uncle Joshua. The moral is that simple home pleasures are best, and you can't blame all your financial ills on Wall Street. The little book achieved a quick popularity. A wag brought out a parody, *A Fourth Experiment of Living,* in which he told how to live without means. Mrs. Lee herself wrote a sequel, *Elinor Fulton,* of which only about a dozen editions were issued.

XVII. THE MUSE IN THE MARKETPLACE

The spirit of poetry is abroad among us. . . . Our constitution and state of society permit no talents to be inactive; they call out genius wherever it lies hid.

American Quarterly Review, December, 1827

THE criterion of sales seems a crude test to apply to the poet's fine frenzy. Literary criticism is not founded directly upon figures of total sales; perhaps not the poet but his public is measured by such totals. Nevertheless, the Muse must sooner or later leave her fields and groves and take her stand in the marketplace, offering her wares for money.

When the first cantos of *Childe Harold's Pilgrimage* appeared in 1812, Scott was the reigning monarch in English poetry.* But when Byron awakened one

---

* Byron had been published in America before 1812. S. & J. Ridge, of Newark, issued *Poems, Original and Translated,* by George Gordon, Lord Byron, in 1808. No discussion

morning in 1812 to find himself famous (to repeat once more his famous boast), Scott had turned to fiction. In America Byron was not so immediately popular: the new poetry was accepted with far more caution and distrust in America than in England. After all, the lively, clear-flowing ballad meters of Scott, with historical incident, forthright clearness, and narrative movement, were much easier for the American readers of the second decade of the new century than the more or less mystical meditations of Harold in Spenserian stanzas. Moreover, the skepticism and immorality of the new poet alarmed many critics. Samuel G. Goodrich tells the story well in his *Recollections:*

> The pulpit opened its thunders against Byron's poems—teachers warned their pupils, parents their children. I remember, even as late as 1820, that some booksellers refused to sell them, regarding them as infidel publications. About this time a publisher in Hartford, on this ground, declined being concerned in stereotyping an edition of them. It was all in vain. Byron could no more be kept at bay than the cholera.

And Goodrich thinks he was quite as dangerous as the cholera.

But the new poet's very misanthropy and cynicism were fascinating, and the beauty of his lines charmed those who censured his morals. Byronism soon became the rage. Even the rolled collar and disordered hair of his portrait were aped, along with his poetic moods. The outburst against him in England in 1816 had no effect upon his American popularity. "The Prisoner of Chillon" took its place as a favorite piece for the "elocutionists," and the longer narratives found eager readers. Admiration for the poet and his work reached its climax with his death on the field of Missolonghi. The struggle for Greek independence was ardently supported in America, and Byron died a hero.

In the year of Byron's death, R. W. Pomeroy, of Philadelphia, brought out his *Works* in eight volumes. But this edition was not complete, for the final cantos of *Don Juan* were not published until the next year. When Carey & Lea received advance sheets of those cantos, they put them into the hands of thirty compositors; and in thirty-six hours the last of Byron's works were on sale in the bookstores. The pirates published edition after edition of the chief works of Byron from that time onward. In the cheap-publishing era of the forties, both Carey & Hart and Burgess & Stringer brought out his complete works in weekly parts at twenty-five cents each. Later in the century, single-volume editions of Byron were published and sold by the hundreds of thousands. Long after the tide of Byronism might have been thought to have receded, Thomas Y. Crowell, a specialist in the publication of the poets, sold 170,000 copies of his Byron.

Thomas Moore's *Lalla Rookh* came in on the Byronic wave but remained popular for a hundred years. The circumstances surrounding the writing of the

---

of poets popular in nineteenth-century America can neglect Burns or Scott, who shared with Byron, Tennyson, Longfellow, and the other poets discussed in this chapter the leadership in popularity among American readers of verse throughout the century. But Burns' following has already been discussed in the chapter on eighteenth-century poets, and Scott's poems with his novels.

poem make a striking story. Longmans, inspired by the success of Moore's *Irish Melodies*, offered the poet three thousand pounds—a record-breaking price—before the "epic" was written. Under the influence of Byron, Moore chose an eastern subject and shut himself up for two years with a library of Oriental books. When the work was finished in 1816, England was in the grip of a post-war depression, and Moore offered to rescind his contract with his publishers; but Longmans stuck to their original offer, paid over the money, and issued the poem the next year. It was a tremendous success and at once made Moore a rival of Byron and Scott in contemporary English poetry.

Moses Thomas, of Philadelphia, brought *Lalla Rookh* out in 1817. Moore was already well known in America, both from his visit to this country in 1804 and his earlier poems. Opinion on the value of his poetry was divided, and the ventilation of extreme views about him at least had the virtue of publicizing his work. Edward T. Channing, writing of *Lalla Rookh* in the *North American Review*, declared that Moore's verse was "little more than a mixture of musick, conceit and debauchery." Indeed the frequent condemnation of his long poem, or rather series of poetical narratives, on the ground of the immorality of some of its lush passages, undoubtedly did much to arouse interest. But only the genuine attraction exercised on the popular audience by the poetical romances of *Lalla Rookh* can account for the many editions of it throughout the whole of the nineteenth century. As late as the 1880's, there was the Lovell's Library edition at twenty cents, and the Estes & Lauriat fine edition the next year at fifty dollars; and there were many other issues in that decade.

Tennyson did not burst upon the world with dazzling Byronic brilliance. He had been before the British public for more than a decade before the first American publication of his work—the *Poems* of 1842, in two small volumes—was issued, under the imprint of W. D. Ticknor, of Boston. Ticknor paid the poet a hundred and fifty dollars for advance sheets and published an edition of two thousand copies, which had "a ready and extensive sale." In a few years the *Democratic Review* was acclaiming Tennyson "the first English poet of his day," and "Carl Benson" Bristed was instructing his compatriots that it was the opinion "of a very large number of the best educated men in England" that Tennyson was a greater poet than Byron.

From then on Tennyson's successive works were eagerly welcomed by an increasing audience in America. Though *In Memoriam* was the most discussed of these slender volumes, the *Idylls of the King* soon became, with the aid of the schools, the most read and best loved. But the single-volume editions of Tennyson had an amazing sale of over a million and a half. Crowell alone sold nearly half a million.

In the year of Tennyson's death, William T. Stead expressed in the *Review of Reviews* a rather bitter regret that the poet had not seen fit to sacrifice a part of the large income which he received from the sale of his works in order to allow cheaper publication of them in his native land. Wrote the English editor:

> He may be a popular poet in America. He is not a popular poet in Great Britain—popular, that is, in the sense of being read and loved by the common people. And this, in great measure, for a very simple cause: for the nation, as John Bright aptly said, lives in the cottages, and Tennyson is too dear for the cottages. . . . There is no shilling edition of Tennyson.

And in the same magazine, as though to emphasize the point, Hamilton W. Mabie wrote:

> Tennyson has been more widely read in this country than in England, and the knowledge of his work is more widely diffused. It has percolated through all classes of society, and much of it has been for many years a possession of the common memory. The poet more than once recognized the fact that he had more admirers in America than in England, and he had more admirers because he had more readers.

And he had more readers because his work was available in cheap editions. As early as 1870 the Harpers were publishing a complete Tennyson in paper covers at seventy-five cents. In the humblest homes, in city and country, on the frontier, Tennyson's poems came into the hands of the people, and to some extent, as Mabie says, into their memories.

Robert Browning's popularity in America was on a somewhat different level. For a good many years Mrs. Browning was more popular in this country than her husband. It was not until literary circles in the cities became interested enough in *Sordello*, *The Ring and the Book*, and the short dramatic pieces to organize clubs devoted to the study of Browning, that great enthusiasm for his work was aroused. The Browning clubs of the eighties constitute one of the most remarkable social phenomena of those times. They created what was called in the magazines "the Browning craze." It was not a fad, however, for it was long-lived and founded on an intellectual interest often very genuine. Came then, naturally, the "required reading" of Browning in the schools. While the distribution of his complete poetical works in this country has been very large (Crowells alone have sold over a quarter of a million), even greater has been the sale of editions of Browning's "selected poems," not only for school use but for home libraries.

Longfellow's popularity is comparable to that of Tennyson rather than to that of Browning. When Longfellow's first volume of verse, *Voices of the Night*, succeeded well enough to sell the first edition of nine hundred copies in a month, the author was delighted; but the little book had a sale, before it was swallowed up in later collected editions of Longfellow, of between forty and fifty thousand—not bad for any book of poems. Each successive volume (except *The Golden Legend*) that Longfellow published in the next fifteen years had just a little better sale than its predecessor.*

---

* See the record of Longfellow's sales to 1857 in *Allibone's Dictionary of Authors* (Philadelphia, 1858), vol. I, p. 1128. Also William Charvat, "Longfellow's Income From His Writings, 1840-52," in *Papers of the Bibliographical Society of America*, 1944, vol. VIII, p. 9.

But it was not until the appearance of *Hiawatha* in 1855 that Longfellow became the great popular poet of America. This poem had an advance sale of four thousand, and sold ten thousand within a month and fifty thousand in five months. This immediate popularity benefited by the controversies which sprang up as to the poet's indebtedness to other works for form and matter, and by the easily imitated, tripping feet of the versification. Hundreds of scribblers—probably thousands, over the years—parodied *Hiawatha*. Marc Anthony Henderson, of Cincinnati, published *The Song of Milkanwatha,* said to be translated from "the original Feejee." Six other full-length parodies were issued in book form, most of them less spiteful. Abridgments for children's reading in the schools have perhaps, in the long run, given the poem its widest circulation.

Longfellow always retained the ownership of his own copyrights; he ordered the printing of the earlier works himself, at the Harvard University Press, and paid his publishers a commission. The early volumes of poetry he sold at seventy-five cents retail, though *Hiawatha* was put at a dollar. Compare the English prices of Tennyson with the American prices of Longfellow: in 1847 the English poet published *The Princess* at five shillings and the American published *Evangeline* at seventy-five cents, while in 1850 *In Memoriam* appeared at six shillings and *Seaside and Fireside* at seventy-five cents. All the older Longfellow volumes were priced by this time at from twenty-five to seventy-five cents. In general, Tennyson in London cost about twice the price of Longfellow in Boston or New York. A collected edition of Longfellow in paper covers was brought out by the Harpers in 1852 at 62½ cents, and Ticknor & Fields' Diamond Edition in 16mo in 1867 at a dollar; while the English collected edition of Tennyson in the fifties was priced at nine shillings.

Meantime, English pirates were selling Longfellow's poems in great quantities at low prices. Bogue paid the poet a hundred pounds for the advance sheets of *Hiawatha,* and sold ten thousand copies of a shilling edition before the pirates caught up with him. *Evangeline* had already had a big sale at the same price, and collected editions of Longfellow were soon available in London at three or four shillings. Altogether, Longfellow seems to have sold quite as well in England as in America.

Through the sixties, seventies, and eighties, Longfellow's publishers kept the flourishing market for the favorite poet's work well supplied with a variety of editions at a great range in prices. James R. Osgood & Company, successors of Ticknor & Fields, published a little "vest pocket" edition of Longfellow's *Favorite Poems* at fifty cents in 1877, as the cheap-publishing war got under way. When Houghton, Mifflin & Company took over from Osgood, they issued the complete poetical works in a very popular edition, and in other forms up to a de luxe set, illustrated by F. O. C. Darley, Edwin Abbey, and others, in forty-five fifty-cent parts sold by subscription.

Longfellow died in 1882. His early works began emerging from copyright restrictions into the public domain in the eighties, and were immediately picked up by such low-price publishers of the time as John W. Lovell, who started his *Library* in the year of the poet's death with his two early prose books, and issued the early poems three years later—all at twenty cents each. From this time forward, Longfellow's "collected," "selected," and "complete" poems were available to American readers at prices ranging from twenty cents up. Hurst sold great quantities of a thirty-five cent edition of Longfellow in the late nineties.

Most popular of the separate poems were *Hiawatha, Evangeline,* and *The Courtship of Miles Standish.* The first of these has sold at least a million copies, and the other two would also qualify, separately, as best sellers in our list. The collected editions of Longfellow's poems in many formats have sold more than a million copies.

No other American poet has ever been as popular abroad as Longfellow. For many years he was more widely read in England than his contemporary Tennyson. The British novelist and Egyptologist Amelia B. Edwards wrote in the *Literary World* in 1881: "Longfellow is in England the most widely read of living poets"—a result, in part, of the work of the London pirating publishers. On the Continent he became almost as well known as in England—especially in Germany, where thirty-five different translations of his poems, separate or collected, have been recorded. Multiple versions have also appeared in Italian, French, Dutch, Swedish, Danish, Polish, and Portuguese. Nor is that all, for he has been translated into at least ten other languages. Brander Matthews, writing in the closing years of the nineteenth century, said very justly: "If we can measure popular approval by the widespread sale of his successive volumes, Longfellow was probably the most popular poet of the English language in this century."

Far different was the publishing history of another leading American poet— Edgar Allan Poe. Poor Poe did not receive more than a few hundred dollars for the copyrights and royalties on all of his ten published books. They all sold slowly, and therefore the author found publishers uniformly reluctant and ungenerous. But by one of the bitterest ironies in the history of American publishing, Poe's works began to sell readily soon after he had been laid in his grave.

Perhaps he had to die to make himself an object of great popular interest; at any rate, the publicity given the tragic end of his erratic life, the attack and defense, a measure of pity, and much general curiosity probably combined to stimulate the sales of his works. Griswold, his literary executor, prepared Poe's writings for printing in four volumes in the year following the author's death; but most of the leading publishers of the day, remembering earlier Poe failures, refused to take the risk of issuing the collected works. Finally, Griswold induced J. S. Redfield, of New York, to print two volumes. These sold surprisingly well, and the publisher immediately added a third, pricing the set at four dollars. Two or three years later, the fourth volume completed the set, of which Redfield had to publish at least fifteen editions within the decade following Poe's death. Before that decade ended, Redfield joined with a London publisher to bring out a sumptuously illustrated edition of the poetical works, of which American readers bought five thousand copies, at six dollars for cloth binding and nine for morocco. Redfield then issued the poems in a little blue-and-gold book at seventy-five cents and sold five thousand copies of that in sixty days. Meantime several shilling collections of Poe's poems and tales had been published in England; and Wiley & Putnam were selling their *The Raven and Other Poems,* originally issued in 1845, at 37½ cents.

Redfield bought the Poe copyrights from Mrs. Clemm, the poet's heir, at an absurdly low price; about 1860 he disposed of them to W. J. Widdleton, his successor, who brought out fifty-cent editions of both the poems and the tales in the low-price era of the late seventies. But as the copyrights expired, the "libraries" of the eighties and nineties issued cheap collections, and more of Poe's works were sold than ever before. The *Tales* have, on the whole, been more popular than the poetical works; but both have clear titles to the best seller list. This has come about partly by aid of the schools, of course; but there is a continuing popular interest in Poe, as witness the large sales in recent years of the Modern Library edition of the tales and poems together and the Pocket Books edition of the *Tales.*

Dr. Rufus Wilmot Griswold, Poe's editor, was responsible for the most popular anthology of American poetry of its century—*The Poets and Poetry of America,* published in 1842. In the eighth edition, issued after Poe had produced nearly all of his work, Charles Sprague is given seventeen pages, Charles Fenno Hoffman eleven, Carlos Wilcox seven, and Poe four. It is not fair, however, to criticise Griswold's choices by the standards and perspective of a hundred years later; and favoritism may be a prerogative of the anthologist anyway. Griswold's handsome book sold some three hundred thousand copies at three dollars each (three-fifty for leather binding), and that was a big sale for those days and those prices.

Whittier received high praise and sixteen pages of space in Griswold's anthology of 1842. It was after the Civil War, however, that the Quaker poet reached his larger audience. *Snow-Bound,* with its homely details and its vividness, did much to endear him to the people; it became a school classic by the eighties. Osgood brought out a dollar edition of Whittier's collected poems in 1876, and a selection of *Favorite Poems* for fifty cents the next year. As copyrights on the early poems began to expire in the eighties, cheap publishers issued paper-bound copies at twenty cents. In the next decade single volume Whittiers were put on the market by nearly a dozen different publishers. For the last twenty-five years of his life, Whittier was one of the best loved poets of America, and there seems to have been no decline in his popularity for ten or fifteen years after his death in 1892.

On the centennial of the birth of Walt Whitman, an admirer of the poet was much disturbed by a statement that his fame was dwindling, his ideology "remembered by a very few." So James Waldo Fawcett sat down and wrote to a hundred representative leaders in America and Europe and asked them if it was so. Among the replies was one from Bernard Shaw: "Whitman is a classic, not a best seller. Curious that America should be the only country in which this is not as obvious as the sun in the heavens!" Curious how the perverse G.B.S. can crowd so many unfounded assumptions into so short a space! A classic may, of course, become a best seller, or a best seller a classic. The former development has taken place in regard to Whitman's work.

For *Leaves of Grass,* long rejected of the American public, then limited in its acceptance for even longer, is at last a popular book. The admirable Doubleday Doran edition of 1940, which was used as a Book-of-the-Month Club "dividend," had a distribution of over a quarter of a million copies in five years. Editions in such active series as the Modern Library, the Blue Ribbon Books, Grosset & Dunlap's Universal Library, Macmillan's Modern Readers' Library, the Penguin Books, Everyman's Library, and Scribners' Modern Students' Library pile up sales for it. *Leaves of Grass* has become a best seller as well as a classic.

The first edition of the *Leaves* appeared in 1855, striking in its quarto size, with ninety-five pages, from the press of Andrew and James Rome, Brooklyn, where the author himself had set the type for it and had doubtless designed the format which fitted the content so well. No name, of author, publisher, or printer, appeared on the titlepage; but the copyright notice named Walter Whitman, and Walt's portrait in unconventional pose faced the title. There was nothing anonymous about the book, after all; quite the contrary, for such readers as it had would discover, on page 29:

Walt Whitman, an American, one of the roughs, a kosmos,
Disorderly flesh and sensual . . . eating, drinking and breeding,
No sentimentalist . . . no stander above men and women or apart from them . . . no
  more modest than immodest.

The book was substantially and handsomely bound, and was priced at two dollars. Probably seven or eight hundred were printed, but not all were bound up at once. The first bookseller who undertook to offer the book found objectionable lines in it before it had been on sale more than a day or two, and told the author and publisher to get it out of the shop. Finally Walt found a firm of publishers and booksellers who were willing to try to sell his *Leaves;* he made the acquaintance of Fowler & Wells, the famous phrenologists, editors and publishers of many books and magazines relating to phrenology, the water-cure, vegetarianism, Grahamism, and so on. Odd as all these "isms" seem now, Fowler & Wells was a good firm (or Fowlers & Wells, as the firm name often appeared, there being two brothers Fowler). They could not force an unwanted product on their trade, however; they cut the price in half, and even bound some in paper covers to sell at seventy-five cents, all to no avail. Three thousand dollars would be a reasonable price for a copy today. The author eventually gave away a considerable part of the edition, and those that were left were "remaindered," doubtless for a few dollars.

Was the young poet crushed by this rejection of his work? Not Walt Whitman. The next year he brought out, through Fowler & Wells, a second and augmented edition, with small pages but 384 of them. Low on the backstrip was printed a sentence from Emerson's letter to Whitman: "I greet you at the beginning of a great career." The young poet had sent the older one a copy of the first *Leaves*, had received a fine, spontaneous letter of laudation in reply, and was following his own notions of what was proper promotion. But not even a plug from Emerson could sell this new edition; and the publishers, whose bumps of Ideality and Firmness were not so well developed as those of Acquisitiveness and Love of Approbation, became frightened at the charges of immorality in their book and resigned the whole edition, less a few copies that had been sold, to the author. Whitman gave it a new titlepage the next year and went on with his struggle for acceptance.

He had more literary friends in Boston, the home of transcendentalism, than in New York; and it was there that he found his first regular publisher. Charles W. Eldridge had become a Whitman admirer, and was to remain a devoted friend of the poet for many years. He was junior partner in the young Boston firm of Thayer & Eldridge, who in 1860 stereotyped a re-augmented and better rounded *Leaves of Grass* and sold two printings—about four thousand copies—at a dollar and a quarter before the firm went into bankruptcy the next year. Richard Worthington, of New York, nicknamed "Holy Dick" by disapproving competitors, got the plates, and continued to issue the book for many years; but Whitman believed that he never received a fair accounting from this new publisher. Though the Boston episode ended in disaster, it did much to found a Whitman public, and it made the author something in royalties.

After Whitman's war experiences he issued two more editions of the *Leaves*, both again augmented, in 1867-68 and 1871-72. For both he was his own publisher, and on both he lost money. The mission of his life had now become not merely the writing of his poems, but the publishing and circulation of them. By 1873 his home was in Camden, and illness had made him old in his mid-fifties. On the streets of Camden and Philadelphia, he was a familiar figure—the big, bearded man carrying in the crook of his arm a basket of his books—his own publisher, his own delivery boy.

The sixth, or "Centennial" edition, of 1876, was the most expensive to date. Bound in half-leather, it sold for five dollars, and an accompanying volume at the same price contained Whitman's prose material and miscellany. To the author-publisher's surprise, it sold rather well, both in America and England. By this time, Whitman had many devoted followers in both countries. W. M. Rossetti, who had come into possession of one of the "remaindered" copies of the first edition, had worked hard to popularize Whitman across the sea.

From diverse classes had come those almost fanatical lovers of Walt sometimes called "Whitmaniacs."

So an established publisher took him up—Osgood, of Boston. This 1881 edition had sold sixteen hundred copies at two dollars each, when the Boston Society for the Suppression of Vice stepped in and threatened to take court action against the book. Osgood surrendered at once and turned over the plates to the author in lieu of royalties, and the second Boston edition was, like the first, abortive.

Whitman thereupon resumed publication risks of his book, and through Rees, Welsh & Company, of Philadelphia, issued other printings from the Osgood plates in 1882. This edition is said to have yielded the poet-publisher thirteen hundred dollars. A special autograph edition of three hundred, with additional poems, was published at five dollars in 1889. Finally, through David McKay, of Philadelphia, Whitman published, still from the Osgood plates though with the addition of more new poems, the edition of 1891-92, prepared when he was on his deathbed. This was the author's eighth edition of his work. What a record! Walt Whitman's persistence in publication as well as authorship, despite misfortune and discouragement of the bitterest kind, is something unique in the annals of literature.

After the poet's death came the era of editions of his "selected" poems, usually omitting those offensive to purists. There can be no doubt that Walt's refusal to expurgate cost him general popularity in his own lifetime. There were, however, several complete issues of the *Leaves* in the twenty-five years following his death. Since the centennial of his birth, celebrated in 1919, there has been a steady and general increase in the popularity of the poems. Now, half a century after his death, Whitman's work has reached that wide, democratic distribution at which he aimed. Walt was right when he published these prophetic lines in the first edition of the *Leaves of Grass:*

> My foothold is tenoned and mortised in granite,
> I laugh at what you call dissolution,
> And I know the amplitude of time.

Whitman's work had behind it the most active group of devotees, and Browning's was supported by the best organized followers, but the book of verse that stirred up the greatest fever of fascinated interest was Edward FitzGerald's version of Omar Khayyám's *Rubáiyát*. That a Persian poem, fatalistic, irreverent, Epicurean, should achieve a spectacular American success at the end of the nineteenth century illustrates the general abandonment of many of the old habits of thought. It also testifies to the effectiveness of FitzGerald's skillful and beautiful verses.

The first edition of this famous translation, or paraphrase, appeared in London in 1859, published, in paper covers, at the author's expense. It was priced at five shillings; but when there were no sales, the little book was repeatedly marked down until it was offered at a penny. It made some friends, however—notably D. G. Rossetti and Swinburne—and by 1868 there was a second and augmented edition. It was this revision that found its way to Columbus, Ohio, in a single copy, and so charmed and fascinated a literary group there that they had an edition of about a hundred struck off for their own use in 1870. But it was not until James R. Osgood & Company, of Boston, published a reprint of the third English edition that the *Rubáiyát* really came to the attention of the American public. This little book, with the verso of each page blank, was reprinted again and again. Osgood, undoubtedly in good faith, placed the words "First American Edition" on the titlepage of his first issue. On the other hand, the true first edition's titlepage bears the words "Second Edition," because it is a reprint of the English volume which bore that legend.

A folio edition of the *Rubáiyát* with illustrations by Elihu Vedder was published in 1885, at twenty-five dollars, by Osgood's successors, Houghton, Mifflin & Company, with some de luxe copies priced at a hundred dollars. The same year the Grolier Club issued an edition in paper covers. But in 1891 the Readers' Library published Omar's quatrains as the second number in its series of twenty-cent classics, and later in that decade many other publishers issued the little book. One of the curiosities of book publication is an edition of the *Rubáiyát* the pages of which measure five-sixteenths of an inch square, published by Charles Hardy Meigs, of Cleveland, Ohio; it is the smallest of all miniature books. By the turn of the century eight publishers were offering Omar at twenty-five cents or less—three at ten cents. One commentator in 1899 declared that American editions were appearing "almost daily." There were other translations of the *Rubáiyát,* as well as parodies: Oliver Herford wrote and drew his *Rubáiyát of a Persian Kitten* in 1904. In the ensuing years scores of American publishers put the book on their lists. It became a favorite for the private presses devoted to fine printing. The climax in cheap publication came when the Little Blue Books sold in the neighborhood of a quarter of a million copies of it at five cents each. More recently, the Pocket Books distributed about the same number at twenty-five cents.

A highly popular narrative poem for half a century was Owen Meredith's *Lucile.* Ticknor & Fields brought it out in Boston, immediately after its first appearance in London in 1860, in a little blue-and-gold volume at seventy-five cents. In the eighties, the cheap publishers sold it by the hundreds of thousands, but the form in which many oldsters today remember it is that of the Crowell edition with padded leather binding designed for the glory of the center-table. Fluent, Byronic, passionate, *Lucile* thrilled many a fair reader, and some not so fair. "Owen Meredith" was the pen-name of the first Earl of Lytton, viceroy of India, later ambassador to France, son of the Sir Edward Bulwer-Lytton who wrote *The Last Days of Pompeii* and other best sellers.

Finally, a word should be said about four women poets—poetesses, in the language of a hundred years ago. The English Mrs. Hemans and the American Mrs. Sigourney were very popular writers of verse, though neither produced a single volume that reached best seller figures, nor did the collected poems of either attain that level. The *United States Review* in 1827 declared that "the popularity of Mrs. Hemans' shorter poems has been almost unexampled." Widely reprinted, they are "read on our seaboard, repeatedly printed in the interior, diligently perused in the little circles of our villages, and, it may be, make their way across Lake Erie to the outskirts of our civilization." The title of "the American Hemans," commonly bestowed upon Mrs. Sigourney, seemed to Poe to point to the imitativeness of the American poetess. Mrs. Sigourney was an indefatigable writer for the magazines and was the author of fifty-six published volumes. She was probably, as one of her admirers phrased it, "the most famous of the female bards of our country" in the first half of the nineteenth century.

Jean Ingelow was widely read in the seventies and eighties. "In thousands of American homes her gracious presence is recognized as that of a fondly cherished friend," wrote an admirer in the *Aldine* in 1871. Similar observations might be made regarding the authors of several "better sellers" of the nineteenth century—the collected poems of Bryant and Holmes, Lowell's *Biglow Papers* and *The Vision of Sir Launfal*, P. J. Bailey's *Festus*, and Will Carleton's *Farm Ballads*.

XVIII. "THIS ILIAD OF THE BLACKS"

Never since books were first printed has the success of *Uncle Tom* been equalled; the history of literature contains nothing parallel to it, nor approaching it: it is, in fact, the first real success in book-making, for all other successes in literature were failures when compared with the success of *Uncle Tom.*

　　　　　　　Charles F. Briggs in Putnam's Magazine, January, 1853

ONE day in the early autumn of 1850 the wife of the Rev. Calvin E. Stowe, of Brunswick, Maine, received a letter from her sister-in-law in Boston. As was her custom when family letters came to hand, Mrs. Stowe gathered her children * about her and read the missive aloud. It was devoted chiefly to telling of the sufferings of escaped slaves under the new Fugitive Slave Act—outrages of which the writer had direct personal knowledge and which had stirred her profoundly. The letter ended: "Now, Hattie, if I could use a pen as you can, I would write something that would make this whole nation feel what an accursed thing slavery is!"

* Her husband had just accepted a professorship at Bowdoin College, but had remained behind to fulfill his contract at Lane Theological School while his wife established their new home at Brunswick.

And Harriet Beecher Stowe, when she read these lines, crumpled the letter in her hand, and with all the energy of a personal dedication, exclaimed, "God helping me, I *will* write something!" Soon afterward she said, in a letter to her Boston brother, the Rev. Edward Beecher: "Tell sister Isabel that I thank her for her letter and will answer. As long as the baby sleeps with me nights I can't do much at anything, but I will do it at last. I will write that thing if I live."

That was the beginning of *Uncle Tom's Cabin.* In a sense, however, it had begun in Harriet's childhood, when she had imbibed religious and antislavery doctrine concurrently from her family and teachers. And later, when she was teaching in Cincinnati and writing her first sketches, she saw something of the Underground Railway, and made some visits, in company with a fellow-teacher, to plantations across the river in Kentucky to see certain phases of slavery at first hand. All this time she was unconsciously storing her mind with characters and ideas for the novel that was to make her famous. In later years, when her book was under attack, she was at pains to point out how this character and that incident sprang from some actual person and occurrence within her knowledge or experience.

After she had taken her solemn vow to write an antislavery novel, plans for it were doubtless much in her mind for several weeks before she began it. In the meantime, she paid a short visit to the Boston Beechers, and there met Josiah Henson, a Negro freedman and preacher, whose story and whose fine Christian spirit made a strong impression upon her. Now she had a hero for her story, for Henson became "Uncle Tom." It was on one Sunday following her return from Boston that Mrs. Stowe, sitting in her pew at church, conceived the whole incident of the death of Uncle Tom. Church attendance is often favorable to literary effort, especially if the sermon is conveniently dull. In this case the whole conception came to the author, rapidly and fully, almost like an inspired vision. That very afternoon she wrote it all out, and in the evening she read it to her children; at the end of the reading they were all in tears, and one of the boys, remembering his aunt's phrase, sobbed, "Oh, mamma, slavery is the most 'cursed thing in the world!"

Then Mrs. Stowe wrote to Dr. Gamaliel Bailey, whom she had known in Cincinnati and who, with the assistance of his wife, now edited and published the *National Era,* of Washington, a leading antislavery weekly. She asked him if he would use a serial story about slavery if she would furnish it, and for what honorarium? The *Era* had printed Hawthorne's "The Great Stone Face," Whittier's *Margaret Smith's Journal,* and other pieces of distinction. Dr. Bailey replied that he would pay Mrs. Stowe three hundred dollars for her story, and they agreed that it was to run for about three months.

So Chapter I was begun, finished, duly read in family conclave, and sent off to the *Era.* With five children to cook and sew for and educate, Mrs. Stowe had little of the daytime for her writing; but after the children were in bed she would toil at the kitchen table, her tears often dropping on the manuscript. She wrote with her whole soul, in the utmost sincerity, and with a complete dedication of her mind and feelings to the task. After the death of Little Eva, she was forced to take to her bed for two days and nights to recover from the ordeal: it was like the loss of her own child.

Meanwhile, Mrs. Stowe's sister Catherine tried to place the story with Phillips, Sampson & Company, of Boston, her own publishers, for issue in book form. But they would not touch it; they feared it would jeopardize their southern business, the profits from which probably amounted to less than a tenth of those which *Uncle Tom's Cabin,* as it turned out, would have brought them. But they were not the first publishers, or the last, to make such a mistake. Later they risked southern disfavor by publishing Mrs. Stowe's *Dred,* her other antislavery novel, but it was not the gold mine that *Uncle Tom* had been.

It was young John P. Jewett who finally offered to put Uncle Tom and his companions between covers. He chanced to see some early numbers of the serial; and though his modest ventures in the publishing field up to this time had included little or no fiction, he was impressed by the moral power of this story and made the Stowes an offer. Indeed, he gave them their choice of two contracts: he would go fifty-fifty with them on costs and profits, or he would pay a straight ten-percent royalty. Professor Stowe went to Congressman Philip Greeley, a friend of the family, for advice, and Greeley said they must not think of risking anything on a novel—and a novel by a woman at that! He pointed out further that antislavery was an unpopular subject in many quarters even in the North. In fact, if a publisher was foolish enough to venture a novel, by a woman, on a controversial subject, and would pay anything to the author—why, then, the author was lucky, said Congressman Greeley; but don't risk anything on it. So the Stowes, swayed by their friend's advice, decided to take the royalty contract, not knowing that they were refusing a fortune.

Jewett became alarmed, however, as the story ran on and on. He had expected to publish it in a slender volume at a low price. He saw a "few sketches" become a novelette and the novelette a full-sized novel, and still the pace showed no signs of slackening. After the serial had been running for six months, he wrote Mrs. Stowe that if it ran much longer it would be a two-volume work, and he could not risk such a venture. Mrs. Stowe, though she had never missed an installment, had found that the work kept her almost in a state of exhaustion; and she wrote to Dr. Bailey and asked what he thought about closing the story now with Uncle Tom's martyrdom and a chapter telling what then happened to everybody. The editor passed the problem on in a guarded query in the *Era* addressed to the readers of the serial. The response was immediate and overwhelming: the readers wanted all of the story, no less. Thus we have what is perhaps the unique example in literary history of the readers themselves making a major decision in the composition of a great work. They were right, of course; and Dr. Bailey and Mrs. Stowe and frightened Mr. Jewett respected their judgment, and the serial went on to the full term of twelve months. Toward the last, Jewett was encouraged by the talk it was creating.

When it was completed, Dr. Bailey wrote in the *Era:* "Mrs. Stowe has at last brought her great work to a close. We do not recollect any production of an American writer that has excited more general and profound interest." But already it was in the bookstores and selling by the thousands, for Jewett had brought it out on March 20, 1852, about two weeks before it finished its course in the paper.

It came out in two large-duodecimo volumes bound in black cloth, with the title in gold on the backstrip. A little vignette of the cabin, showing Aunt Chloe in the doorway and some of the children tumbling about, appeared on the titlepage and was reproduced in gold stamping on the front covers. Three full-page woodcuts illustrated each volume. Altogether, Jewett did himself proud. The price was a dollar and a half per set.

One of the first copies off the press was made a gift from Professor Stowe to Congressman Greeley, who had not read the story at the time he gave his friends the advice which was to keep them from making a fortune from the book. Greeley was just leaving for Washington, and put the volumes in his pocket to read on the train. When he got settled, he opened the first of them, was enthralled from the opening page onward, and soon found himself wiping away tears and blowing his nose. He realized he was attracting the attention of fellow passengers and tried to restrain himself; but in spite of all his efforts, his tears continued to splash on the printed page. So what did he do? He gathered up his parcels and left the train at Springfield, went to a hotel, rented a room, and there sat up most of the night finishing the book, and weeping as much as he wanted to.

The first edition of five thousand copies of the book was sold out within a week. For the next year, the eight presses of George C. Rand, Jewett's printer, ran day and night to keep up with the demand for *Uncle Tom.* After selling over one hundred thousand of the two-volume edition, Jewett in the fall brought out a single-volume edition at 37½ cents, and a copiously illustrated issue for the Christmas trade. The cheap volume stimulated sales which had scarcely declined at all, and brought the total to more than three hundred thousand by the end of the book's first year. Of course, it couldn't keep this rate up indefinitely, but for a long time it maintained a sale of about a thousand a week, mainly in the cheap edition. By the time of the panic of 1857, it had sold half a million copies. Jewett did not weather the panic, and *Uncle Tom's Cabin* went into other hands, and shortly appeared upon the lists of various publishers of low-priced books. One Chicago distributor manufactured and sold, within the space of somewhat over half a century, no less than 740,000 copies. Altogether, it seems reasonable to believe, from such reports as are now available, that only a little less than three million copies of the book have been distributed in the United States. It certainly belongs in the top flight of the list of American best sellers.

But the story of Uncle Tom's misadventures sold even more copies abroad than it did in the United States. It took England by storm. Forty pirated editions appeared in Great Britain and her colonies within a year of first publication. During September, 1852, one firm in London sold ten thousand copies a day of various editions, according to the *Edinburgh Review* of April, 1885. Prices ranged from sixpence to fifteen shillings. Sampson Low, later Mrs. Stowe's London publisher, after "carefully analyzing" the British editions which appeared within a year of the book's first English publication in April, 1852, "and weighing probabilities with ascertained facts," asserted "pretty confidently" that *Uncle Tom's Cabin* sold more than a million and a half copies in England and her colonies during that time.*

Almost as impressive was the book's success in France. In December, 1852, Mme. George Sand wrote Mrs. Stowe that it was "in all hands and in all journals," that it had "editions in all forms," that "the people devour it, they cover it with tears." It continued to be a best seller in Paris for two or three years. In its German versions it had even more readers than in French, if we may judge by the number of recorded editions; there were at least 75 editions of more than 40 different translations, with 11 abridgments for children.

Macaulay, the historian, returning in the fall of 1856 from a visit to Italy, wrote Mrs. Stowe that "your fame seems to throw that of all other writers into the shade. There is no place where Uncle Tom (transformed into 'Il Zio Tom') is not to be found." And this was despite the Pope's prohibition. Before the end of the year 1852 the novel had been translated into Dutch, Swedish, Danish, Flemish, Polish, and Magyar; and shortly thereafter it was made available in many other languages and dialects, so that it now exists in more than forty translations. The array of names of the hero is appalling, from l'Oncle Tom to Tio Tomas, Wuya Tomasza, 'Ewyrth Twm, and so on. No single novel of Scott or Dickens was ever so widely translated.

Wrote an enthusiastic American reviewer:

Mrs. Stowe now holds the popular ear, and holds it as no one else has ever held it. Even the Wizard of the North never so held a *world* spell-bound—never spoke to so many hearts, or excited in each such wondrous enthusiasm. The mightiest princes of intellect, as well as those who have scarcely harbored a stray thought in all their lives before, ascetic scholars and noisy politicians, friends of slavery equally with the haters of that institution, grave deacons, pious persons, and novel-loving misses—all and each bend with sweating eagerness over her magic pages.†

* Quoted by Mrs. Stowe in the introduction to a new edition by Houghton, Mifflin & Company in 1878; also in *Old South Leaflets*, No. 82. George Sand and T. B. Macaulay are quoted in the same place.

† *Free-Will Baptist Quarterly*, vol. II, p. 25 (January, 1854).

There have been few world successes to equal that of *Uncle Tom's Cabin* since its publication. Many estimates of the world distribution of what one English reviewer called "this Iliad of the blacks" have been made; six and a half millions seems fairly conservative. This is probably the top figure for any single American work.

Illustrated editions were common. Cruikshank drew twenty-seven pictures for the London Cassell edition; an ambitious English issue the next year carried one hundred fifty illustrations. European editions often borrowed English pictures. Adaptations and abridgments for the young became common in all the chief languages. Uncle Tom was versified, set to music, made into comic opera. At least twenty Uncle Tom songs were published in the summer of 1852. At least two different publishers brought out card games based on the characters in the story, with pictures of each on the cards; and a London publisher got up an Uncle Tom puzzle. In recent years there has been an Uncle Tom "comic strip" book.

The availability of the story for the stage was at once recognized and dramatic versions were printed in several languages. For a time Uncle Tom shows crowded nearly everything else off the boards in American theatres. In London too, in December, 1852, Legree was cracking his whip in six theatres at once; and in Germany and France popular plays were based on the story. Nor was the public surfeited, for "Tom shows" continued for many years to attract crowds. Eventually they deteriorated into "op'ry house" melodrama, featuring the bloodhounds, Eliza crossing the ice, Marks and the Quakers as comics, and Little Eva wafted to Heaven by means of pulleys; and thence into tent shows, where they long survived.

"Tom shows" became a profession; what actors call "hokum" was grafted upon the old story until the original was barely recognizable. A parade, with local boys fearfully leading the "bloodhounds," Eva in a pony-cart, Marks on his donkey, and a half a dozen darkies tootling in a brass band, was a promotion feature borrowed from the circus. The performance was usually pretty bad, and the following two-line review was a common one in the local press: "Uncle Tom's Cabin played here last night. The bloodhounds were good." Yet many actors later famous on Broadway received some part of their training in "Tom shows"—Joseph Jefferson, James K. Hackett, Denman Thompson, Mrs. Fiske, Maude Adams, Fay Templeton, and so on. One Eva tells of how she was playing her great scene while it was raining outside the tent. There was a hole in the canvas, and a stream of water was falling on her neck as she spoke her dying farewells to the weeping family about her. What with tears and rainwater, there was too much dampness altogether; and St. Clare, without batting a tear, rose from his knees and strode into the wings, returning immediately with Marks' comedy umbrella, which he raised and held over Eva's head, and let her die dry. It is said that the audience did not laugh.*

In more recent years there have been serious revivals of the old play—notably that of the New York Players Club in 1933, with the old Aiken script revised by Augustus Thomas. Otis Skinner was Uncle Tom and Fay Bainter, Topsy; and it was one of the season's successes. Critic Percy Hammond saw tears in the eyes of seasoned theatre-goers at this performance. A few years earlier Universal Pictures had made a two-million dollar production of the play for movie audiences; and it has been made into an opera, and even into a "swing" production. Still more recently Helen Hayes in "Harriet" brought home to theatre-goers the story of the authorship of *Uncle Tom*.

Another byproduct of the tremendous popularity of Mrs. Stowe's book is found in the output of "anti-Uncle Toms." There were some thirty of these books, about half of them fictional in form, which incorporated the arguments in favor of slavery and against abolitionism—all published in the early fifties. None of them ever attracted much attention. One of the more interesting was Mrs. Mary H. Eastman's *Aunt Phillis's Cabin; or, Southern Life As It Is;* much shorter than its prototype, it lacks interest and emotion. Mrs. Eastman not only fails in this little book to equal Mrs. Stowe, but she fails to keep up to the level of her own earlier work. Another was J. W. Page's *Uncle Robin in His Cabin in Virginia and Tom Without One in Boston*.

These books were but one phase of the flood of criticism, railing, and abuse that was let loose upon Mrs. Stowe's devoted head by proslavery advocates North and South. One of the first of the reviews of *Uncle Tom's Cabin* appeared in the *Literary World*, of New York. The editor found the book "neither fish nor flesh, nor yet good red herring." Regarded as a political disquisition, an ethnological essay, or a novel, it was equally unsatisfactory. Perhaps it was a "manual for runaways." At least, it was "capable of producing infinite mischief." † Further south the tone of criticism was even more bitter. The *National Era* reported that some of the southern courts were sentencing men to prison for long terms when the hated book was found in their possession. Mrs. Stowe, thus under attack, published *A Key to Uncle Tom's Cabin*, "presenting the original facts and documents upon which the story is founded, together with corroborative statements verifying the truth of the work." This case-book was Mrs. Stowe's Book of Martyrs.

But Uncle Tom was, of course, greeted far otherwise by the antislavery press, which could scarcely contain its enthusiasm. Within the very week that the book was issued, the *Liberator* predicted a "prodigious" effect "upon all intelligent and humane minds." The *Independent* shouted: "Spread it round the world! . . . thank God! it bids fair to become as familiar as household words."

* The story is told by J. Frank Davis in *Scribner's Magazine*, vol. LXXVII, p. 355 (April, 1925).
† *Literary World*, vol. X, p. 291 (April 24, 1852).

As we all know, it did just that. The actual and precise effectiveness of a given piece of propaganda is always difficult to measure, but Mrs. Stowe is generally credited with having done much to bring on the ultimate decision in the war between the States. She emphasized the moral issue in a conflict which was, as she herself knew, to a large extent economic. When she called upon President Lincoln in the midst of the war, it was certainly not wholly in a mood of badinage that the President greeted her with the question, "Is this the little woman whose book made such a great war?" Yet, it should be remembered that the solution suggested in *Uncle Tom's Cabin* was voluntary emancipation and colonization—a plan which was foredoomed and which the book did not forward in any perceptible degree.

The book's importance in the American slavery controversy is likely to make us overlook, however, the fact of its effectiveness in other directions. It was a plea for the oppressed of all races and nationalities. How much good the passages directed against mistreatment of the poor in England did, we cannot tell; perhaps the English admirers of the book worked off their emotions satisfactorily by signing the address to the women of America in regard to slavery (over half a million English women signed it) and forwarding it to Mrs. Stowe. Perhaps the Scotch people, contributing a thousand pounds by small contributions, achieved a similar catharsis. But it would take a good deal of cynicism to believe that Mrs. Stowe's basic teaching of Christian kindness to the lowly had no effect on her millions of readers. Certain Russian lords are said to have freed their serfs after reading Uncle Tom's Cabin, and there is an interesting passage in Heine's *Geständnisse* in which, referring to his religious reawakening, he says that he has now joined Uncle Tom in his view of the Bible and of prayer.

The literary shortcomings of *Uncle Tom's Cabin* are all obvious. In the first place there is too much preaching—a fault shared with *Pilgrim's Progress* and other well known works of some importance. Also it is sentimental and melodramatic. How much do these sins vitiate the work as a whole? The answer must depend upon critical points of view, which change with the times. Such things annoy today's reader more than they did the men and women of the eighteen-fifties, who were accustomed to Dickens and his imitators. Mrs. Stowe has, indeed, much in common with Dickens.

The immense popularity of *Uncle Tom's Cabin* was not due wholly, or even chiefly, to the fact that it was topical. The ready interest in the slavery controversy certainly gave it a start; but it gathered momentum primarily because it was a vital story, striking with extraordinary directness to the heart of fundamental human feelings and relationships. To this we must add other elements of popular appeal: the suspense in the chase of Eliza and George, which carries through the first half of the novel; the humor, especially in the characters of Sam and Andy, and Topsy; the pathos, which, however overdone in the case of Eva, still has potency in those of Eliza and Tom;

and the characterization, which often has charm and convincingness, uneven though it is. Nor can the omnipresent religious tone and textual quotation be omitted in an inventory of the bases of the book's popularity; indeed the *Edinburgh Review* named this as "the principal cause of its American popularity." And finally, there is the rank sensationalism of the flagellation of Tom, the death of Old Prue in the cellar, the sexual misbehavior of slave owners, and so on.

One can only say, of a good book now unfashionable: if you wish to know why millions once read it, go and hunt it out of the shelves, and, putting aside all modern sophistication, read it for yourself. And do not be surprised if, like Congressman Greeley, you should drop a few tears on its pages.

XIX. AMERICAN FICTION OF THE FIFTIES

America is now given over to a d——d mob of scribbling women, and I should have no chance of success while the public taste is occupied with their trash— and should be ashamed of myself if I did succeed. What is the mystery of these innumerable editions of the "Lamplighter," and other books neither better nor worse?—worse they could not be, and better they need not be, when they sell by the 100,000.

Hawthorne to Ticknor, 1855

THE 1850's saw the biggest boom American book publishing had ever known. Before it ended with the financial crash of 1857, it had seen the appearance of more best sellers than any previous decade. A writer in the "Easy Chair" of *Harper's Magazine* in December, 1857, said that it had been an era

when every book of every publisher was in the twenty-sixth thousand, and the unparalleled demand was increasing at an unprecedented rate; when presses were working night and day; when, owing to the extraordinary demand, the issue of the first edition must be postponed from Saturday to Thursday; when not more than 50,000 copies could be furnished in three days; when the public must have patience, and would finally be supplied . . .

The middle-class American home was one of the chief focal points of the best seller literature of this great book boom. The home, with a saintly mother, a father saintly or otherwise, and a family of growing children one of whom is the heroine formed the basis for many a popular novel. Or to emphasize the home still more, an author sometimes showed an orphan growing up in an alien family. This Home-and-Jesus formula, emphasizing the strains of family life, and the education of youth, with the religious solution for all problems, filled books which found hundreds of thousands of purchasers.

There is a direct line of descent from the behavior books of the eighteenth century, such as *A Father's Legacy to His Daughters*, through such family guides as the Abbott brothers' *The Mother at Home* and *The Young Christian*, to Susan Warner's *The Wide, Wide World* and other domestic novels of the fifties. Of course, the line does not stop there, but continues with *Little Women* and other family stories by Miss Alcott, then with such juvenile best sellers as the *Five Little Peppers* series, and still later with *Pollyanna* and *Mrs. Wiggs*. But this emphasis on family life seems to reach a notable height in the novels of the fifties.

The writing of *The Wide, Wide World* grew out of family difficulties not unlike those which produced *Little Women*. Susan Warner's was a "Pathetic Family," too; her father was not a philosopher, but an unsuccessful lawyer. The Warners were living in even greater penury than that of the Alcotts when the talented daughter wrote, in a kind of desperation, a novel of family life that was to lift them all out of poverty. Though the pattern of production was thus much the same, there was one great difference between the two families; the Alcott children had a saving sense of humor, while the Warners were terribly and unremittingly serious.

The difference between the books themselves is another matter, for *The Wide, Wide World* is, at best, mawkish in its sentimentality and pious to a repulsive degree. The little heroine is literally too good to be true. It was doubtless the abundance of incident and detail of common life which furnished the basis of the book's unusual appeal. Sympathy with poor Ellen's situation and struggles probably had something to do with it, too: the popularity-value of tears is not to be neglected. Tears there were aplenty in this book. A writer in the *Critic* once filled half a column with turns of phrase which describe Ellen's weeping. Here are a few of them:

> Her tears almost choked her, began to drop again, brought no relief, came faster than her words, dropped into the water, fell faster, fell from the eyes, fell much too fast for her eyes to do their work, flowed, flowed faster than ever, followed in a flood, gushed forth, had to be wiped away, kept coming all the time, knew no measure, mingled, poured, ran down her cheeks, ran down her face and frock, ran fast again, ran fast down her face and fell into her lap, rose to her eyes, rushed to her eyes, started, streamed from her eyes, used to flow abundantly when they could unseen. . . .

Worst of all, they would drop down on her Bible. Poor Ellen!

The religious teachings of *The Wide, Wide World* were, of course, an important factor in its success. *The Christian Review* thought that Miss Warner had succeeded "better than any other writer in our language in making religious sentiment appear natural and attractive, in a story that possesses the interest of romance." A Newark paper declared that this book might do more good in the world "than any book outside of the Bible." If it be thought that these were merely comments of obscure "fans," we may turn to the great *North American Review* and find Mrs. Kirkland's statement about *The Wide, Wide World* and the later *Queechy*: "We know not where, in any language, we shall find their graphic truth excelled." No; we cannot laugh off the acclaim which greeted this lachrymose and edifying masterpiece of its kind.

Nor can we laugh off its sales record. In the first place, to be sure, it had been difficult to find a publisher for the book. Anna B. Warner, Susan's sister, later wrote that it had been offered "to nearly every leading book firm in New York" before it found a publisher.* Finally, it was submitted to G. P. Putnam, who took the manuscript home to read. His mother happened to be visiting in his home at the time, and he handed the carefully written pages to her to look over for her amusement if she should find them interesting. She found them more than interesting; she wept over them, and gave her son a report in the form of an explicit command to publish this book if he never published another. It was so decreed, though Putnam had no great faith in the venture.

So *The Wide, Wide World* was issued in December, 1850 (though the titlepage bore the date 1851), in two small volumes at a dollar and a half. The author was named as "Elizabeth Wetherell"—a pseudonym long retained. The book won immediate praise from the critics and sold in quantities which surprised both author and publisher. Thirteen editions were required within two years. The title became a catch-word of the day, used in conversation, in news stories, in advertising. Wrote one enterprising merchant: "In the 'Wide, Wide World' cannot be found better undergarments and hosiery than at James E. Ray's, 108 Bowery." Putnam brought the book out in de luxe form at six dollars in 1854, and zealously kept new and cheaper editions in print. When the copyright expired in 1892, fifty-cent copies brought a renewal of popularity.

It was popular in England as well as in America. When Thomas Ollive Mabbott, the Poe scholar, had some conversations with Professor Saintsbury at Bath in 1927, he found that famous critic and omnivorous reader anxious to talk about *The Wide, Wide World*, which he had read as a boy and still recalled with pleasure.

In all, Miss Warner's opus has sold over half a million copies on this side of the Atlantic. The later *Queechy* sold well, and was highly praised by many, including Mrs. Browning; but it was never quite as popular as its predecessor while under copyright, and much less so in the cheap editions.

Four years after *The Wide, Wide World* was published, and in the year of *Queechy's* appearance, came another novel by a spinster about the experiences of a young girl. Maria Susanna Cummins, of Salem, Massachusetts, had already received the accolade of acceptance into the pages of the *Atlantic Monthly* when she started *The Lamplighter* on its long career as a popular favorite in 1854. It was published by John P. Jewett, of Boston, who, only two years before, had made a big hit with another best seller entitled *Uncle Tom's Cabin.*

The first quarter of the new book—up to the death of Uncle True, the lamplighter—could well have stood by itself. Alone, it would have formed a novelette of considerable pathos, simplicity, and dignity. Readers of the full-

* Anna B. Warner, *Susan Warner* (New York, 1909), p. 282. This biography contains many letters and diary notes about *The Wide, Wide World.*

length novel which the book-trade required still remember better than all the rest the story of poor, miserable little Gerty of the slums, rescued by the kindly lamplighter. In the remainder of the book the heroine is translated to the inevitable middle-class home; she becomes Gertrude, a paragon of virtuous self-sacrifice and all that; in the end she finds her long-lost father, also a paragon; and of course she marries Willie, who has grown up into a third paragon.

Jewett was a good publisher for *The Lamplighter*. He brought it out in a fat volume bound in black cloth and gold-stamped on the backstrip with the title and a picture of the lamplighter on his ladder, and priced at seventy-five cents. Forty thousand copies were sold in the first eight weeks and a hundred thousand within the first decade. Apparently it had copyright protection for only the first term of twenty-eight years, for it was in the cheap quartos and selling at twenty-five cents by the mid-eighties. It was long a popular library book; when Hurst issued it as a number in his Cambridge Classics in 1915, the New York Public Library ordered 250 copies, and later increased the number. Its sales record both within the copyright period and afterward is somewhat higher than that of *The Wide, Wide World*. Like that story, *The Lamplighter* was translated into the leading European languages, and had the distinction of being included in the Tauchnitz library. Both enjoyed large sales in England, in pirated as well as authorized editions.

Another authoress who got her start in the fifties was that prolific favorite of the unthinking—Mrs. Mary J. Holmes. Teacher in a Massachusetts school at thirteen, a scribbler of stories and sketches at fifteen, Mary Jane Hawes was imaginative, ambitious, moral. Her uncle was the Joel Hawes, D.D., who wrote *Lectures to Young Men* and *Looking Glass for Ladies,* and her brother became a well known Chicago judge. Mary Jane married a young lawyer named Holmes, and they went to Versailles, Kentucky, for a few years; but in 1852 they returned to the husband's former home in Brockport, New York, where Mrs. Holmes wrote all of her thirty-odd novels.

D. Appleton & Company published the first two books, *Tempest and Sunshine* and *The English Orphans,* but did not do well with Mrs. Holmes' work, which soon passed to Miller, Orton & Company. Following the bankruptcy of the Miller firm in the late fifties, G. W. Carleton & Company took over the Holmes novels. Carleton was the right publisher for these books; he knew how to reach the great non-literary audience which was developing in the sixties and seventies. By this time Mrs. Holmes had developed her publishing formula; she wrote a novel each year, for which Street & Smith's *New York Weekly* paid her about five thousand dollars for serial rights; Carleton then took the story and put it up in a volume in green cloth with gold stamping which he sold at a dollar and a half.

In 1870 an acute observer wrote in *Appleton's Journal* that Mrs. Holmes had "an immense constituency outlying in all the small towns and rural districts," and that none of the living English novelists could dispute her leadership with this public. By this time, indeed, there were best sellers on different levels of readership at the same time.

In the eighties, Mrs. Holmes' stories got into paper covers. G. W. Dillingham published them at twenty-five cents, and Street & Smith later issued them at ten cents. They were sold largely on the trains. Most popular were her first book, *Tempest and Sunshine,* based on her Kentucky experience, and another early title, *Lena Rivers;* each of these eventually reached the million mark. M. A. Donohue & Company, of Chicago, printers for the national cheap-book combination of the nineties, manufactured nearly half a million copies of each of them. No other story by Mrs. Holmes rivaled the two leaders, though *Meadow Brook, Marian Grey,* and *Ethelyn's Mistake* were among the more popular of the lot.

It is difficult for even the most catholic modern reader to find qualities in these novels sufficient to account for their great popularity. They seem thin and filled with absurd quarrels and misunderstandings; their villains male and female are equally double-dyed, while their heroes and heroines are perfect. But we must think of these stories in terms of contemporary ideas and tastes. A reviewer of Mrs. Holmes' second novel, *English Orphans,* writing in the *North American Review,* thinks its "pathetic element stops short of mawkishness," finds its comic vein successful and not over-drawn, appraises its characterization (especially in rural life) as "exquisite," approves its Christian morality and its assault on the absurdity of "plutocratic" notions, and calls its plot simple and natural. At any rate, Mrs. Holmes' stories do move with a certain simplicity and vigor, and her rural characters often are picturesque and amusing.

A fourth popular authoress of the fifties must be discussed here. She was much discussed in her own day: we should not begrudge her two or three paragraphs. In 1867 that excellent southern magazine, *Scott's Monthly,* said: "We venture to place her at the head of American female novelists. This, if not the decision of contemporary criticism, will be the verdict of posterity." How foolhardy it is for a critic to forecast "the verdict of posterity"! Today we can check on *Scott's* prediction. "Evans?" we hear Posterity asking in puzzled tones. "Eh? Augusta J. Evans? What did she write?"

Well, Augusta Jane Evans, of Mobile, Alabama, was another of those precocious girls with a flair for writing. At fifteen or sixteen she wrote *Inez, a Tale of the Alamo,* and gave it to her father for a Christmas present. Her father got it published by Harpers, but it was not a success. *Beulah,* however, published a few years later by Derby & Jackson, was definitely a "hit." Though it was laden with an amazing amount of literary, historical, and philosophical erudition, stilted in dialogue, and filled with the details of the petty jealousies and little intrigues of social intercourse, nevertheless the book was sincere and valid in its main inquiry into religious doubt.

In *St. Elmo,* published shortly after the Civil War, there are no doubts. Its heroine is another of those paragon-girls; and it is her business to reform a worldly sophisticate, and, of course, marry him in the last chapter. The encyclopedic erudition is even more prominent than in *Beulah*. A visiting English baronet takes occasion to praise the writings of John Stuart Mill, whereupon the heroine makes the following weighty observations on the subject of women's rights:

"At least, sir, *our* statesmen are not yet attacked by this most loathsome of political leprosies. Only a few crazy fanatics have fallen victims to it, and if lunatic asylums were not frequently cheated out of their dues, these would not be left at large, but shut up together in high-walled enclosures, like Sydney Smith's 'graminivorous metaphysicians,' or Reaumur's spiders, when they could only injure one another and destroy their own webs. America has no Bentham, Bailey, Hare or Mill, to lend countenance to the ridiculous clamor raised by a few unamiable and wretched wives, and as many embittered, disappointed old maids of New England. The noble apology which Edmund Burke once offered for his countrymen always recurs to my mind when I hear these 'women's conventions' alluded to . . ."

Then she quotes Burke, and adds, with customary girlish simplicity:

"I think, sir, that the noble and true women of this continent earnestly believe that the day which invests them with the elective franchise would be the blackest in the annals of humanity, would ring the death-knell of modern civilization, of national prosperity, social morality, and domestic happiness! and would consign the race to a night of degradation and horror infinitely more appalling than a return to primeval barbarism."

You would think Sir Roger would be crushed by this bombast: evidently he is not, for he later asks Edna to marry him. But then, nearly every unattached male in the book does that at one time or another.

It is not strange that a humorist of the time, C. H. ("John Paul") Webb wrote a parody of the book. It was published under the title, *St. Twelvemo*; in it the author accounted for Edna's qualities as a conversationalist by explaining that one day during her infancy, when the nurse was not watching her, she swallowed a dictionary. But Webb's travesty was only a tribute to the book's popularity. Children were named "St. Elmo"; towns, streets, hotels were christened with the magic name.

It seems fairly clear that the popularity of the novels of Augusta Evans Wilson (to use her later name) was based upon three factors: the comfortable feeling of the reader that he was being instructed while he was being entertained, the general approval of religious and moral teachings in fiction, and the basic appeal of sensational incident. This last was not too prominent, but it was nevertheless important in these stories. There were other things, too, that gave *St. Elmo* a sale of a million copies and *Beulah* about half as many; there was the success story, in each case, of an underprivileged girl, and a long-drawn-out love affair, and a strong attack on the sins of the rich in comparison with the virtues of simple home life.

Another best seller in this group of sentimental novels about girls making their way into the world and its pitfalls is Mrs. Miriam Coles Harris' *Rutledge*. But the heroine of this story is not such a nonpareil as those of *The Wide*,

Wide World, The Lamplighter, Beulah, and the rest; she is apt to be surly when people do not treat her kindly, and in a fit of injured pride she gets herself engaged to a handsome fellow who turns out to be the illegitimate son of the hero's erring sister and a murderer in the bargain. It was a bad bargain indeed and about ruined the girl's life, but she finally came to an understanding (perversely long-delayed) with her middle-aged admirer, the gloomy but well-nigh perfect Mr. Rutledge of Rutledge. The heroine's troubles are supposed to teach the reader many lessons about the proper deportment of young girls, and especially about the folly of dancing parties (our heroine attended three of them and danced quite too much).

This was a very anonymous book. Not only was the author's name withheld, but the heroine was also nameless. Strangely enough, one is unconscious of the omission in reading the story, since it is told in the first person and many forms of address may be used in the stilted dialogue without exciting attention. When *Rutledge* made its great success, there were plenty of claimants to the authorship. *Vanity Fair,* the humorous paper, promised one week to print a portrait of the author of *Rutledge* in its next issue; but when the picture appeared the lady was holding a fan before her face.

Harpers had refused the manuscript, which was published in 1860 by Derby & Jackson; Carleton later took it over, with Mrs. Harris' other somewhat less successful books; and shortly before 1890 Houghton, Mifflin & Company became its publisher, reprinting it twenty-eight times. It sold well for more than half a century.

For somewhat younger girls was the long popular *Faith Gartney's Girlhood,* by Mrs. A. D. T. Whitney; at least it is less melodramatic and brighter in tone. Faith has her domestic troubles, and her young life is ultimately complicated by the necessity of a choice between two lovers; but there is some humor, and everything comes out all right, as it should in New England village life. Mrs. Whitney continued to write stories for girls until she was eighty, but she is remembered chiefly for this Sunday School library classic. It was issued by A. K. Loring, of Boston, in 1863 and laid the foundation of that publisher's extensive juvenile publishing business.

To the roll of popular feminine novelists of the fifties as recorded in this chapter must be added two who are important enough to have chapters to themselves—Mrs. Stowe and Mrs. Southworth. This makes a list of seven best-selling authoresses—all tearful, all earnest, all religious, all melodramatic. But so far as sheer sentimentality goes, a man carried off the palm.

In 1850 Baker & Scribner brought out Ik Marvell's *Reveries of a Bachelor, a Book of the Heart,* which was so enthusiastically received that the next year they published the same author's *Dream Life.* It soon became known that "Ik Marvell" was the pen-name of Donald G. Mitchell, a young magazine writer, gentleman farmer, law student, and traveler. The first of the "reveries" had been a magazine article in the *Southern Literary Messenger.* Mitchell had something of the charm of Irving in his style, and he was often compared to the author of the *Sketch Book*; but he seems rather to hark back to Crèvecoeur and other writers of the "sensibility" school of the late eighteenth century.

Dream Life, though it had more narrative continuity, never reached best seller heights; but the *Reveries* enjoyed consistent and steady favor for well over half a century. They were imitated and travestied. An anonymous wit wrote the *Reveries of an Old Maid*, which Dewitt & Davenport brought out in paper covers to catch a bit of the gale of popularity fanned up by the original. When the copyright of Mitchell's *Reveries* expired in the nineties, there was a host of editions at twenty-five cents to a dollar. It made a favorite gift-book for birthdays, for Christmas, for lovers' remembrances.

It was a man, too, who wrote the greatest temperance book of the decade. *Ten Nights in a Bar-Room* was the *Uncle Tom's Cabin* of the prohibition movement. T. S. Arthur, its creator, was one of the most prolific authors in the history of American literature. He wrote sketches, novelettes, essays, guidebooks for home life, and tracts of many kinds by the score; not even the Library of Congress catalogue lists them all, but they probably numbered over a hundred. Besides, Arthur was editor and publisher of *Arthur's Home Magazine* and a contributor to many other periodicals. He had already written several temperance books before *Ten Nights*, most popular of which was one called *Temperance Tales; or, Six Nights With the Washingtonians*. The Washington Temperance Society was exciting much interest in the early forties, when this book appeared, by its "moral suasion" techniques.

Ten Nights in a Bar-Room and What I Saw There was first published in Philadelphia under the combined imprint of three publishers, J. W. Bradley, J. B. Lippincott Company, and Grambo & Company. Within a year or two, Arthur, who held the copyright, placed it with distributors in other cities, changing imprints. The book was bound in black, and on the front cover was stamped in gold a striking scene from the bar-room showing several figures, with little Mary Morgan in the foreground grasping her father's arm; beneath the picture is the legend, "Father come Home!" The book was priced at seventy-five cents.

The family tradition that *Ten Nights* "at once leaped to an enormous circulation," second only to that of *Uncle Tom's Cabin*, seems to be based on exaggerations. There were not many editions of it in its first twenty-five years —less than of the *Six Nights With the Washingtonians*. Both books were dramatized. Probably J. C. Derby was not far off in estimating the sales of *Ten Nights* before 1880 at 100,000.*

But at last *Six Nights* fell by the wayside, probably because the Washingtonians were out of date and forgotten. *Ten Nights*, in the current dollar-and-a-quarter editions, was demanded more and more by the Sunday School libraries

* J. C. Derby, *Fifty Years Among Authors, Books, and Publishers* (New York, 1884), p. 719. Cf. *Dictionary of American Biography*.

and temperance societies. When its copyright expired in the nineties, and the book became available at twenty-five cents to a dollar, it took a new lease on life; its sale in the ensuing twenty-five years amounted to two or three times that of the similar period following its first publication. William W. Pratt's stage version, first produced at the National Theatre in New York in September, 1858, was revived and became a popular road show. The book played a part in the prohibition war of the twenties; as counter-propaganda, "T. S. Arthur, Jr." wrote *Ten Nights Without a Bar-Room,* which was dubbed "The *Uncle Tom's Cabin* of Prohibition Slavery."

The old temperance classic has been so much travestied and satirized that we are likely to lose sight of its sterling qualities. The stage version is now usually produced as a comic-piece—a distinction shared with the *Uncle Tom's Cabin* play—though a serious motion picture was made of it as late as 1931. The original story has an extraordinary vitality, based on vivid scenes, sharp characterization, vigorous writing, and utter sincerity.

Nathaniel Hawthorne would, we fear, resent being placed in the same chapter with his "d——d mob of scribbling women," by a presumptuous historian of best sellers. But he was a part of his times. Two novels came out of Salem, Massachusetts, in the early 1850's—*The Scarlet Letter* and *The Lamplighter.* We know definitely that Hawthorne did resent the great popular success of his fellow Salemite; and, her book being what it was, we can only share his indignation.

Hawthorne's first book, *Fanshawe,* published at his own expense, was a failure. His second, *Twice-Told Tales,* did little better; Horatio Bridge put up a $250 guarantee, without the author's knowledge, to secure the publication of a thousand copies by Goodrich's American Stationers' Company, and it took over a year to sell them. A second and enlarged edition of *Twice-Told Tales* five years later, and the publication of *Mosses from an Old Manse* in 1846, added more to his reputation among the knowing than to his financial resources. Late in 1849, after Hawthorne had been dismissed from his position in the Customs Office, the publisher James T. Fields went down to Salem to see him. Let Fields himself tell of the famous interview.

I found him alone in a chamber over the sitting-room of the dwelling; and, as the day was cold, he was hovering near a stove. We fell into talk about his future prospects, and he was, as I feared I should find him, in a very desponding mood.

"Now," said I, "is the time for you to publish, for I know that during these years in Salem you must have got something ready for the press."

"Nonsense," said he; "what heart had I to write anything when my publishers have been so many years trying to sell a small edition of the *Twice-Told Tales?*"

I still pressed upon him the good chances he would have with something new.

"Who would risk publishing a book for *me,* the most unpopular writer in America?"

"I would," said I, "and would start with an edition of two thousand copies of anything you write."

"What madness!" he exclaimed. "Your friendship gets the better of your judgment! No, no," he continued; "I have no money to indemnify a publisher's losses on my account."

I looked at my watch and found that the train would soon be starting for Boston, and I knew there was not much time to lose in trying to discover what had been his literary work during these last few years in Salem. I pressed him to reveal to me what he had been writing. He shook his head and gave me to understand that he had produced nothing. At that moment I caught sight of a chest of drawers near where we had been sitting, and immediately it occurred to me that hidden away in that piece of furniture was a story or stories by the author of *Twice-Told Tales*, and I became so positive of it that I charged him vehemently with the fact. He seemed surprised, I thought, but shook his head again; and I rose to take my leave, begging him not to come into the cold entry, and saying I would come back and see him again in a few days.

I was hurrying down the stairs when he called after me from the chamber, asking me to stop a moment. Then, quickly stepping into the entry with a roll of manuscript in his hands, he said: "How in Heaven's name did you know this thing was there? As you have found me out, take what I have written, and tell me, after you have time to read it, if it is good for anything. It is either very good or very bad—I don't know which." *

It was *The Scarlet Letter;* Fields soon decided it was very good, and most critics have endorsed his judgment. It proved to be a successful novel, both upon publication, throughout its copyright period, and after it reached the "public domain." Published by Ticknor & Fields at seventy-five cents, it sold an initial printing of four thousand copies in ten days; its second printing was sold out before it was ready for delivery; and, stimulated by a lively "press," it kept up a good sale for many months. Editions at higher prices came in later years, but in 1885 Houghton, Mifflin began catering to a more popular audience with an issue at a dollar in cloth and fifty cents in paper. The copyright on *The Scarlet Letter* expired in 1892, and it was immediately incorporated into the "libraries" at twenty-five cents. Brander Matthews, writing of the book in the *New York Times* in 1920, declared, "When it came out of copyright, it had a sale of several hundred thousand copies—probably ten times that on its first appearance." The dictionary says "several" means more than two, and Professor Matthews' statement is therefore surely correct.

There can be no doubt that the scandalous implications of the title and story of *The Scarlet Letter* have had something to do with its large sale, despite its delicacy and lack of passion. *The House of the Seven Gables* had no such appeal as was afforded by an adultery theme, though it was, of course, not without sensational elements. It followed closely enough upon its predecessor to catch the freshening breeze of popularity, and it was better liked by the general reader. It had somewhat the same publishing history in later years as *The Scarlet Letter,* with one important supplement: it got into the secondary schools as required reading. Such was the fate also of *Twice-Told Tales,* which would, however, have reached the best seller list by way of the cheap series and libraries of the eighties and nineties even if the schools had never taken it up.

Herman Melville dedicated *Moby-Dick* to his friend and neighbor, Nathaniel Hawthorne. The inclusion of this masterpiece in our best seller list is simple irony, for it was a very poor seller indeed when it first appeared; and not

* James T. Fields, *Yesterdays With Authors* (Boston, 1871), pp. 49–50.

until the Melville renaissance, thirty years after his death, did it sell the hundreds of thousands necessary to bring it to notice here. Thus it was one of those few late-comers to the best seller list, like the *Leaves of Grass*, which gave no promise of success at the outset but proved their vitality by finding an audience after many years.

Moby-Dick was published by Bentley in London about a month before Harpers issued it in New York in November, 1851. The English edition carried the title *The Whale*, and was in three volumes, priced at thirty-one shillings and sixpence. The American edition was in one thick, ugly volume, and was priced at a dollar and a half; probably less than two thousand copies were issued, of which about three hundred were destroyed in the great Harper fire of 1853. But a second printing was not called for until twelve years later, and that seemed to be enough. Yet the book was not dead. When Melville died, forty years after the original publication of his masterpiece, interest in his work revived sufficiently to suggest two new issues of *Moby-Dick*, one in Boston and the other in Chicago. A few years later Scribners brought out the first illustrated edition, and in 1907 it was adopted into Everyman's Library.

But the great rebirth of interest in Melville came with the publication in 1921 of Raymond M. Weaver's *Herman Melville, Mariner and Mystic*. No less than thirteen new editions of *Moby-Dick* appeared in the twenties, and eight in the thirties; seventeen publishing houses participated in this resuscitation of the great white whale, and prices ranged from twenty-five cents to fifty-two dollars. The most expensive edition was that of the Lakeside Press in three volumes, with illustrations by Rockwell Kent. Warner Brothers made a motion picture of Captain Ahab's pursuit of the whale in 1925, and a movie edition of the book was issued by Grosset & Dunlap. The Book-of-the-Month Club issued an edition with the Kent pictures in 1930, the Book League distributed a Garden City edition in 1940, and four years later GI's overseas were reading the story in an Armed Services edition. Without doubt, considerably more than half a million copies of *Moby-Dick* have been distributed in the United States in the past twenty-five years.

XX. A DOZEN ENGLISH NOVELS
OF THE MID-CENTURY

> There are more writers in France, and better writing in England, no doubt, than among ourselves; but these nations cannot compare with us in the number of intelligent readers. *Putnam's Monthly, July, 1856*

THOUGH probably Hawthorne did not intend to include them in his "d——d mob," three women writers from England furnished best sellers to American readers in the 1850's—Dinah Maria Mulock and Charlotte and Emily Brontë.

John Halifax, Gentleman was published in London in 1856 in three volumes at thirty-one shillings sixpence, and in the same year Harpers issued it in New York in one paper-bound volume at fifty cents. Up to this time, Miss Mulock's books had been published anonymously; but when a certain Mrs. Whyte laid claim to *John Halifax,* Miss Mulock quickly acknowledged her authorship. This sterling story was popular in America from the first. For many years it was possible for the purchaser to choose from a dozen different editions of it, depending on whether he wished to spend a dime, a quarter, fifty cents, or more. John, in the story, was another of those orphan paragons who make their way in the world by sheer excellence; but Miss Mulock's novel has far more freshness and sense than most of the American stories about orphans. Despite its English setting, readers on this side of the Atlantic thought it highly American in its insistence on the importance of middle-class ideas and on the success theme.

Harper & Brothers were also the first American publishers of the Brontë sisters. Early in 1848 they brought out *Jane Eyre,* which had just made a great popular success in London. "*Jane Eyre,* by Currer Bell," said the title-page. At the same time, they brought out another book which had just been published in England: "*Wuthering Heights,* by Currer Bell, Author of *Jane Eyre,*" said that titlepage. It is not strange that such a mistake should have been made. So complete was the anonymity of both books that the London publishers of *Jane Eyre* supposed that Currer Bell and Ellis Bell were men, or a man. Thackeray later wrote Charlotte Brontë that many persons thought his governess wrote *Jane Eyre,* since he himself, like Rochester, had a mad wife.

The freshness and vigor of *Jane Eyre* took the world by storm. The fact that it was the love story of a governess and a married man not only made talk for moralists, but it made curious purchasers for the book. An American reviewer doubted that it would have been so popular "had not some sly manufacturer of mischief hinted that it was a book which no respectable man should bring into his family circle." As a result, said this writer, "every family soon had a copy of it, and one edition after another found eager purchasers." Later, in the cheap-printing era at the end of the century, literally scores of publishers brought out low-priced American editions, Harpers leading the way with a fifteen-cent, paper-covered issue in 1879.

Wuthering Heights enjoyed no such success in those years. Its present popularity affords one of the outstanding examples of what a successful motion picture can do for a book. After the production of Emily Brontë's novel by Samuel Goldwyn in 1939, starring Merle Oberon and Laurence Olivier, enthusiastic fans wanted to read the book. Pocket Books alone sold about 700,000 copies of it. This was no flash in the pan, for it continued to sell: the movies had simply introduced the book to a new public, and it had sufficient vitality to defy dates.

Jane Eyre, in turn, was screened by Twentieth Century-Fox early in 1944; and three reprint houses brought out new movie editions. Said *Publishers'*

Weekly of Charlotte's masterpiece in October, 1943: "An example of its perennial popularity is the fact that so many editions of the book are actively in print today. These range in price from thirty-five cents to five dollars." Random House published a two-volume set of *Jane Eyre* and *Wuthering Heights* late in 1943, of which the Book-of-the-Month Club distributed some 350,000 as a "dividend." Both Charlotte's and Emily's masterpieces are now safely in the "million class."

Another movie-made best seller was Jane Austen's *Pride and Prejudice*. This favorite of the discriminating novel-reader has a curious history. It was really Miss Austen's first attempt in authorship: she began it before she was twenty-one, gave it the title *First Impressions*, and finished it in ten months. Her father, the Rev. George Austen, rector in the village of Steventon, sent the manuscript promptly to a London publisher, who promptly declined it. A few years later Jane wrote another novel, however, called *Northanger Abbey*; it was sold for ten pounds to an eccentric publisher who refused to issue it until he got good and ready and actually did not give it to the world until after the author's death. Despite two setbacks, Jane wrote a third story, *Sense and Sensibility*, which was published in 1811 and was successful enough to warrant bringing out *First Impressions*, which was now given the title *Pride and Prejudice*. For it Miss Austen received a hundred pounds, and it was published in 1813.

It was nineteen years later, and fifteen years after Miss Austen's death, that *Pride and Prejudice* was first published in America. Carey & Lea, of Philadelphia, brought it out then, giving it the title *Elizabeth Bennet: or, Pride and Prejudice*. It must have sold fairly well, for the same publishers issued Miss Austen's other books the next year. For the next hundred years occasional new editions showed that *Pride and Prejudice* still had readers; it got into the leading series and "libraries" and was read in the schools. Then in 1940 a popular motion picture brought it to general attention, and there was a rush to buy the book. Pocket Books alone sold a third of a million copies. The timeless nature of a classic was again demonstrated: the tempo of the twentieth century slowed for a re-appraisal of what Scott called "the exquisite touch" of the Steventon spinster. "The big bow-wow," wrote Sir Walter in his diary, "I can do myself like any one going; but the exquisite touch, which renders common-place things and characters interesting from the truth of the description, and the sentiment, is denied to me."

Another English spinster whose books about home life were popular in nineteenth-century America was Grace Aguilar. She was a Jewess, and her early books related chiefly to the history of her race; but shortly before her early death she turned out a spate of rather sentimental stories about girls in the home. Most popular of them and the only one actually to see print before her death was entitled *Home Influence: A Tale for Mothers and Daughters*. It made a great success in England and was promptly reprinted by Harpers in the United States. Other publishers followed suit, and throughout the latter half of the century Miss Aguilar was a favorite in Sunday School libraries and in many homes. *Home Influence* was one of the most popular titles in the famous Select Library of A. K. Loring, Boston publisher of juveniles.

Vanity Fair was being published in parts when *Jane Eyre, Wuthering Heights,* and *Home Influence* appeared. Thackeray's works had been promptly pirated in America from their first appearance; but none attracted wide attention before the publication of *Vanity Fair,* which made his fame, indeed, on both sides of the Atlantic. Thackeray's two visits to the United States in the fifties did much to enhance his American reputation. The English critic Lewis Melville has asserted that "Thackeray's fame was even greater in America than in England" at the mid-century; and again, speaking of the author's reputation through later years, he says, "In the United States Thackeray has always aroused more interest than in his native land." Henry C. Carey, in his *Letters on International Copyright* (1853), asserted that Thackeray's American sales quadrupled those in England.

Melville tells of Thackeray's habit, on his visits to America, of inquiring at bookstores about the relative sales of his novels and those of Dickens, and of his conclusion "that five copies of Dickens' books were sold for every one of his own." * Four or five to one probably holds as the proportion not only in the fifties but in that later period from 1880 to 1910, when cheap publication in single volumes and sets gave both Thackeray and Dickens an audience much larger than the earlier one. Nevertheless, four of Thackeray's novels must be included in the list of American best sellers—*Vanity Fair, Pendennis, The Newcomes,* and *The Virginians.* The first-named has always been the most popular. Langdon Mitchell's dramatic version, under the title "Becky Sharp," in which Mrs. Fiske and Maurice Barrymore starred, gave the book a new popularity a generation ago.

Thackeray was wont to speak kindly of American publishers and their generous payments to English authors for advance sheets, but Anthony Trollope thought that the purchasers of American rights to his books paid less than five per cent of what his English publishers gave him. Trollope usually drove a hard bargain with his publishers, however, and then allowed them to get what they could for themselves from America. J. Henry Harper declared that his house paid seven hundred pounds for advance sheets of *Sir Harry Hotspur,* while Trollope says in his *Autobiography* that he received only seven hundred and fifty pounds for that novel from his English publisher. Could Trollope, who thought himself so much the business man, have been badly misled as to the large receipts from American publishers of his books?

Trollope's *Barchester Towers* survived the years and has won new readers of new editions down to the present. Throughout most of the nearly ninety

* Lewis Melville, *Some Aspects of Thackeray* (London, 1911), pp. 223, 245, 246.

years since its first publication it has been available in America at twenty-five to fifty cents. Trollope's successive novels through the sixties and seventies had a large popular following as serials and as reprints, but most of them seemed to lose their hold in later years; and *Barchester Towers* alone of that long list can safely be named a best seller.

George Eliot's *Adam Bede* appeared at the very end of the fifties. It and *Silas Marner* doubtless owe much of their great American popularity to their settings of humble family life. It is clearly a mistake to think that the analytical quality in George Eliot's work was repellent to the common reader in this country. Again we quote J. Henry Harper: "Some critics have assumed that the stories by George Eliot would appeal rather to the thoughtful few than to the great world of novel readers, but our experience with the sale of her works shows this supposition to be ill-founded." * Cheap, paper-covered editions of George Eliot's novels at ten to fifty cents were common in the eighties, along with complete sets of her works in cloth at from three to ten dollars. The schools have helped to increase the sales of *Silas Marner*, though *Adam Bede* is a close second. *Middlemarch* and *Daniel Deronda* probably fell just a little short of the best seller level. An interesting edition of *Silas Marner* is the Confederate imprint with wallpaper covers issued by S. H. Goetzel in Mobile in 1863.

XXI. MRS. E. D. E. N. SOUTHWORTH

> It is a truth, sadly attested by the times in which we live, that literature, like human society, is growing more degenerate every year. At the present day the great mass of reading matter of the public is composed of the most worthless and enervating effusions of the many would-be authors whose names fill the annals of nineteenth century literature. . . . Nine out of every ten (nay, we may say ninety-nine out of every hundred) persons prefer the stories of Mrs. Southworth and Sylvanus Cobb, Jr., to the noble productions of Miss Muloch and George Elliott [sic]. *The Hidden Hand* and *The Gunmaker of Moscow* are far more universally read than *John Halifax* and *The Mill on the Floss*. Even the great Bulwer is rated a bore, while Emerson Bennett is considered charming.
>
> *National Quarterly, June, 1860*

The most popular authoress in the annals of American publishing was Mrs. E. D. E. N. Southworth. Her two foremost novels—*Ishmael* and *Self-Raised*—sold more than two million copies each, and *The Hidden Hand* must have come close to that figure. In all, Mrs. Southworth wrote over fifty novels, and nearly all of them sold in six figures. A few years before her death, a newspaper writer interviewed her in her home on the Potomac; the old lady spoke of the many persons she had met since she had begun her writing career, and added,

* J. Henry Harper, *The House of Harper* (New York, 1912), p. 388. In reference to the Trollope figures, pp. 114, 346-347. Cf. Chaps. XVII and XX of Trollope's *Autobiography*.

"I have never found one who has not read some of my books, and I have never heard of one." *

Emma Dorothy Eliza Nevitte was born in Washington in 1819, daughter of Captain Charles Le Compte Nevitte, who had been owner of a fleet of merchant ships until he lost all in the War of 1812-14. At the age of forty-five, Captain Nevitte married a girl of fifteen, and the future authoress was the first child of this union. Her father died when Emma was four years old, and a few years later her mother married Joshua L. Henshaw, of Boston, who had come to Washington as Daniel Webster's secretary and who later conducted an academy in that city. In this school Emma received her education, spending her vacations among relatives in Maryland and Virginia. After her graduation from the academy, she taught school some five years; then she married Frederick H. Southworth, a plausible but impractical gentleman from Utica, who was always about to make a fortune by his inventions or by some clever scheme that did not involve vulgar work. He could not settle down for long, and soon carried his bride off to Prairie du Chien, Wisconsin. Three years later he was gone, following some will-o'-the-wisp, leaving his wife to care for their two children as best she could. Later the wandering husband was, of course, in the California gold rush; occasionally, it seems, he would return to his family, sometimes with full pockets but more often in need.

When her husband first deserted her, Mrs. Southworth took her children and went back to Washington. There she did the only thing she knew how to do to make a living: she got a job teaching in the public schools. Soon she began to supplement her meager pay by selling short stories, which she wrote at night after a day in the schoolroom and an evening of housework. Her very first story was published in the *Baltimore Saturday Visiter*, the paper which printed Poe's first tale. But most of her early stories appeared in the *National Era*, a Washington literary miscellany with strong antislavery bias—remembered chiefly today as the paper which gave serial publication to *Uncle Tom's Cabin*.

Very early in her literary career, Mrs. Southworth met the poet Whittier at the house of Dr. Gamaliel Bailey, editor of the *Era;* he encouraged her and urged Bailey to make her a regular weekly contributor. It was Mrs. Southworth who suggested to the poet many years later the idea of "Barbara Frietsche"; he wrote to her after it was published, "If it is good for anything, thee deserves all the credit." And then Mrs. Stowe, coming to Washington to see Bailey about publishing her work, was introduced to Mrs. Southworth, now a regular writer for the *Era*. A warm friendship sprang up between them and Mrs. Stowe stayed at the Southworth cottage while in Washington. The lifelong friendship of Mrs. Southworth with Whittier and Mrs. Stowe is interesting in

* *Washington Post*, December 2, 1894. Quoted in Regis Louise Boyle, *Mrs. E. D. E. N. Southworth, Novelist* (Catholic University of America Press, 1939). This is the most detailed study of Mrs. Southworth.

many respects. If it seems odd that between them they did not make an antislavery novelist out of Mrs. Southworth at once, it should be remembered that this deserted wife and untried authoress had to make a living, and everyone (including Mrs. Stowe's advisers) thought there was no money in antislavery literature. And so the slaves in Mrs. Southworth's early novels are used for comic relief, and are happy and satisfied with their lot; but immediately after the success of *Uncle Tom's Cabin* she wrote her *India,* with its manumission theme, which Whittier thought her masterpiece. *Broken Pledges,* two years later, also introduces the slavery problem. Yet neither of these are among her more successful novels.

The fact is that Mrs. Southworth was incapable of passionate devotion to an idea. She had her ideals, of course. She believed in God and the Bible; in pity, kindness, and philanthropy; in female virtue and manly devotion; in generous ambition as a key to life. These things did not need thinking out; they were axiomatic, and carried with them certain codes to live by. Illustration of these codes by examples was the formula not only of Mrs. Southworth but of many another successful fictioneer of the time. It is a formula which invites numberless fascinating variations and brings up a constant succession of problems which interest the reader because he (or she; surely most of Mrs. Southworth's readers were she's) has to do the same thing the heroine is doing—apply the code to her own situations and problems. It is a wonderful game, of infinite variety; merely as a new kind of puzzle it has its fascination.

But Mrs. Southworth was a highly successful novelist because of two gifts: she was naturally a good story-teller, and she was a born imitator.

Probably she never set out to imitate anyone. But she read voraciously, and she picked up all the tricks of the popular writers of the day. Her reviewers were always comparing her to other and more famous authors—often favorably. Whittier said that her first novel, *Retribution,* was as good as *Jane Eyre*—better, indeed, because it had a moral. Many compared her humorous passages to those of Dickens, and her work is full of echoes of Scott. *Ishmael,* her best known novel, is reminiscent of *John Halifax, Gentleman.* Her use of minor characters often reminds one of Cooper.

But her imitativeness would not have made her a first-flight best seller without her native gift for telling a story. This was not a talent for structure, in which she was lamentably weak, but a strong feeling for melodramatic incident and an instinct to develop such incidents swiftly and in strong colors. There is something satisfying—to the simple mind, at least—in a villain who is thoroughly evil from his crown to his toes, incapable of a single good impulse. And how gratifying the idea of a hero who is slightly more perfect than King Arthur, St. Francis, and Daniel Webster rolled in one! Now take the elaborate moral codes referred to, invent situations in which villain and hero and other simply-typed characters are brought into the puzzles of the codes, supply the familiar fictional reagents such as irresistible passion, a storm or fire, the effects of ancestral sins, murder or other sudden death, insanity—and you have, well, at least the beginning of a Southworth romance.

This typing of characters, resulting in a dramatis personae all in lily white or Stygian black, was not acceptable to minds somewhat more subtle than that of Mrs. Southworth; but we must remember that by the middle of the nineteenth century there were enough readers in America so that both George Eliot and Mrs. Southworth could have very large audiences without much overlapping. As the *Nation* remarked anent Miss Braddon's readers in 1865, they were drawn from "that public which reads nothing but novels and yet which reads neither George Eliot, George Sand, Thackeray, nor Hawthorne."

There is a great reading public today for the black-white novel, and apparently the chief reason Mrs. Southworth has gone out of print in the last decade is that her moral codes and their puzzles are out of fashion. They are indeed almost incomprehensible today. Ishmael, hero of the novel of that name, though half starved, would not take the dollar urged upon him for holding the horses and defending with his fists the property of the man who later became his benefactor. Then after he had been admitted to the bar, he distresses a modern reader because, though he himself is poor as Job's turkey, he insists on turning down fat fees and taking only the cases of the poor and unprotected who can pay him nothing. He even splits hairs about accepting from clients any part of what he recovers for them if they could not, in the first place, pay him retainers.

Ishmael's first client was a deserted wife whose husband had returned and was trying to get her children away from her. The later novel *The Deserted Wife* enlarges the theme. Mrs. Southworth often repeated situations and incidents in her fifty novels. Many of her episodes were autobiographical, and the settings were nearly all those she knew best in Maryland and Virginia. Occasionally she used a western setting derived from her Wisconsin experience, and later a couple of years in England gave her material. Sometimes, though not so often, she wrote of places she had only read about.

Mrs. Southworth's first novel was published in the *National Era* and issued in book form by Harpers; the second appeared in the *Saturday Evening Post* and was later issued by Appleton. The next dozen or so were divided between these two periodicals and several book publishers. Of this group, the most popular was *The Curse of Clifton*, printed serially in the *Post* in 1852, and published in book form by Carey & Hart. Its central story is that of the love of young Captain Clifton for little Kate Kavanagh; but they are ill-assorted lovers, since he is the heir of old Clifton of Clifton and she is a very poor (but respectable) mountain girl. Again and again these unequal matches make the troubles on which Mrs. Southworth's plots thrive. The "curse" of Clifton is the captain's stepmother—an accomplished villainess if there ever was one. Here, for an example of Mrs. Southworth's more frenzied style, is a soliloquy of Mrs. Clifton, uttered just after she has inadvertently betrayed, for a moment, the malignity which she feels toward her whole household:

"I could tear my heart out! I could bite my tongue off, for thus betraying me! Shall I ever have power to chain and guide the tiger in me? But *he,* with his doting, and *they,* with their dalliance, goad me to extremity! *But,*" she exclaimed, clenching her fist, setting her teeth, and glaring, while all her countenance darkened with rage and anguish—"*But,* before they shall *marry* under my very eyes, and live here, maddening my soul and senses, day and night, by the view of their love and joy, I will pull down ruin on the heads of all! Yes, although I myself should be the first to fall!" She paused in silent thought for some time, then rising, said, "*Down,* tiger heart! *Down!* crouch! Be smooth, brow! Be tender, eyes! Be soft, voice! And now to go and pacify the old man [her husband] before his vexation betrays me to the others. Come! in time I shall learn to curb wild impulses, and only spring upon my prey when time and place is fit."

The readers of the *Saturday Evening Post* thought this was pretty fine stuff; and so did the editor of the *London Journal,* chief English story-paper, who stole the serial, substituted English places and names, with titles, and printed it under the title *Brandon of Brandon.*

Up to about 1853, Mrs. Southworth worked under many difficulties. Teaching, caring for her family, writing weekly installments late at night, she exhausted her strength. Her children had serious illnesses; she herself collapsed, and had to beg her readers to control their impatience and wait on her health. But soon she went on, the indomitable mother making the indefatigable serialist.

Changing to Bonner's *New York Ledger,* Mrs. Southworth wrote *The Hidden Hand,* one of her most popular books. Its readers liked particularly the character of Capitola, the heroine. "Cap" was not of the rather colorless but ineffably good type; she was good, of course, but a hoyden—the stock "romp" of the old theatre. Nine years after the *Ledger* first printed this story, it published it again, and fifteen years later again reprinted it serially for a new generation of readers, calling it "the most popular story ever printed in the *Ledger.*" It is doubtless the only long serial ever published three times in one paper.

The Hidden Hand was very long. Neither the editor of the *Ledger* nor Mrs. Southworth herself ever knew how long one of her serials was going to be when it was begun; and they ran on and on week after week, winding up one dramatic series of episodes only to start another. Sometimes a character who had been supposed dead turned up in the latter part of the story to afford new complications. Two characters did that in *The Curse of Clifton:* Frank Fairfax is killed in the Indian wars, and so his secret bride drowns herself; then when Fairfax turns up safe and sound, it develops that Zuleime was not drowned after all, and she even surprises her husband by contributing a baby to their reunion. Thus sets of characters shift, and the story runs on. Peterson, the book publisher, would bring out the book when the serial had reached a certain length, and then publish the remainder as a "sequel." The first half of *The Hidden Hand,* for example, was published under that name, breaking off without any kind of conclusion; and the second half was issued under the title *Capitola's Peril*.

Many of Mrs. Southworth's admirers have considered *The Hidden Hand* her best work. It has more variety than most, with Cap's pranks, the outlaws and their cave, and a mystery. Le Noir is a model villain. Here he is doing his stagey villainy when the hero has told him off:

Colonel Le Noir ground his teeth in impotent rage, muttering: "Take care, young man! I shall live to be revenged upon you yet for these affronts!" And his dastard heart burned with the fiercer malignity that he had not dared to meet the eagle eye or encounter the strong arm of the upright and stalwart young man.

This novel was translated into the leading European languages, and was especially popular in England. By this time the *Ledger* had agreed to sell the *London Journal* advance sheets of Mrs. Southworth's novels. When she visited England in 1859-62, she found London shops featuring Capitola hats and Capitola suits for girls, and three of the city's theatres producing dramatic versions of her story at once. In one of these plays, John Wilkes Booth was taking the role of Black Donald, the outlaw. In the United States *The Hidden Hand* was long a favorite melodrama.

Mrs. Southworth's next serial in the *Ledger* was called *The Doom of Deville; or, The Maiden's Vow*, but its title in the *London Journal* and often in its book form was *The Fatal Marriage*. Here an outlaw's beautiful daughter is wronged and seeks vengeance; 'tis a wild tale. It was also a best seller, but its popularity was eclipsed by *Self-Made*, of 1863-64. The latter story was published by Peterson in his two-part fashion, the first volume called *Ishmael; or, In the Depths* and the second *Self-Raised; or, Out of the Depths*. Mrs. Southworth regarded this as her best work, and she was probably right. Its rags-to-riches theme is always an interesting one, and its humor sometimes comes off fairly well. Ishmael is quite too wonderful, of course; and Lord Vincent too degenerate to represent even what another American authoress is said to have called "the effete cockroaches of Europe." And, as always, the dialogue is highfalutin. Ishmael has just saved Claudia's life in a runaway (he is always doing chores like that) and the judge visits the injured hero to thank him:

"How do you feel yourself this morning, my lad?" he inquired, putting the usual commonplace question.

"Much easier, thank you, sir," replied the youth in the pure, sweet, modulated tones of a highly-cultivated nature.

The judge was surprised, but did not show that he was so, as he said:

"You have done my daughter a great service; but at the cost of much suffering to yourself, I fear, my lad."

"I consider myself very fortunate and happy, sir, in having had the privilege of rendering Miss Merlin any service, at whatever cost to myself," replied Ishmael, with graceful courtesy.

In spite of that nauseating way of talking, or perhaps because of it, Ishmael keeps on rising "out of the depths" and makes a hit with everybody except his heart's love, the judge's daughter, who will not marry him because of his low birth. She pays for her pride, however, when Lord Vincent carries her off.

Contemporary female readers were no doubt fascinated by Mrs. Southworth's descriptions of ladies' costumes. She always did full and detailed justice to her heroines' ball dresses and wedding gowns. Several of her novels bring in descriptions of President's receptions at the White House. This "democratic court life" fascinated her. The sad fact is that our authoress was a phony democrat: she really thought that the high-born were essentially better than those of humble ancestry.

Mrs. Southworth's popularity continued to grow, in America, in England, in Germany. The *Ledger's* circulation broke all records. In 1877 Peterson brought out Southworth's *Works* in forty-two volumes. But the wider distribution of her novels was still to come. As her copyrights began to expire in the eighties and nineties, the cheap libraries picked up her books and issued them at ten to twenty cents apiece. These were the prices that really brought Mrs. Southworth to her public.

An oddity of the Southworth popularity was the attempt made by other would-be authoresses bearing the charmed name (or borrowing it) to win literary success thereby. Mrs. S. A. Southworth, of Boston, and Ella Southworth and Emma S. Southworth, of nobody seems to know where, capitalized on the magic cognomen; and the *Ledger* had to insist repeatedly that the only genuine trademark was formed by the celebrated initials E. D. E. N.

It is extraordinary how long Mrs. Southworth's vogue lasted. For more than sixty years she had a wide following. When she died in 1899 her books were still selling in great numbers. As late as 1930, eighty years after her first great success, Street & Smith were listing over ninety volumes of her work at ten cents each. Only in the last decade have the most popular of the novels dropped out of print.

The honest inquirer after the reasons for Mrs. Southworth's popularity must forget his own repugnance for her excesses and artificialities. Equipped with the gas-mask of tolerance, he must penetrate into her long and involved romances. He will then be able to discern an indefatigable story-telling talent, a strong feeling for blatant and primitive melodrama, a love for sensational effects in both incidents and characterization, and a faculty for passionate declamation. Add to these things the art of echoing the most respected authors of her day, and add also her good fortune in publishers like Bonner and Peterson; and Mrs. Southworth's success begins to seem less an enigma. It may be said of her, as of so many inferior writers and artists, that she had great gifts, but that they were undisciplined either by the restraints of sense or the subtleties of sensibility.

XXII. SENTIMENT AND SENSATION IN THE SIXTIES AND SEVENTIES

> Granting, as we must, that works of this class merely appeal to the curiosity —that they do nothing more than amuse the vacant or the wearied mind; if they do *that*, it is something. They may be as transitory as fireworks, and raise no loftier emotions. But a frivolous and a wearied public demands amusement.
>
> *Review of "Lady Audley's Secret" in the Cornhill Magazine, January, 1863*

LADY ISABEL VANE has two suitors, the high-souled Archibald Carlyle and the black-hearted Captain Francis Levison. She marries Archibald, but that only strengthens the determination of the captain to have her for himself. The Lady Isabel's jealous disposition, a series of suspicious circumstances, and the wicked captain's cleverness in persuasion combine to bring about an elopement; leaving her two children behind her, the Lady Isabel flies with her lover to France. Thus villainy has its triumph for a time, as is its way in romances (and in life, forsooth); then the captain, having succeeded to a baronetcy, deserts his mistress and child. The child is killed in a train wreck and the mother is reported killed. Carlyle, the wronged but noble husband, had divorced Lady Isabel but would not marry again until he believed himself released by her death; now he weds the girl of whom his wife had been jealous. But Lady Isabel is not dead. She lives to grieve over her deserted children; and finally, disguised as a governess, she returns to her old home, to live unrecognized in the Carlyle household. This situation, though comparatively innocent, is shocking: "we have not become Mormons yet," declares the authoress. So, to save the situation, Lady Isabel expires of a broken heart, recognized and forgiven on her death-bed by the exemplary Archibald Carlyle.

The name of the family estate on which much of this happened was East Lynne, and the foregoing is a summary of the plot of the novel which made that name known far and wide for more than half a century.

Mrs. Henry Wood, a semi-invalid afflicted with curvature of the spine, wrote *East Lynne* as a serial for the *New Monthly Magazine*, of London. Two book publishers rejected it before Richard Bentley decided to take a chance on it. It was thereupon issued as a three-decker in the autumn of 1861; its initial success is said to have been due to a favorable review in the *Times* which created such a demand that the printers had to work night and day to keep abreast of the sales.

In the United States, the New York firm of Dick & Fitzgerald brought it out late that same year in paper covers at seventy-five cents. It became a favorite with the publishers of cheap editions. M. A. Donohue & Company, of Chicago, founded in the year *East Lynne* was first published, manufactured over 400,000 copies of it for various publishers. Street & Smith reached six figures with their ten-cent edition. In 1887, the year of Mrs. Wood's death, the New York *Journalist* declared that "at least one million copies of *East Lynne* have been sold, in cheaper editions, to American novel readers." Certainly the distribution reached that figure before the book stopped selling ten or twenty years ago.

The sale of the novel was stimulated by the popularity of dramatic versions. Few melodramas have ever been so widely and continuously presented. All the old theatrical troupes that traveled from town to town through the country, showing at op'ry houses or in tents, put on *East Lynne* one evening in the week's program. City sophisticates, too, wept at the death of the Lady Isabel and laughed at the hokum of Alfy. Gold miners and cowboys in the West welcomed the play. Charles Chapin, who had to write his autobiography in Sing Sing, told of one evening when "Calamity Jane" came to see the production put on at Deadwood, Colorado, by the touring company of which he was a member. Angered by the behavior of the false Lady Isabel, Jane arose and, with the skill derived from many years of tobacco chewing and spitting, directed a copious stream of tobacco-juice against the erring heroine, ruining her pink satin evening gown. This was calamity indeed, and the curtain was rung down amid confusion. But when it was made clear to the excited Jane that all this was make-believe, she threw a handful of gold on the stage, and in due time the play went on. The movie version of 1931 was about half by Mrs. Wood and half by Hollywood, but audiences found it the same affecting thriller.

The year after the publication of *East Lynne* another "preposterously successful melodrama" was given to the world under the title of *Lady Audley's Secret.* Its author was Mary Elizabeth Braddon. At nineteen she had written a serial called *Three Times Dead; or, The Secret of the Heath* to be printed in penny numbers, with violent woodcuts, by a local Yorkshire printer. But the printer went bankrupt; a few years later Miss Braddon rewrote her story as *The Trail of the Serpent.* Then she received a hurried call from a young publisher named John Maxwell, who was about to launch a new periodical, for a serial thriller of domestic life; and she wrote very rapidly the story that was to be one of the great successes of fourth-rate fiction—the account of the famous reticence of the Lady Audley. But publishers' failures dogged the footsteps of the young authoress, Maxwell's paper went under after twelve numbers, and the serial was transferred to the *Sixpenny Magazine.* Later Maxwell married Miss Braddon, after which he got along very well with his publishing. Meanwhile, Tinsley Brothers brought out *Lady Audley* in book form; it made their fortune, and William Tinsley built him a villa out of his profits and called it Audley Lodge. Miss Braddon, having found her pace, went on furiously all her life, writing and editing her husband's magazines. She wrote some eighty novels and died in 1915.

The same critic who penned the apologia for idle fiction which heads this chapter wrote thus of Miss Braddon's chef d'oeuvre:

> Its characters have no life; its incidents are not simply violations of probability, but are without that congruity which, in a skillful romance, makes the improbable credible. There is no wit, no humor, no passion, no eloquence, no truth of description. But there is the skill which carries a story through a steeple-chase of incidents, and never lets the reader's curiosity flag. By artful suggestions we are made to believe that the woman whose illness, death, and burial seem authentically proved, is still living in triumphant wickedness. Who was buried in her name? And how was the substitution effected? Here is one mystery. Then for another, there is the sudden disappearance of a man: what has become of him? Is he dead—murdered? If so, how and by whom? . . . The author is master of our curiosity, and can take his [her] own time and means for gratifying it. When the explanations of these mysteries are given, it is true they turn out incredible; but by that time you have finished the book!

Miss Braddon was often scolded by the moralists for allowing her heroines to commit so many and such dastardly crimes, such as dropping their husbands in wells, eloping at midnight, and making bigamous marriages. Bigamy, indeed, commonly produced through the machinery of secret marriages and improperly authenticated deaths, was a commonplace of this whole school of writers, including Mrs. Southworth and her compeers in America. Sometimes more than two husbands are involved. The London *Examiner* thus satirized this element in the Braddon romances:

> But think of the shifts and perplexities of a wife with *eight* husbands, being not only mysteriously married, like Aurora Floyd [in Miss Braddon's novel of that name] to her noble husband's horse-trainer, but also to the beadle of whose cane she is in dread, and also to the Emperor of China, who writes compromising letters by each mail, the more compromising as she is also secretly married to the postman, who is of a suspicious temper, and may open any letter addressed to her; also, under peculiar circumstances, to the giant of a show that is coming to be set up at a fair in the neighborhood; also to a maniac whom she keeps in the cellar, for which reason she alone carries the keys of the cellar; and also to the rector of the parish, who believes her to be on a friendly visit at the grand house which must always be in the center of the stories of this school.

In America, *Lady Audley's Secret* was promptly pirated by Frank Leslie for his *New Family Magazine,* and brought out in 1863 by Dick & Fitzgerald in paper covers at fifty cents. Though never as popular as *East Lynne,* it was long one of the leaders in this class of fiction.

More important than either Mrs. Wood or Miss Braddon was a third sensationalist of those years known to the public as Ouida. Daughter of a French master at Bury St. Edmunds named Ramé, she added another *e* to the name and the prefix *de la,* so that her name became Marie Louise de la Ramée; but to the public she was known by the syllables of baby-talk which represented her own infantile pronunciation of her name *Louise.* Her father was continually disappearing into France for longer or shorter absences; from one of them he did not return, and it is supposed he died fighting in the streets of Paris in the Revolution of '48. Mother and daughter moved to London, where Louise began writing tales at an early age. The first of them, dealing largely with "high life," guardsmen and their mistresses, and the intrigues, debts, and pleasures of noble families, appeared in *Bentley's Miscellany* in 1860.

Ouida's most popular story, in America at least, was *Under Two Flags*. Lippincott issued it by arrangement with the English publisher in 1867 at two dollars, but the rise of the cheap "libraries" ten years later made it a popular paper-covered book at ten to twenty cents. It was successfully dramatized, and in recent years it has made a good motion picture with Claudette Colbert as Cigarette and Ronald Colman as Cecil.

Cecil, protagonist of *Under Two Flags*, is a lazy spendthrift and philanderer, to put the best face on the matter, while he is serving under the British flag. Ouida has been much praised for her realism in the portrayal of this kind of life, with its gambling, drinking, love-making with married women and the demimonde; but to the captious critic it is bound to seem too, too brilliant to be true. Then Cecil is ruined and joins the French Foreign Legion, thus setting a fashion for many later heroes of romance. And now he becomes a hero indeed, noble, self-sacrificing, daring, loved after her fashion by Cigarette, favorite vivandière of the Legion, and by the Princess Corona after hers. But Cigarette is a real heroine of high romance, who makes us forgive Ouida for many sins.

The fact is that Ouida did some things extremely well; *A Dog of Flanders, Bimbi,* and *A Village Commune* are exemplary proof that she could write well of dogs, children, and peasants. Her great fault was extravagance; as a writer she indulged in more excesses than her favorite guardsmen. Ouida loved to dress everything in superlatives: diamonds cascaded over the breasts of her society queens, and a handsome guardsman was "a splendid, golden-haired Colossus." It was Ouida's nature to write thus, for all her life she actually lived in the high colors of hyperbole. Her early novels made her rich, and she moved to Italy, with her mother, to live grandly in a villa near Florence. She suffered agony from a disappointment in love; she was Lady Bountiful to scores of dogs of all sizes and breeds; every day she was driven through the Florentine streets attired in orange-colored satin with a mantilla of black lace, favorite canines sharing her carriage, which was lined with turquoise-blue leather. She was probably the richest woman in Italy for a time; but she spent prodigally, years came when her novels did not sell so well, and in her latter years she was plunged into the depths of want. She buried her mother in a pauper's grave; she herself had scarcely enough to eat. When knowledge of her penury reached English acquaintances, overtures of help were made, which she spurned; but she finally accepted a small pension from the English government. The course of her life, the gamut of her emotions, and the art of her writing were all exaggerated and overdone, in the florid style and with a straining after striking effects.

Very different from these lady retailers of sensation was R. D. Blackmore, whose *Lorna Doone* was published in 1869. Though Blackmore was educated at Oxford and later read law and was admitted to the bar, he was an epileptic; and when he was left a small legacy, he retired from the city and devoted himself to fruit gardening and writing. It was gardening that chiefly interested him throughout the rest of his life; he wrote in order to pay his losses from his experiments in horticulture. *Lorna Doone* was his only considerable success.

This romance, beloved of generations of discriminating readers, is by no means devoid of sensation or even of sentimentality. But the story of the changing seasons, the fine, simple, strongly delineated characters, the poetic style, and the rush of narrative in the dramatic parts give to this old favorite a perennial, ripe charm. The story is founded on a legend of the outlaws of Exmoor in the seventeenth century, but the historical element is a minor one: Blackmore wrote, perhaps too modestly, in his first preface, "The writer neither dares nor desires to claim for it the dignity, or cumber it with the difficulty, of an historic novel." Legend is its basis; simple love of nature and character are its theme.

It is said that eighteen publishers respectfully declined the manuscript of *Lorna Doone*. Sampson Low finally undertook it; but his first modest edition of five hundred copies simply did not sell, and about half of them were sent to Australia to be disposed of at a discount. This was the usual three-volume type of edition; but cheap book publishing was bringing its changes in England, and Low, who believed in the book, brought it out in a single volume at a greatly reduced price in 1871. In addition to this inducement, the book was the beneficiary of a piece of promotion. The popular Pincess Louise was to marry the Marquis of Lorne, and newspaper notices suggested that *Lorna Doone* was a story of the bridegroom's family: the upright Sampson Low was, of course, not responsible for such a piece of fakery, but it seemed to afford just the stimulus that the book needed to make it bound into popularity. Harpers pirated the story to publish the first American edition in 1874. Blackmore did ultimately receive some returns from the American sales, and he was doubtless right in thinking the book sold more widely in America than in Britain; its distribution on this side of the Atlantic must have come pretty close to a million, and it still finds buyers.

America, too, had a gardener who wrote best sellers. For Edward Payson Roe gardening, however, was only an avocation once he was well started on the way to bestsellerdom. At first he was a clergyman and a Civil War chaplain. While pastor of a Presbyterian church at Highland Falls, New York, adjacent to West Point, he read of the great Chicago fire of 1871 and was so excited by the accounts that he took the next train for the stricken city, tramped the streets while they were still strewn with ashes and smoldering wreckage, and planned forthwith a novel which should use the great fire as its dramatic climax. The resulting book was *Barriers Burned Away*. It made a great hit, first as a serial in the *New York Evangelist* and then as a book from the Dodd, Mead house. Roe decided to try another novel by the same formula, but using this time a different catastrophe; and if this should also be successful, he would retire from "the active ministry" to devote himself to authorship, with the cultivation of small fruits as diversion. The second book was also popular; and Roe carried out his plan, settling at Cornwall-on-the-Hudson, where he raised excellent berries and wrote in a dozen years as many successful novels.

It would be wrong, however, to say that the Rev. Mr. Roe gave up preaching. He merely changed pulpits. Every story of his was an evangelical sermon. The formula he devised for his first book and thereafter followed with considerable faithfulness called for a religious hero or heroine who labored to convert a doubter, usually of the opposite sex, to Christian beliefs, and succeeded through the intervention of some great disaster. The rags-to-riches element, too, was often important. In *Opening A Chestnut Burr*, Roe's second novel on the over-all best seller list, the shipwreck of an ocean liner furnished the big sensational climax required. This story first appeared as a serial in *Hearth and Home* with the title *The Chestnut Burr*.

E. P. Roe! Once that name was magic. But how stale his chapters are today, how stilted the conversation, how tiresome the sermonizing! Has the virtue gone out of E. P. Roe, or out of us? Even the great catastrophes seem rather flat—except perhaps for that description of the Chicago fire, which, by its successive incidents, has a cumulative effect of considerable power.

Dodd, Mead & Company, Roe's publishers, estimated his total sales a few years ago at four to five millions. Some of the stories were published in cheap quarto editions at twenty cents, to compete with the price-cutting publishers of the eighties; this doubtless helped to establish Roe as a best seller. Besides, his books were great library stand-bys, and who shall say how many millions read them?

XXIII. THE CHEAP "LIBRARIES" OF 1875-1893

There is likely to be a great cheapening of books by and by, and an immense increase of reading in consequence—which, if it were all one (as it is to a dreadful degree all *two*) whether we read sense and truth or falsity and nonsense, would be an indisputable benefit for mankind! Anyhow, we must try it, and *then* see what is next.
> Thomas Carlyle in a letter to Robert Chambers, 1852

A volume of Carlyle can be bought for the price of a glass of whiskey.
> The Hour, April 21, 1883

DURING the thirty years which followed the cheap-publishing outburst of the early 1840's, some established publishers maintained a competition in books priced at less than a dollar. Harpers and Appleton in New York and Peterson in Philadelphia were leaders in such offerings, while at the same time they issued regularly priced books. There was no little publishing in paper covers; English books, pirated or printed from advance sheets, were frequently issued in cloth and paper at the same time.

And then in 1858 a young man from Buffalo came to New York and began a publishing experiment which eventually was to have tremendous effects upon the whole book industry. His name was Erastus F. Beadle. He had published a *Dime Song Book* in Buffalo which had sold like hot cakes, and that success gave him ideas. Having moved in on New York, with his brother Irwin and his later partner Robert Adams, he experimented first with joke books and such collections; and then, at intervals in 1860, he issued a dozen novelettes, dealing chiefly with pioneer life, the Revolution, Indians, and Mexico. Everything he published sold well, and so he increased his output. The times were propitious, for hundreds of thousands of soldier boys in the field wanted reading matter, and here was just the thing for them. So bales of yellow-backs were shipped out to the Union armies in camps, barracks, and hospitals; and Erastus had the satisfaction of knowing that he was maintaining military morale at the same time that he was making a mint of money.

Though Beadle & Company had published over four million dime novels by the middle of 1865, the sales of individual titles ranged from 35,000 to 80,000;* thus few single dime novels ever had really large sales, and only two can safely be placed on the overall best seller list. It may be that Mrs. Metta V. Victor's *Maum Guinea,* an 1861 story of slave life in Louisiana, belongs there; but it is doubtful. Mrs. Victor was the wife of Beadle's editor and author of many popular novels, including *The Backwoods Bride* and *Off With the Old Love.* But the two dime-novel best sellers were Mrs. Stephens' *Malaeska,* which was Number One of the series, and E. S. Ellis' *Seth Jones,* which was Number Eight.

Mrs. Ann S. Stephens was well known as a magazine editor and an indefatigable writer of serials before she made her debut as a dime novelist. She had written two very popular books in the mid-fifties—*Fashion and Famine* and *The Old Homestead*—and it was this success that made Victor ask her to write the first Dime Novel of the Beadle series. *Malaeska, the Indian Wife of the White Hunter* tells of the tragic results of the marriage of a frontiersman with an Indian princess; in the denouement, the son of this union drowns himself when he learns that he is a half-breed. There is plenty of action, Indian fighting, and melodrama. The novel was used to initiate the new publishing venture, said the editor, "from the chaste character of its delineations, from the interest which attaches to its fine pictures of border life and Indian

* See paragraph on dime novels in Appleton's *Annual Cyclopaedia* for 1864, p. 473. The writer seems well informed. Edmund Pearson's *Dime Novels* (Boston, 1929) is of little help on distribution statistics. *The Beadle Collection of Dime Novels, Given to the New York Public Library by Dr. Frank P. O'Brien* (N.Y.P.L. Bulletin, 1922) is valuable, but some of Dr. O'Brien's estimates seem high.

adventure, and from the real romance of its incidents. It is American in all its features, pure in its tone, elevating in its sentiments." This foreword emphasizes the elements which the founders of the series had in mind. Mrs. Stephens' story was highly suitable to their purposes and was immediately successful. Thirteen years later, Beadle & Adams reprinted it in quarto form as the third number in their series of New and Old Friends. In 1929 it was republished as a curiosity, with an introduction by Dr. Frank P. O'Brien, the leading dime novel authority. Dr. O'Brien believes that *Malaeska* sold half a million copies.

He suggests a somewhat higher estimate for *Seth Jones,* which, after its initial sales of 450,000 in the original yellowbacks, became No. 1 in the New and Old Friends series, and took its old "No. 8" in Beadle's Half-Dime Library, begun in 1877. It continued to be reprinted occasionally; as late as August, 1900, it was No. 1104 in the Half-Dime Library, then published by M. J. Ivers & Company. It was translated into seven foreign languages. Edward S. Ellis was only twenty years old when he wrote the book; later he became a historian of sorts, and author, among other things, of a six-volume, richly illustrated *History of the United States,* which was sold by book agents in the years at the turn of the century. The setting of *Seth Jones* is the "Wilderness" of New York in 1785, and the story is filled with rapid adventure, Indian fighting, scouting, and other ingredients of Cooperian romance. In fact, young Ellis seems to have tried to get everything he could think of into his novelette— a love affair, the humor of backwoods characters, miraculous woodcraft, repeated hair-breadth escapes, all kinds of chases (by footrace, by boat, on horseback), a contest with a rattlesnake which "charms" its victim by its baleful eye, and two heroes, each of whom has the athletic prowess of Paul Bunyan, the skills of Leatherstocking, and the cleverness of Davy Crockett.

Beadle & Adams had sense enough to exploit the dime novel idea as soon as it became a pronounced success. They started one new series after another, trying new formats, rallying new authors. Beadle's New Dime Novels, Beadle's Pocket Novels, and Frank Starr's American Novels (Starr was Beadle's head printer) were in the market by 1870. But other publishers were trying their luck, too, by that time—especially Robert M. De Witt & Company, New York, with De Witt's Ten-Cent Romances, and Elliott, Thomes & Talbot, Boston, with their Ten-Cent Novelettes.

The thousands of dime novels were, with very few exceptions, original stories of novelette length written by American authors. They did, however, point the way to cheap publication of full-length reprint novels in series. Two other signposts pointed that way in the early seventies. First, reprints of standard English fiction were being imported from London at prices so low that they could be retailed for twenty-five cents. Second, the *New York Tribune* began in 1873 its Tribune Novels, selling at ten cents for a single number and twenty cents for the double number necessary for an English three-decker.

The *Tribune* published only twenty-six of these in ten years; but many were books by such important writers as Hardy, Blackmore, Besant, and Mrs. Oliphant. The method of publication was much like that which had created such a sensation when it was used by the *New World* and *Brother Jonathan* forty years earlier. The fact is that, just as faster presses and papermaking machines had made the 1842 incident possible, so declining prices of paper and improved presses made the cheap "libraries" a logical development in the seventies.

In 1875 came the first blast of the storm that was almost to wreck the country's established book business. It blew out of Chicago, where, in January of that year, Donnelley, Lloyd & Company issued the first numbers of their Lakeside Library in double-column quartos at ten cents a copy. Later the longer novels were issued at fifteen and twenty cents, though there were always many at a dime. "The great, popular want today is for Cheap, Good Literature," said the prospectus. "Dime novels are issued by the million, and good books by the thousand, but to the mass of readers the one is as distasteful as the other is inaccessible." The Lakeside Library began with semi-monthly issues, then increased the tempo to three times a month, and finally to once a week. It took over much of the standard American literature on which copyrights had expired, but it was made up largely of pirated English novels, with some from the French.

A year or two later Beadle & Adams took up the challenge by founding their Fireside Library in New York. This, as well as Myers, Oakley & Company's People's Library (in which Street & Smith had some interest), and Frank Leslie's Home Library were all modeled on the Lakeside. Then in May, 1877, George Munro began the most successful of all the quarto series, the Seaside Library. Munro's first three numbers were *East Lynne*, *John Halifax, Gentleman*, and *Jane Eyre*. He was not satisfied to issue a novel a week; his presses tossed one out every day.

Other cheap "libraries" now plunged into the fray, until by the fall of 1877 there were at least fourteen of them.

In the 1840's Harper & Brothers had tried to meet the cheap-johns on their own ground, and now they used the same tactics. In 1878 they set up a quarto series of their own, the Franklin Square Library. Other regular publishers issued more of their paper-bound books at fifty and sixty cents, but the Harper house was the only one to get down on the ten-cent quarto level. Isaac K. Funk, later founder of Funk & Wagnalls, noting the large number of trashy novels in most of the "libraries," in 1880 started one of his own which was to include only works of high quality: his Standard Series was founded upon Macaulay, Carlyle, Spurgeon, and so on—chiefly non-fiction. Dodd, Mead published E. P. Roe in quartos at prices ranging from twenty to fifty cents. Holt established his pocket-size Leisure Moment Series in 1883 at twenty and twenty-five cents, and continued it for about ten years. A little later, Houghton

Mifflin, Appleton, Scribners, Cassell, Estes & Lauriat, and other publishers followed suit.

Originally the quartos were sent through the mails at magazine postage, just as the 1842 cheap editions had been. But history repeated, and pressure was brought on the Postoffice Department to refuse them this privilege. The cheap publishers then turned to the news companies for distribution, and these well organized concerns were thereafter the chief retailers of the quartos. Sizes of the editions varied greatly. Raymond Howard Shove, in his study of cheap publishing in this period,* indicates editions of five to sixty thousand. The Seaside Library's average seems to have been about ten thousand, and at the height of its prosperity it would not put a book to press for a smaller run.

John B. Alden, a Chicago dealer in second-hand books, came to New York in the mid-seventies, and in 1879 put into effect a new idea which was finally to drive the ten-cent quartos out of the market. This idea was the publication of cloth-bound books of a size convenient for shelving to sell for fifty cents. That price had long been the low figure for the paper-bound books of the regular publishers. Alden's series was called Acme Editions, and a little later he established his Aldus Editions, with better paper and binding, at one dollar. Still later he began his Revolution Pamphlets, in which he published separate plays of Shakespeare, essays of Macaulay, etc., at only three cents; in 1883 he changed the name to Elzevir Library and varied the prices from two to fifteen cents. Alden published good books, and vast quantities of them, but he went bankrupt late in 1881. He was able to reëstablish himself in a few years, however, and was an important figure in cheap publishing throughout the eighties and the early nineties.

Alden had demonstrated the fact that the buyers of cheap books liked **volumes** they could put on their shelves better than the old quartos; and the movement which he had termed "the Revolution in Books" now turned in the direction of the production of what was variously known as the "twelvemo," "pocket," or "handy-size" paper-covered edition. The Seaside began its Pocket Edition in 1883, and three years later abandoned its quarto size altogether. By that time Munro's business was falling off badly. When an unknown printer stole the name of the Seaside Library for some books he was issuing, Munro appealed to the booksellers to outlaw him. "Why, the fellow's a pirate!" he exclaimed. Munro, now a multi-millionaire, had himself been in the business of piracy so long and so profitably that by this time he had come to regard himself as an honest man.

The paper-covered "handy-size" volume rode the top of the wave in the early eighties, and in the publication of this type of cheap book John W. Lovell made himself the leader. Lovell was the son of a Canadian publisher of reprints. He came to New York in 1875 and began producing sets of English

* *Cheap Book Production in the United States, 1870-1891* (University of Illinois Library, 1937). The present writer owes much to this excellent "spade-work" study.

books at cut prices. In 1882 he founded Lovell's Library, a series of standard and popular reprints in bright paper covers at ten cents, or twenty cents for double numbers. After this series got well under way, Lovell added a new title every day. It is strange to see *Vanity Fair* bearing a date like a daily newspaper. It is strange, too, to find *Pilgrim's Progress* neighboring with the works of Bertha M. Clay and The Duchess. Soon Lovell introduced two other series,— Lovell's Popular Library, which issued cloth-bound books at fifty cents; and Lovell's Standard Library, which furnished better paper and binding for a dollar. A new title was often issued in the three series at once.

Now came a deluge even greater than that of the quarto "broadsides" of the late seventies. Among the series of paper-covered books of the "handy size" established in the next five or six years were Munro's Library, by Norman L. Munro; the Franklin Editions, by Richard Worthington; the Standard Library, by Funk & Wagnalls; the Handy Series, by Harper & Brothers; the Manhattan Library, by Albert L. Burt; the National Library, by Cassell & Company; the Household Library, by Frank F. Lovell; the American Series, by M. J. Ivers & Company; the Echo Series, by Pollard & Moss; and various "libraries" by Street & Smith. And then by the middle of the decade, popularity veered to the cloth-bound books selling from twenty-five to fifty cents; and many of these same publishers established other series for books with the more permanent bindings but with paper and presswork, alas, just as poor. Lovell, Alden, Burt, and Worthington were prominent in this new development; newcomers were Hurst & Company, Porter & Coates, F. M. Lupton, W. B. Conkey, and W. L. Allison in New York; and Belford, Clarke & Company, Donohue & Henneberry, and Rand, McNally & Company in Chicago. The list becomes tiresome. In 1887 the *American Bookseller* reported that twenty-six "libraries" had contributed to the book output of the preceding year. Several of these were devoted to the dime-novel business, but nearly a score were issuing regular novels and general literature.

The news companies still played a large part in the distribution of the cheap books, but the turn toward cloth-bound works had made the product more acceptable in the bookstores. Firms like Belford, Clarke & Company, with their tricky discounts, had got into the department stores. John B. Alden was the leader of a group that sold largely by mail from catalogues. Funk & Wagnalls had a subscription list of sixteen thousand buyers who took a book every other week at four dollars a year—the forerunner of the modern book club.

It seems obvious that such a cheap-book publishing program as has been outlined must eventually result in glutting even such a great market as that furnished by a growing nation with a high percentage of literacy. By the end of the eighties, the publishers were making no profits, great stocks of books were at the mercy of bargainers, and the quality of bookmaking had sunk to new depths. Minna Irving, writing about "The Modern Novel" in the *Journalist*, said, "There is too much of it. It is everywhere. It is hawked on the street, it crowds the El stations . . . until I am conscious of a feeling of nausea at the mere sight of a row of paper-backs." To remedy the whole situation, John W. Lovell brought a majority of the publishers of the "libraries" into a combination which bought up thousands of sets of plates and took over and consolidated many of the leading "libraries." This "trust" or pooling arrangement, under the name of the United States Book Company, might have succeeded if its owner had been less ambitious and visionary; but it failed in 1893. It had cleaned up some of the lists, however; and certain of the companies into which it was divided after its bankruptcy had strength enough to continue for several years.

In the meantime, an international copyright agreement had been signed in 1891, and the pirates at last had been forced to haul down their black flags. But cheap reprint houses continued to flourish for many years. After all, they had at their disposal all the riches of foreign literature published before 1891 and all the earlier American books which had emerged and were now emerging year after year from copyright. Burt, Altemus, Lovell-Coryell, Mershon, Donohue, Street & Smith, and many other specialists in reprint literature continued to publish cloth-bound books at twenty-five to seventy-five cents and paper-covered numbers at ten to twenty-five cents long after international copyright and the collapse of the Lovell combination had ended the orgy of the piratical "libraries." A catalogue of the Street & Smith "libraries" and series published January 1, 1915, contains over thirty-five hundred titles, and this style of publication continued to be important in the creation of best sellers beyond the turn of the century.

We must not neglect the importance of this aftermath of the "libraries" in the nineties in its effect on best sellers. Probably Emerson's *Essays* would not have reached our list without the aid of such publishers as Hurst, Mershon, and Altemus. The first series of the *Essays* was published in 1841 and the second three years later, both by James Munroe & Company, of Boston. They had a small sale; and though Emerson's later publishers kept attractive editions in print through the seventies and eighties, it was not until their emergence from copyright made them available to the cheap-publishing houses that the *Essays* reached their widest distribution. A new and important incident in the history of the sales of these *Essays* is their inclusion in the Bantam Books—a twenty-five-cent series.

Similar is the story of Thoreau's *Walden,* issued by Ticknor & Fields in 1854. Seven publishers issued it in editions priced at less than a dollar the year it came into the public domain. There have been many editions since—some with distinguished illustration by woodcuts and photographs, some in such standard series as the Modern Library and Everyman's, some in simple formats for the schools. "The full significance of *Walden* has never been felt until today," wrote Professor Canby in 1939. The revolt of individualism against regimentation and a fresh emphasis on simple values in living have given the book new meaning for us.

Both of these classics have been promoted by the schools, of course, both have been reproduced in very handsome recent editions, and both have been distributed by book clubs. But they originally got into middle-class homes largely by means of cheap publishing shortly after the turn of the century.

Many features of this episode of the cheap "libraries" are regrettable. Literary piracy, the tricks of price-cutting, the publication of much inane and driveling fiction, and the wretched bookmaking which the movement encouraged are all deplorable. On the other hand, a considerable part of the literature published was of a high class, and much of it probably could have been brought to the attention of the great popular audience in no other way. Certainly these cheap series had an enormous influence upon the creation of best sellers. Alone, they probably made few such successes; but what they added to more regular sales lifted many books to the best seller level.

XXIV. FOR THE YOUNG IN HEART

He cometh to you with a tale which holdeth children from play and old men from the chimney corner.

Sidney's "Defence of Poesy"

BY 1867 the name "Mark Twain" was pretty well known the country over. It no longer stood for just another one of those rowdy western funny men; Mark was known in the East as the author of a little book called *The Celebrated Jumping Frog of Calaveras County, and Other Sketches,* he had lectured successfully at Cooper Union, and he had contributed pieces to the *New York Tribune* and other papers. And the newspapers of those days were in the habit of clipping choice bits of humor from each other, so that good sketches were reprinted hundreds of times and in most of the towns and cities of the country. Readers now got ready to chuckle as soon as they saw that trade-mark of the laughable, "Mark Twain."

So Elisha Bliss, Jr., secretary and manager of the American Publishing Company, Hartford, Connecticut, sat down and wrote Samuel L. Clemens, Esq., a letter in which he proposed to publish, by subscription only, a book to be made up of Mark Twain sketches which had been published in the papers. And Samuel L. Clemens, Esq., who was just back from an excursion to Europe and the Holy Land aboard the steamship *Quaker City,* thought immediately of the papers he had written for the *Alta California* about that trip and decided —how correctly!—that they would make a good book.

Publishing by subscription had enjoyed a long and successful history. It developed along two lines—the underwriting of the cost of publication of expensive books by patrons of literature who agreed in advance to purchase one or more copies as an encouragement to author or printer, and the peddling of books from door to door. The former, a very dignified procedure, still exists, mainly in the field of scholarly publication. The latter, which began with the activities of those chap-book peddlers whom Cotton Mather wished to protect because they carried religious tracts along with other less respectable miscellany, was eventually assimilated into the subscription projects because traveling agents became necessary to get the subscription pledges—and there was little difference between a book-agent selling books already printed and a solicitor selling books from a prospectus in advance of publication. Before the middle of the nineteenth century, the books subscribed for were usually books already issued, though the agent still used his prospectus. After the Civil War, there was a great boom in the subscription business (or selling by book-agents) partly because of inflationary prosperity and partly because army demobilization made it easy for publishers to find plenty of bright young men at loose ends as canvassers.

The American Publishing Company had made a big success in distributing the work of Albert D. Richardson and other popular writers in this way, and had just published Greeley's *American Conflict*. Mark made a bargain with this company for the book which was later to be titled *The Innocents Abroad*. He was to receive a royalty of five per cent; Richardson had received only four. Then he found, to his indignation, that the *Alta California* had copyrighted the articles he had written from abroad, with the view of getting back the thousand dollars they had paid for them by issuing a book themselves. Mark had to make a trip to California to straighten this out, after which he found he had to rewrite most of the copy anyway. But in July, 1869, the book appeared, with 234 woodcuts by True Williams, and "issued by subscription only, and not for sale at the bookstores." It immediately entered upon that phenomenal door-to-door sale of four thousand or more a month at $3.50 a copy which continued for several years.* The book was sold by subscription for thirty-five years; and though it dropped by the end of that term to little more than a tenth of its first rate of sale, it had piled up a total of over half a million by that time.

This made a nice income for Mark Twain, and it helped materially to make the American Publishing Company the most prosperous subscription-book concern in the country. For Mark's next book, *Roughing It*, his royalty was increased to seven and a half per cent, which Bliss claimed represented half of the profits. The new book was also successful, though it never quite reached the best seller level. But *The Adventures of Tom Sawyer,* published in the same fashion in 1876, was destined to reach higher sales figures than any of Mark Twain's other books. Probably the subscription business did no better by it than by *Innocents Abroad;* but after that method was abandoned in 1904

* See *Appleton's Journal*, July 4, 1874 (vol. XII, p. 17) where the sales for five years are given at 241,000.

and especially after many moderate-priced editions were authorized, its grand total rose to two million or more. It emerged from copyright in 1932.

Why *Tom Sawyer* should outsell *Huckleberry Finn* is hard to explain. For the latter, Mark Twain organized his own publishing company, retaining the subscription method which had been so successful in the distribution of his earlier books. Bliss was dead, and Mark was dissatisfied with the way the half-profit royalty system was working. Eventually the new company was to bring disaster upon him, but it did well with *Huckleberry Finn,* building up an advance sale of 40,000 copies as a starter. Interest was stimulated by the action of the Concord, Massachusetts, library in barring the book as unfit for the young readers for whom it was designed. "That will sell 25,000 copies of our book for sure," chortled Mark in a letter to his nephew-publisher, Charles L. Webster. Where the later book about Tom and Huck fell behind the earlier one was in sales after the turn of the century; then *Tom Sawyer* forged far ahead. Both felt the stimulus of movie production: Jackie Coogan played Tom in film versions of both stories, in 1930 and 1931; and David Selznick made a million-dollar film of *Tom Sawyer* in 1938, with Tommy Kelly as star.

The fourth Mark Twain best seller was *Life on the Mississippi* (1883). The earlier and better part of the book was first printed serially in the *Atlantic Monthly;* then it was padded out to make a volume to be sold by subscription. Though it had a good sale in its various cloth-bound editions, it would scarcely have reached the best seller list without the aid of the Bantam Books, which adopted it in 1946 as Number One of its series at a quarter each. Certain newspaper subscription schemes have also added to the total sales of Mark Twain's books in recent years.

In his history of the American novel, Carl Van Doren names *The Adventures of Huckleberry Finn* and *The Scarlet Letter* as the greatest books in that broad field. Strange pairing!—a juvenile, and a novel on the adultery theme. Or is *Huckleberry Finn* a juvenile? Mark Twain denied that *Tom Sawyer* was written for boys. "It is not a boy's book at all," he wrote to Howells. "It will only be read by adults. It was only written for adults." But Howells persuaded him to edit and promote it as a book for boys. If, in the long run, a book is read by children and adults alike, the question of the author's purpose in this regard loses significance. Surely all four of Mark Twain's best sellers are books for the young in heart.

Incidentally, the biggest achievement of C. L. Webster & Co. was the sale by subscription of 312,000 sets of Grant's *Memoirs* at an average of nine dollars a set within two and a half years. Mrs. Grant received nearly half a million dollars on a contract that provided that the author or his heirs should get 70% of the profits.* Her first check was for $200,000. These were the great days of the subscription book business, with professional solicitors organized under

* For the fullest account of the whole episode see Mark Twain's account (in the main reliable) in his *Autobiography,* vol. 1, pp. 27-57 (New York, 1925).

regional agencies which acted as middlemen in dealing with the publishers.

Much more definitely limited to the boy audience than the stories of Mark Twain—limited by intention and by their own immaturity—were the tales of Horatio Alger, Jr. To criticize Alger today is to challenge the widespread and loyal Order of Old Fellows Who Read Alger When They Were Boys. They are apt to forget their author's banality, his typed characters, his bad writing, and his copybook moralities, and to remember only their boyish response to his getting-ahead thesis and their breathless interest in his rapid story-telling. Alger's name has become a by-word for the boy's success story, and that is no mean fame.

Horatio Alger, Jr., though he rose from rags to riches, or at least from the poverty of a parsonage to the affluence of big royalty checks, was himself no Alger hero. He was not moral enough, by a long shot. He had three passionate love affairs—one with a Paris grisette, another with an English art student, and another with a married American lady. In between these torrid episodes he was a Unitarian minister for a couple of years, became a writer, and worked in close association with the New York Newsboys' Lodging House and other benevolent organizations. But most important of all, he wrote. And how much he wrote! and how fast! He could write one of his novelettes in two weeks, and altogether he wrote at least 135 of them.*

His biographer calls Alger "the most widely read writer of the ages," and many other extravagant claims have been made as to his reading public. The jacket of a recent reprint of some of the stories says over a hundred million Alger books were sold, while the introduction says "close to two hundred million." These figures belong to astronomy, not publishing. Let us look at the matter a little more closely. When Alger died in 1899, the obituaries published in the papers gave the total sales of his books as about 800,000, a figure which may be accepted, under the circumstances, as reasonably accurate. But the big sale was to come later. Porter & Coates, of Philadelphia, who had succeeded A. K. Loring as Alger's publishers, had been issuing the books at $1.25 each; now they not only began offering them at a quarter, but permitted Hurst & Company, of New York, and Donohue & Henneberry, of Chicago, to do likewise. From this it was only a step to paper covers at a dime a throw; and soon the New York News Company, Street & Smith, and others had the Alger books on their ten-cent lists. For nearly fifteen years literally millions of boys read these books in the dime-novel form. They passed from one boy to another, and sometimes to their sisters; some boys collected libraries of a dozen to fifty or more of them. But a sale of a hundred million in these years is preposterous. There were only five and a half million boys between the ages of fifteen and twenty in 1910, and certainly not all of them read Alger. Allowing for new-

---

* Herbert R. Mayes, in his *Alger: A Biography Without a Hero* (New York, 1928) lists 119, but the editor of *Struggling Upward and Other Works by Horatio Alger, Jr.* (New York, 1945) gives a list of 135. This latter book is a collection of four Alger novels by Crown Publishers; it includes *Ragged Dick*.

comers in that age-group over fifteen years, the potential market is still too small. In 1910 *Publishers' Weekly* noted that one bookseller had estimated the total current sales of Alger books at a million a year, but dismissed the claim as "probably very greatly exaggerated." * We should be inclined to accept it, however, and to place the aggregate sales at sixteen or seventeen millions.

But one Alger opus sold about as well as another, and if you divide 17,000,000 by 135, it is hard to get much more than 125,000 for a single book; and that is far from enough to make a best seller according to our standards. However, there were a few, such as *Ragged Dick, Luck and Pluck, Tattered Tom,* and *Phil the Fiddler,* which some veteran booksellers think of as leaders; and we venture to place the first-named of this quartette on our list.

Ragged Dick was Alger's first story. Published serially in Oliver Optic's *Student & Schoolmate* and as a book by A. K. Loring, of Boston, in 1867, it was a marked success from the first. Porter & Coates named two series after it, and contemporary writers usually singled it out as Alger's best story. It has more freshness and more value as a depiction of New York street life than most. Dick was a bootblack, and a very enterprising one. He made the most of his chances, and when Mr. Whitney, with whom he had had a fortunate encounter, gave him some good advice, he took it. "I hope, my lad," said Mr. Whitney, "you will prosper and rise in the world. You know in this free country poverty in early life is no bar to a man's advancement." Dick was a bright boy, and every chapter of his history chronicles some new advancement, until finally he saves the little daughter of a rich merchant from drowning and so gets his big chance. At the conclusion we are told:

Here ends the story of Ragged Dick. As Fosdick said, he is Ragged Dick no longer. He has taken a step upward, and is determined to mount still higher. There are fresh adventures in store for him, and for others who have been introduced in these pages. Those who have felt interested in his early life will find his history continued in a new volume to be called—
FAME AND FORTUNE; OR, THE PROGRESS OF RICHARD HUNTER

Thus not only Dick, but Horatio, was launched. The formula was set, and Alger was to use it again and again—about one hundred and thirty times.

When John Habberton sent the manuscript of *Helen's Babies* to publishers in 1875, he was met by the objection that the story was too light for adults and too heavy for children—and also by that most scathing of comments, that making merry with the moral delinquencies of infants was wicked. This book was clearly written for adults; its first draft was indeed prepared for the mother of the two delightful little boys whose antics are there recorded. Mrs. Habberton was ill one day, and separated from the "babies"; but she insisted on being informed of what went on. So her husband became the historian of the children for a day, scribbling hard every moment he could spare from actual attention to the youngsters; and that night he had some ten thousand words

* *Publishers' Weekly,* June 11, 1910.

to read to his wife. She was amused and delighted, and together they plotted publication. Habberton eventually used about half of what he had written that day, added other baby stories he had heard from his friends, and even invented a few.* When the little paper-covered book was finally published by A. K. Loring, in Boston, it bore the richly descriptive title: *Helen's Babies, with Some Account of Their Ways, Innocent, Crafty, Angelic, Impish, Witching, and Repulsive. Also a Partial Record of Their Actions During Ten Days of Their Existence, by Their Latest Victim.* It made a real hit at once. A few years later Hurst in New York and Peterson in Philadelphia were allowed to bring out new cheap editions. After that there were more than a dozen publishers of it, and it remained a popular book through the eighties and nineties. After it went out of copyright in 1932, two or three publishers for the dime-stores took it up. Dated though it is, *Helen's Babies* is still full of charm and chuckles.

Treasure Island was written while its author and his wife were both seriously ill. It was a flat failure as a serial in a boys' paper, and its early sales as a book were slow. It was at first entitled *The Sea-Cook;* but the editor of *Young Folks,* seizing upon the words "Treasure Island" in the opening sentence of the story, made the happy change. The needy Stevenson received only about thirty pounds for the serial; but it was not worth more than that to *Young Folks.* Stevenson did not have the tricks of the serialist: his story had a slow start, and it lacked exciting installment breaks. It was relegated to the back pages of the paper long before its end, and charged up as a dead loss. Luckily, Stevenson used a pen-name, "Captain George North," for the serial instead of the "R.L.S." of his usual signature.

It was more than a year after the serial was finished that Cassell & Company in 1883 published it in book form, paying Stevenson a hundred pounds for it—"a hundred jingling, tingling, gold-minted quid!" he wrote exultantly. The book was greeted with an outburst of praise from critics, but it sold only some five thousand copies in its first twelve months. Roberts Brothers, of Boston, is-sued it early in 1884; within the next ten years it was widely pirated in America and piled up a total in six figures. Its use in schools eventually stimulated sales; and the elaborate M-G-M production of a motion picture version, filmed on Catalina Island, with Jackie Cooper as Jim Hawkins and Wallace Beery as Long John Silver, helped bring the old favorite back to mind. One leading New York publisher has sold over half a million copies of *Treasure Island,* and two others about a quarter of a million apiece. Literally scores of pub-lishers have had it on their lists.

About the same time he was writing *Treasure Island,* Stevenson began the poems later collected in *A Child's Garden of Verses.* Through four or five years of suffering from sciatica, inflammation of the eyes, and hemorrhages from the lungs, he continued to write these sprightly, fanciful pieces that both children

* See Habberton's "My Literary Life," *Lippincott's Magazine,* June, 1886 (vol. XXXVIII, p. 708ff.)

and grownups have loved ever since. Never was there finer example of the triumph of pure spirit over pain and disease than is afforded by R.L.S.—"The sciaticated Bard," as he once signed himself in a letter to Henley. The *Garden* was published in 1885 and was soon popular on both sides of the ocean. Scribners published the first American edition that same year at one dollar. It has since been issued in many formats, from the Blue Books at five cents to the expensive illustrated editions. Rand, McNally & Company, of Chicago, alone has sold a quarter of a million copies of the *Garden*.

A few months later there was published another Stevenson book—by no means a juvenile—which made a more sensational success. *The Strange Case of Dr. Jekyll and Mr. Hyde* had its inception in a dream. Mrs. Stevenson was awakened early one morning by the moans and groans of her husband. She realized he was suffering from a nightmare and awakened him, only to have him exclaim, "Oh, why did you wake me? I was dreaming a fine bogey tale." His publishers had suggested that he write a "shilling shocker" type of story, and now he was sure he had the idea for it in the interrupted dream. He went feverishly to work, and completed the first draft in a few days. But Mrs. Stevenson, who was always his faithful critic, objected that he had covered up the allegory to make a plotted story; so he threw the manuscript into the fire and started all over again.

Longmans issued it in paper covers at a shilling. A favorable review in the *Times* started a brisk demand for it; a sermon based upon it by the Canon of St. Paul's gave it a further boost. Thus in England it was a hit from the beginning. Scribners published the authorized edition in America in cloth at a dollar and in paper at fifty cents, but other firms brought it out immediately at ten to twenty-five cents. It has had a considerable circulation ever since, chiefly at low prices. Concurrently, it has had a great career on stage and screen. Richard Mansfield was the greatest of all Jekyll-and-Hydes in the legitimate theatre. Stock and traveling companies built up the horror elements, and it was standard fare for "ten-twent'-thirt'" melodrama. Three screen versions starred in turn John Barrymore, Fredric March, and Spencer Tracy. It was probably the third of these productions which brought the sale of a recent Pocket Books edition of this perennial thriller to over two hundred thousand.

Let us return to the children's books. In 1884 Cupples, Upham & Company, of Boston, brought out a little translation from the German called *Heidi: Her Years of Wandering and Learning*. It did not sell, and the next year the price was reduced from $2.00 to $1.50. It took several years, and a combination of the author's two books about Heidi into one, to make this charming and sincere story of the little Swiss girl and her companions of the mountainsides well known to American girl readers. Madame Johanna Spyri, daughter of the doctor in a village near Zurich, wife of the town clerk of that city, wrote a score or more of books dealing with child life in Switzerland; but the two that made her internationally famous were *Heidis Lehr- und Wanderjahre* and *Heidi*

Kann Brauchen, Was es Gelernt Hat, both first published in 1881. There have been many American illustrated editions of *Heidi,* and the book still has a steady sale.

Another book that has given pleasure to American children for more than fifty years is *Five Little Peppers and How They Grew.* Harriett Mulford Stone, of Hartford, was thirty-six years old in 1880, when this story of hers ran serially in *Wide Awake,* a monthly juvenile issued by the Boston publishing house of D. Lothrop & Company. Miss Stone used the pen-name "Margaret Sidney," and the next year she changed her real name to Lothrop, having become the bride of the fifty-year-old publisher. In book form, with attractive illustrations, at $1.50, the story of the Pepper children—Polly, Ben, Davie, Joel, and Phronsie —made a great success. Many will yet remember it in square octavo, two columns to the page, bound in board covers with the children all shown in chromolithograph. This was apparently printed directly from the original *Wide Awake* plates and was usually read to tatters. The struggles of the Peppers against poverty, some moderately exciting incidents, and plenty of simple moral teachings, made the story a favorite in hundreds of thousands of families.

Sequels followed—*The Five Little Peppers Midway, The Five Little Peppers Grown Up,* and others—but no other was ever as popular as the first. The Pepper books still sell over the counters of the low-price variety stores.

A serial in another children's magazine scored a resounding success when issued as a book in the mid-eighties; this was *Little Lord Fauntleroy,* by Frances Hodgson Burnett, first given to the world as one of those "continued stories" which kept the young readers of *St. Nicholas* counting the days until the arrival of the beloved magazine each month. Mrs. Burnett was an established author when her young sons persuaded her to write "a book that little boys would like to read." The original of Cedric Errol, the "little lord," was her own son Vivian. Indeed, the illustrations by Reginald Birch, which not only helped to make the book popular but also set a fashion in boys' clothes, were based upon a photograph of Vivian dressed in black velvet knickerbockers, sash, and white collar and cuffs.

Published attractively at two dollars by Scribners in 1886, the story found hosts of readers—among adults as well as among children. The democratic theme, the interesting plot, and the attractive characterization combined to make a strong appeal. Then there was the stimulus of successful dramatic presentation. Mrs. Burnett's stage version was a London success before it was presented in Boston, New York, and Chicago to delighted audiences. Later it was produced in Paris as "Le Petit Lord" and in 1921 it was made into a motion picture with Mary Pickford in the title role.

Very different in nature and in history was another juvenile of the eighties —*Uncle Remus: His Songs and His Sayings.* Shy, diffident, humorous Joel Chandler Harris, a reporter on the *Atlanta Constitution,* wrote some feature material for his paper based on animal fables which he had heard Negroes tell in the days when he had lived, as a boy, on a Georgia plantation. These tales were immediately picked up and reprinted by important papers all over the country, and Uncle Remus, Brer Rabbit, Brer Fox, and the rest were already familiar names to many readers when Appleton brought out a small book made up of the *Constitution* stories. It was illustrated by Frederick S. Church and sold for a dollar and a half. It was welcomed by a good sale, which kept up steadily for a long time. By the end of its first quarter-century the annual distribution had fallen to four thousand, but a new edition with A. B. Frost's inimitable pictures brought sales up again. Appleton later added other editions. Since Harris' notation of Negro dialect is not precisely easy reading, other versions have been made from time to time for the children's own use. These and the abridgments (chiefly taken from the first book) served to swell the total.* Half a dozen important houses put *Uncle Remus* on their lists, in one form or another, as soon as the copyright expired; and it is still a good title from the publishers' point of view.

In 1890 the American Humane Education Society, of Boston, issued a little paper-bound volume with the title *Black Beauty, His Grooms and Companions*. It contained a few illustrations, and sold for twenty cents. The Humane Education Society, sister organization of the Massachusetts Society for the Prevention of Cruelty to Animals, was founded by George T. Angell, reformer and editor of *Our Dumb Animals,* which was the organ of both societies. Angell was a great man; a born crusader, he had courage, tremendous vigor and initiative, and good organizing ability. In no single one of his causes was he more interested than in the fight against men's cruelty to horses; and the only thing that is strange about his adding *Black Beauty* to his society's publications in 1890 is that he had not done it long before.

For this little book, later subtitled *The Autobiography of a Horse,* had been published in England as early as 1877. Anna Sewell belonged to a family well known among Quakers. Her life was filled with misfortunes. Her father failed repeatedly in business, and the family moved from place to place. In childhood, Anna met with an accident to her ankle, which left her a cripple for life in spite of visits to specialists on the continent. Increasing illness kept her confined to her "house and sofa" for the last six or seven years of her life, but through her mother she was brought into touch with many and varied interests. Mrs. Sewell was a remarkable woman—author of many books for the very young (some of them republished in America) and an indefatigable worker among the poor.

It was in the last few years of her life that Anna Sewell wrote *Black Beauty.*

* "Two or three large printings are invariably sold out every year," wrote Grant Overton in *Portrait of a Publisher,* a promotional brochure of 1925. "Large" is an equivocal word in this connection, and the present firm is reticent, to put it mildly, on all such matters; but there can be little doubt that *Uncle Remus* has sold its 500,000 in various forms and editions.

Probably Horace Bushnell's *Essay on Animals* gave her the idea of it. Several years before the writing, a Mrs. Bayly, friend of the Sewells, had spoken to her about the Bushnell book. And incidentally, Mrs. Bayly's account of the end of her visit at the Sewell home should be interesting to all lovers of *Black Beauty*:

The parting came all too soon. In the afternoon it poured with rain. When the carriage that was to take me to the station came to the door, Anna was standing in the hall, enveloped in a large mackintosh. The future writer of *Black Beauty* was to be my driver. I found that she and her mother were in the habit of driving out on most days, without attendance, the understanding between them and their horse being perfect. The persistent rain obliged us to keep up our umbrellas. Anna seemed simply to hold the reins in her hand, trusting to her voice to give all needed directions to her horse. She evidently believed in a horse having a moral nature, if we may judge by her mode of remonstrance. "Now thee shouldn't walk down this hill—don't thee see how it rains?" "Now thee must go a little faster—thee would be sorry for us to be late at the station!"

Anna received twenty pounds for the manuscript of *Black Beauty*. It was thought that her happy excitement over the favorable reviews with which it was greeted hastened her death, which occurred a few months after the publication. When the hearse that was to carry her body to the Friends' burying-ground near Buxton drew up before the house, Mrs. Sewell noticed that the horses hitched to it had their heads drawn high with check-reins; and before the funeral procession moved off to carry the frail body of the world's greatest special pleader for the horse to its final resting place, she ordered that every check-rein in the line should be loosed.

If a Miss Georgianna Kendall, of New York, had not sent Mr. Angell a copy of *Black Beauty*, it is likely enough that the story would have remained a comparatively obscure English bit of propaganda. In the thirteen years since its publication, it had sold less than a hundred thousand copies. Angell had never seen it or heard of it until he received the copy from Miss Kendall about February 1, 1890. As soon as he read it, he proclaimed it "the *Uncle Tom's Cabin* of the horse," called upon all the supporters of the S.P.C.A. for funds to help publish it at a low price, placed an immediate printing order for ten thousand copies, and declared his hope of printing a hundred thousand more "immediately." The first copies went out in March; in two years the Humane Education Society had disposed of 226,000 copies.

Other American publishers seized upon the book, issuing handsomer editions than Angell's, almost always with illustrations. It boomed in England in reaction to its American popularity. Angell had it translated into several foreign languages. The total American sales have sometimes been given as three million, but were probably not much over half that. But a million and a half is a tremendous lot of books. How happy the shy Quaker girl would have been if she could have seen her *Black Beauty* spreading the gospel of kindness in the movies! The total influence of Anna Sewell's book has been tremendous; millions of people have been kinder to horses from having read it.

There have been many popular dog stories. Dr. John Brown's *Rab and His Friends* (1855), though often published separately, is really a short story. Alfred Ollivant's *Bob, Son of Battle* (1898) still sells well. Eric Knight's *Lassie-Come-Home* (1940) is very likely to accumulate, in the next few years, the 1,300,000 necessary to make it a best seller in its decade. The one dog story now on the list is Margaret Marshall Saunders' *Beautiful Joe*, published four years after *Black Beauty's* introduction to the American audience. Joe is mistreated by his first master, so that the early part of the story is rather painful; but he later finds a happier life in a new home. As originally issued by the Judson Press, religious publishers of Philadelphia, the story was a short novelette, but it was later enlarged. The little book has sold steadily for fifty years, and its publishers say that its total now exceeds a million copies.

And now, fifteenthly (if our count is correct) and finally, we must note the popularity of Thomas Bulfinch's *Age of Fable; or, The Beauties of Mythology*. Originally published in London in 1855, it was pirated in the same year by Sanborn, Carter & Bazin, of Boston. It was occasionally reprinted in the ensuing twenty years, but its greatest popularity waited on the edition edited by Edward Everett Hale and published by Lee & Shepard in 1882. More than a score of publishers have issued it, often for as little as twenty-five cents. It was intended for young people, and therefore the sexual misdemeanors of the Greek and Roman deities are handled "delicately." Though it is not a textbook, its comparatively full and extensive treatment has made it useful to students.

XXV. CRUSADERS FOUR

It is a pledge of the destiny appointed for us that the Creator has set in our hearts an infinite standard of achievement, judged by which our past attainments seem always insignificant, and the goal never nearer.
"Looking Backward"

THROUGH 1861 and the first two months of 1862, Parson William G. Brownlow, tall, stern-faced, trumpet-voiced, was a painful thorn in the side of the Confederacy. Though forced to suspend his newspaper in Knoxville, Tennessee, the belligerent editor-parson would not keep his mouth shut or remove the Union flag from his house. He seemed determined to be a martyr to his cause; and when the government at Richmond at last succeeded in arranging to get him through the lines and out of the Confederacy under a flag of truce, Jefferson Davis and his advisers all breathed a great sigh of relief. As for Parson Brownlow, as soon as he reached Union territory and his eyes caught sight of the stars and stripes, he spread his arms wide, lifted his face to heaven, and shouted in resounding tones: "Glory be to God in the highest, on earth peace and goodwill to men, all except a few hell-born and hell-bound rebels down in Knoxville!"

Union soldiers crowded about him, and he began shaking hands with them, praying and crying in good camp-meeting fashion; soon officers appeared, and he introduced himself. They had all heard of him and of his courage and defiance of the Confederacy; they looked upon him as a hero. Soon he was making speeches. Within a week he set out on a grand tour of lectures. He was needed at the great recruiting mass-meetings in the northern cities that summer and fall. His reputation had gone before him; everywhere he was lionized. He became as well known as Lincoln, and more popular.

George W. Childs, enterprising Philadelphia publisher, got the parson's name on the dotted line of a contract for a book about his experiences, in April, 1862, paying him ten thousand dollars in advance for the manuscript. Brownlow settled down in the village of Crosswicks, New Jersey, for a month to write it.

The book turned out to be mainly a compilation of editorials which had appeared in the *Knoxville Whig,* parts of the diary Brownlow had kept while he was confined in the Knoxville jail, and shrill denunciations of his enemies, together with a passionate sermon arguing by history, statistics, and Bible texts that God was on the side of the North. The title of this remarkable book was *Sketches of the Rise, Progress, and Decline of Secession; with a Narrative of Personal Adventures Among the Rebels;* but the backstrip title was *Parson Brownlow's Book,* and by that name it has generally been called. In his preface the author stated that his sufferings had left him "in no mood for the use of softened forms of speech." He continued:

Extreme fastidiousness of taste may, perhaps, shrink with over-sensitiveness from some of the language I have employed. But it is no time for dalliance with polished sentences or enticing words. . . . The traitors merit a sword-thrust style and deserve the strongest epithet I have applied. My persecution by them was such that I have a fair right to handle them roughly: they are not worth any other mode of treatment; and I have written what I have written.

Published in the summer of 1862, *Parson Brownlow's Book* sold a hundred thousand copies in three months. The parson continued with his triumphant speaking tour, chanting his song of hate before roaring audiences in New York, Boston, Philadelphia, and many other cities. The papers were full of the new crusader, pamphlets about him were issued, he was made the hero of a new Beadle dime novel, "The Parson Brownlow Quickstep" set him to music, portraits of "the Apostle of Freedom" found a ready sale.* All of this tremendous personal acclaim made *Parson Brownlow's Book* sell like hot cakes; and it is doubtful whether any other non-fiction best seller, up to this time, had ever had such a large immediate sale. The book continued to sell in the North throughout the ensuing three years of conflict. Today it belongs to the curiosa of those war-fevered times.

* E. Merton Coulter's *William G. Brownlow* (Chapel Hill, 1937) tells the parson's story admirably.

Enthusiast of a more intellectual kind was Henry George. About the time Brownlow was entering upon the last episode of his spectacular career—his service in the United States Senate—George, then thirty years old, was getting established in California journalism. As a youth, he had divided his time between the sea and the type-case. After his marriage, at twenty-two, his struggle against poverty was nothing less than desperate for some years; but after about 1868 he began to find a position for himself in journalism. He continued to develop as a writer, a speaker, and a politician in his adopted state of California.

In 1871 Henry George published an essay on "Our Land and Land Policy" in a little pamphlet of forty-eight pages. This contained the germ of ideas which were later to bring him a world-wide fame, but it was not until the fall of 1877, in the fourth year of the financial depression, that he began to write his *Progress and Poverty*. Finished in about a year, this book was declined by all the publishers to whom it was submitted, and George decided to have it set up and plates made through a printer friend of his. From these plates in September, 1879, he had "something over four hundred copies printed, thinking to sell what I could in order to help pay for the plates." This, then, was the first, or author's edition, of *Progress and Poverty*. D. Appleton & Company decided a month or two later to take the publication over, using George's plates.

The book was issued by Appleton early in 1880 at $2.00—later $1.00 in cloth and 75 cents in paper. It was a success from the start. Five large editions were published within fourteen months. In 1882-83 George made a trip to Ireland as special correspondent of the *Irish World,* of New York, and in the course of his work drew upon himself the suspicion of the British police and was thrown into an Irish jail. He was soon released, but the matter became an international incident and gained the author wide publicity in both the English and the American press. In 1883 he arranged with Appleton to issue a 25-cent edition of his book; it sold rapidly, the first printing of 15,000 being exhausted in less than a week. George's speaking tour of England in the winter of 1883-84 made him even better known in that country than at home, for he drew the fire of the most important men and newspapers of Britain and his book enjoyed a great sale there at low prices.

English interest in American books has always reacted strongly in this country, and it was not long until various American publishers became interested. George, who had retained the copyright from the first, encouraged the widest publication. Lovell's Library issued the book at twenty cents in 1882. Translations were made into German, French, Dutch, Swedish, Danish, Spanish, Russian, Magyar, Hebrew, and Chinese. In this country, *Progress and Poverty* became the bible of all the Land and Labor Clubs which were organized to support the single-tax idea. The Georgist periodicals pushed the sales of the book week in and week out. George himself issued an edition in 1889, and since then some ten publishers have been active in its distribution.

In 1886 Henry George was a successful, though defeated, candidate for mayor of New York. In 1897 he was again a candidate for that office, but died of apoplexy a week before the election. The movement which he had founded was strong enough, however, to continue unabated without his leadership; or, rather, his guidance persisted long after his death. The Duke of Argyll had called him sarcastically, "the prophet of San Francisco"; now his followers bestowed that title upon him in all sincerity.

What was this book that carried a new economic gospel all over the world? Its title was *Progress and Poverty: An Inquiry Into the Cause of Industrial Depressions, and of Increase of Want with Increase of Wealth. The Remedy.* Its chief thesis was that economic rent is robbery. Wealth is the product of labor applied to natural resources; interest is that part of the result of labor paid to capital, but capital is the fruit of labor and not its master; rent is the tax taken from labor and capital by the landholder. Thus labor, capital, and enterprise receive less than their due because of the landholder's levy of tribute. The solution is for the government to take economic rent in its taxes, which would relieve labor and capital of taxation and insure the smooth working of economic laws and make for the equitable division of all wealth. Incidentally, financial depressions, such as that of the seventies, through which the nation had just passed with so much pain and suffering, would disappear when natural resources were regarded as public property. Here, indeed, was presented a panacea for social as well as economic ills.

But this bare and inadequate summary of the thesis of *Progress and Poverty* gives no idea of the persuasiveness and charm of the book. The style is lucid and the arguments well ordered. The whole is pervaded by a sense of the importance of the message—the crusader's veritable Messianic spirit. And this is supported by occasional eloquence and the charm of imaginative language.

In 1929 the Robert Schalkenbach Foundation, of New York, began issuing George's books and has since become their chief publisher. It has printed about a hundred thousand copies of *Progress and Poverty*. The Modern Library and the Classics Club have issued editions in recent years. How many have been sold altogether is difficult to estimate. A British Georgist once claimed a worldwide circulation of 5,000,000. Albert J. Nock's claim of 2,000,000 is more credible. In the United States alone, a conservative estimate of the sale of the book over 64 years would be 700,000 to 800,000.

Our third crusader, like the two already discussed, was a journalist; but in most respects Edward Bellamy was a man of different stripe. Brownlow was a son of strife, and George too was a fighter; but Bellamy was a gentle soul, introspective, retiring. His life was conditioned by a tubercular affliction. After a short service on the *New York Evening Post,* Bellamy became an editorial writer for the *Springfield Union.* After several years of this, he retired from the paper to devote himself to writing fiction. He had written short stories for the *Atlantic Monthly* and other magazines and had published two novels before he wrote his masterpiece, *Looking Backward 2000-1887*. This he began as "a literary fantasy, a fairy tale of social felicity." But he became dissatisfied with this attitude; his long interest in social philosophies suddenly crystallized and determined him to attempt a real contribution to current thinking on economic and social questions. So he rewrote the beginning; "instead of a mere fairy tale of social perfection," he said later, "it became the vehicle of a definite scheme of industrial reorganization."

Julian West, fashionable young Bostonian, after calling on his fiancée, Edith Bartlett, goes home and to bed; but he cannot sleep. He sends for his physician, who hypnotizes him, whereupon he sleeps for 113 years, the doctor having neglected to bring him out of his trance. Awakened, then, in the year 2000, through the good offices of Dr. Leete and his beautiful daughter Edith, he has a wonderful time studying the changes in society, government, and ideas which have taken place while he slept so soundly. America has become a coöperative commonwealth. From twenty-one to forty-five, every person works in the industrial army, at an equal wage, paid not in money but in vouchers which are accepted at the state warehouses. There are horseless carriages, something like radio, and scores of interesting gadgets. Poverty, wealth, crime, even unkindness have disappeared. Julian falls in love with Edith Leete, of course; and is happy when he finds she is a grand-daughter of his nineteenth-century love, Edith Bartlett.

Such is *Looking Backward* in bare outline. Published by Ticknor & Company in 1888, it made a poor showing. Even including a fifty-cent edition in paper covers, it had sold only 35,000 when, early in the next year, it was turned over to Houghton, Mifflin & Company. It is said that a department store which had overstocked threw the whole remainder of its supply of the book into a window with a sign "10¢," and that this produced sales, and the sales new interest, and the new interest reprinting. At any rate, the demand suddenly picked up and swiftly mounted to surprising proportions. Two hundred thousand copies were sold by January, 1890. The book might have saved the faltering house of Ticknor & Company if that firm had kept it a little longer; Houghton, Mifflin ultimately sold well over half a million copies. A recent revival of interest in Bellamy's ideas caused the World Publishing Company to bring out a new edition of 100,000 copies in 1945.

By 1890 the enthusiasm for the socialistic ideas of Bellamy's utopia had blossomed into Nationalist Clubs, Bellamy Societies, and so on. The author, forced out of the semi-retirement which he loved, founded and conducted first the *Nationalist* and then the *New Nation* to advocate the type of coöperative and regimented society described in his book, supporting them by his royalties. He wrote a sequel, *Equality*, which was only moderately successful. In the meantime half a dozen other writers had published answers or supplements, such as A. D. Vinton's *Looking Further Backward*, Richard Michaelis' *Looking Further Forward*, an unknown's *A.D. 2050*, and M. W. Ramsey's *Six Thou-*

sand Years Hence. In 1897, worn out by writing, lecturing, and editing, Bellamy succumbed to the disease from which he had long suffered.*

The last crusader in our present series also met with health difficulties. If William Hope Harvey had not been led to engage in mining in Colorado for his health's sake, it is unlikely that he would ever have become deeply involved in the silver controversy or have written the remarkable little book on that subject which made him famous as "Coin" Harvey, and sold over a million copies.

Born in West Virginia (then part of Virginia) in 1851, Harvey had been admitted to the bar at nineteen and had practiced in his native state and in Cincinnati before he came to Chicago in 1878. He was a moderately successful Chicago lawyer when, in the mid-eighties, he had to give up his sedentary pursuits for more healthful outdoor work. Laboring among the miners of Colorado, he found not only health but a great idea. He became convinced that the free and unlimited coinage of silver at the valuation ratio of sixteen to one would cure the economic ills of the country. When Harvey came back to Chicago after eight years in the Colorado mountains, it was to found the Coin Publishing Company and to begin issuing "Coin's Financial Series." First of these was a pamphlet on bimetallism by Archbishop Walsh, of Dublin; second was *Coin's Hand Book,* a pamphlet compiled by Harvey giving the statistics on which the free silver argument was based; third was *Coin's Financial School,* a book of 152 pages, the publication of which did more than anything else up to that time to focus public attention upon the issue of bimetallism.

It is not easy today to realize what a tremendous interest in the highly technical question of coinage developed among the people of the United States in 1895-96. The suffering caused by hard times and the emotions aroused by bitter labor wars and the hanging of the anarchists doubtless helped to develop a state of mind in which a supposed panacea might enlist fanatical devotion. Free silver was argued wherever men came together; no issue had been so bitterly fought over since the Tilden-Hayes election controversy. The pastor of the First Congregationalist Church in Chicago made a prayer one Sunday morning early in 1895 in which he said: "O Lord, we thank thee that Congress has not issued more paper money than it can redeem; and we especially thank thee, O Lord, that the debased fifty-cent dollar is no longer coined."

Coin's Financial School was a remarkably skillful piece of economic propaganda. To serve as mouthpiece for arguments which were full of mathematics, statistics and close reasoning, Harvey invented a spokesman who was a cross between a Brownie and a university professor. With the help of his artist, H. L. Goodall, Coin was depicted as a spick-and-span little fellow no bigger than a boy, bright-faced, and wearing evening clothes with tight knickerbockers and black silk stockings. This Coin sets up a financial school in Chicago, and

* Arthur E. Morgan's *Edward Bellamy* (New York, 1944) is a comprehensive and enlightening study of the man and his work.

his lectures and blackboard demonstrations are given in full. After he gets well started, all the leaders of Chicago business, journalism, education, industry, and finance flock to his school—bankers like Lyman Gage and John R. Walsh, business men like Phil D. Armour, Potter Palmer, and Marshall Field. These men ask questions which Coin answers easily; they advance arguments which Coin invariably overturns with neatness and dispatch. It is a device, of course, to reply to the stock reasoning of the gold-standard men; and the daring use of these familiar names, as well as the liveliness of Coin's classroom, help to make the book interesting. The pictures are fetching, too—especially the cartoons, big and little, which reduce all of Coin's arguments to the most primitive terms and seem singularly pungent.

A year after the appearance of *Coin's Financial School,* the little book, in editions selling for 25 cents, 50 cents, and $1.00, had reached a circulation of 300,000, and was said to be going at the rate of 5,000 a day. Harvey now issued a sequel, *Coin's Financial School Up to Date,* No. 6 of the Financial Series, which also sold well, especially when bound with the earlier book. The silver excitement mounted. Bryan made the most famous of convention orations, ending, "You shall not crucify mankind upon a cross of gold!" and was nominated to oppose McKinley for the presidency. The campaign was full of pyrotechnics, actual and verbal. Harvey's bright and hard-hitting little book was quoted by a thousand campaigners. The answers to Coin made a considerable literature of their own. When Bryan was defeated, the issue was not dead; but from that time on, the sales of Harvey's books dropped off rather sharply.

In 1900 Harvey went down into the Ozark region of Arkansas, where he financed and built the resort town of Monte Ne, promoted a short-line railroad, and conducted a banking business. He was a busy man. He was associated with Paul's School of Statesmanship, organized the World's Money Educational League, and continued to write books on public questions. He died in 1936. His widow places the sales of *Coin's Financial School* at 1,000,500 in the United States, not including several hundred copies which Harvey distributed free.

Here then are four crusaders—Brownlow, George, Bellamy, Harvey; but this quartette alone does not tell us the whole story of the part that devotion to causes has played in the roll of American best sellers from *Pilgrim's Progress* to *One World.* Immediately there come to mind such other crusade-books as *The Age of Reason, Uncle Tom's Cabin, Ten Nights in a Bar-Room, Black Beauty,* and *In His Steps.* Nor should we forget that long list of best-selling novels with theses, from *Pamela* to *Lost Horizon.*

XXVI. IDEAS IN THE EIGHTIES

The time is wracked with birth-pangs; every hour
Brings forth some gasping truth.
Lines by O. W. Holmes prefaced to "The Heavenly Twins"

FEW decades have been characterized by more turbulent and confusing clashes of ideas in their best sellers than the 1880's. These ten years, to be sure, brought forth less controversial books by Stevenson, Mark Twain, and Conan Doyle; but the distinctive feature of the decade was a procession of intellectually exciting books, such as *Progress and Poverty, Looking Backward,* and *Robert Elsmere.* These three were outstanding; but many others were, if not precisely "intellectual," at least filled with ideas, theses, and a jumble of "notions." Orthodox religion, then under attack both by the atheist Ingersoll and by the social reformers; radical theories of labor and of poverty; curious ideologies in ethics, pseudo-science, women's rights, industry, and so on—the discussion of these matters made a stirring and often amazing decade of popular literature.

Some of the best sellers of the eighties have been discussed already. For the present series, let us begin with *Ben-Hur.*

Immediately upon the successful publication in 1873 of his novel of Aztec life called *The Fair God,* General Lew Wallace began to make some studies for a story of the time of Christ. Within the next two or three years he wrote a narrative of the wise men, the star, and the Babe at Bethlehem, intending it for publication in some periodical as a short serial. But before he submitted it to an editor, an incident occurred which caused the author to change his plans.*

While making a journey by railroad, Wallace happened to encounter Robert G. Ingersoll and to get into an extended discussion with that famous freethinker on the question of the divinity of Christ. Now singularly enough, Wallace had, up to this time, given little or no attention to personal religion. War, literature, and the law had been his three divinities. "The preachers had made no impression upon me," he wrote later; and to the end of his life he never belonged to any church. But now, stirred by Ingersoll's brilliant but shocking talk, he determined to make an independent study of the life of Christ, "if only for the gratification there might be in having convictions of one kind or another." And bethinking himself of the manuscript in his desk, he began to wonder if the best way to consider and investigate the Christ would not be to write a novel about His times, with all the research such a task would entail.

Wallace did not make a journey to the Holy Land a part of his preparation for writing *Ben-Hur.* He revisited Mexico just before he wrote *The Fair God,*

* Wallace's article, "How I Came to Write *Ben-Hur*" in the *Youth's Companion* for February 2, 1893, reprinted in the *Autobiography,* is our best authority; but it should be supplemented by J. Henry Harper's *The House of Harper* (New York, 1912), pp. 267-70.

but he spent the years devoted to *Ben-Hur* in the study of books of history and religion. When, many years later, he followed the footsteps of his hero from Bethany to Jerusalem, he found that his authorities had guided him well. "I find no reason for making a single change in the text of the book," he wrote. Moreover, the library of works that he read led him steadily toward personal religious convictions; and long before his own book was finished he became a firm believer in the divinity of Christ.

Wallace gave up the practice of the law in 1878 in order to devote all his time to *Ben-Hur,* most of which was written at his Crawfordsville, Indiana, home. He was appointed governor of the territory of New Mexico, however, in 1879, and wrote the final section, or "book," at Santa Fe. Harpers accepted the manuscript at once, though George Ripley, then chief literary adviser to the firm, declared he would not have favored its publication had not Wallace already possessed a reputation as a successful novelist. Ripley thought the book too bold and melodramatic; but could the house turn down a manuscript by the author of *The Fair God,* which had made such a success? * It could not, and *Ben-Hur* was published late in 1880.

The book got off to a slow start. Novels that do not show promising sales within a year are usually foredoomed; most of such failures are dead beyond resuscitation by that time. *Ben-Hur* dragged along discouragingly for a second year; then it began to pick up. Its reviews had been good; but long historical novels were out of vogue, and besides, this book was published at a regular $1.50 price and through the booksellers at a time when most of the big sales were being reached by cheap publication in paper covers or by the subscription method. But by its third year enough enthusiastic readers were recommending *Ben-Hur* to other readers who were soon to be its ardent advocates to still another circle, to give the book a steady momentum which carried it along through forty years of extraordinary success. Midway of its sixth year it reached 90,000, in its seventh year 200,000, and in its eighth year 290,000. † The course which this great best seller ran was not like that of its hero against Messala in the famous chariot race—not seven furious rounds of the circus—but a long, sustained achievement.

The Sunday School library movement was doubtless an aid. The spectacular dramatization by Klaw & Erlanger, an immense success for many years after its first production in 1889, helped maintain interest: it was melodrama, religious observance, and circus in one. Its chariot race, with plunging horses on a treadmill track, was a great thriller; and people traveled many miles to the cities where the exhibitions were held. It was a great national spectacle over two decades or more.

---

* It eventually sold 150,000 copies, according to Wallace.

† See New York *Journalist,* May 22, 1886; *Literary News,* vol. IX, p. 126 (April, 1888); Appleton's *Cyclopaedia of American Biography* (New York, 1889), art. "Wallace, Lew."

In 1913 *Ben-Hur* had been in print for a third of a century and was on the verge of a sale of a million copies; in that year Henry Hoyns, of Harpers, sold to Sears, Roebuck & Company in one order one million copies of the book—the greatest book-order in publishing history. *Ben-Hur* has since been distributed largely by this mail-order concern and by Grosset & Dunlap, leading publishers of reprint books.

Nor was the book's success limited to America: it was widely pirated in England, and it was translated into all the European languages and into Arabic. The great screen version of 1926, produced at a reputed cost of four million dollars, was by no means the long-continued success of the great Klaw & Erlanger show, but it did stimulate once more the popularity of the famous story. Ramon Novarro was a satisfactory Ben-Hur, and the picture was "an orgy of huge sets and seething mobs." It had what R. E. Sherwood, writing in *Life,* described as "undoubtedly the most terrific chariot race in history." He continued:

Ben-Hur and Messala have been arguing it out in the Circus Maximus for a matter of forty-five years now, and Messala has been beaten every time; but for all that the old thrill is still there. . . . For some strange reason there is always the vague fear in the heart of every spectator that Messala may win. The fact that the villain's batting average, to date, is exactly .000 has no effect on his big-league standing.

Altogether, *Ben-Hur* has sold about 2,600,000 copies in the United States, and ranks among the top half-dozen best sellers by American authors.

Another classic with a strong religious element which became an American best seller in the mid-eighties was Ludovic Halévy's *L'Abbé Constantin.* In many respects, however, this little book is as different as possible from General Wallace's great historical romance. It is only about 40,000 words in length; it is simple and rural—a modern French idyll; it is thoroughly Catholic.

Up to the time of the publication of *L'Abbé Constantin,* its author had devoted himself to writing for the stage. In a long collaboration with Henri Meilhac, Halévy had produced librettos for many famous operas, both light and tragic, ranging from Offenbach's "La Belle Hélène" to Bizet's "Carmen." With Meilhac, too, he had written such popular plays as "Frou-Frou" and "Tricoche et Cacolet." *Constantin,* his first novel, was an immediate success upon its publication as a newspaper feuilleton and book in 1882; it won him an appointment to the French Academy, and it maintained its popularity for a long time.

Anti-Catholicism had been a factor in many earlier American best sellers; we now come at last to the first of our list which has a strong pro-Catholic thesis. Undoubtedly, however, the element that made *L'Abbé Constantin* immediately popular in this country was its pleasant, not to say flattering, treatment of two Americans who have leading rôles in the story. The good Abbé is in despair because, upon the death of the Marchioness de Longueval, patroness of his little church and benefactress of his poor, the great Longueval estate had been sold—and to a rich American, doubtless a heathen or a Protestant. The story then tells of the delight of the priest and his people when the Americans turn out to be as charming and churchly as they are wealthy, and of the love of the abbé's nephew for the sister of the new patroness. The artless, simple-hearted, fairy-story quality of the tale has charmed readers for more than sixty years.

L'Abbé Constantin was immediately seized upon by the cheap American "libraries." The Seaside and Lovell's brought it out at once at ten and twenty cents respectively. Putnams also published it in paper covers, but at sixty cents; and both Lovell and Putnam issued cloth editions at a dollar. All this was in 1882. The next year other publishers issued the novelette, and the Putnams reduced their paper-bound edition to twenty cents. Since then scores of editions, cheap and expensive, have been published. In 1888 Dodd, Mead & Company brought out a de luxe edition in large quarto at $15, and J. W. Bouton, New York, brought it out in sumptuous format at $17.50. It became a favorite in the schools, and a score of class-room editions were provided.

And so Halévy, once famed as a contriver of naughty situations for French comedies, is today remembered chiefly as the author of a simple religious idyll.

Americans, traditionally sensitive on the point of what the rest of the world thought about them, have often been eager to read books on that subject. In the eighties they made best sellers out of *Little Lord Fauntleroy*, *L'Abbé Constantin*, and *Mr. Barnes of New York*. What a diversity among these three! But of them all, the strange and eccentric book, the freak, the curiosity, was Archibald Clavering Gunter's *Mr. Barnes of New York*.

Gunter, born in Liverpool, was reared in California and became a civil engineer on the Central Pacific and then a chemist connected with various mining concerns. Later he was a successful broker in San Francisco. In 1879 he removed to New York, continuing in the brokerage/business; but he had already begun writing plays. One of these was successful—"Prince Karl," in which Richard Mansfield made his first hit. In the mid-eighties Gunter wrote his first and most famous novel.

Its hero, Mr. Barnes, was a rich, clever, self-assured American who was traveling in Europe when he was led, through his interest in a pretty girl, into the very midst of a Corsican vendetta. It all begins with a duel, in which Barnes demonstrates that he is a crack shot as well as a good surgeon. It continues with a love affair, in which he demonstrates that he has a way with the ladies. It works rapidly into an international complication, involving English, French, and Italians, in which the resourceful Barnes more than holds his own, cleans up the vendetta, and carries off his girl. If you like action, some primitive passion, and a smart hero, and if you do not mind a schoolboyish style of writing, you may find this very entertaining. A great many readers did.

But after all, the episodes were what is today known as "corny," and the writing was lamentable. For example, Gunter was apparently so impressed with the vividness of the historical present that he almost never used the past tense. A sample seems necessary. Marina, a few hours after she has been wedded to her Englishman, is convinced by Tomasso that her husband is the man against whom they have both sworn the vendetta. Take it away:

> She lowers her stiletto.
>
> Her face and her actions make Tomasso suspicious; he screams to her, "Remember your oath!"
>
> "Yes! The one I swore at the altar to-day! *To be his wife!*" is her answering cry.
>
> "But I remember my *vendetta!*" he hisses, advancing to take the dagger from her.
>
> Then she turns upon him with flashing eyes, and standing, her back to the curtains, cries, "Away! you who would have tempted me to eternal infamy and remorse!"
>
> "You will not kill?"
>
> "My husband?—As soon assassinate my God!"
>
> "Then I will do it for you!—I hear him coming—Give me the stiletto!" whispers Tomasso, about to seize the weapon.
>
> But Marina, her eyes filled with dauntless resolution, cries, "Back! or I kill *you!* He is my husband! Against you; against the world; against my vow; *him! I defend!*" and uplifting the dagger stands nerved to strike this human panther as he comes toward her.

When Gunter sent this child of his fancy out among the publishers, it was unanimously rejected. Cassell & Company, to be sure, would have published it if they had been able to persuade Gunter to omit certain lines. Cassell's New York branch had just been rebuked by the parent house in London for publishing inelegant Americanisms in another book, and was therefore insistent on the deletion of "certain unnecessary lines" in *Mr. Barnes;* Gunter was offended, withdrew the manuscript, and went on trying the other publishers. Finally he arranged with Deshler, Welch & Company to issue the book in March, 1887, at fifty cents in paper and a dollar in cloth, at author's expense. It was popular as "hammock reading" that summer, and began to sell well on trains and boats. Soon it caught on, became "all the rage." A traveler reported in *Current Literature* for July, 1888: "From San Francisco to Paris and from Paris back to New York, I saw nothing but *Barnes of New York.* . . . Foreigners persist in regarding it as 'the great American novel.'"

Now, Archibald Clavering Gunter, as a matter of plain fact, was a better business man than writer. His portraits show him wide-faced, wearing the heavy mustache of the period, and with an impressive "corporation"—more the broker than the man of letters. At any rate, Gunter proceeded to organize a publishing concern solely for the production of his own work. Mrs. Gunter became manager of the firm, which was called the Home Publishing Company, while her husband devoted himself to writing two novels a year to feed the production line. Thus *Mr. Potter of Texas, Baron Montez of Panama,* and many others—thirty-nine in all—were issued in the remaining twenty years of Mr. Gunter's life. They were advertised as "the most successful novels ever published." As public taste appeared to veer, Gunter books veered with it, and all types of novels went into the long series; but none was ever quite as popular as the first.

Figures on the sales of *Mr. Barnes of New York* are not now available. Fantastic rumors of its enormous distribution, probably encouraged as good promotion by the Gunters, were common. The Home Publishing Company sold to Hurst & Company, and perhaps other such firms, the right to issue cheap reprints. The book was pirated in England, and immediately imitated by dozens of clever American writers. The title created a vogue for *Mr.'s* and *Misses* of *This* and *That*. Of these perhaps H. B. Milman's *Mr. Lake of Chicago* (Street & Smith) was the most successful; but it remained for Gunter himself to top all these title efforts with his *Miss Nobody of Nowhere*. It is probable that *Mr. Barnes of New York* was the only one of Gunter's productions to reach a sale of half a million, though *Mr. Potter* may have come close to that figure.*

Another book of melodramatic adventure published in the same year with *Mr. Barnes of New York* was H. Rider Haggard's *She*. The Englishman's romance was somewhat better written than the American's, but the success of both was clearly due to their absorbing and vivid narrative. *Mr. Barnes* did not pretend to have any ideas except that of American superiority in everything; but *She* boasted a good many of them, mostly false. Certainly the central thesis—that a person who lives for hundreds of years among ordinary mortals, and in full possession of his powers, must surely become very wise and very powerful—is nonsense. Incidentally, Ayesha's own consistent follies contradict the thesis. But most of the readers of *She* had the feeling that they were gleaning some facts from the fields of archeology, ethnology, geography, and ethics; whereas the "facts" were quite as romantic as the story. And it was all embellished with such passages as this:

Above me, as I lay, shone the eternal stars, and there at my feet the impish marsh-born balls of fire rolled this way and that, vapor-tossed and earth-desiring, and methought that in the two I saw a type and image of what man is, and what perchance man may one day be, if the living Force that ordained him and them should so ordain this also. Oh, that it might be ours to rest year by year upon that high level of the heart to which at times we momentarily attain! Oh, that we could shake loose the prisoned pinions of the soul and soar to that superior point whence, like to some traveler looking out through space from Darien's giddiest peak, we might gaze with the spirit eyes of noble thoughts deep into Infinity!

Sunsets also inspired Haggard to purple composition, and Ayesha talks for pages in blank verse of a hollow, resounding kind. But obviously, the pretensions of *She* must not lead us to regard it as a serious book. It must be read for its romantic narrative vigor or not at all.

King Solomon's Mines is more satisfying because it was designed and written as a boys' story, without any philosophical nonsense. The author had lived for some years in Africa, in the British colonial service; and, like most of his

* An apparently informed writer in the *Author*, W. H. Wills, stated in 1889 that *Mr. Barnes* had sold 180,000 copies in its first two years, and *Mr. Potter* 140,000 in about fifteen months (quoted in *Journalist,* June 22, 1889). Since *Mr. Barnes* continued to be issued by both Home and Hurst for many years and its large sales are often mentioned in the press, it seems safe to credit it with half a million. The statements in the sketch of Gunter in the *Dictionary of American Biography* regarding the success of *Mr. Barnes* seem to the present writer to be greatly exaggerated.

heroes, he had been a traveler and a sportsman. In his old age he performed services for English and colonial agriculture for which he was knighted.

She was published in the United States very early in 1887, by Harper & Brothers, who sent the author ten pounds as a kind of honorarium. Most of the cheap "libraries" immediately issued it in their piratical fashion, at least ten editions (most of them priced at twenty or twenty-five cents) being published during 1887. Catch-penny writers hastened to bring out parodies and echoes. In its issue for April 30, the New York *Journalist* observed: "A host of imitators has sprung up, like toadstools, in a single night. *He, It, Me, Her* are on the news stands in gaudy covers." The next winter a dramatization by William Gillette was produced with great success at Niblo's Garden in New York. This was long popular. Almost forty years later a motion picture version starring Betty Blythe renewed public interest in the old favorite, and was the occasion for a new Grosset & Dunlap edition. But it was the old cheap "libraries" that brought *She* a circulation of more than a million in the United States. Wrote a rhymester in *Clips* in 1896:

> Where is there man who has not been staggered
> by the great *She*-demon of Rider Haggard?

King Solomon's Mines, published only a few months before *She,* had almost the same publishing history and sold (if we can trust the figures it is possible to gather at this time) almost as well. *Allan Quatermain* and other Haggard adventure books also were popular in America.

If the Ideas of the eighties (with a capital I) are noticeable in Haggard's masterpiece, they hit the reader like a ton of bricks in Marie Corelli's novels. Miss Corelli's first novel, *A Romance of Two Worlds,* was an extraordinary mystical farrago of spiritualism, pseudo-science, mesmerism, social reform, evangelistic religion, angelology, amateur psychology, cosmogony, and physical therapy. Its enormous popularity in this country can be explained only by the fact that great numbers of readers were much interested in all or most of these subjects and ill informed upon them. To this must be added the same kind of interest that made *She* such a favorite—the perennial popular appeal of that outrageously bold imagination which makes mystical melodrama. For the narrator of *Two Worlds* is, by the labors of a great master and sage named Heliobas, lifted up far above the world and shown the mysteries of life here and hereafter, the beings of the air, the meaning of existence, and, especially, the secret of the Electric Ring, which is later elaborated with care in the document, "The Electrical Principle of Christianity."

Mary Mackay, daughter of the poet and journalist Charles Mackay, took the name Marie Corelli when she entered upon a London musical career. She long maintained the fiction of Italian birth and of a kind of isolated individualism, but she was English-born and had family and friends. She was a talented improviser on the piano, as was the heroine-narrator of *A Romance of Two Worlds.* Indeed, her own story of the writing of that novel shows that she thought of it all as happening to herself; and certainly many of her readers believed that she had actually had the "experience" therein narrated.

But it was Marie Corelli's second novel, *Thelma,* which made her one of England's leading writers of fiction. This work does not carry such a heavy freight of half-baked ideas as *Two Worlds,* and its story value is higher. *Thelma* is really two novels. Book I, "The Land of the Midnight Sun," tells how a rich young baronet discovers and woos the daughter of a descendant of Viking kings among her native fjords; it drives home the thesis that not only were the old-timers greatly superior to a degenerate posterity, but the old Norse religion of Thelma's father compares pretty favorably with modern churchly corruption. Part II, "The Land of Mockery," tells how Sir Philip brought his lady back to England; it emphasizes the immorality and vacuity of English social life, which drive Thelma back in flight to her former home. This is really a sequel to the rounded, romantic story of Part I. The two are tied together, however, by a brief Part III, in which we have the lurid description of the old Viking's flaming death, and the reconciliation of Philip and Thelma.

It was *Thelma* which won Marie Corelli her American as well as her English public. Issued in 1887 by M. J. Ivers & Company, of New York, as an "extra" in their American Series, it did well enough to suggest the similar publication the next year of *A Romance of Two Worlds.* Soon other cheap "libraries" picked up both novels, as well as the other Corelli books written before the international copyright agreement of 1891. Throughout the nineties *Thelma, Two Worlds,* and *Ardath* had a great run. In England *The Sorrows of Satan* (1895) was Miss Corelli's most popular book, breaking all publishing records for a new novel. That was at least partly because its publishers issued it in a single volume instead of the customary three, so the English people could afford to buy it instead of borrowing it from the circulating libraries; but it was also because of the sensationalism of a story in which Lucifer was the tragic hero and the authoress a heroine. But in America *The Sorrows of Satan* never approached the record made by the first two Corelli romances. *Thelma* was issued by a score of publishers for two decades, and by some much longer. It was sold by Street & Smith at ten cents (and so was *Two Worlds*) up to about 1930, but it was also issued in fine bindings. And finally, thousands of mothers paid their sincere tribute of affection to the story by naming their baby girls after the Norwegian princess.

In her will, Marie Corelli provided that her estate at Stratford-on-Avon, purchased with the almost fabulous royalties she had received from her books, should be kept as a literary shrine, neighboring, as it did, with that of an admittedly greater writer, and that future royalties, as they were paid over, should go to maintain the home of the author of *Thelma* for future generations of English and American readers to visit. In 1943, royalties having fallen to a figure insufficient for such maintenance, the place was put up at auction. Sic transit.

For two decades after the Queen's Jubilee year of 1887, the two leading woman novelists of England were Marie Corelli and Mrs. Humphry Ward. It was a curious juxtaposition, for Miss Corelli's mind was disorderly and her talent undisciplined in comparison with Mrs. Ward's keen and calm intelligence.

Mrs. Ward was a granddaughter of Dr. Arnold of Rugby, a niece of Matthew Arnold, the wife of a famous scholar and anthologist. Her intimate association with Oxford from childhood did much to form her mind and character. The germ of *Robert Elsmere* was a little pamphlet which Mrs. Ward wrote in reply to a Brampton lecture at Oxford, though several years and much study intervened between the two: the point is that Oxonian religious controversy was at the root of this most important fictional contribution to the current movement to change the emphasis in religion from forms and supernaturalism to Christian ethics and social reform.

Perhaps this gives the impression that *Robert Elsmere* was stuffy. Certainly its readers did not find it so. Its genre pictures of English country life seemed equal to those of George Eliot or Mrs. Gaskell, its discussions of religion were vital as a part of a sincere and passionate current controversy, and the story of Robert and Catherine was stirring and impressive. The book was an immediate success upon its English publication in three volumes in 1888. In that year it was reprinted by the Macmillan Company in New York in three editions ranging in price from three dollars to fifty cents, and by the pirating "libraries" at twenty cents to a dollar and a quarter. At least nine American editions were brought out that year, and several in the years immediately following. In her autobiography, Mrs. Ward estimates the American sales "from the data I have" at half a million for the first year only.

Robert Elsmere was one of the great controversial books of its times. In pulpit and press, on the street and in drawing rooms, the questions raised by Robert's career were debated from all points of view. Gladstone's famous discussion of the book in the *Nineteenth Century* furnished a rallying point for the antis, but the sales went on and up. William Gillette dramatized the story as a problem play. Oliver Wendell Holmes wrote Mrs. Ward that her book was "beyond question, the most effective and popular novel we have had since *Uncle Tom's Cabin*." Another observer, identified only as "an American man of letters," wrote:

No book since *Uncle Tom's Cabin* has had so sudden and wide a diffusion among all classes of readers, and I believe that no other book of equal seriousness ever had so quick a hearing. I have seen it in the hands of nursery-maids and of shopgirls behind the counters; of frivolous young women who read every novel that is talked about; of business men, professors, and students. . . . The proprietors of those large shops where anything —from a pin to a piano—can be bought, vie with each other in selling the cheapest edition. One pirate put his price even so low as four cents—two pence! *

* Mrs. Humphry Ward, *A Writer's Recollections* (New York, 1918), vol. II, p. 91.

George P. Brett once told of a firm which did not ask even four cents for the book, but gave it away as a premium with a bar of washing soap—no doubt with the conviction that godliness should be next to cleanliness.

It seems fairly safe to say that the book sold a million copies in the United States. Mr. Brett put the figure at "upwards of a million." * Its big sales continued for only two or three years, after which it settled down in the lists of the cheap "libraries" to enjoy a diminishing but considerable sale for nearly a decade. Thus its publishing history was the opposite of that of the slow-starting, long-prosperous, full-priced *Ben-Hur,* which many people considered an antidote for Mrs. Ward's "free-thinking."

Some of Mrs. Ward's later novels, published after international copyright, had big sales in America, such as *The History of David Grieve* (1892) and *The Marriage of William Ashe* (1905), but none of them reached half a million. Meantime Mrs. Ward was active in public affairs, worked in London "settlements," founded the English Anti-Suffrage League, and devoted herself to war work in the World War of 1914-18. She died in 1920.

The chief woman's rights novel of the period was *The Heavenly Twins,* by Mrs. Frances Elizabeth (Clarke) McFall, who wrote under the name of Sarah Grand. This was more like Marie Corelli's work than Mrs. Ward's—ill constructed, crammed with ideas and opinions and prejudices, and often overwritten. The stories of the twins (*enfants terribles*) are less important than that of the marriage of the heroine, Evadne. Here the thesis is the evil of sacrificing a fine young girl by marrying her to a rake, reformed or otherwise. If Mrs. McFall had made three novels out of her material, at least one of them would doubtless have been more satisfying to the critic, though what the result as to great sales might have been, none can guess.

In some respects the book was shocking to the sensibilities of the time. Plain talk about syphilis was taboo. When Harry Thurston Peck tried to talk to women's clubs about the problems raised by the author in unvarnished terms, he was rebuffed. "They simply froze me alive," he reported. "The woman's movement will never get along very far until women get down off the high horse and become rational in such matters."

Mrs. McFall had sent her manuscript to most of the London publishers without success, and finally decided to publish it herself. After it was in printed sheets, however, Heinemann took it over and issued it in 1893 in the old three-decker form at a guinea and a half. Cassell & Company, New York, had no hesitation in accepting the book for American publication; they expected the disapproval of the parent house in London but remembered how deference to such conservatism had cost them a best seller in *Mr. Barnes of New York,* and went ahead on their own. The book proved an immediate success on both sides of the Atlantic; but, published by Cassell at one dollar.

* *Outlook,* vol. LXXVI, p. 514 (February 27, 1904).

it sold at least five times as many copies in the United States as in England the first year. "Just now *everybody* is reading *The Heavenly Twins*," wrote a commentator in *Munsey's Magazine* in October, 1893. It continued to be a highly popular book for many years. In 1901, Street & Smith, having bought the plates from Cassell, brought out a new edition at twenty cents, giving the book a new lease on life.

Mme. Sarah Grand, as she preferred to be called, wrote other books, but none highly successful. She was a pioneer British suffragette, she served the city of Bath as its Mayoress for six terms, and she died in 1943 at the age of eighty-eight.

Another English writer who made a considerable sensation in the American reading world in the late eighties and the nineties was Hall Caine. It was *The Deemster*, published in this country by Appleton in 1888 at fifty cents and immediately pirated by three or four other publishers, which introduced this melodramatic and often powerful writer to an audience which was destined to increase both in size and loyalty for the next decade or two. *The Deemster* was one of those full-bodied, earnest, sombre, highly-colored novels for which Hall Caine became famous. Like its successors, it dealt much with the church and its problems, for Caine was deeply religious and fond of biblical themes. His close friend Rossetti had suggested that he use the Isle of Man, where he had spent his boyhood, as a setting for fiction; and this he did in *The Deemster*, *The Bondman*, and *The Manxman*.

Though *The Manxman* was fourth on the *Bookman's* list of 1895 best sellers and *The Christian* sixth on that of 1897, *The Deemster* was the only Caine novel to reach the over-all best seller list. The reason is clear: the absence of copyright restrictions made numberless cheap editions of the earlier works possible. Caine himself wrote: "Fifty-one editions of the novel have been published in England, about one hundred (chiefly unauthorized), in America (where it was refused by the Harpers), and nine or ten in foreign countries." * *The Bondman* was also published before international copyright restrictions went into effect and was reprinted by several American publishers, but it never won the popularity which fell to the lot of *The Deemster*. Caine himself was a good promoter of his own work, and his critics were wont to call him "The Boomster."

It remains to say something of the vogue of Tolstoi in these years. Though Scribners had published a translation of *The Cossacks* in 1878, and Crowell had brought out *My Religion* in 1885, it was not until *War and Peace* created a furore in Paris upon its publication there that Tolstoi really became known in western Europe and America. In September, 1885, Auguste Laugel told of this book and the French interest in it in his Paris letter in the *Nation*; early the next year, the first section of an English translation of the French version ap-

* *New York Times Book Review and Magazine*, August 21, 1921, p. 17.

peared in New York in two editions—one by William S. Gottsberger, which was completed in six volumes at $5.25 in cloth and $3 in paper; and one by the Harpers in three numbers of the Franklin Square Library at 20 cents each. This was just twenty years after the first volume of *War and Peace* was published in Russia.

Crowell brought out *Anna Karenina* that same year, and the Dole translation of *War and Peace* a few years later. There can be little doubt that the former was somewhat the more popular in the United States for the next two decades or more. During that time Tolstoi gained a remarkable following in this country through his religious and social theories as well as by his literary genius. At the time of the world-wide celebration of his eightieth birthday in 1908, American periodicals were full of evaluations of his work; and there were many to hail him as the greatest of living writers. Upon his death two years later, there were even greater outpourings from admirers and critics. Again in 1928, when the Soviets celebrated the centenary of Tolstoi's birth, there was a renewal of interest.

By this time *War and Peace,* generally regarded as its author's masterpiece and by not a few as the world's greatest novel, was showing remarkable strength for a book which had been on the American market for forty years and had received little if any help from the schools or the movies. It was, for example, one of the Modern Library's best sellers. When Hitler's armies invaded Russia, there was a sudden wave of interest in a book which told more vividly than any other how Napoleon had failed in a similar attempt; and Simon & Schuster published a handsome edition of *War and Peace* with an introduction by Clifton Fadiman pointing the Hitler-Napoleon analogy. Thus this great novel, with its epic sweep, its vivid narrative, and its new meaning for successive generations, continues to be bought and read. It is an active title on the lists of half a dozen publishers today.

XXVII. LITERARY FEVERS OF THE NINETIES

> When the Rudyards cease from kipling
> And the Haggards ride no more.
>
> *J. K. Stephen, 1895*

The intellectual and spiritual climate of the early nineties was well adapted to literary fevers. Enthusiasms for certain books and authors gathered force suddenly and spread widely through the country, with all the exaggerations and the delirium of eulogy that follow upon such epidemics.

Various factors made the rapid spread of literary ardors possible in the nineties. The growth of compulsory-attendance schooling and the great increase of high schools, as well as a steady rise in college enrollment, had helped to make a more literate American public. The acceleration of the library movement, with Andrew Carnegie's help, was increasing readership.

In addition to these educational movements, and to some extent a result of them, was the wide-spread fashion of organizing seekers after culture. This vogue doubtless had its comic aspects. Mrs. Wharton began one of her most famous short stories with a satirical description of her heroine: "Mrs. Ballinger is one of the ladies who pursue Culture in bands, as though it were dangerous to meet alone." But these clubs were important in the development of our American reading public. Many independent clubs had studied art and literature more or less seriously, and on the eve of the nineties the General Federation of Women's Clubs had been organized. The gentlemen joined the ladies in the Chautauqua Literary and Scientific Circle, which had a hundred thousand members by 1892. Individual authors and books had clubs dedicated to them: such were the Browning clubs; the Omar societies; the Land and Labor Clubs, devoted to the propagation of the ideas of Henry George's *Progress and Poverty;* and the Nationalist Clubs and Bellamy Societies, inspired by *Looking Backward.*

These various factors operated on what may be called the "demand" side of the mass distribution of books; on the "supply" side we have the great cheap-publishing business of the twenty years ending in the mid-nineties, supported before July, 1891, by the absence of an international copyright agreement. This movement had given the middle classes a first lesson in the pleasure of owning books, poorly printed and bound though they usually were. It had brought millions of books into American homes. Though the flood of cheap series subsided in the early nineties, low-priced books by no means disappeared; and they continued an important influence in the publishing business.

To this proposition that schools, libraries, clubs, and cheap publishing had created an American reading public which could be swayed by literary enthusiasms on a national scale, one must add two corollaries. First, though these fevers may seem to have spread swiftly, they bear no comparison in that respect with the quick-acting book developments which were to come later. The clubs were conservative, and a book which might sweep the East in a season would require a year or two more to reach its peak in the Middle West. Second, best sellers did not all come up through the clubs or the libraries. The growth of various reading publics in the eighties has already been mentioned; as the century drew to a close, multiple best-seller publics became more noticeable and significant.

Rudyard Kipling was the object of one of the great literary "crazes" of the nineties. He was a young Anglo-Indian journalist of twenty-three, almost unknown in this country, when he landed in San Francisco in 1889. He made the grand tour through the West, swept on to Chicago, visited a Pennsylvania village, and called on Mark Twain at Elmira, New York. He kept his eyes and ears, and (to a certain extent) his mind open; and he sent lively, brash, rapid-fire letters back to the *Allahabad Pioneer* in India. These letters were clipped out of the *Pioneer* a couple of years later, after their author had developed his first popularity in the United States, and issued by piratical publishers as *American Notes*. The title, the free and easy criticism,* and the smarting American reception of the book remind us inevitably of the Dickens travelogue of half a century before.

Kipling tried to sell some of his literary wares in San Francisco and New York, but he had no success. He felt his rebuff by Harper & Brothers most keenly, for they kept close touch with English literary movements and he had recently made a sensation in London. That was, indeed, the chief reason he was going "home."

A few months later the English Kipling "craze" did reach America, like a gale blowing across the Atlantic. American cheap publishers began issuing Kipling in twenty and twenty-five cent paper-covered editions right and left. There were authorized editions by John W. Lovell's United States Book Company, but the American editions of the early Kipling books were mainly piracies. *Barrack-Room Ballads* (with *Departmental Ditties*), *Plain Tales From the Hills, Soldiers Three, The Story of the Gadsbys, Mine Own People,* and collections under other titles, such as *Indian Tales,* were added in 1890 to the lists of the "libraries" and "series" issuing cheap and popular books. By the fall of 1890, about a year after the young author's unsuccessful visit to their office, Harpers put a Kipling collection to press; bound in blue paper covers, it contained six stories recently published in English magazines. Kipling shouted "Piracy!" but Harpers explained that they had bought serial rights of all the stories but one, and for it they tendered a ten-pound payment. When their money was indignantly rejected, they substituted another story which had been bought for *Harper's Weekly*.

Lippincott's Magazine bought Kipling's first novel, *The Light That Failed,* for two hundred pounds and published it in its number for January, 1891. This was in the years when a full-length novel was the monthly feature of *Lippincott's*. This and ten other Kipling books were available to the pirates before the international copyright agreement went into effect on July 1, 1891. Though later works, such as the *Jungle Books, The Day's Work, Captains Courageous, Kim,* and certain of the later poems fed the Kipling vogue in America, none of them reached the best seller figure; in the top list we have only *Barrack-Room Ballads, Plain Tales From the Hills, Mine Own People,* and *The Light That Failed*.

Here is an interesting example of the purely commercial factor in the creation of best sellers. In a competition not affected by copyright restrictions, surely *Captains Courageous* would have forged well ahead of *The Light That*

---

* Yet Kipling liked the Americans: "Let there be no misunderstanding about the matter. I love this People, and if any contemptuous criticism has to be done, I will do it myself. My heart has gone out to them beyond all other peoples . . ."

Failed in total sales. It did add to Kipling's fame in America by its serial publication in *McClure's*, its circulation in its regular edition, and (much later) its movie version, accompanied by a cheaper reprint; but it never caught up with the runaway sales of *The Light That Failed*, the first long story of a popular new writer, unhampered by any copyright restrictions. *The Light That Failed* is not a first-rate novel; nor does it appear to have elements of great popular appeal, except perhaps for the pathos of its central situation and its authorship by a writer that everybody was reading. Editions based on the *Lippincott* publication had a weak but sentimental ending; others carried a melodramatic ending which was far better Kipling. A dramatic version, with Forbes-Robertson in the leading rôle, was popular both in England and America; it used the *Lippincott* ending.

Mine Own People, first gathered together and published in a pirated edition by Hurst & Company, of New York, contained some of the best of the early Kipling stories—some of the best short stories, indeed, in the English language. The Hurst "enterprise" led Kipling to authorize an edition which was published by the United States Book Company, with an introduction by Henry James. These stories were later included in the collection called *Life's Handicap*.

The vogue of Kipling's verse in America was tremendous. Some critics praised it and some denounced it, but the people read it. As *Time* remarked many years later, when T. S. Eliot made the matter an issue again by writing an essay "In Praise of Kipling's Poetry," there was a time when "Americans and Britons who would not be found dead with a book of poems in their pockets read Kipling." Thousands of young people loved to spout the resounding lines of "If—" and "L'Envoi." Tags like "East is East and West is West, and never the twain shall meet," "a rag, a bone, and a hank of hair," and "You're a better man than I am, Gunga Din!" became part of the current small-change of the language. Many of Kipling's poems were set to music, and "On the Road to Mandalay" and "Danny Deever" early became program favorites. One of the chief events of Queen Victoria's Jubilee was the publication of Kipling's "Recessional" in the *Times;* and a high spot in modern Congressional oratory was the occasion when Robert G. Cousins delivered to a crowded House of Representatives his speech on the sinking of the *Maine,* ending with a recitation of the second stanza of the great poem, which held the audience in breathless silence and at the end brought prolonged cheers. A little later "The White Man's Burden" gave American expansionists their most resounding argument.

The most widely distributed volume of Kipling's verse was commonly published under the title *Barrack-Room Ballads;* but it contained *Departmental Ditties*, originally published in India in 1886, and all the ballads and other poems by Kipling which diligent search of English and Indian periodicals could turn up. The poems as well as the short stories, indeed, were made up in collections with many mutations of content and title, according to publishers' hopes of profits. The "Little Blue Books," of Girard, Kansas, included three

Kipling collections—*Gunga Din and Other Poems, Mandalay and Other Poems,* and *The Vampire and Other Poems,* whose sales ranked in the order in which they are named, but averaged about 90,000 each.

Kipling was the object of controversy from the time that his early stories first "caught on" in London. Both his political views and his literary practice made him enemies; but attacks in prose and verse, in review articles and full-length books, stimulated rather than checked the growth of interest in his work. The sharp and bitter little poem from which the epigraph prefaced to this chapter is taken described Kipling's early work as "a boy's eccentric blunder": is not youth the unforgivable sin in a genius? The periodicals were full of notes and anecdotes about Kipling. Paul Elmer More, beginning an essay on "Kipling and Fitzgerald" in the *Atlantic Monthly,* later included in his *Shelburne Essays,* tells of a magazine editor who wagered that he would keep Kipling's name out of his pages for six months, only to lose his bet with his next issue. More continued:

> Apart from this journalistic notoriety, none of our poets, not even Byron, has enjoyed just the kind of popularity that Kipling has achieved. Other poets have received equal or greater honor from the cultured public, but our new Anglo-Saxon bard appeals with like force to the scholarly and the illiterate; his speech has become, as it were, the voice of the people.*

This was in 1899, year of the zenith of Kipling's popularity. In February of that year, he lay in a New York hotel critically ill with pneumonia, while the whole world watched anxiously the bulletins from his bedside. The extraordinary interest aroused by his illness, and the relief of millions of readers when it was announced that he would recover, served to point up his importance. The *Journalist,* of New York, issuing a Kipling number on March 4, 1899, to celebrate the author's recovery, said:

> We have just passed through ten days of anxiety and suspense during which we were threatened with the greatest calamity which could fall upon English literature. It seemed more than likely that our greatest living writer—many of us believe the greatest writer the English language has ever known—was to be taken from us at the very beginning of his career—a writer who has won the love and personal regard of his readers as no other writer in any language has done.

And the *New Voice* asked, "Is it too much to say that in his hands, more than in the hands of any other one man, lies the destiny of the world for the next quarter century?" Small wonder that the conservative *Dial,* in May of that year, referred to "this hysteria of unreasoned admiration, this toy tempest of flatulent adulation" of Rudyard Kipling. Yet it continued for months. Twelve numbers of a magazine devoted wholly to facts and anecdotes about Kipling were published. *Thro' the Year With Kipling* furnished a quotation from the great author for each day in the year. William Dean Howells, writing in the *North American Review,* noted the world-wide rejoicing over Kipling's

* Quoted by permission of Houghton Mifflin Company.

recovery, and declared him "at this moment possibly the most famous man in the world . . . all must own this, whatever any man think of his work." Mark Twain, speaking in the summer of 1899 to the London Authors' Club, perpetrated his famous pun: "Since England and America have been joined together in Kipling, may they not be severed in Twain!"

Though *Kim*, considered by some to be his greatest work, was published in 1901, and Kipling continued in full tide of writing up to 1919, there was a gradual subsidence of interest in his work after the turn of the century. He is said to have remarked bitterly that the Americans never forgave him for not dying in New York in 1899. Yet his works continued to sell: some managers of standard bookstores told a *New York Sun* reporter in 1913 that they were then selling ten times as many volumes of Kipling as they were in 1903. At the time of the author's death in 1936, the authorized American publishers, Doubleday, Doran & Company, were selling some 100,000 volumes of Kipling's works each year.

The sin of callow youth, so often charged against Kipling in the early nineties, was one with which critics could not tax his chief rival in the best seller market of those years. George du Maurier was fifty-seven when he made his debut as an author, and sixty when he scored his great success with *Trilby*. Son of a French industrialist who had become an English citizen, du Maurier was educated chiefly in France, became an accomplished artist in black and white, and won an important place on the staff of *Punch*. In that position he had enjoyed a long and distinguished career before he turned to authorship. He had lost the sight of one eye in his middle age, and was threatened with total blindness; it was partly in order to provide another vocation against such time as the light should fail (to revert to Kipling) that he tried novel-writing.

According to a story that du Maurier told his American publisher, J. Henry Harper, Henry James urged him to put the plots with which his mind teemed to the proof; among other ideas, du Maurier described to James the one which later took form in *Trilby*. James was delighted, and du Maurier offered him the idea. "No, no; it's yours. You do it!" urged James. Thus encouraged, du Maurier set to work; but he took up first another plot with which he had been toying, and *Peter Ibbetson* was the result. He had been a contributor of pictures to *Harper's Magazine*, and it was natural that he should offer his novel to that magazine. It was accepted and published both serially and in book form by the Harpers, but it was not very successful.

There was some searching of hearts in the Harper organization when *Trilby* was offered to the magazine. The pictures of studio life in Paris, and "the thin slimy layer of sorrow and shame" which (the author confessed) lay at the bottom of Trilby O'Ferrall's soul, gave them pause. But Editor Alden overruled the doubters on the grounds of the "essential purity" of the story.* There

* John Corbin, "Henry Mills Alden," in *New York Times Book Review*, October 19, 1919.

were some deletions, however, in the serial version—chiefly references to models posing in the "altogether," to mistresses, and to matters of religious belief. These were allowed to stand in the book version, on the theory (which still obtains) that book readers are more tolerant than magazine readers.

The story was a hit from the first installment. Its vividness, its grace and lightness, its sentiment, and, by no means least, its delightful illustrations by the author, enraptured its readers. Howells sat down and wrote a glowing letter of congratulation to du Maurier long before the serial had run its course—which was lucky, because he did not like the latter part of the story very well. One incident must be told in the nice grandfatherly phrases of J. Henry Harper:

> As the novel drew near its conclusion in the *Magazine*, we received a most pathetic letter from an afflicted mother telling us that her daughter was desperately ill and would probably survive but a few weeks, and that she was anxious to see the final chapters of *Trilby* before she died. We sent her the last installment, and before its appearance in our *Magazine* the young woman had passed through the portals of earthly fiction to the great realities of the unknown.*

The book was published in the summer of 1894. By the end of the year it had sold 100,000 at $1.75 (a high price for a novel), and in six months more it had nearly doubled that. Justin Huntly M'Carthy, who was in this country at the time of *Trilby's* first popularity, described it two years later in the *Gentleman's Magazine*:

> Never in our time has a book been so suddenly exalted into a bible. It flowed in a ceaseless stream over the counters of every bookshop on the American continent. It was discussed in the dialect of every state in the Union. Clergy of all denominations preached upon it from their pulpits. Impassioned admirers, for the most part women, formed societies and debated over the moralities and the possibilities of the altogether. . . . Finally, somebody made a play of it and fanned an adoration that had not yet begun to flag higher and higher above the fever line of the human thermometer. The delight of the Republic became delirium when *Trilby* took incarnation in the body of Miss Virginia Harned.

Trilby "programs" were worked up in many cities and towns, with readings and music and "living pictures." The Oliver Ditson Company published a pamphlet of the Trilby songs. Mary Kyle Dallas wrote a parody called *Drilby,* and a burlesque opera entitled "Thrilby" was produced. The play, with Miss Harned as Trilby of the beautiful feet and Wilton Lackaye as the sinister Svengali was immensely successful, and touring companies were soon organized. A circus with a ringmaster made up as Svengali and a bareback rider as Trilby attracted attention. A new town in Florida was named Trilby, with streets called after Svengali, Little Billee, and the others. A new three-dollar shoe was named the Trilby, and there were Trilby hams, Trilby sausages, and a Trilby hearth-brush. "Trilbies" became a slang word for feet. A patent medicine

---

* J. Henry Harper, *The House of Harper* (New York, 1912), pp. 536-37.

company published a pamphlet containing a rhymed synopsis of the story, ending with the lines:

> Had she spurned Svengali's offer
> When her headache made her sick
> And just taken Bromo-Seltzer,
> 'Twould have cured her just as quick.

But the advertiser made the mistake of using some of du Maurier's pictures
as illustrations for his brochure, was sued at law, and had to withdraw the whole
edition. The *Critic* chronicled these aberrations of a great national fad in a
special column from week to week, and later published some of the material
in a pamphlet called *Trilbyana*.

One of the chief items in this pamphlet was an account of the libel suit
against author and publisher threatened by the artist J. McNeill Whistler. It
was generally thought that Whistler was merely trying to get a share of the
publicity that seemed to be going to waste; at any rate, he had recognized himself as the original of a minor character in the story, and wrote to the papers and
threatened to sue. Harpers apologized handsomely and then du Maurier
changed the offending passages for the book publication, and even put a beard
on the character in question where he appeared in the illustrations. And
Whistler gloated over the way in which he had humbled his former studio-
companion.

As a matter of fact, as Alfred Ainger has pointed out in the Dictionary of
National Biography, all the artists portrayed in *Trilby* were formed upon
originals whom the author had known in Paris. The vividness and clarity
and high spirits of these characterizations constitute a chief charm of the
story. As a picture of the bohemian life of artists it is certainly far better than
that which Kipling had recently presented in *The Light That Failed*—nor is the
difference to be accounted for by the fact that the one scene is laid in Paris and
the other in London. As a novel, however, *Trilby* suffers from sentimentalism,
from the unconvincingness of the hypnotic element, and from the failure of the
plot to hold up in the last two "parts."

It was, of course, attacked for these faults, but even more for its alleged
immorality. As a rhymster in the *Literary World* observed,

> Now every paragraphing prude
> Sneers at "these studies from the lewd,"
> Its pages ne'er a charm reveal,
> And Trilby's but a new Camille.

But this kind of controversy did little more than encourage the great *Trilby*
epidemic, which continued to rage for a decade or more. Harper & Brothers
had bought the novel outright for $10,000, but they sent the author an addi-
tional check for $40,000 in 1895. This must have had a soothing effect on the
growing impatience which du Maurier is said to have felt toward some of the
extravagant absurdities of the *Trilby* mania in the United States. A third

novel, and a much less successful one—*The Martians*—was running in *Harper's* at the time of du Maurier's death.

Englishmen writing of India, of Paris, and of Scotland were responsible for the great fevers in American readership in the early nineties. The writers who exploited the humble life of Scottish villages came to be called the "Kailyard School," after the lines from an old Jacobite song which were prefaced to *Beside the Bonnie Brier Bush:*

> There grows a bonnie brier bush in our kail-yard,
> And white are the blossoms on't in our kail-yard.

The first of the Kailyarders to find popularity in America was James M. Barrie, whose *Auld Licht Idylls* was published in New York early in 1891 by the Macmillan Company, later in the same year by Cassell, and then in the next year or two by half a dozen of the publishers of paper-bound books in series. Having thus discovered Barrie three years after the publication of the *Auld Licht* stories in England, American publishers promptly picked up his other books, including two which became best sellers in the United States— *A Window in Thrums* and *The Little Minister*.

It was *The Little Minister* that made Barrie's first great popularity in the United States. Its combination of humor, sentiment, and melodrama in portraying the weaver folk of Thrums suited popular taste perfectly, and Barrie became a prime American favorite forthwith. Though it was published in London three months after the international copyright agreement went into effect, half of the novel had appeared serially in an English periodical before that time; and besides, the copyright in book form was defective.* It did not take American piratical publishers long to discover these facts, and in the course of a few years a dozen editions were in print in paper and cloth bindings. *A Window in Thrums,* a continuation of the *Auld Licht* stories which had been published in England in 1889, was not issued in the United States until after *The Little Minister;* and then for a time the two books seem to have been almost equal in popularity. De luxe editions of both appeared in 1892; one two-volume edition of *The Little Minister* sold for twenty-five dollars. But there were also all sorts of waifs and strays containing pieces by Barrie which got into the cheap-book "libraries." In the preface to the first collected edition of his works (Scribner's, 1896) Barrie wrote:

> I know not how many volumes purporting to be by me are in circulation in America which are no books of mine. I have seen several of them, bearing such titles as *Two of Them, An Auld Licht Manse,* and *A Tillyloss Scandal.* They consist of scraps collected and published without my knowledge, and I entirely disown them.

All of which made no difference to his readers, who took their Barrie with or without benefit of copyright. New editions of the favorites continued to ap-

---

* "His publishers were so pressed for time that they had to copyright *The Little Minister* minus its last chapter."—J. A. Hammerton, *Barrie, The Story of a Genius* (New York, 1930), p. 268.

pear throughout the nineties. The immense success of *The Little Minister* as a play, when it was produced in 1897 by Charles Frohman at the Empire Theater in New York, with Maude Adams as Babbie, brought out a spate of new editions of that novel.

S. R. Crockett's *The Stickit Minister*, with its pathetic and humorous stories of Scottish village life, also won a following in the United States. But the greatest American success of all the kailyard literature was Ian Maclaren's *Beside the Bonnie Brier Bush*. Here again a defective copyright threw the book into the public domain; and Dodd, Mead & Company, the authorized publishers, reckon that it "probably sold nearly a million copies within a few years." *

Like *Auld Licht Idylls, A Window in Thrums,* and *The Stickit Minister,* this latest candidate for favor was a collection of sketches and tales of Scottish village life which combined pathos and humor with strong characterization, which poked a little fun (always judiciously) at the religiosity of the older and stricter Calvinism, and which made lavish use of the Scottish dialect. Maclaren seems definitely inferior to Barrie as one rereads the stories today, but there was something about the simple and unpretentious annals of Drumtochty that caused American readers to take Maclaren's book to their hearts as they took no other of this group. Possibly the appetite for this type of reading had merely worked up to its height when *Beside the Bonnie Brier Bush* appeared.

Critics were free in their condemnation of the surfeit of dialect in these books. *Life* announced a project to translate Maclaren into English. One of its smart writers, having noted the author's lecture trip in the United States (as who could not?), gave an account of the visit of Donald Macslushey, author of *In the Bonnie, Bonnie Brier Pipe* and *My Wee, Wee Galoot*. "He employs dialect to a great extent," writes our satirist, "which, of course, renders his books incomprehensible to American readers, but this has no evil effect upon the sales." Of course, Maclaren's dialect did not make his books incomprehensible to American readers, who had been well schooled in dialect fiction by American writers and who doubtless found some pride and pleasure in being able to take the conversation of Drumsheugh and Dr. MacLure in their stride.

"Ian Maclaren" was the pen-name of the Rev. John Watson, a successful Church of England clergyman of Liverpool, who came of a Scotch Highlander family and had served a parish in Scotland early in his clerical career. He visited the United States in 1896 on one of the most successful lecture tours ever enjoyed by an English notable in this country. In ten weeks Major J. B. Pond, his manager, cleared $35,795.91 on his lectures, readings, and sermons. Everywhere in the East, Middle West, and Canada, he was welcomed by audiences which overflowed the halls when he spoke. Major Pond offered his star $24,000 for twelve weeks more, but the good doctor had had enough for the time

---

* Dodd, Mead & Company, *The First Hundred Years* (New York, 1939), p. 24.

being. He did come back later, however, and he died in 1907 at Mt. Pleasant, Iowa, while making his third lecture tour in the United States.

Other books by Ian Maclaren followed his biggest hit—*The Days of Auld Lang Syne, Our Neighbors,* and some collections of religious essays; but they were in a descending curve so far as popularity went. The last of the Kailyard series to achieve considerable popularity was the *Auld Lang Syne* book, though the three best sellers of the group—*A Window in Thrums, The Little Minister,* and *Beside the Bonnie Brier Bush*—continued to sell well through the first decade of the new century. Alexander Woollcott's enthusiasm over the *Bonnie Brier Bush* is still remembered by his followers.

XXVIII. IN HIS STEPS:
THE MYTH OF THIRTY MILLIONS

For hereunto were ye called: because Christ also suffered for you, leaving you an example, that ye should follow his steps.

I Peter 2:21

IN JANUARY, 1889, a young minister named Charles M. Sheldon came out from an eastern pastorate to found the Central Congregational Church of Topeka, Kansas. He was profoundly convinced of the duty of the churches to take a decisive part in the solution of social problems on a Christian basis. He had been in Topeka only a few months when he put on old clothes and a disreputable hat and spent a week tramping the streets of the city hunting a job. He really entered into the rôle he assumed; it was not play, and he felt deeply the disappointments of the honest man out of work.

This and similar experiments with social questions furnished lively material for Sunday morning sermons. But the Sunday evening sermons were still a problem. The need was two-fold: the young preacher had to find a way to fill his church auditorium twice on Sunday, despite the feeling of his congregation that their duty was done for the week when they had gone to church once; and he also felt the necessity of teaching his social creed to the young people of nearby Washburn College, who were less attracted to the morning services than to those of the evening. The resourceful minister found the answer in a new homiletic technique—the sermon-serial.

His first attempt at fiction from the pulpit was the serial *His Brother's Keeper.* It was the story of a miners' strike, and in the first chapter the strikers seized the engine-house and pulled up the pumps so that the mine would be flooded, leaving the hero at the bottom of the mine with the water rising fast to his knees. There the first installment ended. Of course those who heard the first chapter came back the next Sunday evening to find out how the hero got out of his predicament, and with them came others who had heard about the story. In the meantime the young author had managed to devise a means for getting his hero out of the wet place in which he had left him the first Sunday night; and so it went on for twelve weeks, each chapter ending serial-wise with a suspense break. Evening congregations overflowed the auditorium, and Christian principles were conscientiously applied to the labor problem —to the edification, surely, of the students of the College.

This was in 1890. The experiment was so successful that the Rev. Mr. Shel-don tried it again in the fall of the next year, and again every fall throughout most of the nineties. The third of the series was *The Crucifixion of Philip Strong,* and this story the Chicago *Advance,* a Congregational weekly of which James A. Adams was editor, published serially from May to October, 1894; and afterward A. C. McClurg & Company, of Chicago, brought it out in book form. It apparently enjoyed only a very moderate sale. Two years later the Congregational Sunday School and Publishing Society, of Boston, issued the story which had been first in the series—*His Brother's Keeper*—in book form. In that year also, the *Advance* published serially the story which Sheldon was currently reading to his evening congregation. This one was called *In His Steps.*

The new story was destined for world-wide distribution. Its subtitle "What Would Jesus Do?" indicated its theme. A young minister is shocked by the indictment of practical Christianity one Sunday morning when a starving, out-of-work tramp rebukes the congregation at the close of the service and then falls dead before them. He asks his people to pledge themselves for a year to do as they think Jesus would do in all their relationships. Many of them take the pledge. A newspaper publisher removes sensation and liquor ad-vertising from his paper; fortunately an heiress in the congregation stands by to endow his business. An industrialist reports a case of rebate manipula-tion on the part of his own company to the Railroad Commission. A girl with a beautiful voice turns down an opportunity to go into comic opera in order to sing at revival meetings. A college president goes into politics against the saloon power. The whole series of reform elements finally merges more or less in a settlement-house project. The last third of the story changes the scene from a city like Topeka to the larger framework of Chicago. The idea is to show the possibility of the spread of such a movement; the new leadership is in the hands of a doctor of divinity and a bishop, and there is more emphasis on the social settlement as a means of reform. But the story itself would be much better without the Chicago epilogue, for a novelist cannot successfully change characters and scene so completely and keep any plot unity.

Missionary work among the poor of the great cities was attracting much attention in the nineties. *Robert Elsmere,* with its challenge to orthodox churches and its emphasis on the Christian in the slums, was still debated. William and Catherine Booth were beating the drums of the Salvation Army, and their "slum brigades" were active. Jane Addams' Hull-House in Chicago was widely discussed, and social settlements had been established in other cities. William T. Stead's *If Christ Came to Chicago* had created a sensation in 1894, though its opinions were challenged the next year in Edward Everett Hale's *If Jesus Came to Boston*. In the same year which saw the publication of *In His Steps,* Hall Caine's *The Christian,* with its thesis of the inadequacy of the church, was making a resounding success on its first publication.

So far as theme is concerned, *In His Steps* is a naïve *Robert Elsmere,* though with respect to literary art it is so far inferior to the earlier novel as to bear no comparison. Its success came largely from Sheldon's stroke of genius in expressing the inquiry into social responsibilities by the incisive, direct question, "What would Jesus do?" The novel, or tract, is all theme: it has little to commend it in characterization, setting, or plot.

When serial publication was finished, the *Advance* itself put out the story in book form, with paper covers. This was in 1897. As the author wrote in his preface for the first cloth-bound edition, issued late that year, the story had been "warmly and thoughtfully welcomed by Endeavor societies, temperance organizations, and Y.M.C.A.'s." By 1899 the Advance Publishing Company had four editions in the market at ten, twenty-five, forty and seventy-five cents, and a fifth (illustrated) at $1.25. It was in 1899 that watchful publishers of cheap editions, having cast envious eyes on the successful venture of a religious weekly new to the book-publishing game, discovered that though the book was properly copyrighted, the serial had been printed in the *Advance* without such protection. Immediately they descended in force, and no less than ten of them brought out editions of *In His Steps* in that year. Seven more publishers have reprinted the book since 1899.*

How many copies of the book have been sold in the United States? Dr. Sheldon wrote in his autobiography:

> From figures of publishing firms sent the author within the last five years by a number of the publishers who issued "In His Steps" all the way from twenty-five cents to two dollars a copy, it seems like a fair estimate to make, not counting the sales of the publishers who have refused to tell how many copies they have made, that over 8,000,000 copies of "In His Steps" have been printed and read in America up to the present time [1924].

Then he goes on to estimate ten million copies for Great Britain, two million in British possessions, and two million in other countries—a grand total of "over 22,000,000." Following the general law that big begets bigger, the claim has been made repeatedly that *In His Steps* has sold a total of thirty million copies—"the largest sale of any book ever printed, with the exception of the Bible."

---

* Eighteen American publishers have had the book on their lists, as follows: Advance Publishing Co. (1897), H. M. Caldwell (1899), Smith-Andrews (1899, apparently authorized by Advance), D. C. Cook (1899), Street & Smith (1899), Altemus (1899), Western News Company (1899), Ketcham (1899), Munro (1899), Ogilvie (1899), Revell (1899), Laird & Lee (1900), Burt (1910?), Christian Herald (1920, certainly authorized), Sears (1923), Grosset & Dunlap, Winston, Books, Inc. (1943). At least four of these have paid royalties.

Fourteen years after the autobiography appeared, Dr. Sheldon published a little booklet entitled *The History of "In His Steps,"* in which he wrote:

People are constantly asking how many copies of *In His Steps* have been printed and sold. . . .

As to American and British editions, it is a question I am not able to answer with exactness, as the different publishers of the book, whom I have written occasionally purely out of curiosity, refuse to report the sales (with one exception that I am going to mention).* But the Editor of the *Atlantic Monthly* is my authority for stating that over eight million copies have been published and sold in the United States and over twelve million in Great Britain and Europe. The same estimate has been given by Mr. Seldes in the *Saturday Evening Post.* These figures do not include the sales of translations . . .

But the editor of the *Atlantic* and Mr. Gilbert Seldes got their figures from Dr. Sheldon's autobiography! As to those figures "sent the author" in the early twenties, upon which that eight-million total was based, one can only surmise they must have been irresponsible estimates. As the claimant of royalties, Dr. Sheldon was not in a good position to get the information he sought. Much more credible is his later statement that the publishers "refuse to report the sales."

The present writer went out to Topeka to talk with Dr. Sheldon about the sales of *In His Steps* in 1942. He spent a pleasant May afternoon with the aged author, who was in excellent physical and mental vigor at eighty-five. A finer old gentleman would be hard to find. He talked freely about his famous book, but when his visitor attempted to cross-examine him about sales, he had nothing to offer save some anecdotes of miscellaneous guesses which enthusiasts had made. Typical was the one concerning his visit to a bookshop in Melbourne, Australia. He had dropped in to see if he could buy a copy of *In His Steps.* The clerk found him a copy and sold it to him for three shillings. Then Dr. Sheldon introduced himself, and asked how many copies of the book had been sold by that shop. "Oh, I should say we have sold 150,000 copies," answered the clerk. (What an extraordinary sale of one book by one shop!) "How many copies do you suppose have been sold in Australia altogether?" pursued Dr. Sheldon; and the clerk, now fully in the spirit of the interview, answered, "Oh, no doubt at least a million copies!" And down went a million copies for Australia in the good doctor's notebook. His visitor did not then believe, nor does he now, that there was any guile in any of Dr. Sheldon's representations of the record sales of his book: he simply had no mind for exact statistics, while at the same time he had a strong feeling for the romance of fine round numbers.

The writer of these pages has obtained estimates from five † of the eighteen American publishers of *In His Steps,* and they total 540,000 sales. It is an

---

* But when he mentions this exception he does not give the figures, nor could he give them to me when I asked him for them.—F.L.M.

† Grosset & Dunlap, Street & Smith, John C. Winston Company, David C. Cook Publishing Company, Books, Inc.

insufficient basis for a satisfactory estimate, but enough to make us fairly sure that the grand total for the United States did not greatly exceed two million.

It is very probable that Dr. Sheldon was right in thinking that the sale of his book was greater in England than in the United States. It was sold on the streets of London in a penny edition, and it had a tremendous vogue with English religious societies. It was translated into at least twenty foreign languages. Though one comes too close to the field of pure speculation in estimating the world-wide sales of a book published quite without restrictions, six million seems a not unreasonable guess. That *In His Steps* has done a vast amount of good in the world by bringing home to readers of good will the world over a new sense of their responsibility to society, and especially to the underprivileged, cannot be denied. As literature, it is nothing less than amateurish; as a social document, it has first-rate importance.

A striking sequel to *In His Steps* was Dr. Sheldon's attempt to publish a newspaper as Jesus might have done it. One of the most interesting episodes in his book had told of an editor's efforts to conduct his paper according to that ideal, and the *Topeka Capital* invited the author to put his ideas to the proof for a week. The inexperienced editor performed, on the whole, a good piece of work under great difficulties. The paper was undeniably dull during his week's editorship, but it was certainly virtuous. It did not omit all news of human depravity, but it "played down" scandals, crime, and vice. Editorials and news stories were signed. The national interest in the experiment brought the paper's normal circulation of 15,000 up suddenly to 360,000, editions being published simultaneously in Topeka, Chicago, and New York. After it was all over, Editor J. K. Hudson observed editorially that he did not believe in the Christian daily idea, and promised that the *Capital* would, in the future, "go forward on the lines it has worked in the past, as a Republican newspaper."

Another preacher-novelist of the late nineties whose work broke into the best seller ranks was the Rev. Charles W. Gordon, a Canadian minister and missionary, who wrote under the pen-name of Ralph Connor. His first novel was *Black Rock,* the story of the crusade of a preacher called Craig against the drink evil among the miners in the Canadian Northwest. Many of the characters and events were taken directly from real life, and the whole narrative is vivid and interesting. It was published in New York, Chicago and Toronto by Fleming H. Revell Company in 1898 and made a considerable success. And once more the publishers of cheap editions discovered a defect in the copyright, and within the next three years (chiefly in 1901) eight other publishers brought out editions ranging in prices from twenty-five cents to a dollar. Still others joined the scramble later, so that eventually at least twelve publishers issued editions of *Black Rock,* and the sale went well beyond half a million. The following year the same author's *The Sky Pilot* made a success; but without the stimulation of piratical competition, its sales amounted to about half of those of *Black Rock.*

Two shorter religious pieces which were commonly published in book form in the nineties were Henry van Dyke's short story, *The Other Wise Man,* and Henry Drummond's address, *The Greatest Thing in The World.* Each doubtless exceeded the half-million mark, but neither is long enough to be fairly included in a list of full-length books.

A long popular book of religious essays is Mrs. Hannah Whitall Smith's *The Christian's Secret of a Happy Life.* Mrs. Smith was born and died in England; but she spent most of her life in the United States, lecturing and writing on religious subjects. Her volume of essays was first published in 1883 by the Fleming H. Revell Company. It was based on deeply consecrated religious feeling and was widely distributed, through many church channels and otherwise. It is still a popular book in its field.

XXIX. "HUMAN NATURE IN SOME FOLKS"

> I guess the' 's about as much human nature in some folks as the' is in others, if not more.
>
> *David Harum*

THE American people like to take their comic heroes seriously. It is all very well to "laugh consumedly" at Davy Crockett's adventures, at the letters of Petroleum V. Nasby, or at the stories of Artemus Ward. But it is not empty laughter; and Tennessee sent Crockett to Congress, Lincoln read Nasby at Cabinet meetings, and A.W. ended his career as an emissary of good-will to England. There are many serious facets to popular American humor. Political and social satires of obviously serious intent have occasionally reached best seller stature in the United States. The comedy of the backwoods has been accepted not merely for its boisterous fun but also for its interpretation of pioneer culture. And the American people have taken to their collective heart certain eccentric characters of fiction because they were not merely "amoosin' critters" but homely philosophers as well. To tickle the risibilities is one thing, and the therapeutic value of a good belly-laugh is indisputable; but the American people will not often buy humor in best-seller quantities unless they see, or think they see, something serious behind it.

It was as a humorist interpreting the new, romantic Far West that Bret Harte made his first resounding success with "The Luck of Roaring Camp." He had been made editor of the *Overland Monthly,* a new San Francisco magazine which was designed to equal the best, in form and content, which the effete East could produce. For the second number of the *Overland* (August, 1868) its editor wrote his most famous story. He highlighted the incongruity between the rough miners of Roaring Camp and the new-born infant, for incongruity is always a reliable ingredient of humor; but he showed that there were good hearts that beat beneath red flannel shirts and a basic kindliness underlying bad grammar and "cuss words."

The "cuss words," incidentally, got into print only over the protests of some of the magazine staff. A maidenly proofreader was deeply shocked by the introduction of a "dissolute, abandoned" woman in the second paragraph of the story; she was indignant when she read that while Cherokee Sal was suffering the pains of childbirth the miners made bets whether Sal "would get through with it," and when the proofreader found the profane exclamation that Kentuck made when the babe took hold of his finger, "He rastled with my finger, the d——d little cuss!" she grasped the proofsheets determinedly in one hand and, manipulating her long skirts with the other, swept into the publisher's office, red with outraged modesty. The dash between the *d's* did not placate her; pure though her mind was, she strongly suspected that here lay hidden a swear word, and she thought it her duty to communicate her suspicion to her employer. It took an editorial conference to settle the issue, and indeed the editor's threat to resign if his work was bowdlerized, before the story finally went in, *d——d* and all.

"The Luck" made an immense success. The *Nation* immediately declared the tale was not "mere magazine writing," but "literature." The editors of the *Atlantic Monthly* wrote asking for contributions from the new author. His work for the next year or two went into his own magazine, however; "The Outcasts of Poker Flat," "Miggles," "The Idyl of Red Gulch," and "Tennessee's Partner" showed the same combination of humor and pathos and the same skill with the short story form. *The Luck of Roaring Camp and Other Stories* was a logical book venture in 1870. Fields, Osgood & Company published it, and though it apparently got a slower start than might have been expected, more than thirty editions were issued within the first dozen years, and steady sales continued long thereafter. It went into the *Everyman's Library* in 1914, and enjoyed big sales in the *Riverside Library* of Houghton Mifflin. After copyright expired, other publishers took it up. The stories were sometimes reshuffled, and such titles as *Tales of the West* and *California Tales* have been used; but the five *Overland Monthly* stories have always formed the nucleus of such collections.

Less than two years after the appearance of Bret Harte's first and most popular book, another portrayal of pioneer life, from a different frontier, was welcomed with less beating of the critics' tom-toms but with almost as striking a popular response. Edward Eggleston's *The Hoosier School-Master*, which was to become a classic of regional literature, was written in a situation similar to that which prompted Harte to produce "The Luck of Roaring Camp." Eggleston had been made literary editor of *Hearth and Home*, a family weekly published in New York. The paper had been started in 1868 under the distinguished editorship of Donald G. Mitchell and Harriet Beecher Stowe; but

Mrs. Stowe gave up after a year and Mitchell somewhat later, and now circulation had fallen off and the weekly seemed pointed for the toboggan slide to oblivion. In an effort to give it more variety and attractiveness, Eggleston wrote for it the first installment of what he planned as a three-part serial dealing with a pioneer community in Indiana and emphasizing certain comical backwoods characters. That first part of *The Hoosier School-Master* attracted so much favorable attention that the editor-author decided to change his plan, work in a love-story and some melodrama, and make it a full-length novel.

So it was done; and when serial publication was completed late in 1871, Orange Judd & Company, publishers of *Hearth and Home,* proceeded to bring this story out in book form themselves. They took the brevier type which they had kept standing after it had been used in the paper and reset it to a wider measure for book use, and they took the woodcuts done in the crude comic vein of the time by Frank Beard, which had lent interest to the serial, and published the whole in a fairly presentable little volume at a dollar and a quarter. It sold twenty thousand copies in its first year, was pirated by English publishers, and soon translated into French under the title *Le Maitre d'Ecole de Flat Creek* by Mme. Blanc. It has had a remarkably steady sale ever since. The Orange Judd issues did not reach 100,000 until 1892; but in 1913 Grosset & Dunlap published the first of their editions of the book, which have now run well over the quarter-million mark. Since the expiration of its copyright, other publishers have issued the book. It has been popular in amateur theatricals, and two acting versions are in print. It has probably sold half a million copies.

Eggleston was later to write novels much superior to the *School-Master*— *The Circuit Rider* and *Roxy*—but none which won such popular response. Crude and full of caricature and melodrama though this first novel was, its hundreds of thousands of readers, young and old—perhaps millions, at home and abroad—have thoroughly enjoyed it. They have enjoyed its comedy and pathos, its religious teachings, its story of the struggle of a young man to master a difficult situation, and its picture of a rude frontier society.

The young master subduing the disorderly lunkheads of a backwoods school reappears in Opie Read's *The Jucklins,* a best seller of the nineties. Read had gained some fame as editor of the *Arkansas Traveler,* a paper famous for its sketches of back-country scenes and characters; but he had given offense to some of the rustics who had unwittingly posed for their portraits in print, and when a man was elected to the legislature for having said he would like to tie a rope around the editor's neck and lead a mule from under him, Read decided to make the paper justify its title and moved it to Chicago. There he wrote two novels for serialization in the paper, the second of which—*A Kentucky Colonel* —achieved wide popularity.

But it was Read's third attempt which made the biggest success of his long writing career—the story of a Carolina backwoods community entitled *The Jucklins.* It was written, shocking to relate, in order to raise money to satisfy a debt incurred at poker; and Laird & Lee paid seven hundred dollars for it. It was published January 28, 1896, in the paper-bound Pastime Series, with a good colored picture of Lim Jucklin encouraging his fighting cocks in a battle royal on the cover. It had a runaway sale in that form, leaping quickly to six figures; and in the same year it was issued in cloth binding, dramatized by Dan Hart, and produced successfully by the Stuart Robson company in Chicago and by Augustus Thomas in New York.

Opie Read, always a raconteur of great ability and endless resources, loved to tell of the cockfight in the first presentation of the play at McVicker's Theater in Chicago. The cocks were imported from Havana and did not arrive until nearly curtain time the evening of the first performance. Robson was skeptical as to whether they would fight, and imagined himself urging a pair of listless roosters to combat before a laughing audience. As the curtain went up on the cockfight scene, he held one beneath each of his arms, and neither seemed in the least interested. "Damned fools won't fight, I tell you," he muttered to Hart, who stood in the wings; but as he bent over and raised his arms,

the roosters fell and hit each other before striking the mat. The air about them was soon full of flying feathers. The audience shouted. It was a new thrill, a cockfight in a drama. No actors ever knew their parts better. There was no need of a prompter.*

Lim's famous "Hike, there, Bob! Hike, Sam!" must have been drowned in the uproar of the audience.

Read claimed that *The Jucklins* sold over a million copies, but that was probably only a guess. It had some success in a London edition, and was translated into German. Ten years later Read wrote a sequel called *Old Lim Jucklin;* it was comparatively unsuccessful, though all the novels of his later years were warmly welcomed by a small army of readers who eagerly seized upon everything that Opie Read wrote. *The Jucklins* suffers from a style which is as flowery and oratorical as the natural language of Read's own Kentucky colonel. It suffers also, by present-day standards, from melodrama; but it is studded with incidents and dialogue which the reader chuckles over and then remembers forever after. As when the telegraph operator, who always refers to girls as "calico," gets married and then remarks to our hero, "Without calico there ain't much real fun in this life. But enough of calico's society is about the enoughest enough a man can fetch up in his mind." And with all its faults, *The Jucklins* must be commended because it is written from the inside out: unlike any of the other four best sellers discussed in this chapter, its author does not look down upon his folk but writes as one of them. But it is to be noted that it never appeared on any of the *Bookman's* best seller lists, since its chief early sales were in its cheap paper covers rather than in the standard editions such as were reported to that magazine by the regular bookstores. It

* Opie Read, *I Remember* (New York, 1930), p. 231.

sold in newsstands, on trains, and by mail, though its cloth-bound edition went into the more conservative shops.

While *The Jucklins* was enjoying its humble but widespread success, an unknown writer was trying to sell his first novel to a publisher. Edward Noyes Westcott was a banker at Syracuse, New York. He had written this novel in 1895-96 while on an extended vacation forced upon him by tuberculosis. He had entitled it *David Harum* (after a village banker character modeled on one Dave Hannum,* of Homer, New York), who, though not the hero of the enveloping plot, had nevertheless taken the book over pretty thoroughly after about ten chapters. He sent his manuscript to at least six other publishers before Ripley Hitchcock, of D. Appleton & Company, discovered the charm and chuckles in the central character and decided that something could be done with the book. The trouble was that it began like an imitation of a third-rate Edgar Fawcett society novel, with the mawkish love affair of the narrator, and David Harum himself was not introduced until the eleventh chapter; by that time publishers' readers had become discouraged or given up entirely. But Hitchcock suggested that one of the best episodes in the book—the story of how Dave got the better of Deacon Perkins in a hoss-trade—should be put into the first two chapters. He was convinced that after readers got a taste of the strong and authentic Harum flavor, they would not be disheartened by the stilted love-making of John Lenox but would skip through it looking for more Harum.

It was an inspired suggestion. Westcott consented to the revision, and even to the deletion of some chapters of the "society" part of his novel, and Appletons got it ready for the press. Westcott's condition grew worse, however, and he died six months before his novel was published. After the book came out on September 23, 1898, at a dollar and a half, the first readers chuckled at David Harum's shrewdness, wept over his Christmas kindness to the Widow Cullom, and quoted (probably misquoted) his version of the golden rule and other characteristic Harum sayings, to all their friends—and their friends went out and bought the book, and the process began over again. It is said that Governor Flower, of New York, carried a copy about with him and introduced it into every conversation. Few books have been so widely and quickly promoted by spontaneous recommendation of friends: this is the best advertising, and the cheapest.

David Harum appeared first in a *Bookman* best seller list in December, 1898, when it occupied fifth place in a list from Rochester, New York, and sixth in one from the Wall Street district in New York City (banking interests must stick together!). In January it was in the best seller lists the country over; and in February it took over the top of the list, which it held for six months. It remained in the lists for nineteen months more, by which time the half-million mark had been reached. In 1900 its publishers brought out a de luxe edition

* See Arthur T. Vance, *The Real David Harum* (New York, 1900).

to sell at ten dollars, and also *The Christmas Story from David Harum*, illustrated by pictures from the Frohman stage production, which had just begun its long run with William H. Crane as Dave. In February, 1904, the book was credited with sales of 727,000 in Harriet Monroe's careful list in the *Critic*. On its twenty-first birthday it was still selling well, and the publishers brought out a new anniversary edition. In 1927 Grosset & Dunlap began their series of reprint editions of the book, and Appletons brought it out at a dollar. It was in the movies, with Will Rogers taking the title role in 1941, and a new edition was issued at that time. The novel still sells, as does the Ripley Hitchcock acting version. Its total sales were 1,190,000 before the issue, in 1946, of a printing of 241,000 copies in the pocketbook format.

All this indicates imperfectly the deeply-rooted popularity of *David Harum* over a long period. Some of the sayings of the old hoss-trader and banker became as well known as those of Poor Richard himself, and his name was permanently fixed as the designation of a type of character. Philosophical essays were written to point out the significance of the book's subtitle, *A Story of American Life;* John Oliver Hobbes declared that there was a David Harum in every real American family.

Many imitations of Westcott's masterpieces have been written and published, and it may be that it afforded Irving Bacheller some suggestion for his own best seller, *Eben Holden*. Bacheller was a newspaperman temporarily out of a job in the summer of 1898. He had written some fiction, and now he began a novel of country life in up-state New York which featured a loyal and tough old farm hand who was a great story-teller, a character formed upon that of a hired man the author had known in his boyhood. The story was first designed as a juvenile, and the narrator told of his childhood; but when the author offered the early chapters to *St. Nicholas* they were declined. Meanwhile Bacheller accepted a job as Sunday editor of the New York *World* and laid his book aside for a time. It seems probable that the great success of *David Harum* prompted him to take it up a year or so later, finish it on slightly more Harumlike lines, and offer it to the Lothrop Publishing Company, of Boston. When it was selling sensationally at the end of 1900, R. W. Gilder, of the Century Company, asked Bacheller why he had gone to Boston to get it published; and the author was considerate enough of the editors of *St. Nicholas*, a Century periodical, not to point out that Gilder's organization had once rejected it.

Eben Holden was published July 2, 1900; in three months it sold 50,000 copies and in four months 125,000. By Christmas time it had reached 300,000, which included one record week in which 105,000 copies were shipped out to the trade. It continued to sell heavily in 1901, making fourth place in the *Bookman's* list for that year. In Miss Monroe's list of 1904 it was credited with sales of 400,000. Later Grosset & Dunlap and Harpers brought out cheaper editions, and nearly a quarter of a century after its first publication the book was still selling some 3,000 a year. It seems likely that its sales in the United States have totaled at least 750,000.*

Sententious wit was having quite a run in the nineties. *Mr. Dooley in Peace and War* was on the monthly best seller lists in 1899, but did not pile up large enough sales totals to make it an over-all best seller. Elbert Hubbard, whose *Message to Garcia* sold vastly as a pamphlet, also specialized in wise maxims. But neither of these aphorists was a countryman or backwoodsman.

From first to last, the bumpkin has played a notable rôle in American best-sellerdom. He appears and reappears all the way from Moses Primrose, the unfortunate horse-trader in *The Vicar of Wakefield*, down to Private Hargrove. He always strikes a rich chord in the memory of readers among the people. Why, this fellow in the book reminds me of old So-and-so, that I knew when I was a boy! And many of the bumpkins—perhaps the best of them—are full of sententious wisdom and dry humor. They serve to emphasize the frequent popular response to homespun materials in literature.

XXX. THE MONTHLY LISTS

There is no best seller list which can have any validity to justify its use. . . .
Best-sellerism is one of the major curses of the industry.
        O. H. Cheney, in "Economic Survey of the Book Industry, 1930-1931"

EARLY periodicals devoted to reviews and literary comment gave little attention to best sellers as such. The old Boston *Literary World* and Chicago *Dial* were inclined to regard popularity as a sign of a book's mediocrity, or worse. The New York *Critic* was a little more liberal. The *Publishers' Weekly* was orthodox in its early years; it was interested in popularity, but not enough interested to gather systematically the news of unusual selling records.

But when the monthly *Bookman* was founded in New York in February, 1895, it adopted from the first the plan of publishing titles of books "in the order of demand" which had been used for some years by the London *Bookman*. It obtained reports from the leading bookstores of sixteen cities in the United States (dividing New York into "Uptown" and "Downtown"), from which it listed the six best selling books in each city. These lists were presented in the back of the magazine under the heading, "Sales of Books During the Month: New books in the order of demand." The lists were eventually extended to include some thirty cities in the United States and Canada.

These reports were not limited to fiction, and occasionally a city list would contain a non-fiction title or two; but more than nine-tenths of the mentions were of novels. Consequently non-fiction did not appear in the national sum-

* See Irving Bacheller, *From Stores of Memory* (New York, 1938), pp. 9, 143-61; A. J. Hanna, *Bibliography of Irving Bacheller* (Rollins College, Fla., 1939).

maries in the years when the *Bookman* was gathering reports—with the exception of four years during which it collected special reports on non-fiction. These years were 1912, 1913, 1917, and 1918. The *Bookman's* successors in the work of gathering best seller data recognized the growing importance of non-fiction in the reports and made separate lists.

At first there was no national summary, but for the issue of November, 1897, James MacArthur, associate editor of the *Bookman*, began such a résumé, which was printed at the end of the separate lists under the heading, "Best Selling Books." Then in 1899 came a new departure—a series of annual lists. It was introduced by the following paragraph:

An esteemed subscriber in Madison, New Jersey, has compiled a tabulated list of the best selling books for each year of the *Bookman's* existence, beginning with 1895. These tables of successful titles and authors have been drawn from the lists appearing every month in the department, and although these lists must be regarded as largely arbitrary, it may be claimed that the results are fairly approximate and represent the books that are most popular at the time. We have found Dr. W. H. Martin's compilation of decided interest: it has enabled us to present a summary of the six best selling books during 1895-1898. The figures opposite the titles indicate the number of times each book has been quoted on the lists of the six best selling books for the period under survey.*

But the method of compiling lists by number of mentions was unsatisfactory, though it was the same by which the monthly summaries had been made up. When Arthur Bartlett Maurice, who had succeeded MacArthur as associate editor, compiled his monthly lists in 1900, he occasionally had to record two books as having tied for first or second place; and when he paired *Eben Holden* and *Alice of Old Vincennes* in that way, he received on the same day telegrams from the publishers of both books, each declaring that the sales of his own book were running far ahead of the other man's. Maurice then devised a point system by which each first place on a city list received 10; each second, 8; each third, 7; each fourth, 6; each fifth, 5; and each sixth, 4. This plan was used for the monthly lists from 1900 onward.

The *Bookman* remained content with an annual résumé which merely recapitulated the monthly lists; but in 1911 *Publishers' Weekly* began what it called its "Best Seller Consensus," in which it applied the Maurice system to all the *Bookman's* city lists for the preceding year, and obtained an annual list in order of rankings. This kind of computation can, of course, be made by any industrious statistician for any year from 1895 onward, using the *Bookman's* city lists for each year. Such lists for 1895-1910, with the *PW's* annual continuations, are standard computations of best seller rankings which are based on booksellers' reports.

There were criticisms of the *Bookman* lists. It was pointed out that too much trust was placed in the reports of bookshops, which could not be expected to keep careful statistics of their own sales; and that it was too easy for a bookseller to try to boost a book in which he had a special interest. Perhaps he had

* *Bookman*, April, 1899 (vol. IX, p. 187).

been oversold on a given title and was anxious to give it the prestige of the lists. Also it was said that small stores and limited markets were given too much weight in comparison with the larger outlets. The only answer was that the *Bookman* made no claims to infallibility in its reports: it made their basis clear, and one could take them or leave them. And after all, they did give a good idea of the trends.

The *Bookman* continued its lists until it was purchased by the George H. Doran Company in 1918, when it substituted "Books in Demand at Public Libraries." But the task of collecting booksellers' reports was immediately taken up by *Books of the Month,* a trade imprint journal published as an adjunct of the *Dial* by H. S. Browne & Company. Under "Best Selling Fiction" it listed ten books each month, and under "Best Selling General Books," six. These lists were based on reports from sixty-two booksellers distributed over the United States. In 1920 *Books of the Month* was taken over by the *Publishers' Weekly,* but it continued its lists until 1932. Then the *Publishers' Weekly* itself, which had reprinted the monthly summaries first of the *Bookman* and later of *Books of the Month,* accepted the job of compiling the reports, doing it weekly instead of monthly. It listed non-fiction as well as fiction, and before the end of 1936 had settled on the custom of naming five of each every week. At first it devised the interesting form of a racing chart for its list, but beginning in April, 1933, it used the term "best sellers" for the first time in any heading of such a regular list—"Current Best Sellers," and later "Weekly Best Sellers." Ever since 1911 it has continued its annual summaries.

Other periodicals have compiled similar weekly lists, as the New York *Herald Tribune's* supplement called *Books,* and the *Book Review* of the New York *Times.* Some newspapers have printed lists of best sellers in their own cities. The *Retail Bookseller,* Baker & Taylor's *Outstanding Books,* the *A.L.A. Bulletin,* and the *Wilson Library Bulletin* have carried national lists.

It must always be remembered that these lists include only the books issued by regular publishers. Reprints and cheap editions, book-club issues, pocket-size books, and "libraries," all of which play such a large part in over-all totals, are not included in the booksellers' reports.

All such lists are a matter of journalism. They are not printed to aid the book industry or to guide readers or to promote the fame of successful authors; they constitute mere reporting of news facts about new books. They have a certain importance: sometimes it is ephemeral, in the case of a brief popularity, and sometimes it is real and worthy of careful study, as in the case of an indicated trend. At any rate, they are guide-posts in any serious study of the history of best sellers.

XXXI. THE ROMANTIC PARADE

The long procession of historical novels from *The Adventures of François* down to the last one by Robert W. Chambers marched on the right side of an avenue whose left side was made gay by the parade of Graustarkian fiction.
Grant C. Knight, in the Saturday Review of Literature

PRECURSOR and color-bearer of the procession was Robert Louis Stevenson, who rode down the avenue singing

> Fifteen men on a dead man's chest—
> Yo-ho-ho and a bottle of rum!

Followed a motley but high-spirited company—the men handsome, booted and spurred, with rapiers in hand, long cloaks floating in the breeze; the women gentle but clearly courageous, in taffeta and lace, and beautiful enough to move any red-blooded man to give his life in their defense.

Half the top best sellers of the years 1894-1902 were novels of high romance. But the fact that the year 1894 saw the publication of Anthony Hope's *The Prisoner of Zenda*, Stanley J. Weyman's *Under the Red Robe*, George W. Cable's *John March, Southerner*, and Captain Charles King's *Waring's Peril* is nothing very surprising, and certainly does not mark that year as the beginning of a "new romantic era." Historical fiction, often rococo in style, had been popular in America for a hundred years. Ouida was still widely reprinted in the paper-bound libraries, and in this very year Sylvanus Cobb, Jr.'s *The Shadow of the Guillotine* was reissued in an illustrated fifty-cent edition. Lew Wallace's *The Prince of India* had appeared the year before, and *Ben-Hur* still sold well. F. Marion Crawford, who was to contribute at least two not-quite-best-sellers to the new procession of romantics, had been producing historical fiction with melodramatic variations for a decade. Captain King's military yarns had long enjoyed a sub-literary success.

No, the romance of rapier and rhetoric was not new among best sellers. But what the turn of the century did see was a series of historical and cloak-and-sword novels, ranging from serious works to hammock thrillers, which caught the general attention of the reading public about 1894 and then for nearly a decade raged up and down the *Bookman's* monthly best seller lists, which had been furnished by booksellers from Portland, Maine, to Portland, Oregon. After such novels had made an initial success and won a public, they prospered by falling in with the great American expansionist ideology of the turn of the century. Although these books did not deal directly with the Spanish-American War or Funston in the Philippines or the white man's burden or McKinley's imperialist policy, they did sublimate the fighting and the politics in easy emotional satisfactions. They suited the moods of the times.

First of the procession on the left side of the avenue was *The Prisoner of Zenda*. Anthony Hope Hawkins was a London barrister of thirty-one who had been writing unsuccessful novels for five years or more before he made a resounding success with *Zenda*. It was a rapid, competently written story of a handsome and accomplished young Englishman who visits the mythical Balkan kingdom of Ruritania, is caught up in an intrigue against the king, and is crowned in his stead in order to circumvent the king's enemies. The heart-throb comes from Rudolph's devotion to the Princess Flavia, the suspense-chills from the sword-fight on the drawbridge. Here are echoes of Gothic romance, and here is that most fascinating of comic-opera motifs—the king-for-a-day theme. And here are color and daring and badinage and tender sentiment, all done up in a pretty package. It is still good hammock reading—if you have a hammock.

Zenda was a hit in England and America in 1894-95, and was soon translated into the leading European languages. Henry Holt was its American publisher, and it was one of his best sellers for twenty years or more. It was a stage success, and has been repeatedly produced for the movies. Indeed it is a hardy perennial, and as late as 1946 one of the publishers of twenty-five cent reprints produced a new edition of no less than a quarter of a million copies.

Anthony Hope Hawkins (to whose name King George later prefixed a Sir) now resigned his mild interest in the law and devoted himself to fiction. He wrote several other romances in the Zenda vein. His *Phroso* was serialized in *McClure's Magazine* in 1897, and got into the monthly best seller lists a little later. That was the year in which the author made a lecture tour in the United States. In 1898 *Rupert of Hentzau,* a sequel to *The Prisoner of Zenda*, was published with somewhat less success than its predecessors. Meanwhile other writers tried their pens on similar inventions. Richard Harding Davis' *The Princess Aline* (1895) may have derived some of its popularity from the *Zenda* vogue; it is no imitation, however, for the hero never finds his princess or her kingdom.* Davis' *The King's Jackal* (1898) was more like.

But it was inevitable that a good American writer should attempt to show to the world that if any hero was born to save thrones, win the hearts of princesses, and set the affairs of mythical European kingdoms to rights, he should be a red-blooded, hard-fighting American. That was A. C. Gunter's idea in *Mr. Barnes of New York*, which was still a best seller in the paper editions. But Gunter's fiction was too wild and unlicked; George Barr McCutcheon was to do it somewhat better.

Graustark did not have the light touch of *The Prisoner of Zenda*, but it had something which was more precious to literally millions of American readers in the first decade of the twentieth century—an outspoken conviction that the young American male was far and away the best type of biped the good Lord had ever created. When Lorry and Anguish visited Graustark, it was noted that

---

* Nor was Davis' even more popular *Soldiers of Fortune*, with its action in the midst of a South American revolution, quite in the *Zenda* pattern, despite similarities.

"they were taller, broader, and more powerfully built than the swarthy-faced men about them, and it was no wonder that the women allowed admiration to show in their eyes." Or that the Princess promptly fell in love with Lorry and the Countess with Anguish. The Princess, while she was still masquerading under the name of Miss Guggenslocker (a rose by any name), told Lorry in her charmingly candid way that he was her "ideal American"; but he modestly replied, "There are a great many better Americans than I. You forget our President and our statesmen." William McKinley was top American when the book was published, but Czolgosz was already nursing a plot as villainous as any ever begotten in Graustark. In a dramatic scene near the close of McCutcheon's opus, after the fighting is over and the villain unmasked, Lorry speaks this piece:

Count Halfont, every born American may become ruler of the greatest nation in the world—the United States. His home is his kingdom; his wife, his mother, his sisters are his queens and princesses; his fellow citizens are his admiring subjects if he is wise and good. In my land you will find the poor man climbing to the highest pinnacle, side by side with the rich man. . . . The woman I love is a Princess. Had she been the lowliest maid in all that great land of ours, still would she have been my queen, I her king. . . . We recognize little as impossible. Until death destroys this power to love and hope, I must say to you that I shall not consider the Princess Yetive beyond my reach. Frankly, I cannot, sir.*

And he not only marries her but he takes her to Washington on a honeymoon—a naïve denouement impossible to Anthony Hope.

McCutcheon was a newspaperman of thirty-three, city editor of a paper in Lafayette, Indiana, when he wrote *Graustark*. He sold his manuscript to H. S. Stone & Company, of Chicago, for five hundred dollars. Herbert Stone bought it with some reluctance and edited it rather severely. He cut it down to little more than half its original length. He deleted certain gaucheries, as when Lorry removed his detachable cuffs before fighting a duel. The hero's name, by the way, was originally John Noble—too obviously thematic, decided Stone. Published early in 1901, the book soon reached the best seller lists. Stone stimulated sales by a large advertising campaign in the magazines and newspapers; and before he retired from publishing and turned *Graustark* over to Dodd, Mead & Company late in 1903, he had sold nearly 300,000 copies. The Grosset & Dunlap reprint sold nearly 600,000 copies. Altogether the book's sales totaled close to a million and a half. A successful play was made from the book.

McCutcheon gave up journalism and devoted himself to authorship, writing nearly fifty novels before his death in 1928. Two of these were in the *Graustark* pattern; *Beverly of Graustark* made the best seller lists in 1904. So did *Brewster's Millions*, popular in book and on stage in the first decade of the new century. McCutcheon always had his following of readers, but *Graustark* was his only book to reach the top rank of best sellers.

Harold MacGrath's *The Puppet Crown* was published in the same year as

* Reprinted by permission of Dodd, Mead & Company from *Graustark*, by George Barr McCutcheon. Copyright 1901, by Dodd, Mead & Company.

the great McCutcheon hit. Like *Graustark,* it used the perils of a small principality's national debt as part of the plot complication: the mortgaged kingdom
bade fair to become as hackneyed in fiction as the mortgage on the old homestead. *The Puppet Crown* outranked *Graustark* in the *Bookman's* summary of
1901 best sellers, but could not keep the pace in later competition. And there
were many others in the now familiar formula, none of them successful enough
to be mentioned here.

In the meantime, on the right side of the avenue, the parade of historical
romance was on the march. In 1895 *In Defiance of the King,* a story of the
American Revolution by C. C. Hotchkiss, won some critical praise. The next
year Mark Twain's admirable *Joan of Arc* made a modest success. But it was another book published in 1896 that was to arouse the popular enthusiasm.

Little, Brown & Company, of Boston, had been publishing the work of
Henryk Sienkiewicz, the Polish historical novelist, in the translations of Jere-
miah Curtin, for several years before one of them rewarded James McIntyre's
editorial faith by achieving any notable success. Critical opinion ranks Sienkiewicz's Polish historical trilogy well above *Quo Vadis* in literary quality; but
there were two elements in this long novel with a forbidding Latin title, by a
Pole whose name was hard to pronounce, which immediately caught the popular attention. Both of these elements were emphasized in the early reviews, set
forth in the advertising, and bandied about in word-of-mouth comment. First,
it was a religious book, for it dealt with the life and sufferings of the Christians
in Rome in the first century A.D. Second, it was shocking, for it dealt with the
decadent society of Nero's reign. This combination of religious interest and
sex-sensation made a strong appeal.

Besides, the circumstances of its publication led to runaway sales. *Quo Vadis*
was published in October, 1896, at two dollars, its size warranting the increase
of fifty cents over the usual price of a new novel. By the next spring, it was
leading the best seller lists, and by May it had sold fifty thousand copies. Now
our copyright agreement with Poland required that a book should be published
in the United States in the original Polish within six months after its appearance at home in order to have protection in this country, and Little, Brown had
not taken that precaution. In view of their previous experience with the works
of Sienkiewicz, the copyright of Curtin's translation seemed enough. But with
sales in the hundreds of thousands in sight, it was inevitable that the pirates
should seize upon the original and put their own translators to work. This was
done first by Henry Altemus, of Philadelphia, who published the book at $1.25
in November, 1897, and began selling it at the rate of 10,000 copies a week.
Little, Brown then brought it out in paper covers to retail at twenty-five cents,
selling it at wholesale as low as nine cents per copy. Street & Smith followed
with an illustrated edition at fifteen cents and one without pictures at ten, and
others joined the fray. Department stores competed in offering *Quo Vadis* as
a special, cutting the retail price sometimes as low as seven cents. The best seller

lists, made up on the basis of regular bookstore sales only, carried *Quo Vadis* for nearly two years; and in the first twenty-five years of such lists, it has been reckoned best seller Number One.* A dramatic version competed with Wilson Barrett's *The Sign of the Cross* on the stage.

At the end of eighteen months, Little, Brown advertised that they had sold 600,000 copies—a total which it had taken *Ben-Hur* more than a dozen years to reach. The original publishers now had *Quo Vadis* for sale in half a dozen forms, including one at twenty-five cents and another at twelve dollars. It was still being sold in paper covers as late as 1915; by that time it had probably reached a sale considerably beyond a million and a half.

Quo Vadis led the *Bookman's* annual list for 1897; Number Two was James Lane Allen's *The Choir Invisible,* which, though not historical romance in the pattern which was so soon to become popular, was notable for a vivid and fresh depiction of pioneer Kentucky. Allen's charming story did not reach the top ranks of over-all best sellers, nor did Number Two for the following year— S. Weir Mitchell's *Hugh Wynne, Free Quaker.* Dr. Mitchell's masterpiece was perhaps the best of the novels of its type in this period, and for a two-volume book it had a remarkable sale. It dealt with the American Revolution, while his *The Adventures of François,* which tied for tenth place in the *Bookman* list of that same year of 1898, had the French Revolution for its setting.

History in motley came on tumultuously in that year. There was Robert W. Chambers' *Ashes of Empire,* which used episodes of the Franco-Prussian War; it was only moderately successful. Chambers had played with the Zenda novel, and he was to make some hits later with the society novel, but he never quite achieved even the *Bookman's* yearly lists. Crawford's *Via Crucis,* though published in 1898, did not reach the monthly best seller lists until late the next year. It profited from its title in a language which, in view of the wild popularity of *Quo Vadis* at this time, one hesitates to call "dead."

Came 1899, and with it Charles Major's *When Knighthood Was in Flower,* Winston Churchill's *Richard Carvel,* and Paul Leicester Ford's *Janice Meredith.* Now everybody was aware of the parade of historical romance. The past was advancing upon them, with all its drama and melodrama, its picturesque pageantry, its portraiture of famous men and passionate women. History was coming alive—the history of Rome and knighthood and the French Revolution and (best of all) the history of the American Revolution and the American pioneers—and how the American reading public loved it all! It was, like the enthusiasm for Scott and Cooper almost a hundred years before, the reader could enjoy the thrills of romance and at the same time congratulate himself that he was improving his mind by storing it with history and biography. Blessed amalgam!

*This is according to a system devised by Irving Harlow Hart in which points are assigned for each appearance in the lists according to the ranking given each time. See *Publishers' Weekly,* January 29, 1921 (vol. XCIX, pp. 269-272).

When Knighthood Was in Flower fell somewhat short of the sale of 625,000 necessary to put it into the top-selling bracket of the nineties, but it was second in the *Bookman* list for 1899 and ninth in 1900. By the end of that year it had sold over 300,000. It went back to the reign of Henry VIII, and used the tempestuous Mary Tudor as its unruly heroine. It had enough that was shocking to a "mauve decade," and enough that was melodramatic, to make it a fascinating novel and a good stage-play for Julia Marlowe to star in. Major returned to the best seller lists in 1902 with *Dorothy Vernon of Haddon Hall*, which dealt with Elizabethan times and was on the whole better done than his first novel; but again he failed to reach the top rank.

Winston Churchill's historical novels were of different texture. Their author himself admitted they were mid-Victorian in an era in which critics were already resenting the restraints, the leisureliness, and the surface quality of the older novelists; and Churchill was far more like Bulwer-Lytton or even Thackeray than like Stephen Crane or Theodore Dreiser. But for all his conservatism, he had something to offer the American reading public of the turn of the century which they read patiently and applauded in the most practical way—by buying his books by the hundreds of thousands. Into these historical novels—*Richard Carvel*, *The Crossing*, and *The Crisis*—Churchill wove the national moods and ideals, the pageantry and portraiture, the half-epical movement of people and events, which make up a popular story of American development. Much of it was uncritical, to be sure, but it did suit the patriotic climate of its times. Throughout fifteen years or more, during the publication of his historical romances and of four novels dealing with social and political problems which followed them, Churchill was the great popular novelist of middle-class American readers.

It was *Richard Carvel* that really made its author's fame. Its pictures of Washington and John Paul Jones, of Charles James Fox and Horace Walpole, and better yet its story of the great sea-fight between the *Bonhomme Richard* and the *Serapis* won it a host of admirers. Churchill, educated at the Naval Academy at Annapolis, had resigned his commission immediately after graduation, but he did the Navy a fine service in this story. His depiction of Captain Jones is superior in every way to Cooper's in *The Pilot. The Crossing* tells of western exploration and pioneering, introducing George Rogers Clark and David Crockett. *The Crisis* centers in St. Louis, the city of the author's birth and boyhood, in the years of Civil War; and it adds Lincoln, Grant, and Sherman to the gallery of Churchill portraits.

Two of Churchill's books reached the top rank of best sellers—*Richard Carvel* and *The Crisis*. Both were published by the Macmillan Company, priced at the usual dollar and a half; but the liberal trade discounts and unrestrained bookstore competition reduced the retail price sometimes as low as eighty or ninety cents. Both were dramatized; E. E. Rose made the stage version of *Carvel* and Churchill himself prepared *The Crisis* for James K. Hackett. The former, as a book, sold nearly half a million by the end of its first year, and more in the regular edition through two decades; in the Grosset & Dunlap reprint and Macmillan's Pocket Classics it added some 200,000 more. *The Crisis* did even better, and its popularity has been durable; it has now passed the million mark. All three of the Churchill historical romances are still in print.

But we must go back to 1899, when *Richard Carvel* was published. In that year also appeared *Janice Meredith*, one of the best novels dealing with the American Revolution. In its story, General Washington is an important character, the hero is a dashing adventurer, and the heroine is beautiful, intrepid and fascinating. Indeed, one could multiply adjectives in speaking of Janice. The history was reasonably good as history, and the fiction was good storytelling.

The author, Paul Leicester Ford, was a historian of note, and he had already demonstrated his ability as a novelist by *The Honorable Peter Sterling*, a popular book of the mid-nineties. He was an interesting personality—a hunchback, a man of wealth and refinement, belonging to a family of bibliophiles and scholars. He had one brother, Worthington, who became a famous bibliographer and librarian, and another, Malcolm, whose athletic prowess contrasted sharply with Paul's physical deficiencies. When the father died, he disinherited Malcolm, who blamed his brother Paul and shot and killed him before turning his pistol against himself. This tragedy took place in the summer of 1902, when Paul was thirty-seven, and while *Janice Meredith* was still in the best seller lists.

Published by Dodd, Mead & Company in the summer of 1899 after serialization in the *Bookman*, the novel began leading the monthly best seller lists by October and was prominent in them for more than a year. Girls wore the "Janice Meredith curl" over the right shoulder, according to the medallion portrait shown on the book's cover, and for a time at least the pompadour of the Gibson girl was superseded. Mary Mannering captivated audiences in the title rôle of the stage version. Like *The Crisis, Janice Meredith* has worn well, is still in print, and has sold more than a million copies.

In 1900 the *Bookman's* ten best sellers included *Janice Meredith, Richard Carvel,* and *When Knighthood Was in Flower,* as well as two newcomers in historical fiction—*To Have and to Hold,* by Mary Johnston, and *Alice of Old Vincennes,* by Maurice Thompson. Thus half the list consisted of fiction displaying the past—from the England of Mary Tudor in the sixteenth century to the Wabash Valley of Alice Roussilon in the eighteenth. And then there was Booth Tarkington's delightful novelette of swords and lace and hopeless love—*Monsieur Beaucaire*—which did not make the annual list but sold well and long nevertheless. *To Have and to Hold,* which is set in Virginia in the seventeenth century, passed the half-million mark in sales; but neither it nor Maurice Thompson's story of the American Revolution in the West ever climbed to the topmost rank in distribution. To do this in the decade beginning in 1900, a book had to sell over 750,000 copies. But, as the writer on "Fiction,

American" in Appleton's *Annual Cyclopaedia* for that year pointed out, the million-circulation book was now becoming common. "The idea," he wrote, "that audiences could be found for several novels at one time, running well into the millions, was not born until within the past two years."

The next year (1901) the three top titles on the *Bookman* list were those of historical novels—*The Crisis, Alice of Old Vincennes*, and Bertha Runkle's *The Helmet of Navarre*. Maurice Hewlett's *Richard Yea-and-Nay*, a story which went back to the twelfth century, when knighthood really was in flower, to follow the adventures of Richard Coeur de Lion, was in eighth place in the annual résumé. But neither of the two newcomers to the list made a total sale of more than a few hundred thousand.

Again in 1902 five historical romances were among the *Bookman's* ten best sellers; thereafter no such list contained more than one or two novels of that type until the mid-thirties. The great procession of fictional history and historical fiction ended in a grand splurge in that year. Owen Wister's *The Virginian* headed the roll: its author maintained it was a historical novel, but it seems rather to belong to the great tribe of "westerns." The list included also Charles Major's *Dorothy Vernon of Haddon Hall*, Emerson Hough's *The Mississippi Bubble*, Mary Johnston's *Audrey*, and Booth Tarkington's *The Two Vanrevels*. Many other historical novels were published in 1902, and a few of them reached the monthly best seller lists; the only one of the group that requires mention here is Gertrude Atherton's *The Conqueror*, an excellent fictionized biography of Alexander Hamilton, which has sold at least half a million copies to book-buyers of two generations. But no historical novel of 1902 can be said to have reached the ranks of over-all best sellers unless we admit *The Virginian* to that category.

Another best seller which, though historical, was definitely not of the cloak-and-sword variety was *The Little Shepherd of Kingdom Come*. John Fox, Jr., had already published two novels before he made his big success with this one, but he was better known for his short stories of the Cumberland mountain folk. It is to this genre that *The Little Shepherd* belongs. The orphan Chad, who prays God to help him "ack like a man," is an appealing hero; and the fact that he grows up into the complications of the Civil War is more or less incidental. The story of a boy's fight against odds recurs again and again in the best seller list, and here we have an Alger theme transferred from New York streets to the Cumberlands.

The book was published by Scribners in 1903 and was a success from the first. It was dramatized by Eugene Walter in 1916. A questionnaire to librarians as late as 1932 showed that *The Little Shepherd*, as well as its author's other great hit, *The Trail of the Lonesome Pine*, were among the older books in chief demand at the public libraries. It has had a total sale of about 1,225,000 copies.

The Trail of the Lonesome Pine came in 1918, after the great procession of historical novels had passed. It belongs more to the Gene Stratton-Porter school:

here is a poor mountain girl who loves nature and also an engineer from the North, and they get mixed up in a political feud. The theme of the unequal love-match is even more common in fictional best sellers than that of the success story: from *Pamela*, the first novel on our list, to *Zenda* and *Graustark*, *The Virginian* and *The Trail of the Lonesome Pine*, and on to the latest big romance of today, the device appears and reappears. Fox was never original or profound, but he knew how to combine the old sure-fire materials; and his two great successes were happily integrated with current fashions in fiction. The second one, also put on the stage by Eugene Walter, had even larger sales than the first—which was no surprise to the publishers, who had given it the record-breaking advance printing of 100,000 and advertised it well.

One more historical novel of the times has been reserved to the end of this chapter because it falls outside the general pattern. Stephen Crane's *The Red Badge of Courage* was a success when it was published by Appleton in October, 1895. It ranked eighth among the best sellers of the annual bookstore computation of 1896. It brought comparative prosperity and greater opportunity to a hitherto neglected genius. But it was a realistic presentation of Civil War experience, and it did not fall in with the current romantic enthusiasms. It eventually reached the top best seller bracket not because of sales in the nineties, but by reason of the appreciation of its values over a full half-century. During the second World War, for example, it was reprinted in the Modern Library and in the Heritage Press series; it has averaged nearly ten thousand annually for the last forty years. Apparently it will continue to sell, along with the more important works of American literature, for many years to come.

XXXII. THE FAMILY NOVEL
IN THE NEW CENTURY

> Now what do I care for the newspaper or magazine critic yammering that there is not such a thing as a moral man, and that my pictures of life are sentimental and idealised? They are! And I glory in them! They are straight, living pictures from the lives of men and women of morals, honour, and loving-kindness. . . . Am I the only woman in this broad land so born and reared? Was my home the only one with a moral code and religious practice? Are there not homes by the thousand in which men and women are true to their highest ideals?
>
> *Gene Stratton-Porter*

NOVELS of home and family life have been a staple commodity on our best seller list from the time when fiction first made an appearance there. From *The Vicar of Wakefield* to *A Tree Grows in Brooklyn* the pattern has not varied greatly: homely characters and incidents, pathos, humor, a love affair within or without the family, a touch of melodrama when the sophisticated outside world impinges on the moral security of home life, growing pains of children, love of the family circle. Such stories are by nature suitable for the young, and they gain in readership by that appeal; but they also attract adults of the great middle class who have themselves grown up in homes such as those described with so much intimate detail in this family fiction.

It was natural that these books should be written most often, though not always, by women, and that they should center upon the experiences of girls oftener than upon those of boys. We have had two great outpourings of such novels. The first came in the middle of the nineteenth century, when Grace Aguilar's *Home Influence,* Mrs. A. D. T. Whitney's *Faith Gartney's Girlhood,* Susan Warner's *The Wide, Wide World,* and the stories of Louisa May Alcott were so popular; and the second in the first decades of the twentieth, with Kate Douglas Wiggin, Gene Stratton-Porter, Alice Hegan Rice, and Eleanor Porter.

Alice Caldwell Hegan was a social worker in Louisville, Kentucky, when she became acquainted with the courageous and humorous mother of an interesting brood who later became known to the world as Mrs. Wiggs of the Cabbage Patch. Miss Hegan had already written some lively character sketches, and her new acquaintances challenged her faculty for literary creation. She wrote out her story on the blank pages of an old ledger, partly in pencil and partly in ink; and because the ledger contained only sixty-eight pages, the story was a novelette. It was declined by one publisher on account of its comparative brevity, but Joseph B. Gilder, of the Century Company, liked it so well that his house published it, in September, 1901. It was sold for a dollar, and began a series of shorter books at that price which later included *Lovey Mary, The Lady of the Decoration,* and *Daddy Long-Legs.*

Mrs. Wiggs of the Cabbage Patch was published in an initial edition of two thousand, but six thousand more were called for before the end of 1901. The next year 170,000 copies were issued, and in 1903 it sold quite as well. For twelve consecutive months it was one of the *Bookman's* best sellers. It became successful as a play, and touring companies eventually showed it all over the English-speaking world. It has been produced four times for the movies and was long a radio feature. Translated into seven foreign languages, it spread the fame of Mrs. Wiggs all over Europe. It is still in print, both in a school series and in a two-volume de luxe edition; and the wit and originality and courage of the mother striving to rear her family properly without any income to speak of are as refreshing today as they were when the story delighted its first readers. There is a Harumesque quality in some of the observations of Mrs. Wiggs, as when she says: "I'm just wore out, that's all. It'll be with me like it was with Uncle Ned's ole ox, I reckon; he kep' a-goin' an' a-goin' till he died a-standin' up, an' even then they had to push him over."

Shortly after the publication of her first and most popular book, Miss Hegan was married to the poet Cale Young Rice. Her *Lovey Mary* joined *Mrs. Wiggs* in the best seller lists for 1903, but never reached the top rank in over-all sales.

Late in that year's lists was another family novel destined to outstrip both—Kate Douglas Wiggin's *Rebecca of Sunnybrook Farm.*

The author had been born a Smith, was educated in New England schools, and founded San Francisco's first kindergarten in 1878. To raise money for this project, she wrote in 1882 *The Story of Patsy,* a little tale which was privately published, sold three thousand copies, and made a neat sum for the Silver Street Kindergarten. Four years later she did another short story for the same purpose; it was called *The Birds' Christmas Carol,* and was so successful that the author sent it to Houghton, Mifflin & Company, who gave it a much larger success in a booklet long popular in the holiday trade. Meantime Kate Douglas Smith had married Samuel Bradley Wiggin and moved to New York. She wrote some more little stories about children; and after her husband's death she spent several years abroad, sight-seeing and writing the Penelope series, half fiction and half travel. She had been married again, to George C. Riggs, a wealthy New York merchant, before the publication of *Rebecca of Sunnybrook Farm;* but the new book's title-page had the author's name as Kate Douglas Wiggin, the form in which it was now well known to many readers.

Rebecca was a lively little girl who belonged to a poverty-stricken family; sent to live with her aunts while she went to school, she encountered a good many trials but kept her cheery disposition and usually emerged triumphantly from the troubles she got into. The village characters are drawn without exaggeration, and the whole atmosphere of the place is convincing; but it is Rebecca herself who makes the simple story appealing. The book was published in October, 1903, by Houghton, Mifflin & Company, and was a steady success for many years. A dramatic version, in which the author collaborated, was produced in New York in 1910 and in London two years later, with Edith Taliaferro in the title role; and it was played by stock companies for many years. Mary Pickford played Rebecca in a screen version. The book is said to have sold over 1,100,000 copies in the United States and has been translated into several foreign languages.

Another little girl—and "such an interesting little thing," as Mrs. Cuthbert justly observed—was Anne, of Green Gables, on Prince Edward Island in the Gulf of St. Lawrence. Like Rebecca, she comes to a new home in the very beginning of the story, and has to make her way against odds. But red-haired Anne, the chatterer, comes directly out of an orphan asylum—and under very unfortunate circumstances, for Mr. and Mrs. Cuthbert had sent for a boy, and there had been a mistake. But the Cuthberts decide, against their sober judgment and the advice of neighbors, to keep her, and the rest of the story is about how Anne, who finds everywhere such "scope for imagination," adjusts herself to her new home, and school and church and friends. The characters are excellent, the enthusiasm for nature is contagious, and there is charm even for grown-ups in the story. Mark Twain declared Anne "the dearest and most moving and delightful child since Alice in Wonderland," and many other readers have felt a similar affection for her.

Lucy M. Montgomery, the author, said her book was designed for teen-age girls. She was born on Prince Edward Island, became a teacher, and later married a Presbyterian minister, the Rev. Ewan MacDonald, and lived in Toronto. *Anne of Green Gables* was published by L. C. Page & Company, of Boston, in 1908, and entered immediately upon a long career of popularity. Its sales are now between eight and nine hundred thousand. Mary Miles Minter starred in a motion picture version; and three sequels were called for, each of which found a receptive but decreasing audience among the friends of the witching Anne.

But the most successful writer of novels about children and the home in all our best seller history was Gene Stratton-Porter. She was the twelfth child of a Dutch-American mother and a father of English ancestry who divided his time between the cultivation of a farm and preaching in a Methodist country church. Geneva (or Gene, as she later preferred to be called) ran wild in the fields and woods until her eleventh year, when the family moved to the nearby town of Wabash, Indiana. There Geneva went to school, scribbled essays, read romances and poetry, and at twenty-two married a druggist who was her senior by fourteen years. Her husband prospered, what with banking and oil interests, and they built a large house on the edge of the great Limberlost Swamp just south of the town. Here Mrs. Porter was able to indulge her love for nature, especially for birds, by careful observation in which the camera aided her own sharp eyes. Her first writing was in the form of natural history sketches, which she sold to *Recreation* and *Outing,* accompanied by original photographs.

Mrs. Porter's first book was a sentimental story of the courtship and marriage (let us not be so crude as to call it mating) of a young cardinal and his bride. It was called *The Song of the Cardinal,* and belonged to a considerable mass of literature in which animals were humanized. Two best sellers, *Black Beauty* and *Beautiful Joe,* had helped to win general acceptance for the idea; and Kipling and Thompson-Seton had more recently given it added vogue. In a few years now, President Theodore Roosevelt would charge into the whole battalion of "nature-fakers" and batter some of them rather severely. In this onslaught, Mrs. Porter was to escape attention, though *The Song of the Cardinal* did receive some adverse criticism from naturalists. On the whole, however, her first book was a popular success, and was eventually widely translated into the European languages.

This encouraged the author to a more ambitious attempt, and the result was the first of her five top-bracket best sellers. Five—count them—five: *Freckles* (1904), *The Girl of the Limberlost* (1909), *The Harvester* (1911), *Laddie* (1913), *Michael O'Halloran* (1915). Up to this time only two authors had made a higher score—Dickens and Scott—though a contemporary writer by the name of Harold Bell Wright was soon matching Mrs. Porter bull's-eye for bull's-eye.* *Freckles,* the first of the lot, got off to a slow start. Doubleday, Page & Company was enthusiastic about it and printed ten thousand copies, but it sold slowly and the bookstores began "unloading." It was only after the publication of Mrs. Porter's second book, and also after some urging by the original publishers, that Grosset & Dunlap issued the fifty-cent reprint of *Freckles* which eventually sold about 1,400,000 copies and inaugurated Mrs. Porter's career as a leading best seller writer.

This was in 1910, after the publication of *A Girl of the Limberlost.* That, too, was taken over by Grosset & Dunlap, and sold only a little less than *Freckles.* Reprint sales did not count in the *Bookman* lists, so *Freckles* never got a mention there, and *A Girl of the Limberlost* made only a few scattered appearances; but by the time *The Harvester* was published, Gene Stratton-Porter's was a name which sold even the original dollar-and-a-half edition in great quantities, and that book ranked fifth in the annual list for 1911. Also Grosset & Dunlap sold 800,000 copies of it, and total sales ran over a million. *Laddie* gained a much larger total, close to a million and a half, of which the original edition furnished more than half. *Michael O'Halloran* made about the same total as *The Harvester.* At the time of her death between eight and nine million copies of Mrs. Porter's nineteen books had been sold. Grant Overton once estimated that she made two million dollars out of her literary activity.

What was there in these books which won readers by the millions? What were they like? They kept rather closely to a common formula or recipe, but each varied in some particular ingredient. A child grows up, and perhaps learns to collect birds' eggs or orchids or moths; he or she goes to school, likes to read fairy stories and poetry, and learns the moral code from various experiences; falls in love, but finds plenty of troubles in courtship before the inevitable happy ending. Very important is love of nature, which is usually given a practical turn, as where the Girl of the Limberlost earns the money for her education by collecting moths. Important also is religious teaching, though the children (like Little Sister in *Laddie*) are inclined to poke fun at the queer prayers and church doings of some characters: it is the author's father-was-a-preacher attitude. The child element is important in all of these books except *The Harvester.* Not only do they deal with children's affairs, but they are written so completely on the childish level that they seem rather banal to any active adult intelligence. Doubtless grown-ups once read them because they liked to recall, through them, their own childhood experiences. Finally, the stories always preach the gospel of cheeriness, keeping a stiff upper lip, seeing the silver lining, and so on. There can be no doubt that they were helpful to many

---

* Cooper had also made a score of five. Erle Stanley Gardner was later to surpass Scott (numerically) with seven. Thus Porter ties with Cooper and Wright for fourth place in number of over-all best sellers. After these come Mark Twain, Kipling, and Mrs. Southworth with four each.

readers, as the multitude of letters that the author received from enthusiastic admirers testified again and again.

That Mrs. Porter wrote according to a formula she freely acknowledged. "My formula for a book was damned by three of our foremost publishers in the beginning," she once wrote, "and I have never changed it a particle." Nor was she ashamed of the liberal admixture of sweetness in that recipe. A paragraph from her long reply to one of *The Harvester's* critics is worthy of quotation:

> Today a criticism of *Laddie* by a minister of the Gospel was sent me in which he wrote of it as "molasses fiction." What a wonderful compliment! All the world loves sweets. Afield, bears as well as flies would drown in it. Molasses is more necessary to the happiness of human and beast than vinegar, and over-indulgence in it is not nearly so harmful to the system. I am a molasses person myself. So is my family. So was my father's family. So are most of my friends—all of them who are happy, as a matter of fact. So I shall keep straight on writing of the love and joy of life I have found in the world, and when I have used the last drop of my molasses, I shall stop writing. Forever the acid of life will have to be doled out by those who have enough in their systems to be accustomed to it. God gave me a taste for sweets and the sales of the books I write prove that a few other people are similar to me in this.*

Mrs. Porter made a shrewd observation in an article in the *American Magazine* in 1919. She said that she had never called her books novels and did not regard them as such: she knew that the buyers and readers of the leading realistic novels of the day never bought or read her stories. Clearly, the family-circle story of the period had a public of its own. Moreover, this was a public in the low-income brackets, since it took a cheaper reprint to start her books moving.

Mrs. Porter felt keenly the criticism of the leading reviewers, nor was she able always to fall back on the comfortable defense of popular endorsement. William Lyon Phelps once wrote of her: "She is a public institution, like Yellowstone Park, and I should not think she would care any more than a mountain for adverse criticism. She does, though." And she did turn to what she called "stark realism" for one novel, *The White Flag*, published the year before her death. Neither this book nor her versified romances were successful.

In 1915 the Porters moved to Philadelphia; but after 1919 Mrs. Porter spent most of her time in California, writing and supervising the production of her stories for the movies. An early motion picture of one of the established producers displeased her, and about 1920 she set up her own company with her son-in-law as director. In the midst of her busy life of writing and picture-making and nature-study, in December, 1924, the automobile in which she was driving on the streets of Los Angeles collided with a street car, and Mrs. Porter received injuries from which she died some hours later in a hospital. Her books still enjoy a considerable sale.

Unlike the other family fiction of this period, and yet definitely a part of it,

* Jeanette Porter Meehan's *The Lady of the Limberlost: The Life and Letters of Gene Stratton-Porter*, p. 159. Copyright 1928 by Doubleday & Company, Inc.

was Kathleen Norris' novelette entitled *Mother*. It was first written as a short story, and was so published in the *American Magazine*. The author's husband was Charles G. Norris, brother of Frank Norris, and at that time a member of the editorial staff of the *American;* later he became a well known novelist. He urged his wife to expand her story for book publication, and she did so one summer in a crowded resort boarding-house. A small baby took most of her time that summer; but when it was asleep, she stole downstairs to the noisy boarding-house parlor, set up her typewriter there, and completed a story which was to move the hearts of millions of readers.

It was published by the Macmillan Company in 1911 at one dollar and began a large and steady sale which eventually reached nearly a million copies in their edition. President Theodore Roosevelt, recognizing it as an effective tract in his campaign against "race suicide," endorsed it. It was serialized in the *Ladies' Home Journal* after its appearance in book form. Doubleday, Page & Company, which had refused a chance to issue the original edition, later put out a reprint which, with those of Grosset & Dunlap and the Pocket Books, added almost a half-million to the book's grand total.

Mother is sentimental, and it is doubtless too much a sermon on motherhood and lots of it; but it gives us a good common-life picture of a crowded, busy household—the kind so many readers had known intimately in childhood —and it is safe to say that few readers have finished it with dry eyes.

If you think Kathleen Norris a sentimentalist, try Eleanor Hallowell Abbott, whose *Molly Make-Believe* adorned the *Bookman's* best seller lists in 1910 and 1911. Mrs. Abbott seems to the present jaded reader of romances about little girls and their trials in the family circle to reach the nadir of the whole business. Even *Pollyanna* is better.

All the books considered in this chapter, except perhaps *Mother,* make cheerfulness in the face of troubles a primary virtue. Intellectually considered, neither optimism nor pessimism affords a proper basis for thinking; both represent romantic attitudes which, in comparison with a realistic frame of mind, seem unsound and unreasonable. But to Mrs. Wiggs, Anne of Green Gables, and Pollyanna, optimism was not a philosophy but an available mechanism of escape. Escapism may be condemned by the rigorous intellectual, but it is often a very good thing practically. It is indeed an integral part of courage, and enables one to endure situations otherwise unbearable. But the great danger, of course, in employing an escape mechanism is that you may do it so easily and so often that it becomes an unconscious habit, and perhaps even one so essential to you that a pathological condition is induced—in other words, you go off your rocker. Now, Mrs. Wiggs did not go off her rocker, because she was a strong-minded woman and knew what she was doing; her optimism was a form of wit. So it was with Anne's euphoric "scope of imagination." So it was with Pollyanna's "glad game."

Pollyanna works at her game rather seriously, to be sure, but it is always a

game; and the reader is amused by it—until, at length, if he has what is sometimes called adult intelligence, he is likely to be bored by it. Because a game
is all right for a while, but "glads" on almost every one of a three-hundred-
page book are almost too much of a very good thing.

Pollyanna is another one of those stories in which a little girl gets off the
train or stagecoach in the second chapter to begin life in a new and difficult
home, and (in about the fifteenth chapter) by her cheery disposition and
essential goodness melts the hard heart of her new guardian. Pollyanna is
scarcely as engaging a sprite as Anne or Rebecca, but she plays her "glad
game" even more persistently.

The author signed herself "Eleanor Stewart" at first, but the titlepage of
her book later bore her real name, Eleanor H. Porter. She was born Eleanor
Hodgman, and was a direct descendant of Governor William Bradford, who
was grim rather than glad. She taught school for a time and later became
a singer on the concert stage. She published five novels before Pollyanna,
including the successful Miss Billy.

But it was Pollyanna, which was published serially in the Christian Herald,
and issued in book form by L. C. Page & Company, that made her one
astounding success. Published in February, 1913, new printings were called
for weekly through March, and monthly or oftener for the next year. After
that it went on and on until it piled up sales of over a million. Its title became
a by-word, and now pollyanna and pollyannish are in the dictionary. A sequel,
Pollyanna Grows Up, has sold close to 400,000 copies. In reviewing it, the
Boston Transcript said that Pollyanna, "having made glad everyone in Beld-
ingsville, Vermont, enlarges her sphere of activity and attempts to bring joy
to all in Boston, a prodigious and, of course, quite impossible task." The publishers registered the Pollyanna name as a patent trade-mark and have brought
out eleven volumes in their series of "Glad Books," most of them by Harriett
Lummis Smith and Elizabeth Barton. Mrs. Porter continued to publish a
novel every year until her death in 1920, and her Just David was in the best
seller list in 1916.

The same list contained Jean Webster's Dear Enemy. More popular in the
long run was the same author's Daddy-Long-Legs (1912), a sentimental,
clever little epistolary romance about an orphan girl; but neither book sold
half a million copies.

Leading the Bookman's lists for 1910 was Florence M. Barclay's The Rosary.
It was really closer kin to Jessie Fothergill's The First Violin, which had been
published in 1878 but was still read in America, than to the "home novels" of
1910; but it appealed to the same women's public that liked Laddie and
Rebecca of Sunnybrook Farm. Mrs. Barclay belonged to the English sentimental school, but her characters were artists and duchesses. She herself was
the daughter of one clergyman and the wife of another; she was a sister of
Mrs. Ballington Booth, with whom she once shared the platform on a tour

of American Chautauqua circuits. In *The Rosary* she fashioned a touching love-story around and about Ethelbert Nevin's popular song. It was published by Putnam's on the insistence of the wife of a member of the firm and it appeared simultaneously in England and America. It sold slowly at first, but picked up suddenly when the publishers broadcast a postcard advertisement bearing a few bars of the song. In a little over three years it sold half a million copies; it has now passed the million mark and still sells.

Consideration of the whole group of family novels suggests some tentative conclusions. Probably the expansive mood of the first two decades of the new century provided a kind of emotional climate which was kindly to books embodying optimistic philosophies. This was the age of self-confidence before the deluge—before war and depression and bewilderment—when personal courage was sure to win out, and the way to be happy was to be good, as Laddie maintained. It was also a time when nature-study was coming more and more into the schools—a development in which Gene Stratton-Porter was much interested—and that may have had something to do with the popularity of these books, most of which emphasize the love of nature.

But another conclusion is also forced upon us. Most of the readers of these books came to them with childish attitudes and appreciations. Of course, to some extent all except *Mother* and *The Rosary* were directed toward the teen-age audience, and especially toward girls; certainly all of them were read eagerly by millions of girls. But they were also read by millions of adults, and in that connection we must not forget that the average educational attainment of American readers was not then, and is not now, very high. In 1910 less than half of the population twenty-five years of age had completed a grade-school education, and only about four per cent possessed college diplomas.* The IQ testers have never invaded the Census Bureau (thank heaven), but even without their help we can be sure that a large proportion of our population gets along on rather meagre quotas of what our psychologists are pleased to call intelligence. As Ed Howe once observed, the man who invented the designation "common people" was very nearly right.

All of which constitutes no indictment of our reading public or our educational system, but it may help to explain the popularity of the Mesdames Porter, Gene Stratton and Eleanor H.

* The Census did not record figures on educational attainment until 1940, when the median was 8.4 years, with 4.6 per cent of the population having finished college. Considering the census reports that school attendance for 5-10 year-olds increased from 1910 to 1940 from 59.2% to 70.8%, there can be no doubt of the above statement.

XXXIII. CHILDREN'S BOOKS AGAIN

Backward, turn backward, O Time, in your flight.
Elizabeth Akers Allen

THIS chapter is in the nature of a postscript to the foregoing discussion of the family novels of the first two decades of the twentieth century. There are a few books of the period which were written for or about children, but which fall so distinctly outside the Porter-Wiggins group that they require separate consideration.

There was, for example, L. Frank Baum's *The Wonderful Wizard of Oz*. It never quite reached the best seller scale we have set up, but it was the most popular juvenile of the turn of the century and established a long line of Oz books. Published in 1900 by Bobbs Merrill, it was a great success both in the book-stores and on the stage. Two obscure vaudeville actors, Fred Stone and Dave Montgomery, became scintillating stars of the comic opera stage in this medium. A bosom friend of the author, F. K. Reilly, became the publisher of nearly forty sequels bearing the imprint of Reilly & Lee, Chicago.

Collections of Bible stories for the young have long been popular. One of them appears on our list as early as 1745. In the latter part of the nineteenth century, Charles Foster's *Story of the Bible*, first issued in 1873, was widely distributed. But it remained for Jesse Lyman Hurlbut's *Story of the Bible* to break all records in this field. Dr. Hurlbut was editor of Sunday School literature for the Methodist Church and a leader in the Chautauqua movement. His biblical narrative, told in simple language and divided into 168 stories, was first published by the John C. Winston Company, of Philadelphia, in 1904, with copious illustration. After about fifteen years of steady sales, some 200,000 copies having been disposed of, the book was reset and issued in even more attractive form. And now it began to boom. By 1930 it had reached the million mark, and in 1946 the Winston Company was advertising it with the line: "More than 2,000,000 copies have been sold." The latest editions carry handsome pictures in color.

A great favorite at the turn of the century was "the children's poet," James Whitcomb Riley. Wrote William Dean Howells in 1899: "Riley has known how to endear himself to a wider range of American humanity than any other American poet." * Be that as it may, the original 1883 collection of Riley, in that form and in the many enlarged and re-arranged editions, certainly rates a best seller listing. That first slender volume was entitled *The Old Swimmin' Hole and 'Leven More Poems by Benjamin F. Johnson, of Boone*. It was published by Merrill, Meigs & Company, of Indianapolis, later the Bowen-

* *North American Review*, May, 1899 (vol. CLXVIII, p. 588).

Merrill Company, and now Bobbs-Merrill. This house has published most of the editions of Riley, though collections have appeared in such series as the Blue Ribbon Books, Grosset & Dunlap series, and the Pocket Books. There was a time when "The Old Swimmin' Hole," "An Old Sweetheart of Mine," and "Little Orphant Annie" were memorized and recited by thousands, and the Bowen-Merrill illustrated editions were on half the parlor center-tables in the land.

Riley won his first fame as a newspaper poet on the Indianapolis *Journal*. A little later Eugene Field made a great reputation with his poems in the Chicago *Daily News*, and other writers of verse became popular "colyumists." In 1899 Edgar A. Guest, exchange editor of the *Detroit Free Press*, began writing occasional verses for that paper; and in 1906 he began producing a daily column the chief feature of which was a homely sort of "pome" about common, homely things. Ten years later a syndicate began furnishing "Eddie" Guest's daily verses to a number of papers—as many as three hundred at the height of his popularity. What with daily syndication, weekly radio programs, royalties on books and greeting cards, movie rights, and so on, Guest's annual income for a long time was in the neighborhood of $100,000 a year —which marks him as a good business man at least. Sales of well over a million have been repeatedly claimed for his first and most popular book, *A Heap o' Livin'*, published in 1915 by Reilly & Britton, later Reilly & Lee, of Chicago.

Though Booth Tarkington's novels have appeared again and again on weekly, monthly, and yearly best seller lists, only *Penrod* has sold enough copies to win a place on the over-all lists. The adventures of the inimitable twelve-year-old who gives his name to this book appeared first in short stories in various magazines in 1913. The next year Doubleday, Page & Company published the book, which was recorded as a best seller in the *Bookman* lists. Doubleday sales, together with those of Scribner, Grosset & Dunlap, and Armed Services editions, have brought its total to the neighborhood of a million.

XXXIV. HAROLD BELL WRIGHT

Uncounted Americans whose ancestors looked to the church as the chief inspiration of their daily existence no longer attend any church. Other thousands, though still nominally members or attendants, have ceased to admit the church or its ministers as a really vital influence in their lives. With expensive equipment, large funds, an educated clergy, often costly music, and other attractions, the church, taken as a whole, no longer leads or even deeply stirs the American people.
Ray Stannard Baker in American Magazine, December, 1908

ONE of the most disturbing factors of the social and economic unrest at the turn of the century was the changing attitude toward the churches. Proletarian movements, political crusades against the trusts and intrenched wealth in general, muckraking writers in the periodicals, and many other elements labored to arouse the social conscience of the people; but the churches were quiescent. Rebels sprang up all over the land to assert that all was not well with the American system, that the poor and underprivileged were not always to blame for their condition but were the victims of injustice, and that something ought to be done about it; but the churches, by and large, kept their silence on such questions. The bitterest critics of the churches, like Upton Sinclair in his *The Profits of Religion,* charged them with being the tools of the moneyed interests; many others who would not go as far as that attacked them for their insensitiveness to the actual social abuses around them.

In the first decade of the new century there was some tendency on the part of the churches to study current social questions and interpret them in the light of the teachings of Jesus. The Congregationalists, the Presbyterians, and the Methodists had made some beginnings in the study of labor problems before the Federal Council of the Churches of Christ in America assumed the leadership in such activities upon its organization in 1908. But an institution in which tradition and forms are basic cannot be changed easily or quickly, and the slowness of the churches' response called forth the impatient accusations of hypocrisy and smugness.

There was a flood of literature on the subject. People still read and discussed *Robert Elsmere* a decade or two after its first publication. Another book of the eighties which long retained its popularity was Josiah Strong's discussion of social Christianity called *Our Country.* Books and articles about the social settlements in the cities, the Salvation Army and "institutional" churches were numerous. *In His Steps* continued to pose its intimate question, "What would Jesus do?" Ralph Connor's successive novels portraying a rugged and pragmatic Christianity were popular. In 1908-1909 the *American Magazine* printed Ray Stannard Baker's enlightening and hard-hitting series entitled "The Spiritual Unrest." Four years later Winston Churchill's *The Inside of the Cup* led the *Bookman's* best seller lists; it was a thematic novel embodying an argument for recognition of the social values in the teachings of Jesus. One cannot dip into the popular literature of the first two decades of the twentieth century without being impressed by the emphasis on the church and its problems. Street & Smith, always responsive to popular interests, began in 1910 a new ten-cent series in paper covers called the Alliance Library, which included Dr. Sheldon's *In His Steps,* Rev. Cortland Myers' *Would Christ Belong to a Labor Union?,* Rev. D. L. Moody's *What Is Christ?,* Rev. C. H. Spurgeon's *John Ploughman's Talk,* Rev. C. W. Gordon's (Ralph Connor's) *Black Rock,* and so on.

Into the midst of this flood the Rev. Harold Bell Wright launched his first novel, following it with others, timed at proper intervals and prompted by extraordinary advertising campaigns, until he eventually made one of the most amazing records in the history of American best sellers.

Wright was born in Rome, New York, in 1872. His mother died when he was ten, and shortly thereafter he was put out to work on a farm. His educational opportunities were limited to irregular country schooling and two years of study, after he had reached manhood, in the preparatory department of Hiram College. He learned the trade of house-painting; paint fascinated him, and some years later he tried his hand at landscapes on canvas. He left Hiram on account of illness, and at that time began his lifelong and successful struggle against tuberculosis. He went first to the Ozarks, in Missouri, searching for health, painting landscapes, doing odd jobs for a livelihood. There, like his own Shepherd of the Hills, he became interested in the people around him and began preaching in a schoolhouse and giving religious instruction. Having begun thus as a preacher, without benefit of college or seminary, he spent nearly twelve years in the ministry of the Church of the Disciples. He occupied briefly pastorates in Pierce City and Lebanon, Missouri, one in Kansas City, another in Pittsburg, Kansas, and finally one in Redlands, California. The number of his "moves" within twelve years is significant; he spent more than two years in only one of his five pastorates. He began his career as novelist during his preaching days; and shortly after the publication of *The Shepherd of the Hills,* he retired from the ministry and devoted himself thereafter to his writing. His latter years were spent first on a small farm ranch at the edge of the desert near Tucson, Arizona, and later in the mountains at Escondido, California, some thirty miles north of San Diego and as far west of the Anza Desert. He had married during his Kansas pastorate and was the father of three sons; later he was divorced and remarried in California. He died in 1944.

Though the parallel must not be pushed too far, Wright's career is reminiscent of that of an earlier writer of best sellers—E. P. Roe. Both were humbly born and poorly educated, both entered an orthodox ministry and later resigned to devote themselves to the ministry of print, both employed themes of great immediate and topical interest, both were strongly didactic and religious in their writing, and both knew how to tell a story that would interest multitudes of middle-class readers.

Wright was thirty years old and engaged in his most successful ministry— at Pittsburg, Kansas—when he wrote his first novel, *That Printer of Udell's.* Before the story was quite finished, he was called to assist in a revival meeting in Chicago, during the winter of 1901-1902, and there met Elsbery W. Reynolds, a Chicago mail order bookseller. Reynolds had been reared in Missouri and Kansas; he had much in common with Wright, including strong religious interests. The two men became fast friends, and they went over the manuscript of *That Printer of Udell's* together and made some revisions. In 1903 Reynolds published the novel through his organization, the Book Supply Company, of Chicago, with nine full-page illustrations, at a dollar and a half.

"Each chapter interwoven with sweet sentiment and thrilling adventure," said the advertisements. "Inspiring and uplifting."

The plot of *That Printer* bore no small resemblance to that of *In His Steps,* but it was better in nearly every respect. It tells of a high-minded young tramp, a drunkard's son, who is hunting desperately for a job, which he finds at last in a printing office in a town like Pittsburg. The hero is immediately in contact with church influences and there are many pages of discussion of the church— all rather skillfully managed, with different characters representing varying points of view. Under the influence of certain dramatic events, as well as the ideals of a forceful young minister who plays an important part, the printer at last decides that not all church members are hypocrites, and he not only joins a congregation but becomes a leader in the establishment of an Association which is a kind of cross between a community settlement and the Salvation Army. The story maintains interest, largely by means of stirring incidents which seem so artificial that we have to call them melodrama. Some episodes are so naïvely related as to be funny, as the starving tramp-printer's refusal of a saloon's tempting hot lunch because a glass of beer went with it, and his later rescue of his sweetheart from a house of ill-fame (which is never called by such an indelicate name).

"*That Printer of Udell's* will place Rev. H. B. Wright's name close to that of Rev. Charles M. Sheldon and 'Ralph Connor,'" declared the reviewer in the St. Louis *Globe-Democrat*. It was a moderate publishing success, though it never passed 450,000 in sales. Its reception inspired Wright to go to work on a new novel. He went down to the Ozarks again for his 1905 vacation, and there began *The Shepherd of the Hills,* his best book and the one that was to make him famous. He finished it at nearby Lebanon, Missouri, where he had taken up a new pastorate, the next year; and it was published by the Book Supply Company in 1907. Its early sales were encouraging, but not startling. It made little showing in the *Bookman* lists. But *The Shepherd* had an excellent "press," and many readers compared it favorably with Fox's *The Trail of the Lonesome Pine,* another popular mountaineer story.

The Shepherd of the Hills is the story of an old man who comes into the Ozarks as a Mysterious Stranger, becomes a shepherd and loved teacher of the hill folk, and is very much involved in the fights with the bad men of the community and in the melodramatic denouement of the plot. Sammy Lane, the heroine, is a robust beauty upon whose perfections the author insists too much. The best things in the book are those which are most Ozarkian: the descriptions of morning and night in the hills, and the sayings of the hill people.

"Preachin' Bill," who runs the ferry, says, "When God looked upon th' work of his hands an' called hit good, he war sure a-lookin' at this here Ozark country. Rough? Law yes! Hit war made that-a-way on purpose. Ain't nothin' to a flat country nohow. A man jes' naturally wear hisself plumb out a-walkin' on a level 'thout ary down-hill t' spell him. An' then look how much more there is of hit! Take forty acres o' *flat* now an' hit's jes a forty, but you take forty acres o' this here Ozark country an' God 'lmighty only knows how much 'twould be if hit war rolled out flat. 'Tain't no wonder 't all God rested when he made these here hills; he jes' naturally *had* t' quit, fer he done his beatenest an' war plumb give out." *

The theme of the book again involves a criticism of the churches, for the shepherd turns out to be a famous city preacher who has escaped from folly and hypocrisy to find true virtue and religion in the hills.

Fortified by the success of his two novels, Wright now resolved to resign from clerical duties and devote himself to a wider ministry through writing. Reynolds had urged him to do this, promising, on his side, to devote all his resources to promoting the books which his friend wrote. The first novel under the new all-out plan was *The Calling of Dan Matthews* (1909). An advertisement in *Publishers' Weekly* carried statements of author and publisher, as follows: " 'I have done my best—another chapter in my ministry to the race.' —Author. 'We will make the voice of Dan Matthews heard 'round the world.' —Publishers." The firm of Wright and Reynolds was now fully functioning; it knew what it was doing and where it was going.

As a mail-order merchant, Reynolds had a good understanding of advertising. He had used some newspaper and magazine space in promoting Wright's first two books, but now he decided to plunge and announced a first printing of 100,000 copies of *The Calling of Dan Matthews,* backed by an advertising appropriation of $48,000. Though strong book advertising had been fairly common for several years, these figures were nothing less than revolutionary. Full-page advertisements in the newspapers and the magazines not only announced the new book but also promoted its two predecessors. Results were immediate. A second printing of *Dan Matthews* equal to the first was announced within eight months of publication, and the aggregate sales of the other two books passed the half-million mark by the end of 1909. The *Bookman* lists, ruled by the regular publishers, reflected this popularity but slightly; but Reynolds now made arrangements with Reilly & Lee to distribute the Wright books to the regular book trade through their organization. "Billy" Darst, Reilly & Lee "traveler," became famous among bookstore owners as a promoter of the list, placing gigantic stocks of Harold Bell Wright wherever he went.

The Calling of Dan Matthews was its author's bitterest attack upon the churches. Its heroine, the nurse, speaking to Dan before she knew he was a clergyman, said deliberately:

This selfish, wasteful, cruel, heartless thing that men have built up around their opinions, and whims, and ambitions, has so come between the people and the Christianity of the Christ, that they are beginning to question if, indeed, there is anywhere such a thing as the true church.

The plot is built around the evil machinations of two elders of Dan's church. Dan finally leaves them to their folly and retreats to the Ozarks, where the last

* Quotations from Wright's novels are by permission of the D. Appleton-Century Company, Inc., their publisher.

plotted incidents occur, and where he begins a new life with the plain-spoken nurse. We can scarcely escape the conclusion that the author, having left the ministry himself, and retreated to the mountains, was writing the bitterness of his own heart into this novel.

A new book every other year seemed the proper pace for Reynolds' great campaign, and so 1911 saw the publication of *The Winning of Barbara Worth*. For this book the first printing was 175,000 and the advertising appropriation exceeded $75,000. A barrage of full-page ads the country over told nearly everyone who could read about the new Harold Bell Wright offering, with insets about the older ones. A second printing only a month or so after the first brought the total to half a million. This time Wright hit the *Bookman* lists with a bang, and *Barbara Worth* was third in the annual rankings for 1911 and sixth in 1912. Wright also began to receive more serious attention from the critics, who were inclined to be severe with him. The thinness of his talent was too evident in the new book, in which he attempted a large and complex novel instead of a comparatively simple tale. He had abandoned the church as a theme and had turned to a consideration of the soul of capitalism. He pitted a benevolent capitalist, Jefferson Worth, against a hard-hearted plutocrat from the East: the two become rivals in a great reclamation project in the Colorado River Valley. Thus when Harold Bell Wright, having said his say on one theme of great popular interest, chose another field, he was smart enough to find one which, by 1911, had a strong hold on the popular mind and imagination. Besides, he could bring together in one book such elements as Colorado scenery, cowboys, engineers, Mexican laborers, mysteries of the desert, problems of the small farmer, and a beautiful, high-riding heroine. What fictional riches! The author fitted them all together to make a glittering show.

The next incident in the Wright-Reynolds saga was a misstep. It was the publication of *Their Yesterdays*, and represents a misjudgment of both author and publisher. Wright's work was always disproportionately strong in theme; he was essentially a preacher and incidentally a fictioneer. His leading characters were always types because the plan of each and every story required that these personages represent the moral elements which he was really writing about; only the minor characters in a Wright novel were realistic and convincing. He had tried pure allegory once before, in a short book, *The Uncrowned King*, which had been a good item for the Christmas trade for several years. Now he tried it in a full-length book, which the New York *Times* well described as "a vaguely personalized sermon upon the intimate affairs of mind and heart and soul." The leading characters—a man and a woman—were not even given names. Reynolds published half a million copies in the fall of 1911, which gave the Wright public two books in one year. It was too much, on all counts. Though *Their Yesterdays* eventually sold some 700,000 copies, comparatively it was a failure; and there was a halt in the production of the Wright books for the next three years, as the publishing campaign was reorganized.

The Eyes of the World, which had been announced for 1913, was postponed a year.

The first three books had been issued at $1.50, but the liberal discounts and the bookselling customs of the times had placed the actual retail price considerably lower. The Book Supply Company itself mailed the Wright books postpaid at $1.17, and they were usually sold in the stores at $1.20. David B. Clarkson, a mail-order book-seller, was sued by Reynolds for selling *The Shepherd of the Hills* at 38 cents, but defended himself successfully. In 1911 A. L. Burt & Company made arrangements with Book Supply to issue 50-cent editions of the early books, and announcements of these cheap editions were carried in all the Book Supply advertising of *The Winning of Barbara Worth.* *Barbara* was originally issued at $1.35, and went into the Burt editions in 1913. By 1914 *The Shepherd* and *Dan Matthews* had each sold about a million and *Barbara's* sales were about a million and a half.

The Eyes of the World was published in August, 1914, with an advertising appropriation of $100,000. Wright and Reynolds were now in big business. They advertised that they had sold 750,000 copies of the new book by the end of September, and in November that they were selling 8,000 daily. Their promise that there would be no cheap edition of it was not kept, for Burt brought one out in 1916.

The Eyes of the World was an attack on meretricious art and letters. It gave the author a chance to strike back, if not at his critics, at least at the kind of literature that some of them were praising. A leading character, Lagrange, declares:

> I am a literary scavenger. I haunt the intellectual slaughter pens, and live by the putrid offal that self-respecting writers reject. I glean the stinking materials for my stories from the sewers and cesspools of life. For the dollar they pay, I furnish my readers with those thrills that public decency forbids them to experience at first hand. I am a procurer for the purposes of mental prostitution.

But he turns out a pretty good fellow, at that. Most of the book is directed against dishonest art and art critics. The characters and incidents, however, are so unconvincing, and even ridiculous, that one feels that only a confirmed Harold Bell Wright fan—and there were millions of them by this time—could bear to read it.

When a Man's a Man came on at the regular two-year interval. Another advertising appropriation of $100,000 was announced for it. There was an advance sale of 600,000, of which 21 carloads were shipped before publication. In this story we find "Patches," a young millionaire, masquerading as a vagabond on an Arizona cattle ranch in order to get away from the stupid and immoral life of the effete East. It is the same kind of escape from the city to the hills, mountains, desert, or what have you, which is so common in all the Wright books. The author captures something of the tonic quality of western life and lands, and this story is probably better than *The Eyes of the*

World; but it is inferior to the westerns of Zane Grey, which were by this time winning a wide popularity.

The Re-Creation of Brian Kent (1919) was the last of the books issued by the Wright-Reynolds combination under the name of the Book Supply Company. Its total sales of 702,000 showed a marked decline in Harold Bell Wright's popularity. The old era was past; the First World War had changed ideas and tastes and had brought new interests. About 1910 Reynolds had suffered a physical break-down and had followed his friend to southern California. From his ranch home near Pomona he had directed the publication of the Wright books in Chicago. As his health improved, he organized a film company for the production of pictures founded on these books and superintended the dramatization and booking of stage versions of the same stories. By 1920 he had become interested in the raising of citrus fruits and other local affairs, and he decided to sell out his book business.

He disposed of the Harold Bell Wright copyrights to D. Appleton & Company, who published seven new novels by that author between 1921 and 1932, one regularly every other year. Then Harpers took over, and published *Ma Cinderella* in 1932 and *To My Sons* in 1934. In this long line of stories Wright made some attempt to adapt the old style to new ideas, but his audience dwindled progressively. When *The Man Who Went Away* was published in 1942, after a silence of eight years, it was still-born. Harold Bell Wright was a man who had gone away.

There have been many exaggerated statements about the total sales of certain of Wright's books, especially that of *The Shepherd of the Hills.* In a letter addressed to the present writer in 1942, with which he enclosed a summary of the sales of his books as compiled by a certified public accountant from his royalty statements, Harold Bell Wright remarked upon how easy it is to misrepresent such things. "May I add," he wrote, "that you are the first person ever to ask for the facts?—A statement which of itself is something to think about when considering those who write about writing." The report he furnished was as of 1932, but he pointed out that "sales during the depression years 1933-1941, while I have not been writing, have been small." Making allowance for these depression sales and for new printings of three titles in 1941, we have the following totals: *The Winning of Barbara Worth,* 1,635,000; *The Shepherd of the Hills,* 1,125,000; * *The Calling of Dan Matthews,* 1,085,-000; *When a Man's a Man,* 965,000; *The Eyes of the World,* 925,000. These five are all that qualify as top-bracket best sellers. The grand total for all nineteen of Wright's books was a little over ten million.

Probably America is better off for having read a lot of Harold Bell Wright. His stuff is wholesome, occasionally somewhat stimulating in ideas, and very often picturesque; and millions found it entertaining. Critics' who were

* This will be increased by the 1947 Pocket Books edition.

annoyed at his obvious shortcomings were wrong in calling him "stupid" and "illiterate," as they frequently did.

His greatest faults were his artificiality in characterization and plotting, and his everlasting sermonizing. He once told a writer for the *Bookman* how he made up cards for every incident and sub-incident, for every character and place, and arranged them on a great burlap-covered screen—all before he began to write a novel. But the basic reason for his artificiality was that all his characters and incidents were theme-ridden; they sprang not from reality but from the lesson the author desired to teach. As he once confessed to an interviewer, his novels were merely themes—"arguments," he called them— "presented through the medium of characters, plots, incidents, and the other properties of the story." Up to the last typing of *Eyes of the World,* no character in that novel had been given any name except that of his or her chief quality, as Greed, Ambition, Hypocrisy, etc.—as in an old mystery play. As for the sermonizing, Wright usually put it in the conversation of his characters; but it was tiresome, nevertheless, and not less tiresome because well intentioned and uniformly good doctrine. As William Lyon Phelps once said, to his lasting shame, "Harold is always Wright."

His success was based upon a fortunate combination: the timeliness of his sincere comment upon social problems which were already exciting wide interest, his native skill and understanding in addressing his great middle-class audience, and the powerful advertising campaign put behind his work by a sympathetic friend and publisher.

He keenly felt the adverse criticism heaped upon him, and resented especially the frequent implication that it was wrong of him to be so popular. He closed a letter to the author of these pages, written shortly before his death and dealing with the data of his popularity, with these words: "I have given you the terrible, the monstrous, the disgraceful facts. Make of them what you will, and may God bless you and have mercy on my poor, illiterate soul."

XXXV. THE GREAT OPEN SPACES

I wish to preach, not the doctrine of ignoble ease, but the doctrine of the strenuous life, the life of toil and effort, of labor and strife; to preach that highest form of success which comes . . . to the man who does not shrink from danger . . . In the last analysis a healthy state can exist only when the men and women who make it up lead clean, vigorous, healthy lives.
Theodore Roosevelt

THEODORE ROOSEVELT was the outstanding spokesman for all that was fresh and vigorous at the beginning of the twentieth century. He was so varied in his interests, so hospitable to new ideas, so courageous in leadership, and so constantly articulate, that his personality dominated that first decade of the new century to an extraordinary degree. John Morley, visiting the United States in 1904, reported: "I have been chiefly impressed in this country by two things—Niagara Falls and the President of the United States."

Deeply interested in popular reading, the President often tried to direct it by recommendations from the White House. An outstanding example of this advertisement by testimonial was his praise of Charles Wagner's *The Simple Life;* as a result uncounted thousands of that mediocre book were sold —perhaps as many as half a million. Roosevelt's own books sold well, especially *African Game Trails* and *The Winning of the West.* The latter had the advantage of cheap editions; Putnam issued it in paper covers at twenty-five cents a volume.

The Roosevelt-La Follette reform movements produced no top-rank best seller, but they were reflected in a number of novels which reached the monthly, and even the yearly, lists. Frank Norris' *The Pit* ranked third in 1903, and in 1906 Winston Churchill's *Coniston* stood first and Upton Sinclair's *The Jungle* sixth. William Allen White's *A Certain Rich Man* was in the lists of 1909 and Vaughan Kester's *The Prodigal Judge* in 1911.

Professor Pattee has pointed out that this Rooseveltian decade was an era of the superman in fiction—the strenuous, red-blooded man "who does not shrink from danger" and who triumphs over terrific hardships by miraculous endurance and courage. T. R. himself, leading his Rough Riders in their charge up San Juan Hill, was prototype of them all. Only one other personality compares with Roosevelt's in weight of influence on the "strenuous school" of writers—that of Rudyard Kipling. Roosevelt and Kipling were the twin deities of the rough-and-tough fictioneers of the beginning of the twentieth century.

This group and the "family novelists" of the same period seem at first glance to have functioned at opposite literary poles. Yet both used the out-of-door scene very commonly, both employed some melodrama, and both were immensely popular. In general, the "strenuous school" was composed of men writing for men and boys, while the "home school" was made up of women writing for women and girls. Yet undoubtedly many readers devoured the stories of both Gene Stratton-Porter and Jack London.

Among the writers for he-men, Jack London was outstanding. He had read Kipling in those formative, hard years when he was trying to teach himself the art of writing short fiction. As with Kipling, his first successful writing grew out of his contacts with a rude and violent society. Gold was discovered in Alaska in 1917, and Jack was on his way to get a share of it soon after the news of the strike arrived in his California home. He was one of the few to get through Chilkoot Pass that bitter winter of 1898-1899; but his strength and courage won no gold for him, and scurvy finally sent him back to the States. Yet he did not return without booty; in place of gold-dust, he brought home a pack full of story-nuggets. Now at last he sold his short stories, and in a few years he was active in the best markets.

His great success came with the publication of one of his Alaskan stories, *The Call of the Wild.* Though he was to write many other novels in the dozen busy and adventurous years that remained before his death at forty years of age, this small book remains his best. It has a directness, a tonic quality of primal strength, and a fresh vividness that make it as good reading today as it was when its public was avid for Klondike adventure. Realistic so far as the life of the frozen North is concerned, it is romantic in its basic theme—that of Buck's kinship with the wolves.

The Call of the Wild was first published as a serial in the *Saturday Evening Post* in 1903; for the serial rights London received seven hundred dollars. Later that year Macmillans issued it as a book, paying the author two thousand dollars for it in a lump sum. It did very well from the start; though it made no impression on the best seller lists, it had a steady and growing sale. Critics praised it; and when *The Sea Wolf,* a longer novel, was published the next year, first serially in the *Century* and then as a Macmillan book, it was apparent that London's fame was assured. His personal picturesqueness, his lectures, and his books on social issues kept him before the people; and he had the faculty of developing an enthusiastic loyalty among his more youthful readers. His books were widely translated, and it is said that in Russia "Yacklunnen" became the best known and most admired of American writers.

The Call of the Wild is the story of a super-dog; *The Sea Wolf* portrays a superman. Though Wolf Larsen meets disaster in the end, he is a thoroughly Nietzschean *Übermensch* up to the hour of his death. The depiction of his brutality as captain of the whaling schooner *Ghost* repelled many readers; but the combination of romantic adventure and apparently realistic sea life (though the seamanship was challenged), with a dash of philosophy, was a strong one, and the book made a great success.

Both of these leaders of the Jack London list have maintained steady sales for forty years, and are definitely popular books today. They were favorites in the Armed Services Editions. *The Call of the Wild* is widely used in schools, and *The Sea Wolf* has been a good number in the Pocket Books series. The total sales of the former have passed a million and a half, and those of the latter are in the neighborhood of a million.

Rex Beach was another popular writer whose work stemmed from the Klondike rush. None of his books appears to have reached the top bracket of best sellers, but three of them were very prominent in the *Bookman* lists—*The Barrier* (1908), *The Silver Horde* (1909) and *The Net* (1912).

Then there was the "Sourdough Poet," Robert W. Service, with his immensely popular book entitled first *Songs of a Sourdough,* but later and more commonly *The Spell of the Yukon and Other Verses.* Service had grown up in Glasgow, and there had been trained in the banking business. But he tired of routine, crossed the Atlantic in steerage, and spent some years of unstable life in western Canada. He joined the Yukon rush, and engaged in banking in Alaska for eight years. It was Kipling's example that moved him to the composition of ballads which won such immediate vogue. Crude and vigorous, some of them are not without power; but most popular were those which made comedy out of the rough life of the North. "The Shooting of Dan McGrew" and "The Cremation of Sam McGee," with their swinging lines and outlandish jocularity were committed to memory and repeated with effect by thousands of stage comedians and parlor entertainers.

Barse & Hopkins, of New York, made seven printings of *The Spell of the Yukon* before publication in 1907. It was prominent in the *Bookman's* non-fiction lists in 1909. Many editions were issued by the original publishers before the book was taken over by Dodd, Mead & Company in 1933. It has probably sold at least 750,000 copies and is still in print. Service's *Rhymes of a Red Cross Man* topped the *Bookman's* non-fiction best seller lists in 1917 and 1918, but did not reach the total sales of the earlier volume.

But the "great open spaces" which furnished the literature of the strenuous life in this period were by no means limited to Alaska. The plains of the great West, which had long afforded the setting for many hundreds of dime novels about Buffalo Bill and his compeers, now came to be used for fiction which, if it did not always display quality superior to that of the old thrillers, was at least sold at a higher price.

Owen Wister's *The Virginian* had quality, though not precisely of the kind its author always claimed for it. "It is strange," muses Douglas Branch,

that Wister could have called his *Virginian* a historical novel of the cattle country when there is not one scene set on the range among the cattle, when the cowboys seem throughout to spend their days in playful pranks, in love-making, in thief-hunting, in anything except work.*

The fact is, there is not a cow in the book, except some the illustrator put in. Yet as a story of Wyoming in the latter seventies and eighties, *The Virginian* has some historical significance; as a series of amusing incidents, it has high entertainment value; as a story, it holds its reader's interest. Certainly the humor, vigor, and wholesomeness of the book made an instant appeal when it was first published in 1902, and have kept a certain popularity for it ever since. Wrote President Roosevelt to the author: "I really think you have done for the plainsmen and mountainmen, the soldiers, frontiersmen and Indians, what nobody else but Bret Harte or Kipling could have done." Wister confessed to the Kipling influence on his writing; certainly the sway of T. R., who was his intimate friend and to whom he dedicated his book, is obvious.

Macmillans issued it in April, 1902, and had to reprint it fourteen times before the end of the year. In two years they sold over 300,000 copies at a dollar and a half; then they published it in paper covers at twenty-five cents.

* E. Douglas Branch, *The Cowboy and His Interpreters* (New York, 1926), p. 198.

The story was a success on the stage, and a "theatrical edition," including music for the songs which occur in the story, was published. (Wister, by the way, had once studied musical composition in Paris.) Illustrations by Frederic Remington and Charles M. Russell adorned a new issue in 1911, Grosset & Dunlap put out a seventy-five cent edition about the same time, and a few years later the book was edited for Macmillan's Pocket Classics. It passed the million mark about 1920, and has sold some hundreds of thousands since. It has been used in the schools, and is by way of becoming a classic.

And now we come down a good many pegs to discuss another writer of best-selling westerns. Zane Grey was born in Zanesville, Ohio, son of a father who had been backwoodsman, farmer, hunter, doctor, and preacher, and a mother who was a descendant of the famed Quaker frontiersman, Col. Eb Zane. He studied dentistry and practised it in New York for six years. Like millions of others, he was a reader of the historical novels published about the turn of the century. He had an old journal which had been kept by Colonel Zane, and the idea of using it in writing a story of the frontier took possession of him. So between intervals of pulling teeth he wrote chapters of novels. His first one was called *Betty Zane;* no publisher would accept it and he issued it privately. His second novel, *The Spirit of the Border,* also based partly on the Zane exploits, was published by A. L. Burt & Company in 1906 at one dollar. It had an encouraging sale, as did *The Last of the Plainsmen* in 1908. The latter book was the result of his first trip to the West, made in company with "Buffalo" Jones. Ripley Hitchcock, of Harpers, now ventured to accept *The Heritage of the Desert* (1910) and then, hesitantly and reluctantly, *Riders of the Purple Sage* (1912). But by this time Zane Grey began to have a public and he had given up the dental drill for the typewriter. St. Louis liked his next book (*Desert Gold*) well enough to put it in one of the monthly best seller lists from that city. In 1915 his current offering was in the *Bookman's* annual list, and from 1917 to 1924, inclusive, no such list was without a Zane Grey book. Twice, with *The U. P. Trail* in 1918 and *The Man of the Forest* in 1920, he topped that annual list.

After a Zane Grey reading-public had been formed, one of his books could be expected to sell around half a million copies over a series of years. The earlier books had some advantage, because for ten years or more this public was constantly augmenting and newcomers liked the older books as well as the new ones. Altogether Grey wrote fifty-four novels, and Henry Hoyns, of Harpers, once estimated his total sales at fifteen and a half millions.

Figured on the over-all basis, however, only two of Zane Grey's stories qualify for top-bracket position as best sellers—*The Spirit of the Border* and *Riders of the Purple Sage.* The former benefited by its early position and by a tremendous sale in its Pocket Books edition. It is a violent, bloody, and crudely written story of fighting against the Indians and their renegade allies. "The author does not intend to apologize for what many readers may call the 'brutality' of the story," begins the Introduction. Apology was not what was required. The story of the death of Girty is revolting in the extreme, though one might accept it if it were supported by historical authority. *Riders of the Purple Sage* was also an early number. It has a sensational Mormon theme in connection with the love story, and more than the usual amount of hard riding and miraculous shooting. It sold better both in the Harper edition and in the Grosset & Dunlap reprint than any other Zane Grey book and probably passed the million-and-a-half mark.

Grey's stories were stimulating to boys who wanted imaginative excitement and to men without developed literary taste who wanted only escape. Their plots displayed an unusual talent for invention, and the narration was swift. Grover Alexander, the famous baseball pitcher, was once asked by a reporter about his literary predilections. "I like Zane Grey," said Grover. "He puts a lot of zip into his things. He's sure got something on that fast one!" It was true; he had. He was also a product of his times. Though unliterary, he belonged definitely to the rough-and-tough school of letters of the Roosevelt-Kipling era, whose typical hero was described by a writer on "The Strenuous Literary Method" in the *Bookman* for June, 1906, as a superman whose will was iron, whose nerves were steel, and whose manners were brass. And if Dr. Grey mixed blood plentifully with his ink, that too was part of the technique of his school. His love passages are far too often downright funny, not in intention, but in their naïve attempts to depict passion. Have a look at the heroine of *Riders of the Purple Sage* at a purple moment:

When she had spoken, the strength and the blaze of her died, and she swayed toward Venters. She leaned against him, and her body was limp and vibrated to a long, wavering tremble. Her face was upturned to his. Woman's face, woman's eyes, woman's lips—all acutely and blindly and sweetly and terribly truthful in their betrayal!

Less crude in most respects were two other writers of the era who produced popular novels about the West—Emerson Hough and Stewart Edward White. Both of them won places on the *Bookman's* annual list; but no book by either —not even Hough's *The Covered Wagon,* with the help of a great motion picture—reached the lofty pinnacle of the top best sellers. White's careful nature studies, as well as his good marksmanship with a rifle, endeared him to President Roosevelt.

Tarzan made the top bracket, however. Tarzan could do anything. *Tarzan of the Apes,* by Edgar Rice Burroughs, was not a very remarkable story as such things go—a typical pulp-magazine serial in its extravagant imagination, its good story-telling, and its mediocre writing—but the way it developed into big business in the amusement world makes a story almost as incredible as that of the ape-boy himself.

Burroughs was the son of a Chicago distiller. He attended a private school and then Phillips Andover; when he left that school, by request, he was sent to Michigan Military Academy. Later his father, who had been a major in the Civil War, got him an appointment to West Point, but he failed the examinations. Thereupon he added three years to his age (he was big for eighteen) and enlisted in the Seventh Cavalry of the regular army. He expected to fight Indians in the Southwest, where Geronimo was at large, but all he did was dig ditches. After a year of that, his father obtained his release. Then came work as a cattle-drover in the West, then a spot of employment on a gold-dredge in Oregon, then "settling down" in a job with Sears Roebuck in Chicago, and marriage. But he soon thought he saw a chance to get rich running an aluminum-peddling concern, and when that failed he got into advertising. So it went. But at last fortune beckoned him. He had placed some advertising for an alcoholism-cure in the "pulps," and when he checked the insertions he got to reading the stories. He liked that sort of fiction and decided to have a try at writing it. He was successful from the first, and soon he was a valued contributor to *All-Story Magazine*. The third serial he wrote was *Tarzan of the Apes*, for which he received seven hundred dollars.

Burroughs knew nothing about the locale of his story except what he had gleaned from Stanley's *In Darkest Africa*. But research was unnecessary; the yarn is the thing. Read as a boys' story, it is not bad. It is far inferior in every respect to Kipling's *Jungle Books*, to be sure, but it does bear comparison with Rider Haggard's novels. It has vigorous imagination, plenty of suspense, and an interesting setting. Of course the idea is "impossible," if you want to be pedantic about it; but it is a convention of "pulp" reading that one accepts the basic improbability, however extravagant, and confines his carping to details. One reader, for example, objected to tigers in Africa, and Burroughs later changed his Sabor to a lioness. On the whole, the first Tarzan is a pretty good story of its kind. It is better than most of its sequels, because it is simpler.

A. C. McClurg & Company brought out *Tarzan of the Apes* in book form in 1914, and the next year *The Return of Tarzan*. They were immediately syndicated in the newspapers, and the development of the great Tarzan audience began. The first movie based on the story was produced in 1917. Harry Reichenbach, the famous press-agent, always claimed he made the success of the first Tarzan movie by dressing up a big ape in neat tuxedo and shiny top-hat and turning him loose in the fashionable Knickerbocker Hotel on a Saturday night "while the lobby was aglitter with New York's élite." The masquerader landed in the police court, but also, more importantly for Harry's purposes, in the front pages of the newspapers. Tarzan has long been a success in a series of elaborate productions; Johnny Weissmuller was the ninth player of the title rôle. Meantime more sequels appeared, until there were twenty-five Tarzan books altogether. Tarzan programs held the air-ways, Tarzan picture strips gained in popularity year after year, Tarzan stories were translated into nearly all known languages. A new name for wild strength was given to the language. The Tarzan theme made its way into the intimate life of the American people more thoroughly than any other fictional idea of its generation. Edgar Rice Burroughs, Inc., of Tarzana, California, became a big business concern. It possesses what a sports writer recently called "a sensamazuma."

The Burroughs company itself took over the publication of the Tarzan books in 1931 from Metropolitan Books, Inc., which had published them for two or three years after McClurg had given them up. McClurg had issued eleven Tarzans and seventeen Burroughs books about life on Mars, Venus, and the moon, and so on. When the output ceased in 1942, there were fifty-three Burroughs books, about half of them Tarzans. How many copies have been circulated it is impossible to tell, because limited copyrights were often sold outright; but Edgar Rice Burroughs, Inc., estimates *Tarzan of the Apes* has exceeded five million the world over and has reached a million and a half or more in the United States. Perhaps four or five times those amounts would give the grand totals for all the Tarzan books.

Outdoor adventure, especially in the form of "westerns," continues a staple of our sub-literature. The "pulp" magazines have been hatcheries for much fiction that has later appeared in full book plumage. The twenty-five-cent books have sometimes given very wide distribution to such stories. One "western" which has been hoisted into the top bracket of best sellers by such means is Max Brand's *Singing Guns,* a fast-moving, straight-shooting favorite of young clerks and mechanics and tired business men who never sat a horse or handled a gun except by proxy. It was published by Dodd, Mead in 1938 and reprinted by Grosset & Dunlap, but had its biggest sales in the Pocket Books edition; altogether it has sold a little less than a million and a half copies. Max Brand's real name is Frederick Faust. He has been called "the king of the pulp writers" and is said to have produced twenty-five million words in twenty years' dictation. At last report his books numbered over ninety. Also he does the Dr. Kildare scripts for the screen, writes poetry, and travels. He is as diligent as a bee, as busy as a cranberry-merchant, as industrious as a farmer in wheat-harvest; he is a superman with the dictaphone as his heroes are with their guns.

XXXVI. THE FIRST WORLD WAR AND AFTER

A desire of knowledge is the natural feeling of mankind, and every human being whose mind is not debauched will be willing to give all that he has to get knowledge.

Samuel Johnson

NECESSARY to achieve a place on the list of top-flight best sellers for the decade in which the First World War fell was a total sale of 900,000 copies, and no book published during the three years in which the United States was in the war reached that figure. Nor did any book definitely inspired by that conflict but published later attain such a sale. There were, however, half a dozen war books of those years which were prominent in the monthly and yearly lists of best sellers and which sold in the neighborhood of half a million copies.

H. G. Wells' *Mr. Britling Sees It Through*, which topped the *Bookman* lists for 1917, helped Americans to understand the popular English attitude toward the war. Service's *Rhymes of a Red Cross Man* led the non-fiction lists in 1917 and 1918. Both of these books fell a little short of half a million in sales in this country. The first war book by an American to make a real hit was Arthur Guy Empey's *Over the Top*, a vivid narrative of trench fighting, which sold over 300,000 in its first year, and some 200,000 later. The big success of 1918 was a collection of amusing letters telling of army life and purporting to be written by a doughboy to his sweetheart, entitled *Dere Mable*. The humorist was Edward Streeter, and his little book sold over 600,000 copies. A spy story of the war held top place in the *Bookman* lists in 1919—*The Four Horsemen of the Apocalypse*, by Blasco Ibáñez, the Spanish novelist, editor, politician, and promoter. In America the book sales benefited by the screen production, which starred Rudolf Valentino; the book eventually sold about half a million copies at the price, high for those days, of $1.90. It was not until ten years later, in 1929, that the greatest novel of the First World War appeared—Erich Maria Remarque's *All Quiet on the Western Front*. It also was made into a "colossal" motion picture. Some 300,000 copies of the English translation of this realistic German work were bought in America during the first year after its publication, and almost as many later.

It is symptomatic of widening American horizons that of these six books, one was written by an Englishman, one by a Canadian, one by a Spaniard, one by a German, and two by Americans. It is worthy of note, also, that two of the six were non-fiction, and a third—*Dere Mable*—was compounded rather more of truth than imagination. Following the war, popularity swung steadily toward non-fiction, until by the mid-thirties it was outselling fiction. The biggest sellers, however, what with detective stories and book-club selections, kept the proportion among top best sellers at about what it had been ever since Scott and Cooper entered the lists, with three or four novels to every non-fiction title.

The amazing popularity of the big historical and philosophical "outlines" was perhaps a sign of the wider interests of the postwar period. In considering such a phenomenon, one must beware, however, of too easy simplification. Here was no sudden transformation of the reading tastes of the people. History, both in romance and in sober non-fiction, had always been definitely popular in America; readers of these pages will recall the gigantic circulation of the work of such writers as Macaulay and Prescott. In the latter decades of the nineteenth century the earlier popularity of Macaulay's *History of England* was matched by that of John Richard Green's *A Short History of the English People*. Published first in London in 1874, it met with immediate success in that country—so great indeed that Alexander Macmillan repented of having paid the author only three hundred pounds for the copyright and generously offered him a royalty contract. It was printed in the United States by Harpers in 1876, and then issued at low prices by many of the cheap publishers of the eighties and nineties. The Useful Knowledge Publishing Company, later the Alden Book Company, issued it at thirty-seven cents in 1882. It was published in four paper-covered parts by Munro for his Seaside Library. Altogether, more than a dozen publishers issued it, some in repeated and varied editions. The readability of its narrative and its availability in low-priced editions made Green's *Short History* the leading best seller in its field for many years. Its chief competitor was Justin M'Carthy's *History of Our Own Times,* also cheaply published and widely popular in the eighties and nineties.

So the extraordinary welcome given in the years after the Second World War to H. G. Wells' *Outline of History* was by no means singular. Wells had long been known to American readers as a writer of romances of science-fantasy and novels of social import, and he had recently been prominent on best seller lists with *Mr. Britling,* when the Macmillan Company brought out, in 1920, his *Outline of History.* In England it had first appeared in fortnightly parts; in the United States it appeared in two volumes, first priced at $10.50 and later in the year at $7.50. It was greeted with enthusiasm by reviewers; and in 1921, after a single-volume edition at five dollars was brought out, it led the non-fiction best seller list. After ten years of good sales at the five-dollar price, some 600,000 copies of a dollar edition by the Garden City Publishing Company were sold. In 1926 a revision, with color plates, was published by Macmillans in twenty-four parts at fifty cents each, followed by a two-volume edition at fifteen dollars. Altogether the *Outline* has sold about a million and a quarter copies in the United States. This does not include the sales of a shorter work based on the *Outline* and variously entitled, with revisions, *A Short History of the World, A Short Story of Mankind,* and *Pocket History of the World,* which would bring the grand total up pretty close to two million.

Wells himself said that his book was "an attempt to reform history teaching by replacing narrow nationalist history by a general view of the human record." It was written with clarity and force, and was, from the general reader's point of view, as fascinating a piece of historical composition as modern times have afforded. In his *Companion to Mr. Wells' Outline,* Hilaire Belloc attacked its rationalistic and materialistic attitudes, and others have criticized it for its neglect of certain favorite historical figures; but on the whole it has met with a remarkable critical and popular acceptance. It was much flattered by imitation, and for a long time we had "outlines" of this and that— including even *An Outline of Wells.*

On the heels of Wells' *Outline* came Willem van Loon's *Story of Mankind* in 1921. It was attractively illustrated by the author's drawings in the original Boni & Liveright edition, as well as in the Pocket Book and other reprints.

It was vastly popular—but not quite vastly enough to place it among top best sellers.

A success second only to that of the *Outline of History* was scored in 1926 by Will Durant's *The Story of Philosophy*. Durant was a Columbia Ph. D. who had taught in certain libertarian schools which were conducted in New York under socialistic and labor auspices and had lectured widely to general audiences on philosophical subjects. He was a genius in the popularization of learning. He did not talk down to his public, but he illumined his material by a wealth of illustration and human interest—all without cheapening it. A course of lectures on the great philosophers was seized upon by E. Haldeman-Julius and published in his Little Blue Books, the remarkable series of five-cent booklets issued from Girard, Kansas. The Durant lectures were popular numbers in this series during the early twenties, enjoying an average sale of about 150,000 apiece. Dr. Durant persuaded Simon & Schuster, a new firm which had hitherto specialized, very profitably, in cross-word puzzle books, to put the Little Blue Book lectures into one volume and try the high-class market with it. The volume was a handsome one, with portraits, and was priced at five dollars. From five cents to five dollars was a big jump, and the publishers were a bit dubious: their first printing was only fifteen hundred copies, and they dared that much largely on the basis of one advance order for five hundred. The venture made a great success, however, which amazed both author and publisher; and when the book was issued in a dollar reprint by the Garden City Publishing Company, its grand total soon passed the million mark. The five-dollar price was suitable to the inflation years, and the cheaper edition was tempered to the depression.

These books illustrate the possibilities that had now developed in an era of multiple best seller publics of vast proportions. In the twenties Edith M. Hull's *The Sheik* could find over a million half-ashamed purchasers; the Rev. Lloyd Douglas's *The Magnificent Obsession* could find a different public of similar size; P. G. Wodehouse, Thorne Smith, and E. Phillips Oppenheim could cater to millions of escapists; and at the same time serious books like the *Outline of History* and *The Story of Philosophy,* issued originally at five or ten dollars, by skilful promotion and proper reprint handling, could be brought to totals above a million. Of course, audiences overlapped, and a catholic and insatiate reader might devour all these books; but the fact remains that here were three or four publics all of which could develop simultaneously best sellers in the million class.

XXXVII. SUB-ROSA

Licentiousness is a vastly over-rated activity. Only Puritans think of the Devil as the most fascinating figure in the Universe. Terrified holy men believed that he could be repulsed only by stout fasting and hearty prayer, while the one complete and perfect exorcism is to face him squarely and yawn.

Heywood Broun

THE succès du scandale is a perennial feature of popular literature. Books which the librarian keeps under her counter or in a locked case, and which self-conscious readers devour on the sly, may be important works of literature but at the same time owe much of their large sales to certain ribald or obscene elements. Condemnation of a book on the grounds of loose morals has frequently been regarded as good advertising, and promoters have been known to invite comstockian censorship in certain quarters for the sake of the demand which news of such action would produce the country over. Certainly there have been scores of cases in which the attacks of moralists have stimulated the popularity of books—especially when they were first "catching on." On the other hand, objections on moral grounds have sometimes checked-the sales of books.

We are not concerned in this chapter with the stock-in-trade of the "book-legger." His books do not reach best seller proportions. Unless a work has other elements of popular interest than the merely erotic, it has little or no chance of reaching an audience large enough to make it a best seller. We are interested here in those popular books, whether "literature" or not, which have achieved best seller levels largely because of erotic elements which have been rather generally regarded as making them improper for general circulation.

Boccaccio's *Decameron* is a good example. However important its stories have been in the development of English literature, its circulation has always been restricted in one way or another because of the licentiousness of its incidents; yet scores of American editions of it in the last hundred years testify to a wide readership which certainly has not been limited to scholars.

It is said that Giovanni Boccaccio himself condemned his *Il Decamerone* in his old age as lascivious, and attempted to check its popularity. Though many of the stories were reproduced in Painter's *Palace of Pleasure* (1566), where Shakespeare found them, fortunately for us all, they were not published in full English translation until 1620—the year in which the Pilgrims set up a colony far away from such follies. John Mein, the Scotch bookseller and printer who later got into trouble with the Patriots and had to flee the country, did bring a tale from Petronius to Boston, for he advertised *The Matrons* in the *News-Letter* September 11, 1766, and that book contained the story of "The Matron of Ephesus." Rivington imported the same book for his stores in New York and Philadelphia, as well as another called *The Amorous Friars*. But when a relatively complete *Decameron* was first issued by an American publisher is hard to tell; perhaps it was not until the publication of Thomas Wardle's Philadelphia edition in two volumes (at one dollar) about the middle of the nineteenth century.* Similar editions followed fast upon this one. The publication of Bohn's edition in London seems to have set off several reprints in the United States, and another lot of them came in the seventies. There have been more than a score of editions since 1900. Four Little Blue Books made up of tales from the *Decameron* sold from 85,000 to 400,000 according to the sensationalism of the titles: *Illicit Love* ranked highest. How many copies of more or less complete editions have been published or sold in America it were rash even to estimate; one can only say that the book has probably earned a place on the best seller list.

The popularity of *Gil Blas, Tom Jones*, and *Roderick Random* toward the end of the eighteenth century was bemoaned by the moralists; but none of the trio appears to have piled up sufficient sales to reach the top list. Chesterfield and Sterne were expurgated, but *Tristram Shandy* ultimately gained its position among the best sellers with all its naughtiness; it seems probable that the timeless charm of Sterne's whimsy put it there rather than the elements that once seemed too indelicate for chaste readers. Byron was once anathema to the virtuous, and there can be no doubt that the immoralities depicted in some of his narrative poems played no small part in the "Byron craze" of the twenties. Moore's *Lalla Rookh* also came under attack, and Bulwer was roundly abused by many a *censor morum* for his glorification of fops and criminals.

These were all sustained and long-read favorites. In 1836 came a book which shocked many, piled up a sale of some hundreds of thousands in a few years, and was then forgotten. It was entitled *Awful Disclosures of Maria Monk, as Exhibited in a Narrative of Her Suffering During a Residence of Five Years as a Novice, and Two Years as a Black Nun, in the Hotel Dieu Nunnery at Montreal.* Its publication was an incident in the political, religious, and literary war against the Catholic Church which enlivened the eighteen-thirties and forties. Two years before, rumors of the immorality of priests and the harsh treatment of nuns in an Ursuline convent in Charlestown, Massachusetts— only a short shay-ride from Faneuil Hall—roused the mob spirit and resulted in the sacking of the convent. During the controversy which followed, Rebecca Reed, whose complaints of harsh penances inflicted had done much to incite the violence, published her book, *Six Months in a Convent*.

A highly profitable pre-publication fracas was stirred up before *Awful Disclosures* was actually issued by Howe & Bates, New York. The *Protestant Vindicator* of that city, which had made a business of Catholic-baiting for a long time, printed a story about the revelations which Maria Monk was about to

* Listed in Roorbach's *Bibliotheca Americana*, 1820-1852, without date.

make; and Montreal papers immediately took the matter up and collected affidavits to prove Miss Monk had never been in a nunnery, but was a bit touched
in the head. This brought excited rejoinders from Miss Monk's backers in New
York and a set of affidavits from the lady herself. The whole thing was by way
of becoming an international incident even before the book was available.

When it did appear, it was found that the "disclosures" were awful indeed,
though the author was careful to avoid lascivious details. She told of underground tunnels which enabled priests to visit the convent (and in an enlarged
edition she provided a plan of the buildings and secret passages) and she told
of the murder of the infants which resulted from those visits, and so on. At
length she had escaped, pregnant, and sought help from the Magdalen Society
in New York. "But the virtuous reader," she declared, "need not fear, in the
following pages, to meet with vice presented in any dress but her own deform-
ity."

An incredible controversy ensued, in which, as Ralph Thompson has observed, "facts were regarded as something of a nuisance." * Many persons of
considerable distinction were involved. The impressionable Samuel F. B.
Morse was one of Miss Monk's champions, and his friend James Fenimore
Cooper feared for a time that he was going to marry Miss Monk. A joint Pro-
testant-Catholic commission made an investigation and reported that Maria
was an impostor. Col. William L. Stone, author and editor, made a trip to
Montreal, went through the convent of Hôtel Dieu, and returned to report that
the Monk story was all a tissue of lies—whereupon the Rev. Dr. Brownlee said
the colonel was another. The Montreal group got out a book called *Awful
Exposure of the Atrocious Plot Formed by Certain Individuals Against the
Clergy and Nuns of Lower Canada, Through the Intervention of Maria Monk.*
So Miss Monk and her clerical friends issued *Further Disclosures by Maria
Monk Concerning the Hotel Dieu Nunnery of Montreal.*

After awhile there were rumors of improper relations between Maria's guardian, the Rev. Mr. Slocum, and his ward; and when J. Watson Webb, of the
Courier, printed the reports, Slocum promptly sued him for libel. But partisans
of Maria and her story stood by her until the group of clergymen who had exploited the matter got to quarreling over the profits of *Awful Disclosures.*
Slocum was sued for a share by one of his associates; Maria claimed she was
being robbed by all of them, called them "Protestant Jesuits," and ran away to
Philadelphia. There she made a new sensation by claiming to have been ab-
ducted by six Catholic priests. Soon after this she dropped out of sight. She is
said to have died in 1849 on what is now called Welfare Island, where she had
been confined on charges of petty thievery and immorality. The *Awful Disclosures,* which had been issued by several publishers, continued to sell for
a good many years; but today, according to Mr. Thompson, Maria Monk's

---

* See his "The Maria Monk Affair," in *The Colophon,* Part XVII (1934).

name "is known only to a few rascals, antiquarians, and churchmen." Readers of the foregoing may now choose their category.

"Exposures" of polygamous life among the Mormons enjoyed much popularity a few decades later. Most famous of these was *Wife No. 19; or, The Story of a Life in Bondage*, by the apostate wife of Brigham Young. It was published in 1876, with introductions by John B. Gough and Mary A. Livermore, and was sold by subscription.

Extravagant claims have been made with regard to the circulation of Eugene Sue's *The Mysteries of Paris*. But everything about that book is extravagant and fantastic. It lacks the magnificent sweep of *The Wandering Jew;* both are about as melodramatic as can be imagined, but the *Mysteries* seems cheaper and more superficial. Both were generally condemned by moralists; but the *Mysteries,* with its heroine Fleur-de-Marie, a girl of the streets, and its sadism, received and deserved more criticism than the masterpiece which Sue was to produce a year or two later. Said the *American Whig Review* in 1846:

Sue's success as a novelist has been almost unparalleled since the days of Richardson. . . . The popularity of Scott, and more recently of Dickens, great as it was, was nothing in comparison to that of Sue; and not only were his works eagerly expected in the original, in Paris and the provinces, but the arrival of a new number in this country, to be translated and issued from the press of Harper's, was regarded as a matter of public interest, and those individuals who could procure an early number were considered peculiarly fortunate.

The success of *The Mysteries of Paris* doubtless motivated the writing and publication of the several novels which soon entered into a friendly competition to show which was the wickedest American city. The palm seems to have gone to Philadelphia, on the basis of George Lippard's *The Quaker City*. Lippard was designed for the Methodist ministry, but left his studies in disgust with the hypocrisy he encountered; he tried the law, but gave it up because of its perversion of justice. He became a newspaper reporter, but soon found his forte in melodramatic stories for the *Saturday Evening Post* and other periodicals. He wrote *The Monks of Monk Hall* in ten fortnightly parts in 1844; published in book form the next year, it was given a new title, *The Quaker City,* but retained the old one as a subtitle. Thirty editions were called for in four years, and it was dramatized, translated into other languages, and imitated. In 1849 Lippard conducted an unsuccessful weekly, most of which he wrote himself, called *The Quaker City*.

An edition published in 1876 carries a titlepage "blurb" which begins:

No American Novel has ever commanded so wide-spread an interest, as this work. It has been made the subject of criticism wherever the English language is spoken. On the one hand, it has been denounced as a work of the most immoral and incendiary character; on the other, it has been elaborately praised, as a painfully vivid picture of life in the Great City.

Certainly the author spared no pains to make his seduction scenes voluptuous; but today it all seems preposterously awkward, labored, and artificial. Lippard had an annoying way of dropping in a note occasionally urging the reader not to skip the passage about to be presented, e.g.: "The Reader who desires to understand thoroughly, the pure love of an innocent girl for a corrupt libertine, will not fail to peruse this passage." All right, Mr. Lippard, we perused the passage; but we still don't understand the phenomenon discussed, and we don't think you do either. Indeed, we think your book is a big, melodramatic humbug.

Newspapers and magazines frequently commented on the popularity of "Satanic literature" in the forties and fifties. The *New York Herald* in 1848 claimed that "Our highly respectable booksellers and publishers are serving the devil better than the devil was ever yet served. One day to God and six to Satan is doing very well to demoralize the rising generation." The writer mentioned Sue as one of the Satanists. Other French novelists, including Charles Paul de Kock, were winning some sub-rosa following. And two non-fiction books on woman by the indefatigable historian-naturalist Jules Michelet which were neither naughty nor nice won a remarkable popularity. *L'Amour* was a sudden success in 1859, and when *La Femme* appeared the next year, G. W. Carleton, New York publisher, hired Dr. John W. Palmer to translate it, contracting to pay a thousand dollars for the job if it was done in seventy-two hours; if the translation did not meet the deadline, ten dollars was to be deducted for each hour over that time. It did, and Carleton sold ten thousand copies a week before rival publishers could catch up with him. Balzac appears never to have been really popular in America. Carleton tried publishing his work, but gave it up. The *Droll Stories* have had some circulation—possibly more than recorded editions would indicate. Hugo, represented on our list by two best sellers, was long considered a "bad" writer by many.

But it was not until the eighties that best sellers developed among what were generally "forbidden" French novels. Then Zola's *Nana* and Flaubert's *Madame Bovary*, both studies of courtesans' lives, were brought into the cheap "libraries." Of course, *Madame Bovary* had been published many years before in France; but it received its chief impetus in America when Peterson, Munro, Rand McNally, and other publishers of cheap novels took it up. Including recent sales in the twenty-five-cent editions, it is probable that each of these novels has reached the million mark in America, or come close to it. If the multitudes who have read them have pursued these stories to the bitter end, they have found the teachings moral in a high degree. The greater novel, with its study of moral decline, is Flaubert's; it ends fittingly in suicide. The lesser one is Zola's, with its sharply etched details of fashionable vice; it ends with a loathsome picture of Nana dead of smallpox.

Maupassant's real popularity in the United States began in the nineties. Harper's *The Odd Number,* containing thirteen of the short stories, with an introduction by Henry James, was published in 1889, and has been highly esteemed ever since. But it is only when we lump all the collections of Maupassant's tales, as put together by different publishers, that we get a proper idea of how widely his work has sold. There have been more than fifty such collections published in the United States; one of the more recent of them has sold 900,000 copies. Some have omitted "objectionable" stories, as *The Odd Number* did; others have prospered by printing even the most shocking tales by this master of short fiction.

Cellini's *Autobiography* has long enjoyed a considerable sale in many editions. How much the popularity of this masterpiece owes to its reputation for naughtiness is hard to tell.

Meantime American writers, high and low, were defying Mrs. Grundy and losing nothing by their boldness. How large a part the interest in the sex passages in *Leaves of Grass* played in Whitman's slowly won popularity is hard to say: possibly a genuinely important part, though, on the other hand, they retarded the early acceptance of that great work. Mark Twain was regarded by many as improper, though scarcely indecent. Said Louisa Alcott of *Huckleberry Finn:* "If Mr. Clemens cannot think of something better to tell our pure-minded lads and lasses, he had best stop writing for them."

Some writers of far lower capacity won widespread publicity by their incursions into sensationalism. *Poems of Passion,* by Ella Wheeler Wilcox, really had more passion in the title than anywhere else; as a contemporary reviewer observed, these verses could not disturb the morals of a lady-bug. The furor over them was largely projected by the newspaper boys. The book sold well enough, for fourth-rate poetry, though it probably never reached a hundred thousand; the author's earlier *Maurine* did better. Amélie Rives' *The Quick or the Dead?* gained notoriety a few years later; it was a novelette with a morbid theme and some scenes of hysterical passion. Parodied, attacked by moralists, adored by sentimental young ladies, it did not fall far short of the top rank of best sellers.

Readers of the nineties, by and large, accepted more frankness about sex than had those of preceding decades; *The Heavenly Twins, Trilby, Quo Vadis* were general favorites. The sub-rosa circulation of Daudet's *Sappho* flourished around the turn of the century by reason of the scandal caused by the arrest of Olga Nethersole, who played the part of the courtesan in Clyde Fitch's dramatic version. Olga was arrested because she allowed herself to be carried up a circular staircase on the stage to what Thomas Beer called "a theoretic bedroom." This happened in 1900. But criticism, on the whole, grew more liberal. Frederic Taber Cooper, a conservative writer for the conservative *Bookman,* declared in 1904, "The plain truth is that the majority of novels, instead of having too much sex in them, fail to have enough." So, in 1907, Elinor Glyn gave the world *Three Weeks.*

The charming, red-haired author, a younger sister of Lady Duff Gordon, was well known in London society circles. She had written two or three novels before *Three Weeks* became an English best seller. Published in the United

States by Duffield & Company, it immediately became the subject of controversy, its defenders emphasizing its romantic appeal ("an example of the most brilliant twentieth century fiction," said the *Baltimore Sun*); its critics condemning its immorality ("fit only for the garbage pail," said the *St. Paul Pioneer Press*). The first three weeks of *Three Weeks* saw "five large editions" distributed, or about fifty thousand copies. In three months it was selling more than two thousand copies a day, and Duffields advertised it as "the most talked-of book in America." In January, 1908, it headed the best seller lists in half a dozen cities. Then the Watch and Ward Society of Boston forced the booksellers of that city to refuse it, and the demand the country over rose beyond all expectations. Duffields ran advertising in the Boston papers offering to send the book postpaid for $1.50, the regular retail price. Anthony Comstock, of New York's Society for the Suppression of Vice, then appealed to the United States District Attorney to take action under the law which forbade sending obscene, lewd, or lascivious matter through the mails. Duffields, unwilling to desert their bookseller friends in Boston, made a test case, and their agent was arrested and fined. But they could pay a fine easily, for the book was now in the midst of what publishers call a "runaway sale." A burlesque by James S. Metcalfe, of *Life*, entitled *Another Three Weeks*, made people laugh at the book but did not stop their buying it. Mrs. Glyn wrote other short romances, also daring; she visited America to arrange for movies based on her books, in which Gloria Swanson and Rudolf Valentino starred; she popularized the term "It" as a synonym for sex appeal; she became an international figure, and *Three Weeks* was translated into most of the European languages. How many copies were eventually distributed in the United States nobody knows; the cheap reprint by the Macaulay Company alone ran to several hundreds of thousands.

In her autobiography, *Romantic Adventure*, Mrs. Glyn says that she wrote some of the more passionate episodes of *Three Weeks* during a visit to Venice a year or two after her marriage, when she felt herself neglected by her husband. "My romantic soul," she writes, "constantly sought in flights of unfettered imagination an escape from the limitations and deprivations of my married life, and *Three Weeks* was the product. My head was a little turned, perhaps, by the amount of attention which almost all men except my husband gave me at that time." It is a stirring thought that if Mr. Glyn had been more attentive on that holiday in Venice the world might have been spared *Three Weeks*.

The story has a certain relationship to the Zenda school, since the heroine is a queen of some unnamed principality taking a vacation from her husband and other affairs of state when she meets Paul, the godlike young Englishman, and decides to invite him to share the tiger-skin rug he has thoughtfully provided. Though the scene shifts from Switzerland to Venice in the midst of the three weeks' honeymoon, the story grows repetitive. That is the way with such things. Mrs. Glyn was incapable of portraying any psychological complications; she had no subtlety or humor. She was interested in animal passion and picturesque settings and little else. She knew her story was immoral, coyly referred to "this bad book" in the first chapter, and put various speeches justifying illicit passion into the mouth of her heroine. Well, "Imperatorskoye" finally packs up her tiger-skin and departs after an incandescent last night, leaving Paul only a jeweled collar for his pet dog—and memories. He later learns that the result of their three weeks' dalliance is the Baby King of Wherever-it-is. Mrs. Glyn always maintained that she had made it all nicely moral by having the lady stabbed when she was trying to meet Paul again, but we must be allowed our skepticism as to what she accomplished by that plot device.

It was two years before the publication of *Three Weeks* that Robert Hichens' *The Garden of Allah*, appeared, to sell, within a few years, some 700,000 copies in England and America. Hichens' *Bella Donna* (1909) was also successful; both made excellent films. Other writers were inspired by these two romantic novels about love in the desert, including Edith M. Hull.

Miss Hull, whose private life has always remained something of a mystery, and who always signed her novels simply E. M. Hull, had done a lot of fairly profitable fiction before she wrote *The Sheik*; but this became, and remains, the one big success in a prolific output. It was published in the spring of 1921 by Small, Maynard & Company, and became, as advertisements proudly announced, "the phenomenal best seller of the year." Of two years, as a matter of fact. The story told how Diana Mayo, beautiful and haughty daughter of Sir John Mayo, while touring in Egypt, was carried off into the desert by an Arab chieftain, and how she was finally brought to yield to his masterful love-making. The central idea, as the *Literary Review* protested, was "poisonously salacious," but the picture of the desert and desert life was interesting and convincing. The author had undoubtedly been there. The silent movie featuring Valentino (once more) was a hit. *The Sons of the Sheik* was a successful sequel in 1925. A parody subtitled *The Shriek* by Charles Somerville was published. The word "sheik" came into the language to describe any young fellow who had a way with the ladies. Including the Burt reprint, sales of *The Sheik* are said to have amounted to about 1,200,000.

James Milne, the English critic, once found a lady of his acquaintance reading *The Sheik*, and rallied her about wasting her time on a story about such a perfectly impossible person. "That's just it," she replied. "The impossible man! A woman can always meet—maybe even get—the possible man. But the impossible man is only possible in the impossible story!" To afford romantic escape is, within limits, a useful function. The escape to the desert was rather overdone, however, after the smashing success of *The Sheik*. Joan Conquest's *Desert Love*, Louise Gerard's *A Son of the Sahara*, and many another story of torrid love in the Torrid Zone eventually brought surfeit, disgust, annoyance. Arthur Guiterman expressed this last feeling admirably in his rhymed review of *Bella Donna*. Summarizing the story in breezy fashion, he comes to the last episode, in which the heroine flees into the desert in pursuit of her lover. But at the last,

> He cast her off. In blinded haste,
> Before the birds began to twitter,
> She staggered far across the waste—
> I hope to God a lion bit her!

There were many other books in the twenties to shock the moralists and challenge the censors, but none of them reached the top rank of the best seller. Not even Cabell's *Jurgen*, in spite of all the publicity its banning procured for it, became really popular. The twenties were the decade of *Flaming Youth*, *Bad Girl*, *The Beautiful and Damned*. The thirties were tamer, as though America were "sobering off" after a spree.

In 1944 two of the first four books on the *Publishers' Weekly* best seller list were banned in Boston, where the censors of books are busier than in any other American city. They were Lillian Smith's *Strange Fruit* and Kathleen Winsor's *Forever Amber*. The former was a serious and often poignant study of the race problem in the South. It was attacked because it employed, realistically and incidentally, words which have been commonly regarded as obscene. That it received much of its initial impulse toward large sales from the publicity given this feature, through the coöperation of Boston authorities acting under the Massachusetts law, there can be no doubt. It seems probable that hundreds of thousands of copies have been sold because of the curiosity thus aroused, or largely by such motivation. But readers who came to smirk have usually remained to praise. *Strange Fruit* at this writing has sold somewhat less than is necessary to place a 1944 book in the over-all list of best sellers.

Forever Amber, however, with an initial advertising appropriation of $20,000, made the extraordinary record of a million copies in print within a year of its first publication, and this without the aid of book clubs or reprints. Its sales were arbitrarily limited during the war, but they are well on their way toward a million and a half at this writing. *Forever Amber* is a big historical novel of England in the period of the Restoration; that was a bawdy era, and Amber flourished in its bawdiness. The chapters about the Great Plague are probably the best in Miss Winsor's novel. Her heroine's egocentric amorality reminds one forcibly of Defoe's Roxana. An action originating in Springfield, Massachusetts, was brought in the Superior Court of that state in 1947 to have *Forever Amber* adjudged "obscene, indecent, or impure"; the Court's ruling cleared the book of these charges.

XXXVIII. GIANTS OF THE THIRTIES

There were other signs of change, too, as the nineteen-thirties began. . . . The freedom so desperately won by the flappers of the now graying "younger generation" had not been lost. . . . What had departed was the excited sense that taboos were going to smash, that morals were being made over or annihilated, and that the whole code of behavior was in flux. The wages of sin had been stabilized at a lower level.

Frederick Lewis Allen in "Only Yesterday"

HISTORY is a continuous process rather than a series of leaps and jumps, yet sometimes there comes what seems a sharp break with the past. The financial crash of 1929 appears to have made some such break, for as we look back upon the third and fourth decades of the twentieth century they seem remarkably differentiated. In the Coolidge era confidence had grown, expansion had become the rule of business, and the word "colossal" was overworked not only in the amusement world but in industry. The Roosevelt era, on the other hand, was filled with struggle against depression, with NRA, WPA, the baffling problem of unemployment, and fears of want and of war. The one decade was full of extravagances in styles, manners, and morals, with its speakeasies, its defiant gangsterism, its "monkey trial," and such outstanding personalities as Lindbergh, Valentino, Capone, and Aimee Semple McPherson. The other decade brought "planning," the TVA, "technocracy," and the Dionne quintuplets. In the twenties we had the revolt of youth and a gleeful assault upon the old standards; in the thirties, a tired withdrawal from the most "advanced" positions. If these antitheses do not represent the deeper movements in the minds and hearts of the people, they at least point up the surface phenomena. The moods of the two decades were different.

In literature, *The Sheik* was more typical of the twenties than *Outline of History*; the former gained its best seller standing within the decade, while the latter was a long-time best seller. Gertrude Atherton's *Black Oxen*, Percy Marks' *The Plastic Age*, Michael Arlen's *The Green Hat*, Anita Loos's *Gentlemen Prefer Blondes*, Sinclair Lewis's *Elmer Gantry*, Viña Delmar's *Bad Girl*, and Julia Peterkin's *Scarlet Sister Mary* were all high on the *Publishers' Weekly* best seller lists in the twenties; and all represented, with various degrees of depth or shrillness, the revolt against the ancient mores. So did Scott Fitzgerald's *The Beautiful and Damned*; so did Theodore Dreiser's great *American Tragedy*. And Warner Fabian's *Flaming Youth* supplied a catchword for at least a part of the movement.

In the chastened mood of the thirties, the American people were ready for a change. They would never go back to the days before the World War: never again would they welcome a Gene Stratton-Porter or a Harold Bell Wright with open arms. They were weary of strident rebellion, though they would tolerate bolder comment on sex and more criticism of intrenched ideas than they had been used to in pre-war years. As Frederick Lewis Allen has written, "The wages of sin had been stabilized at a lower level."

And so, when the young publishing firm of Farrar & Rinehart gave the world Hervey Allen's *Anthony Adverse* on June 26, 1933, the American people were ready for it. It had plenty of sex, but it was not stridulous or saucy. It afforded escape from the worries of the depression in the travels and adventures of a picaroon hero at the end of the eighteenth century, thus leading readers back to a favorite best seller field—that of historical romance—and giving them a travelogue to boot. Mr. Allen, who had made his living as a teacher of English, and was chiefly known to the public as a poet, had taken five years to write this book, which was his first novel. In those five years he had used up all his savings, so that his bank balance was reduced to thirty dollars when he sent his manuscript off to the publishers. He had no first-hand knowledge of the scenes of his story: his information about places as well as times had to be derived from books, yet it was all convincing enough.

Anthony Adverse was published at three dollars, but the price was later reduced to two. The advance sale was about 20,000, and then the Book-of-the-Month Club gave it a big boost by using it as their July selection. As sales increased that summer to 10,000 a week, and in the fall to 15,000, the publishers began to use more advertising space, and by the end of the year 275,000 copies had been sold—an amazing total for a depression year. In January the demand became a stampede, especially when some of the retailers got to cutting prices on the book below cost in order to make a bargain feature of it. Price wars of this kind sometimes brought it down to 89 cents.

It was a big 89 cents' worth, for the volume ran to 1,224 pages. It had been planned as a "three-decker," but the publishers had finally decided to issue it in one volume. Many were the "gags" about its size. One man was said to have dropped his copy on his foot and then sued the publishers for the broken bones that resulted. A member of the Byrd expedition, according to another story, took a copy with him in order to have reading for the long antarctic nights. One library patron was said to have piled up $47 in over-due fees before he had finished the book.

But the big sales continued. *Anthony* led the best seller lists in 1933 and 1934. In the latter year it sold 176,000. The publishers issued a two-volume edition at five dollars in 1934, and a de luxe set in three volumes at ten dollars in 1937. The story made a big success on the screen in 1936, when produced by Warner Brothers with Fredric March as Anthony. A 75-cent movie edition of the book, limited to 97,000 copies, was published, after which the two-dollar price was resumed. Total sales were about 600,000 by the end of the book's fourth year, and it was said to have "taken the edge off the depression." In 1938, when the grand total had passed 700,000, came a Grosset & Dunlap reprint at 69 cents.

Meantime the novel had been translated into nine European languages, and its sales in England had mounted to important figures. Thereafter the reports of its publishers are understood to include its sales abroad—a grand total of over a million by 1939 and two million by 1946. Rinehart & Company are too busy selling the book to gratify our curiosity about what proportion of these totals belong to the United States, but a careful guess would place the American sales a little short of a million and a quarter.

While *Anthony Adverse* was still on the top of the wave, the Macmillan Company published *Gone With the Wind*, which was destined to become one of the greatest best sellers of publishing history.

The author, Margaret Mitchell, was the daughter of an Atlanta lawyer who was president of the Historical Society of that city. The whole family was interested in history, and "Peggy," as she was called, grew up in an atmosphere of historical reminiscence and pride in Atlanta's past. She was ten years old before she knew that the Confederacy lost the war; it was a crushing revelation, she says. After completing a course at Washington Seminary, in Atlanta, she entered Smith College in order to prepare for a medical course; but she was recalled to Atlanta by the death of her mother. For four or five years she worked on the *Atlanta Journal,* and the by-line of Peggy Mitchell became familiar to readers of the Sunday edition of that paper. In 1925 she was married to John R. Marsh, advertising manager for the Georgia Power Company. The next year she met with a serious injury to an ankle and was forced into semi-retirement. Then it was that she began to write down a series of romantic incidents which she devised about a green-eyed, tempestuous heroine she named Scarlett O'Hara. Her work on the story was rather disordered: she scarcely thought of it as work, for she had begun it for her own amusement and had no very clear thought of immediate publication.

Then one day in the spring of 1935, H. S. Latham, Macmillan editor, came to town, and Peggy Marsh met him at a luncheon. Mr. Latham was on a trip through the South and West scouting for new books and authors. This was a comparatively new technique in fiction publishing; traditionally, the editor sat at his desk in the home office and waited for new authors to come to him. But now friends had furnished Mr. Latham with contacts in various literary centers—Lois Cole, Macmillan's representative in Atlanta, had put him in touch with writers in that city—and he went out on a literary safari.

At the Atlanta luncheon given for Mr. Latham and attended chiefly by newspaper people, Mrs. Marsh was present. In the course of the conversation, someone said,

"If you're looking for a novel of the South, Mr. Latham, you ought to get Peggy Marsh's!"

"Oh, have you written a novel, Mrs. Marsh?" asked Mr. Latham.

And Mrs. Marsh, looking demurely at her plate, replied, "Oh, no, Mr. Latham."

The next day Mr. Latham attended a meeting of the Georgia Federation of Authors, and there again he heard rumors about a wonderful Civil War story that Peggy Marsh had written, or was writing. When he met her at a tea that afternoon, he said,

"I keep hearing about that novel of yours, Mrs. Marsh. Are you sure you haven't something you want to show me?"

"Oh, no, Mr. Latham," said Mrs. Marsh.

That evening his friends took the editor on a little trip out to Stone Mountain. Mrs. Marsh was in the party. The dogwood was in bloom, and it was a beautiful drive. When they had returned to the city and Mr. Latham was making his adieux to his hosts, he said to Mrs. Marsh:

"And you really haven't any novel, Mrs. Marsh?"

"Oh, no, Mr. Latham," she replied.

When Peter denied his Lord thrice, there was a cock that crew, and that broke him down. Whether Peggy Marsh heard any crowing is as yet undisclosed, but sometime that night she heard some kind of voice that told her this was Scarlett O'Hara's chance. The next morning when Mr. Latham was fastening his luggage preparatory to leaving his hotel, his telephone rang, and the desk clerk told him a lady was waiting in the lobby to see him. He came down at once and found Mrs. Marsh standing there, unsmiling.

"There it is, Mr. Latham," she said, pointing to a great pile of manuscript stacked on a chair nearby; "take the stuff!"

The editor had to hurry out and buy a big suitcase to pack his booty in. As soon as he got settled in the train, he opened it and began to read. He knew from the first that he had a prize. He read all the way to the West Coast, with growing enthusiasm. The first chapter was not yet written, and the story had no name, and there were two or three experimental versions of the ending; otherwise the story was complete.

Gone With the Wind was published in June, 1936, at three dollars, with liberal newspaper and magazine advertising. The first printing order was for 10,000 copies. Adoption by the Book-of-the-Month Club in July brought an order for 75,000 or more; that helped start the boom. Orders for over 100,000 piled up before publication. Early reviews by enthusiastic critics helped start the landslide. "In narrative power, in sheer readability, surpassed by nothing in American fiction," wrote J. Donald Adams in the Book Review of the New York Times. This was a good "quote" for the advertising of "the book which became a national best seller the day it was published." Runaway sales reached the million mark in six months and on one hectic day at the Macmillan office totaled 50,000. In two years sales passed a million and a half.

Everybody discussed Scarlett O'Hara and Rhett Butler. The general interest reached such a point that if you confessed you had not read the book you were regarded curiously, as though you were deformed, or had only one ear. You were left out of half the conversations that went on. You missed the points of most of the jokes. You were an illiterate outsider—the man who had not read *Gone With the Wind*. In self-defense you rushed to the nearest book-shop. *Gone With the Wind* became popular as a gift: one woman departing on a European voyage received nine copies from zealous friends. The author was besieged with thousands of letters, all of which she answered, with the aid of two secretaries. Many of them asked about the ending: did Scarlett get Rhett back? "How am I to know?" came the puzzled answer. "I really have no idea." A women's columnist referred in a New York paper to "Scarlett O'Hara green," and the stores had to lay in stocks of fabrics of that color— or of one that passed for it. An enterprising reporter interviewed scores of peo-ple as to how long it took them to read the book, and gave the palm to a taxi-driver who had done it all in eighteen hours and thirty minutes.

Not that there were no critical or dissenting voices raised. Some very nice persons thought Scarlett an improper heroine; some not so nice called her by harsher names. Some complained of superficiality. There were critics who asked in distressed tones, "Why do they read it?" but there were others to answer, "Because it is a good story." So it is. Moreover, the characters seem real enough, and they are full of life and feeling and lusty action. The Civil War romance had long been popular, and the public the country over had grown to like the southern view-point. *Anthony Adverse* had conditioned readers to the long novel, and there were enough high points in *Gone With the Wind* to hold the interest without perceptible drops. After all, the Ameri-can public has liked long novels in nearly all periods of our readership. *Gone With the Wind* is only about a fifth longer than *David Copperfield*.

David O. Selznick bought the picture rights to *Gone With the Wind* for $50,000 soon after its initial success as a novel, but he delayed the production for nearly three years. There was no doubt about the choice of Clark Gable for the part of Rhett; the popular voice demanded it, and Selznick had to bor-row him from Metro-Goldwyn-Mayer, and cut them in on the profits. The rôle of Scarlett was finally assigned to Vivien Leigh, an English actress. The pro-duction cost $3,850,000, and the showing of the film required three hours and forty-five minutes. The première was held in Atlanta, where, as the *Constitu-tion* said, it was the greatest news event since Sherman. The governor of Georgia proclaimed a state-wide holiday, and the mayor of Atlanta went further by urging his people to make it a three-day festival, for which the men were to grow goatees and beards in the Civil War fashions, and the women to dress in crinolines. Said *Time*: "To Georgia it was like winning the battle of Atlanta seventy-five years late." Once released to the country at large, the picture was given special showings at advanced prices in every city and village. It is said to have made thirty million dollars in profits to the producers.

A motion picture edition of the novel was issued by the Macmillan Company in 1939; printed in double columns and bound in paper, with illustrations in color, it sold for sixty-nine cents. A Grosset & Dunlap reprint at fifty cents came the next year. There was a limited edition in two volumes, with color plates, in 1939, selling at $7.50. Translations have been made into all the European languages, and the book has sold especially well in Germany, France and Denmark, as well as in Canada and England. The foreign sales have considerably exceeded a million and a half copies.

In the United States they have amounted to double that figure. The distribution of *Gone With the Wind* in this country has now surpassed that of *Uncle Tom's Cabin,* its nearest rival for the topmost position among novels in all the history of American readership. Moreover, it is one of five or six books which, by virtue of sales of about three million, lead the entire list of works designed for general reading.

A small book in comparison with the bulk of either *Anthony Adverse* or *Gone With the Wind,* but a great book in its interpretation of a people and of life in general is Pearl S. Buck's *The Good Earth.* Published by the John Day Company early in 1931, it had made an immediate success and had led the best seller lists for the two years preceding the appearance of *Anthony.* In March, 1931, the Book-of-the-Month Club adopted it, and its sales in the original John Day edition soon ran into six figures. It received a Pulitzer Prize in 1932; and six years later Mrs. Buck became the third American author to receive the Nobel Prize for Literature, an award based largely on *The Good Earth.* A stage version in which Alla Nazimova starred, and a remarkable M-G-M motion picture, helped to make this modern masterpiece genuinely popular. Reprints have been published by Grosset & Dunlap, P. F. Collier, the Modern Library, and Pocket Books; and total American sales approached a million and a half.

The author was born in West Virginia, daughter of Absalom and Caroline Sydenstricker, Presbyterian missionaries, who took her to the far interior of China while she was still an infant. Pearl grew up in that great country, seeing many parts of it and becoming well acquainted with the Chinese life and people. She was educated at a Shanghai boarding-school, at Randolph-Macon in Virginia, and at Cornell; but her most valuable early training in writing was received from her mother. She married a scholarly missionary, had two children, and taught English literature in Nanking University. She was thirty-eight when her first novel, *East Wind: West Wind,* appeared from the John Day press. It was not very successful; but Richard J. Walsh, president of the publishing company, believed firmly in Mrs. Buck's genius and the next year published *The Good Earth,* which had been written shortly after the Chinese Revolution of 1926. Never was publisher's faith more fully justified.

During the height of the book's popularity, Mrs. Buck, who was in the United States on an extended visit, made a public criticism of missionary policy which provoked a stormy controversy and resulted eventually in her resignation from all connection with the Presbyterian Board of Foreign Missions. Since then she has devoted herself to authorship and has lived chiefly in this country. After divorcing John Lossing Buck, she was married in 1935 to Mr. Walsh, her publisher.

The Good Earth, with its epical sweep, its deeply satisfying characterization, and its dramatic power, has been accepted as one of the great novels of its generation. With its two sequels, *Sons* and *A House Divided,* it presents a trilogy of the family of Wang; and the three have been published together as *House of Earth.* The original novel has been translated into twenty languages and widely distributed in twenty-seven countries of the world.

In the last year of the decade came the fourth great and successful novel of the thirties—*The Grapes of Wrath.* Its author, John Steinbeck, had been born in Salinas, California, and had become acquainted as a boy with the ranches and lettuce fields of that region. A roamer over the United States for many years, day-laborer, gardener, watchman, harvester, and so on, he learned to know the workers and to share their problems. Then he turned to fiction, and he was already a successful novelist when he wrote *The Grapes of Wrath.*

This story grew out of its author's interest in the problems involved in the situation of the migratory workers in his native Salinas Valley. Living with the migrants, writing about them in a series for the *San Francisco News,* helping a *Life* photographer get pictures of them, Steinbeck gathered the materials which made his novel so vivid. The Viking Press published the book April 14, 1939, and it took the country by storm. Its relentless commentary on the Dust Bowl and migratory-worker problem, its poignance and realism, and its narrative power brought it a large and earnest audience. Critics praised it, editors discussed it, Congress took notice of it, President Roosevelt made a speech based on it, and California undertook to cope with the situation which it had brought to national attention. It was accepted as a great social document as well as a good novel.

Well over half a million copies were sold before the book went into the cheaper editions. It ranked first in the *Publishers' Weekly* summary of best sellers for 1939 and eighth the next year. Then in 1946 it became the actual best seller of the new Bantam Books series, and its grand total rose to at least a million and a quarter.

The fifth top-seller of the 1930's was Dale Carnegie's remarkable book about how to get ahead in the world. The theme is a familiar one to the reader of American best sellers. History and biography emphasize it: Franklin's and Barnum's autobiographies are full of it. The theme is even more frequent in fiction, from *Pamela* to *The Girl of the Limberlost,* and all up and down the long line of stories of ambitious boys ranging from John Halifax and David Copperfield to the Alger and Southworth heroes. We find it in more didactic form, too, in many best sellers—in Chesterfield's *Letters* and the less remembered behavior books. There has never been a time when plenty of such books of counsel and guidance were not available. Samuel Smiles' *Self-Help* and its sequels were widely read in Britain and America in the latter half of the nineteenth century. Orison Swett Marden's success books were popular for two decades, beginning with *Pushing to the Front* in 1894. In 1906 Marden published *Power of Personality,* his most successful book; and the next year appeared a book by Frank C. Haddock whose sales were to surpass those of all the other turn-of-the-century success books.

This was *Power of Will,* issued by the Pelton Publishing Company, of Meriden, Connecticut. Haddock was a lawyer and a lecturer on popular psychology, and his book is full of illustrative anecdotes and suggestions for practical exercises. The book was undoubtedly helpful to many, and sounder, on the whole, than those which followed it in the author's Power-Book Library. Though Haddock did not belong officially to the New Thought movement, it is hard to separate his work from that cult. *Power of Will* was sold at three and four dollars, chiefly by agents, and in twenty years piled up sales of about 750,000.

Like Haddock, Carnegie was a popular lecturer, less scientific than his predecessor but even more practical. He was a Missouri boy, who had come to New York to study dramatic art; eventually he got a rôle in a company which took *Polly of the Circus* on tour. But he had trouble finding another engagement and began giving public-speaking lessons at a New York Y.M.C.A. It was not long before his success in this venture was impressive, and he enlarged his work to include other courses, wrote a textbook on public speaking, and took some important clients (one was Lowell Thomas, then a Princeton teacher) for private coaching. The First World War interrupted his activities; but after his uneventful tour of duty, he resumed his work, built it up again, and organized the Carnegie Institute of Effective Speaking and Human Relations. In his classes, some of which met in the grand ballroom of the Pennsylvania Hotel, he now enrolled many important business men; and almost without exception they became enthusiastic Carnegie fans.

Among Carnegie's students in 1934 was Leon Shimkin, of the Simon & Schuster publishing house. Shimkin was not long in becoming a Carnegie fan himself, and suggested a book which should embody the materials of the Institute lectures. The result was *How to Win Friends and Influence People.* It is a practical, readable book, crammed with illustrative anecdotes and quotes from famous men and women, instrumented with exercises which the reader was urged to try—all given in a rapid-fire, talking style. It was so convincing that readers were converted in spite of themselves and went about making friends and influencing people as a kind of game. Part I presents the fundamental thesis that you have to get the other fellow's point of view. Part II gives "Six Ways to Make People Like You," Part III "Twelve Ways to Win People to Your Way of Thinking." Later we have "Nine Ways to Change People Without Giving Offense or Arousing Resentment" and "Seven Rules for Making Your Home Life Happier" (the author was married once but is now divorced).

The book was published November 4, 1936, with a first printing of 3,000 copies and an advance sale of 1,506. An eight-inch, double-column advertisement in the New York *Times* on November 16, with coupon, brought in 192 orders; and Simon & Schuster, who never sleep on a job, then risked a full-page ad, which yielded 1,488 coupons returned. In the next two years S & S spent a quarter of a million dollars advertising *How to Win Friends,* and sold a million and a half dollars' worth of copies at $1.96 apiece.*

Important as this paid advertising was, it was the word-of-mouth recommendation of readers that made the book a continuing success. That, and the author's own activities; for Carnegie wrote a syndicated column, made regular radio broadcasts, and went on with his lectures, and everything he did won friends and influenced people to buy his book. It was close to the million mark when Pocket Books issued their first printing of it in July, 1936; at the end of six years it had sold nearly two million copies in that form and was second only to *Private Hargrove* on the PB list. Thus *How to Win Friends & I.P.* has today sold over three million copies, which puts it at or near † the top of the non-fiction of our entire best seller list—exclusive always of bibles, textbooks, manuals, and so on. Of course, it might be argued that Dale Carnegie's masterpiece is a textbook or manual, but that would be straining a point: it was intended for general reading.

The trademark of the Pocket Books is conspicuous on the decade of the thirties. *Anthony Adverse* and *Gone With the Wind* are the only top-rank best sellers of the decade which did not sell half a million or more in that format. *How to Win Friends, The Good Earth,* and *Lost Horizon* were PB leaders. Seven Erle Stanley Gardners, three Ellery Queens, and one other detective story, together with a western and *The Best of Damon Runyon* reached places on the top best seller list largely by virtue of Pocket Books sales. *The Grapes of Wrath* reached that position with the aid of Bantam Books. What part the economic depression played in the history of the best sellers of the decade is a matter for interesting speculation: all the top leaders were either big books or cheap books, and in either case purchasers got a lot for their money.

* George Stevens, *Lincoln's Doctor's Dog and Other Famous Best Sellers* (Philadelphia, 1938), pp. 46-48.

† One hesitates at estimates within some hundreds of thousands of such a long-time classic as Shakespeare's *Plays,* or of such a multiform juvenile as *Mother Goose;* but it appears that these two, with *Gone With the Wind, Uncle Tom's Cabin, How to Win Friends, Ivanhoe,* and *Ben-Hur* are the seven books on our list which have sold well over two and a half million copies. So we tuck them together modestly down here in this footnote.

XXXIX. THE CASE OF THE
BEST SELLER MYSTERY

The mental features discoursed of as analytical are, in themselves, but little susceptible of analysis. We appreciate them only in their effects. We know of them, among other things, that they are always to their possessor, when inordinately possessed, a source of the liveliest enjoyment. As the strong man exults in his physical ability, delighting in such activities as call his muscles into action, so glories the analyst in that moral activity which *disentangles*. . . . It will be found, in fact, that the ingenious are always fanciful, and the *truly* imaginative never otherwise than analytic.

Edgar Allan Poe in "The Murders in the Rue Morgue"

"Escapism!" snorts the censor of our reading morals, as he surveys the well filled shelves of crime-mystery writers from Edgar Allan Poe to Erle Stanley Gardner. "What of it?" we reply impudently.

What is this crime of escapism? Escape from what? Apparently it is escape from work and worry. Escape *to* what? Apparently to play and fun. Now the difference between work and play is that the one consists of activities performed under the compulsion of duty after the freshness and novelty have worn off, while the other is activity which is not compulsory but is engaged in because its novelty is not exhausted to the point of boredom. Thus big-game hunting is still play despite its fatigue and hardship, but professional baseball is work for the "player" because the sport has, for him, passed from the status of an activity enjoyed for its own rewards to that of a job required by duties under a contract. And so reading, if required and onerous (as professional study may often be) becomes work; but if done for pleasure, as most of our reading is, it is play—whether it is in the light literature of romance and adventure or in the heaviest dissertations in science and philosophy. In other words, all general reading is escapism.

To be sure, there are degrees and gradations in such escapes. As was observed in connection with the discussion of *Pollyanna* in an earlier chapter, escapism may, like other good things, be carried too far; but to make a sweeping condemnation of it—to use it as a "smear word"—is pretentious and snobbish criticism.

The comparative values of different kinds of play are by no means obvious. Our censor is quick to condemn our "morbid" interest in crime, but we shall have to remind him that what may be actually morbid for him may be merely invigorating for us. Curiosity with regard to evil is not itself evil. And monitorial and even self-righteous as the contemners of detective tales sometimes are, they would scarcely wish to screen the crime out of literature from the Old Testament through Aeschylus and Shakespeare down to Hawthorne and Ellery Queen.

No, neither their escapism nor their preoccupation with crime affords grounds for frowning upon the whole class of detective fiction. If we condemn them, let us discriminate against such as are ill-written, superficial in the portrayal of scene and character, and neglectful of the "rules of the game" which to ignore is the real crime of the mystery-weaver.

Eighteen murder mysteries find places on the top best seller list. This total does not include Poe's *Tales,* since only four of them were stories of ratiocination—to use his term. Nor does it include Gaboriau's *File Number 113* or *M. Lecocq;* both have sold widely in American cheap editions, but evidence of a distribution that would put them in the top bracket is not at hand.

Wilkie Collins' *The Moonstone* was printed serially in *Harper's Weekly* in 1868, and then brought out in a dollar edition. The Harpers apparently paid £750 for it, but it was soon pirated by competing publishers. The *Citizen and Round Table,* of New York, declared in 1869 that "after Dickens, there is no living novelist who enjoys a popularity which approaches that of Wilkie Collins." He visited this country about the time the cheap, paper-covered "libraries" were getting started: most of them included *The Moonstone.* The story is a hardy perennial, and it still has many readers and admirers. Sergeant Cuff is a thoroughly convincing detective, and his sayings stick in the mind. Dorothy Sayers, in her introduction to the badly titled *Omnibus of Crime,* wrote: "Taking everything into consideration, *The Moonstone* is probably the very finest detective story ever written." Harpers still publish it; it is in the Modern Library, Everyman's, Armed Services Editions, and other series.

Just ten years after the publication of *The Moonstone,* a young lady, accompanied by her lawyer father, called at the publishing house of G. P. Putnam's Sons, bringing the manuscript of a novel written in pencil on yellow paper. The young lady was Anna Katharine Green, and the novel was *The Leavenworth Case.* Putnam decided to publish it, and thus the portly and fatherly-looking Ebenezer Gryce joined the ranks of the great detectives. The story became very popular. In the eighties the publishers got out a cheap quarto edition to compete with the "libraries," and sold it for twenty cents. The story was dramatized and successfully produced, and the author married one of the actors in the cast, Charles Rohlfs. Woodrow Wilson, inveterate reader of detective novels, told Carolyn Wells that his favorite writers of this type of literature were Anna Katharine Green and Emile Gaboriau.

Twenty-five years after the first publication of *The Leavenworth Case,* its publishers announced that they had worn out two sets of plates reprinting the regular edition and were making another. It has probably sold at least half a million copies. Mrs. Rohlfs continued to write mysteries until she was seventy-seven, always using her maiden name. She lived to see her most famous story pass out of copyright.

Long before that, the detective story had been dominated by a greater deductive genius than Mr. Gryce. It was *Lippincott's Magazine* that first brought

Sherlock Holmes to America. It had an arrangement with Ward, Lock & Company, of London, New York, and Melbourne, to distribute the magazine in England, and they were the publishers who had bought Dr. Arthur Conan Doyle's *A Study in Scarlet* for twenty-five pounds and printed it in *Beeton's Christmas Annual* for 1887. The next year they issued it separately in paper covers, and in 1889 reprinted it. It was doubtless with their cooperation that Dr. Doyle, then an unsuccessful physician at Southsea, near Portsmouth, was asked to do a novelette for *Lippincott's.* The result was *The Sign of the Four,* which appeared as the chief feature of the February, 1890, number of the magazine and was later included in a book called *Six Complete Stories from Lippincott's,* which was simply the semi-annual bound volume of the magazine. Lippincott's also published *A Study in Scarlet* in 1890—one edition in paper covers at fifty cents and one in cloth at seventy-five.

Thus was the tall, sinewy, sharp-faced detective known as Sherlock Holmes introduced to the American people. It would be pleasant to say that he immediately took the country by storm, but such was not the case. It was three or four years before he won a large audience. Some of Doyle's early work was published in America in cheap bindings in 1889 and 1890; but it was not until Harpers issued *The Adventures of Sherlock Holmes* in 1892, after its publication in London in the preceding year, that there were signs of the popular enthusiasm which was later to develop around Conan Doyle's great creation.

But the vogue for Sherlock Holmes, when it did develop, simply swept the country. The first two Holmes books were "in the public domain," and they were issued in paper-bound volumes at ten cents, published in cheap sets (sometimes along with some of Doyle's non-detective novels which were also unprotected by copyright), syndicated to Sunday papers, and run as "boilerplate" in country weeklies. William Gillette starred in *Sherlock Holmes,* a melodrama made from three of Doyle's stories, at the Garrick Theatre in New York in 1899, and continued in that part now and again for thirty years. John Barrymore played Sherlock in the movies, and later Basil Rathbone starred in a series on the screen and also took the part of the great detective in some hundreds of radio broadcasts. Stage, screen, and the standard illustrations by the English Sidney Paget and the American Frederic Dorr Steele had made the hawk-nose, keen eyes, fore-and-aft cap, dressing gown, and slippers of Holmes as familiar as Lincoln's beard and shawl. Few characters in fiction have become so universally known. "Sherlock" became a synonym for "detective." "Elementary, my dear Watson!" has been a catchword for half a century. In more recent years Sherlock Holmes has become the center of a cult, with a considerable literature, clubs, and a serio-comic bibliophilic scholarship of amazing proportions.

The three books recording the exploits of the immortal Holmes to reach the top rank of best sellers in the course of years were *The Sign of the Four, A Study in Scarlet,* and *The Adventures of Sherlock Holmes.* In 1902, *The Hound of the Baskervilles* attained high popularity and the best seller lists, but its totals did not place it in the topmost bracket. In recent years the Doubleday *Complete Sherlock Holmes* in various editions, including those for the Book-of-the-Month Club and the Literary Guild, has had a large distribution. The *Sherlock Holmes Pocket Book*, containing two novelettes and most of the short stories, has fared well. The Modern Library issued a Holmes book in 1946. Thus the great detective strides on, through London fog and the dreams of readers new and old. If the three leaders among the books that portray him have not reached the million mark as yet, they are close to it.

Sherlock Holmes did much to stimulate the production of good detective stories. Of course, the weekly "Old Sleuth," "Old Cap Collier," and "Nick Carter" nickel novelettes antedated Sherlock Holmes, and they continued through the nineties and some of them even later. But the Holmes influence was felt upon magazine literature of a higher grade: Arthur Morrison's Martin Hewitt, Jacques Futrelle's Thinking Machine, G. K. Chesterton's Father Brown, and Israel Zangwill's Grodman may be cited. And yet only one detective novel published in the United States between Doyle's *Adventures of Sherlock Holmes* (1892) and Ellery Queen's *Dutch Shoe Mystery* (1931) reached the top rank in sales, and it has attained that distinction by means of long-continued demand which has piled up the necessary total only as these pages are written. That book is *The Circular Staircase*.

It was the first book in a long series of successes by Mary Roberts Rinehart, and was published in 1908 by the Bobbs-Merrill Company. The middle-aged spinster narrator, of a type later to become common in such stories, mixes in an exciting murder investigation; and the puzzle is worked out with care. The regular edition enjoyed what seemed a fine sale of some thirty thousand copies, but it was when Grosset & Dunlap put it into a reprint edition (or rather, into three of them) that it really showed its paces—to the extent of nearly a quarter-million copies. Later it went into the Triangle Books; and in 1941 it joined the Pocket Books, which accounted for half of its grand total. Mrs. Rinehart's books have since been on the best seller lists so frequently that Irving Harlow Hart's computations place her first in the list of authors of the best sellers of the last fifty years; * but none of her other books has reached the top rank.

The Great Impersonation, by E. Phillips Oppenheim, is a novel of intrigue and adventure rather than a detective story. Published by Little, Brown & Company in 1920, it soon got into the best seller lists and finished in eighth place for that year. It was later in Burt's reprints and the Triangle Books. But it was the Pocket Books edition that brought it into the over-all lists and contributed the lion's share to its grand total of over a million.

From 1926 onward, indeed, the Pocket Books have played a dominant part in the making of detective best sellers and "better sellers." In this latter class

* See *Publishers' Weekly* for Jan. 19, 1946, p. 288.

during the six years beginning with 1926 we find stories by some of the most important authors of recent mystery fiction—Earl Derr Biggers (*The Chinese Parrot, Behind That Curtain, Charlie Chan Carries On*), Dashiell Hammett (*Red Harvest, The Maltese Falcon, The Glass Key*), Frances Noyes Hart (*The Bellamy Trial*), S. S. Van Dine (*The Canary Murder Case*), Agatha Christie (*The Murder of Roger Ackroyd*), E. C. Bentley (*Trent's Last Case*), and Leslie Charteris (*Enter the Saint*). But none of these rang the bell which meant top placing.

Ellery Queen rang it, however. In fact he (or they) rang it four times, thus surpassing the record of Conan Doyle. Ellery Queen is the name adopted by a busy team of writers—Frederic Dannay and Manfred B. Lee—cousins, both born in Brooklyn in 1905, and enough alike to be twins. Theirs is probably the most successful collaboration in literary history, for the aggregate sales of the Ellery Queen books in America are said to exceed ten millions, and *Ellery Queen's Mystery Magazine,* the radio, and the screen increase their fame and profits.

Their first novel was *The Roman Hat Mystery,* which they wrote in competition for a prize of $7,500 offered by *McClure's Magazine* and the Frederick A. Stokes Company. The judges were unanimous for the Queen manuscript, but shortly before the decision was to be announced, *McClure's* went into bankruptcy. Such was the ill-starred beginning of the great career of Ellery Queen; but Stokes published the book, it made a modest succcess, and the collaborators were encouraged to do another. Fourth of the mysteries with the geographical names was *The Dutch Shoe Mystery;* it was the first Ellery Queen to reach the top bracket of best sellers. In it the murder was committed in a hospital, and for years doctors and nurses have been writing to Ellery telling him about technical inaccuracies in the book. But if the medical details were bad, the mystery was excellent, and the *Dutch Shoe* has sold about a million and a quarter copies.

Since the Queen books have been published in the 1930's and 1940's they must reach totals of 1,200,000 and 1,300,000 to be listed as first-rank best sellers. These four are now in the list—*The Dutch Shoe Mystery, The Egyptian Cross Mystery, The Chinese Orange Mystery,* and a volume of short stories called *New Adventures of Ellery Queen.* As a writer of detective short stories, Ellery Queen is easily the most popular performer since Conan Doyle. His original *Adventures* had a big sale, but the new book eclipsed the old one, selling over a million copies in the Pocket Books alone.

The method of "processing" an Ellery Queen novel is illustrated by the publishing history of *The Chinese Orange Mystery.* It was serialized in the *Red Book,* and then issued in a two-dollar edition by Stokes. After that it went into reprints by Grosset & Dunlap and the Triangle Books at reduced prices. Then, five years after its original publication, it was included in the Pocket Books. Finally, there was a ten-cent condensation. They squeezed a lot of juice out of that orange, said *Life.*

But the King of Anodynists, the most popular whoduniter of his times, is Erle Stanley Gardner. Son of a mining engineer, he spent much of his boyhood and youth in mining camps, including some months in the Klondike in 1906; so that, while he achieved a continuing love of outdoor life, his education was irregular. But he has tremendous vitality and capacity for work, and when he got around to it, he studied hard. He was admitted to the California bar at twenty-one, and practiced law in Ventura County for more than twenty years. He specialized in trial work, was defense attorney in some spectacular cases, and became the Perry Mason of the California bar. He was thirty-five before he began writing in earnest; within a few years he was, to use his own words, "established as a quantity producer in the pulp field," writing over a million words a year—and he was still conducting an extensive law practice! He had some Chinese clients and through them became interested in China; he began to study the Chinese language—in addition to his other occupations—and in 1931 dropped everything to go to the Orient, where he lived for a year or two. Upon his return to this country, he decided to quit his law practice and devote himself to writing and travel. He is an enthusiastic traveler, and once spent two years living in a fleet of house trailers, in which he maintained offices as well as living quarters for his staff. He requires a staff wherever he goes, for he uses dictaphones for his composition, and commonly keeps three to five secretaries busy. We need a higher-powered word than "indefatigable" for Erle Stanley Gardner.

Besides the popular, and frequent, Perry Mason stories, he has a series about Douglas Selby, the D.A., and another about Terry Clane. He is said to have two or three pen-names. They told us not long ago that he was A. A. Fair, author of the Harold Lam and Bertha Cool stories. We shall not be surprised now if they tell us he is Agatha Christie and Dashiell Hammett: we can believe anything about him.

All of Gardner's top-bracket best sellers belong to the series in which that smart, fast-moving lawyer called Perry Mason and his faithful secretary Della Street (always in love; never to marry) befriend some underdog who looks as guilty as Tophet, involves Mason dangerously, and then turns out to be innocent because Mason has found, in the midst of the trial of his client, who the real murderer is. It is a marvelous and durable formula. Here are the great successes, all of them having sold at least 1,200,000 copies: *The Case of the Sulky Girl, The Case of the Curious Bride, The Case of the Counterfeit Eye, The Case of the Stuttering Bishop, The Case of the Lame Canary, The Case of the Dangerous Dowager,* and *The Case of the Substitute Face.* These have all been published by William Morrow & Company at two dollars, then by Grosset & Dunlap at fifty cents, then by Pocket Books at twenty-five cents. The Pocket Books sales of five of them have passed the million mark, and the other three are, at this writing, not much below that.

One other detective story to reach the top rank in sales was published in the late thirties—Marco Page's *Fast Company*. Marco Page is Harry Kurnitz, and his swiftly moving, clever, "tough" story of a rare book dealer turned sleuth won Dodd, Mead & Company's thousand-dollar Red Badge Mystery prize in 1938. It later followed the path of a Gardner story, going to Grosset & Dunlap for a fifty-cent edition, and then to the Pocket Books, where it has sold almost a million copies.

The thirties were a great decade for detective stories. It takes several years for one of them to reach its full stature, so that the figures for those of the forties as we have them at this writing do not tell what this decade will do; but already three Christie novels published in 1939-1941, as well as Eric Ambler's *A Coffin for Dimitrios* and Helen MacInnes' *Above Suspicion,* are "better sellers." And *Publishers' Weekly* tells us that one-fourth of the new fiction titles now published in the United States are those of detective and mystery stories.

So if this type of escapist literature is evil, we are going to the dogs—and fast.

XL. THE NEW ERA IN BOOK PUBLISHING

One thing is certain—that books have been selling in totals never before reached, possibly double the pre-war figures, in fact as fast as they could be produced, with the output limited by the supply of materials and the capacity of plants.
Frederic G. Melcher: "1945 in Retrospect" in Publishers' Weekly

AN OLD era in book publishing ended in the early 1940's, and a new one began. The changes which defined the new era were not brought about by the Second World War, but occurred in spite of it. War conditions—shortages of labor, linotype-metal, paper, and binder's cloth—actually retarded that expansion of mass markets for books which is the chief characteristic of the new era.

Early in 1943 several book-publishing records were broken. Wendell Willkie's *One World,* through heavy Simon & Schuster advertising and the use of news-stand outlets, sold 800,000 copies in one month and 1,100,000 in two months. Random House, with a book club order and a large advance sale, ordered 440,000 copies of Captain Lawson's *Thirty Seconds Over Tokyo* printed in advance of publication. The advance printing of a book already in the best seller lists, *See Here, Private Hargrove,* in the Pocket Books reprint, was 850,000; and it sold a million copies in that form in less than a month. These incidents all broke records, but they were to be broken again and again within the next few years, not only for war-born books but for others. Though the phenomena here recorded developed in war years, the means by which mass sales were obtained originated before the war.

Since then the mass markets have grown steadily. The record for advance printings of new books rose to 800,000 before the end of 1946, and million-copy sales in short periods are not uncommon. "A million-copy sale is peanuts today," wrote Richard Mealand in *Publishers' Weekly* in the early weeks of 1946. A million-copy sale is never peanuts, but it certainly is far commoner today than anyone could have imagined ten or twenty years ago.

Some observers have maintained that this phenomenon is ephemeral, and that with a return to normal economic and social conditions it will disappear. But an examination of the reasons for the mass market in books leads to the conclusion that, so far as anything can be certain in the troubled forties, a very large distribution of books is sure to continue. We can divide these reasons into two classes: those on the side of demand, and those on the side of supply.

The increased demand, based on growing readership, springs obviously from augmentation of such factors as population and schooling on all levels. But it is so smoothly retroactive with the supply elements as to make a continuous circle: the new supply techniques have educated and built up the demand, so that readership desires increase by what they feed on. Millions have discovered books in the last decade or two. The book clubs and the 25-cent series have taught people to buy books easily, and having them in the home has made more readers who want more books. The Armed Services Editions have made book readers of hundreds of thousands of young men who otherwise would have tasted the pleasures of books seldom and gingerly.

The demand is also controlled, to a degree not yet fully apparent, by the economic situation. Certainly gasoline rationing had some favorable effect on reading habits during the war, but resumption of automobile travel has not produced, as yet, any disastrous effect on the book trade. War "prosperity," bringing plenty of money but little to spend it on, helped the mass sales. Post-war inflation had not, by the end of 1946, damaged the book business, despite the fears of publishers who recalled their misfortunes after the First World War, when higher book prices and the social developments of the dizzy twenties had made a difficult selling situation. Finally, the educational boom, based on the "GI Bill of Rights," seemed likely to be effective in fostering new reading habits.

On the supply side, the chief factors to be noted are the improvements in fast printing and binding, particularly in connection with the production of cheap books; the development of new, superior designs in cheap formats; the lavish use of advertising, especially in the forties; the growth of the book clubs as a new technique of distribution; the contribution of the reprint houses to the sale of books a year or two old; and the amazing development of the 25 cent book business.

The Book-of-the-Month Club was the brain-child of Harry Scherman, who had earlier been associated with the Little Leather Library. It sent out its first book, Sylvia Townsend Warner's *Lolly Willowes*, in May, 1926, to 4,750 members. Sinclair Lewis' *Elmer Gantry* was offered in March of the next year to 50,000 members, and in another year the number was doubled. This does not mean that the Club was selling that many books each month; it began that way, but soon changed to plans which allowed members to pass a given number of the monthly selections, and finally settled on the idea of requiring the purchase of only four books a year to maintain membership. As a matter of fact, between 40% and 65% of the members may be expected to accept a given month's selection; the average is probably a little less than half.

When the depression struck the Club in 1930, it had 110,000 members. It lost nearly a third of them, but resumed the upward curve by adding the "book dividend" inducement—a special gift book for every two books accepted. By 1939, despite the depression and all its works, BOMC had 200,000 members. From then it went on steadily to half a million in 1940. At the beginning of 1944, the membership was halted at 600,000 on account of war shortages, but increases were resumed in the fall of 1945, and in a year's time the membership was raised to a million.

Nearly a third of BOMC's books are non-fiction. Rather frequently in these latter years, two books are offered together. In 1942, for example, sixteen books were offered, ten of them fiction. Altogether, in its twenty years the Club has distributed some 70,000,000 books, including dividends and substitutes. In 1945 the retail value of the books it distributed was about $25,000,000.

This is certainly big business. But the Book-of-the-Month Club is only one of about fifty such organizations, and not, in 1946, the largest. The Literary Guild was incorporated in 1921, but did not get its distribution of books started until in 1926, a few months after the Book-of-the-Month Club had made its beginning. In 1929 Doubleday & Company purchased a 49% interest in the Guild; the membership was then about 70,000. It suffered from the depression, like everything else. In 1934 Doubleday took over complete control. Tie-ins were made with the bookstores, which promoted Guild memberships. The Club grew to 100,000 in 1938, adopted the Book Bonus device in 1940, increased to 300,000 in 1942, and then skyrocketed to nearly a million during the war. It was said to be 1,250,000 by the summer of 1946. In later years the selections have been nearly all fiction. Doubleday's own books are not favored over those of other publishers.

The Dollar Book Club, with a membership in 1946 of half a million, as well as the Book League, also belong to Doubleday & Company. Both began as mail-order devices for handling the Doubleday "remainders," but since 1940 the Dollar Book Club has issued reprints of the "best sellers" of other publishers. All of the Doubleday clubs are advertised in the catalogues of Montgomery Ward & Company.

The selling device involving an alliance with a great mail-order concern was first used by the People's Book Club, founded in 1943 by Simon & Schuster, the Consolidated Book Publishing Company, and Sears, Roebuck & Company. Their books are reprints of recent successes. They devised a new system of selection: whereas the Book-of-the-Month Club choices are made by a board of literary authorities, and those of the Literary Guild and Dollar Book Club are made by shrewd John Beecroft, the decisions of the People's Book Club are arrived at by collecting the preferences of cross-sections of the reading public.

There were said to be over fifty book clubs by 1947. One of the oldest is the Scientific Book Club, founded in 1921, which was taken over in 1946 by Henry Holt & Company's new Science Book Club, later to be called the Non-Fiction Book Club. The Religious Book Club and the Catholic Book Club are well established. The Book Find Club began in 1943 in the midst of the difficulties of war-time publishing. The Detective Book Club offers three successful mysteries in one volume each month. In the same field is the Unicorn Mystery Club. The Classics Club, the Limited Editions Club, and the Heritage Club specialize in reprints of older books. There are a dozen juvenile book clubs. The History Book Club, the Jewish Book Guild, and the Frederick Douglass Book Club are comparative newcomers.

Advertising is the life-blood of the book club system. Properly adjusted campaigns can control the size of the membership, within the limits of competition and a chosen field. In the largest clubs there is a big turn-over, and constant advertising is necessary to recruit new members in order to keep to the size attained, while a higher goal calls for increased appropriations. In 1945 the Literary Guild spent $400,000 in newspaper advertising alone, the Book-of-the-Month Club $145,000, and the Dollar Book Club $117,000. Advertising has also played a large part in the establishment of the market for the 25-cent books, though the similarity in format of the four leaders in that field in 1946 seemed to have made it impossible for one publisher to promote his own books without benefiting equally those of his competitor.

Pocket Books, Inc., was founded by Robert F. de Graff in 1939 to publish reprints of popular books, bound in stiff, glazed paper covers, at twenty-five cents each. De Graff's contribution to modern publishing rests on three accomplishments: the selection of genuinely popular and creditable books for his series, his achievement in devising and manufacturing a presentable and readable format for a cheap book, and the opening of a multitude of new outlets for retailing his product.

O. H. Cheney, in his famous survey of the book trade in 1931, bewailed the fact that there were only five hundred real bookshops in the United States. Of course, the cheap-book publishers of the 1880's had availed themselves of all kinds of outlets, but conditions had changed in fifty years. The book clubs, which began in the twenties, by-passed the whole problem of retail outlets to use mail-order selling.* But now, in 1939 and 1940, de Graff went out into cities and villages the country over and placed Pocket Book racks in drugstores, in variety and dime stores, in cigar stores, and in newsstands wherever they

---

* Later most of the clubs made agreements with the bookshops for taking memberships and delivering books.

are found—and they are scattered everywhere. At this writing Pocket Books has close to 80,000 outlets.

By the summer of 1946 there were 420 full-length, unabridged Pocket Books in print, and aggregate sales had mounted to 150,000,000. Twenty-three of the books had passed the million mark. The leader was *See Here, Private Hargrove,* with 2,175,000; and in second place was *How to Win Friends and Influence People,* which was only 75,000 short of the two-million goal.

Readers of these chapters will agree that the cheap-book idea was by no means new in American publishing. They will recognize Pocket Books as an adaptation to modern merchandising of the ten-to-twenty cent book of the 1880's. Cheap paper-covered books had never entirely disappeared in the intervening years; Street & Smith books were still on some newsstands after the First World War. A little later the Bonibooks and the Modern Age Books were noble experiments. The Penguin Books were successful in England before de Graff set up his organization, and they probably gave him ideas and encouragement. Since the Pocket Book success in this country, the publishers of the Penguin and Pelican Books, which have long been available in some American stores, have established a New York house and have entered into the competition for the quarter-book trade in all varieties of outlets. Other competitors, such as the Avon and Dell Books and the Popular Library, are largely devoted to detective stories, and there are several "Mystery" series. The Bantam Books, with initial printings of 400,000 to 500,000, began in 1946 a sharp competition with the Pocket Book, Penguin, and Avon series.

Allied with the book clubs and the publishers of 25-cent books in the assault on the mass markets were the reprint publishers. Grosset & Dunlap, founded in 1899 by Alexander Grosset and George T. Dunlap, had long been the chief reprint house; it was sold in 1944 to Random House, Harpers, Scribners, Little Brown, and the Book-of-the-Month Club. Blue Ribbon Books, originated by Frank C. Dodd in 1932, eventually came under the joint control of Dodd Mead, Harpers, Harcourt Brace, and Little Brown. Freeman Lewis founded Triangle Books in 1938, to furnish 39-cent books to the variety stores; Doubleday Doran later bought the enterprise from Reynal & Hitchcock, and Lewis in 1942 started the New Home Library to distribute 69-cent non-fiction. The Modern Library, begun by Boni & Liveright shortly after the First World War, and composed of older classics as well as more recent books, is now published by Random House. Thus there has been, in the forties, a constant shifting and reshuffling of the leaders in the reprint industry in competition for the low-priced markets.

Important for their general effect on readership were the Armed Services Editions begun in September, 1943. They were published by Editions for the Armed Services, Inc., a non-profit corporation established by the Council on Books in Wartime, sold to the Army and Navy at cost, and distributed free to men in the services. The series began with the issue of thirty titles a month; by January, the number had been increased to forty. The printing order at first was for 50,000; it had been raised by the summer of 1945 to 155,000. By that time some 75,000,000 books had been distributed.

One other contribution to the mass merchandising of books which must not be overlooked is the "soft format." Improvement of the design of cheap books, especially as to covers, was one of the chief causes for the success of the Pocket Books. Similarly, the quarto-page, double-column, paper-covered form of *One World* and *I Never Left Home* was a leading feature of the record-breaking sale of those books. Macmillans had used a similar format for *Gone With the Wind* some years earlier. Such books can be piled on the newsstands like magazines. Indeed, as a merchandising technique, the "soft format" harks back to the "extras" of the *New World* a hundred years ago, and to those of the *New York Tribune* in the 1880's.

The influence of the book clubs, reprints, and newsstand formats on the making of best sellers has been tremendous. During the twenty years which have followed the establishment of the book clubs in 1926, only two titles have reached our over-all best seller list without the aid of the clubs, the Pocket Books, or the "soft-format." * To attain that height required a total of 1,000,000 copies in the twenties, 1,200,000 in the thirties, and 1,300,000 in the forties—goals difficult to achieve without book club or Pocket Books aid, or both. In other words, these mass-marketing techniques have taken over the creation of our top-notch best sellers.

Lest anyone should view with alarm such appearance of literary fascism, it should be emphasized that Scherman, Beecroft, and de Graff compose no triumvirate of dictators. They hold their jobs while they can (a) pick the winners, (b) keep ahead of competitors in the merchandising game, and (c) retain the respect and confidence of the reading public for their output. A best seller is still determined by the number of people who buy it.

Yet there is a real danger to proper book publishing in the emphasis on mass distribution. Only a small proportion of new books are potential best sellers. The thousands of valuable works which ought to be published but which cannot be depended upon for more than a very modest return on the investment must not be forgotten in the scramble for mass markets. It is alarming to note that while total book-sales mount, the number of titles issued declines year by year. Fortunately, we still have conscientious publishers who use profits from occasional best sellers to bring out works for the scholar, fiction by promising unknowns, and books appealing to special tastes and interests. Mass publication performs a genuine social and cultural service; but it would be unfortunate if overemphasis on these techniques, especially in the midst of paper shortages,

---

* Even *One World* was included in Pocket Books and in a Book-of-the-Month Club dividend, though it would have made the top list without that aid. The two titles which made the grade in their original editions were *Forever Amber* and *The Egg and I*. Of the forty-two best sellers since 1926, twenty-eight are in the Pocket Books series, six were Literary Guild books, six BOMC, and two were People's Book Club offerings.

should prevent the publication of the more modest books which, in the long run, are necessary for the development of American culture.

An idea of the quality of one section of our mass-production may be obtained by taking note of a few books which have been elevated to best seller rank mainly through the agency of million-copy sales of Pocket Books. The *Pocket Book of Verse* was No. 62 of the series, issued in 1940. A first-class anthology, filled with old favorites, this book has been carried about in hundreds of thousands of pockets, for odd-times refreshment. It was originated by Pocket Books, and had no previous publication. Much the same can be said of another anthology, the *Pocket Book of Short Stories,* issued in 1941. It contains twenty-two well known tales, from Poe to Benét. M. E. Speare, the editor, had no fear of well-worn stories; what he wanted was the best, and the book maintains a very high level. The *Pocket Book of Boners* was published by the Viking Press in 1940 and by Pocket Books the next year; it has sold very nearly 1,400,000 in the reprint. Ripley's *Believe It or Not!* was first published by Simon & Schuster in 1929. They sold 150,000 copies, and later included it, with a second series, in the *Ripley Big Book;* in all forms, it has built up a total of a million and a half copies sold. It is based on one of the most popular of newspaper features, and illustrated by Ripley's drawings.

George H. Doran Company published *Jeeves,* by P. G. Wodehouse, in 1924, selling 7,000 copies; then A. L. Burt & Company sold 16,000 in a reprint edition. In 1939 *Jeeves* became Number 29 of the Pocket Books and in that form has sold nearly a million copies. Wodehouse is an author who has—or has had—an army of "fans," who are attracted by his funny characters and plots. If you are one of the chappies who have a liking for the jolly old blighter, I mean to say, you will toddle up to the counter every time a new Wodehouse comes out. Of the sixty or more amusing and facile Wodehouse books, *Jeeves,* which is really a collection of short stories, has had far the largest American sale. Another Doubleday Doran book to reach the highest rank of best sellers largely by virtue of 25-cent sales is Thorne Smith's *Topper.* Published in 1926, it had Sun Dial and Grosset & Dunlap reprints, and became Pocket Book Number 4 in 1939. Thorne Smith was a master of modern light fantasy. Superficial, just naughty enough to add a bit of spice, always amusing, his books were well adapted to the screen, where they were highly successful. *Topper Takes a Trip* also had a big Pocket Books sale. *The Best of Damon Runyon* was originally published by Frederick A. Stokes Company in 1938. Two years later it appeared in both the Triangle Books and the Pocket Books, and made quite some coconuts, if we may be allowed to say it in Runyonese. The book had an excellent introduction by E. C. Bentley. A second collection called *Damon Runyon Favorites* went into the Pocket Books only a few months after Stokes published it early in 1942; it has sold its million and more, but not quite enough to put it in the top rank for books of the forties.

The lighter and more amusing books dominate the Pocket Books list, but many serious works have made records of over half a million in this format. Among them are *Lost Horizon, The Good Earth, Microbe Hunters, Mrs. Miniver, The Magnificent Obsession, Mutiny on the Bounty, One World, Here's Your War, Mission to Moscow, The Steinbeck Pocket Book,* and *Five Tragedies by William Shakespeare.* All this will give some idea of the Pocket Books trend; but the direction, or directions, in which the best sellers of the new era of mass book production are going is shown best in the general list from 1926 to 1946.

XLI. WAR-BORN

... put down somewhere, too, everything you see and hear which will help later on to recapture the spirit of this tragic, marvellous, and eye-opening time: so that, having recaptured it, we can use it for better ends.
Jan Struther, in "Mrs. Miniver"

For two or three years at the end of the 1930's Jan Struther contributed little sketches of family life to the court page of the London *Times.* Their charm and sincerity won them a loyal following. Some of these pieces were gathered together at the end of 1939 to make a book called *Mrs. Miniver,* which was published the next year in New York by Harcourt, Brace & Company, chosen as the July offering of the Book-of-the-Month Club, and received with genuine popular appreciation by the American public.

The simple sketches of the life of the Minivers derived added poignance from the fact that England had just gone into the war and such quiet family life as the author depicted was facing disruption and disaster. Jan Struther did not labor the point, and most of the sketches have nothing to do with the war threat—but the fact was there, to be faced calmly. When the book was re-worked for the movies, the Minivers were brought more fully into the war; but that was nearly two years later. The screen version was a great success, and about the same time reprints of the book were issued by Grosset & Dunlap and by the Pocket Books. The book and the picture together undoubtedly did much to create a sympathetic admiration for the English people in war-time.

American readers were wont to think of Jan Struther as Mrs. Miniver: the stories are so real that they must be autobiographical. But the author denies that she and her husband and children are the originals of the Minivers. She is Mrs. Joyce Maxtone Graham. Her maiden name was Joyce Anstruther, whence her pseudonym. Mr. Maxtone Graham is an insurance broker, served in the Scots Guards in North Africa, and was taken prisoner by the enemy.

The first war-born book by an American to reach the top rank of best sellers was another series of sketches, dealing this time with the experiences of a rookie in a basic training camp at Fort Bragg. Marion Hargrove, a young man of twenty-three who had been employed on the *Charlotte News,* in North Carolina, wrote a series of letters to his home paper telling in an amusing but un-exaggerated style about the trials of a raw recruit. Always he is the butt of his own humor, and he takes his misfortunes philosophically. The book is full of information about the army life he observes about him, and the characters and most of the incidents seem to be actual.

Maxwell Anderson was down at Fort Bragg one day in the spring of 1942, met Private Hargrove, and accepted from him a big bunch of clippings to look over with a view to finding a publisher. Anderson turned them over to Henry Holt & Company, and the result was a book entitled *See Here, Private Hargrove*. It was an immediate hit. An abridgment was published in *Life* in September, and another in the *Reader's Digest* the next month. Holt sold about 350,000 copies at two dollars in the fourteen months before the issue of the Pocket Books edition in March, 1943; then the book broke all records by selling a million copies in the 25-cent form in less than a month. By 1946 it had sold about two and a half million copies altogether.

Hargrove's book emphasized the humors of camp life; the *Pocket Book of War Humor* picked up the good stories of camp and dugout and ship and plane, together with some old ones from the Civil War and the First World War, as well as extracts from the funny books, and put them all together for a quarter. The editor was Bennett A. Cerf, one of the shrewdest and most tireless of modern anthologists. The little book was published early in January, 1943, sold half a million by August, and became one of the ten best sellers in the Pocket Books list.

It was in April, 1943, that Wendell L. Willkie's *One World* was published. During his 49-day trip around the world in the fall of 1942, Willkie had made four or five addresses, and mutual friends proposed in behalf of Simon & Schuster, New York publishers, that he should make a book out of those speeches. He agreed to do so, but when he got down to the work of editing the material, he found that he could make it much more effective if he told in some detail about his trip—incidents and experiences, observations of people and conditions. Therefore he called upon Gardner Cowles, Jr., and Joseph Barns, his traveling companions, both newspapermen, to furnish him with such notes as they had accumulated on the trip; and working from those notes, his own memoranda, his speeches, and half a dozen articles he had previously published in magazines, he wrote *One World* in about six weeks.

Willkie made a wager with an enthusiastic member of the publishing house that the book would not sell over 150,000 copies. The advance sale was only 55,000. But in one month it sold 800,000 copies, and in two months the total was 1,100,000. Printers worked on a 24-hour schedule, using five sets of plates; the book was printed in two plants and bound in a third. The record-breaking speed of the sale was due in large measure to brilliant merchandising: Simon & Schuster offered a dollar edition in "soft format" along with the handsome two-dollar book. Great piles of these appeared on the newsstands; nevertheless, two or three hundred thousand of the cloth-bound edition were sold.

The Book-of-the-Month Club included *One World* in its *Prefaces to Peace*, a compendium which was distributed as its dividend for July and August, 1943. In January, 1944, *One World* was added to the Pocket Books series. When the author died in October of that year the approximate sales of his book were: Simon & Schuster, 1,300,000; Pocket Books, 500,000; BOMC, 300,000. The book had also been translated into sixteen foreign languages, and was being circulated "underground" in the occupied countries.

It was a great publishing feat and a remarkable record. As for the result, one can only surmise that the influence of *One World* must have been very great. To translate its doctrine of internationalism into governmental policy was another matter.

Another great non-fiction book of 1943, *annus mirabilis* of modern publishing, was Ernie Pyle's *Here Is Your War*. Pyle had come to the Washington *Daily News* from Indiana journalism and had worked up to the managing editor's desk. In a short time the routine of that job became slow poison to him, and he contrived to get a job as a Scripps-Howard roving reporter, traveling all over the country by automobile, bus, and plane and writing easily and realistically about what he saw—common people, common things. He came to have a following among newspaper readers, which increased when he went to England to report London under the bombs. *Ernie Pyle in England* did not make much of a stir as a book. It was the Ernie Pyle letters about the Tunisian campaign in the fall and winter of 1942 that really made a legend out of their author. The reporter who lived with the boys, sharing all their hardships and dangers—their chow, their own reactions under fire, their rough joking, their homesickness, cold, insects, disease—and who got next to the real heart of the GI as no other writer ever did: that was Ernie Pyle. And he put down names and addresses like a country correspondent for the home paper. Wrote John Steinbeck:

> There are really two wars, and they haven't much to do with each other. There is the war of maps and logistics, of ballistics, armies, divisions, and regiments—and that is General Marshall's war.
>
> Then there is the war of homesick, weary, funny, violent, common men, who wash their socks in their helmets, complain about the food, whistle at Arab girls, or any girls for that matter, and lug themselves through as dirty a business as the world has ever seen, and do it with humor and dignity and courage—and that is Ernie Pyle's war. He knows it as well as anyone and writes about it better than anyone else.

Here Is Your War was published by Henry Holt & Company at the end of October, 1943. It had four big printings before it was adopted by the People's Book Club in May, 1944. In August of that year it went into the Pocket Books series. In April, 1945, United Artists founded their motion picture "The Story of GI Joe" on it; and about the time that film was released, the World Publishing Company issued a dollar movie edition in the Forum Books which went to

350,000 in a month. In July, 1945, *Publishers' Weekly* reported that the book had sold over a million and a half in all editions.

In the meantime Holt had published a second series of Pyle's war stories under the title *Brave Men* in November, 1944, and the Book-of-the-Month Club had made it their December selection. Advance orders, including that of the book club, were for half a million copies. The advertising campaign in 1944-45 cost $50,000. Paper shortages caused Holt to design a double-column page for a new edition, and later to turn the book over first to Grosset & Dunlap and then to the World Publishing Company; Holt took it back in January, 1946, when more paper became available. It led all books on the best seller lists for 1945. At the end of that year it had sold 1,297,450 copies, somewhat less than half of which had gone to the book club.

A monument on Ie Shima bears this epitaph: "At this spot the 77th Infantry Division lost a buddy—Ernie Pyle, 25 April, 1945."

Another civilian who won the affection of enlisted men during the war was Leslie Towner Hope—Bob Hope to you. He was born in England, but grew up in Cleveland, Ohio. He sold newspapers as a boy, and tried several occupations, including that of the prize ring: he says he was "the only fighter who ever had to be carried both ways." He got into vaudeville when he was twenty-one (1925) and eventually made a big hit in both radio and the movies by his ready "gags" and his likable personality. Among the many entertainers who went overseas to give shows for the men in service, Bob Hope was probably the most popular. He won the men because he was funny, friendly, indefatigable. His tours were never pleasure jaunts: he often put on six or seven shows a day. One incident is typical. When he was playing in England, six hundred men once tramped across ten miles of moors to hear him at a neighboring camp; but when they reached the great outdoor auditorium where he was showing, they could not get within earshot. So they had to turn around and start back. When Hope finished his show, he was told about the disappointment of the six hundred; he immediately loaded his troupers into jeeps and set out after the soldiers, and when he overtook them he clowned for them through forty minutes in a pouring rain.

I Never Left Home is Bob Hope's account of his experiences as an army entertainer—full of jokes, high spirits, and stories about the boys. Published by Simon & Schuster in June, 1944, in the two formats used in the sales of *One World*, it sold 1,385,000 copies in four months, of which 185,000 were bound in cloth. This includes sales of the Home Guide edition brought out by a Chicago publisher during the paper shortage. The book had unusually good advertising, humorous in style. By the end of 1946 it had increased its sales by nearly 300,000. The author contributes his royalties to the National War Fund.

There were several other war-born books which rode high on *Publishers' Weekly* best seller lists and later showed impressive totals, but which have not, at this writing, sold the 1,300,000 necessary for top rating in the forties. William

L. Shirer's *Berlin Diary* was *avant-coureur* of the correspondents' stories in 1941. The next year came John Steinbeck's story of the German occupation of Norway, *The Moon Is Down*, and Pearl S. Buck's *Dragon Seed*, with its memorable scenes of war in China. In 1943 Walter Lippmann's *U. S. Foreign Policy* gained a large circulation through almost simultaneous publication by Little, Brown & Company, the Book-of-the-Month Club, and Pocket Books. In the same year appeared the most popular of the many correspondents' narratives of warfare, Richard Tregaskis' *Guadalcanal Diary*, as well as John Roy Carlson's sensational exposé of subversive activities at home entitled *Under Cover* and promoted by Walter Winchell's broadcasts. John Hersey's story of the AMG in Italy, *A Bell for Adano*, was published in 1944, and was later highly successful on stage and screen.

XLII. BOOKS OF THE NEW ERA

Success, as I see it, is a result, not a goal.
Flaubert to du Camp, 1852

THE system of making up a top best seller list of only such books as sell one per cent of the total population of the United States in a given decade places the hurdle pretty high for the 1940's. The figure has reached 1,300,000. But the arbitrary device does precisely what it was intended to do: it screens out for us the few topmost books of each year.

The chief best seller published in 1941 was James Hilton's *Random Harvest*. Any Hilton novel was bound to be a best seller of sorts after the hit-parade of *Goodbye, Mr. Chips, Lost Horizon*, and *We Are Not Alone*.

This is the way the Hilton success began. The *British Weekly* wanted a long short story for its Christmas supplement, and in the fall of 1933 its editor wrote Hilton, who accepted the commission with pleasure and alacrity. He was a Cambridge graduate of thirty-three, and had been writing with a good deal of regularity for just half of his life; his first novel was published when he was nineteen. But even the practiced writer sometimes falls upon evil weeks when his mind seems empty and the creative faculty dead. So it was now with Hilton, who came down to his deadline with the story unwritten. Then one day he went out for a bicycle ride and got to thinking of his schooldays. Suddenly his imagination was galvanized into life, and he pedaled for home and typewriter: in four days he had finished *Goodbye, Mr. Chips* and sent it off to the editor, who liked it so well that he suggested an American market. Hilton sent the story to the *Atlantic Monthly*. *Mr. Chips* was too long for a short story, and the *Atlantic* did not use serials; but the editors liked it so well that they ran it all in their April, 1934, issue by "tailing" it into the advertising section. America at once took the old English school teacher to its heart. In the magazine, in book form, in the movies, it made a great success. Moreover, it carried with it into the best seller lists a Hilton novel which had been published by William Morrow the year before, called *Lost Horizon,* which was destined to surpass it in popularity.

This was the story of a lamasery in the lofty mountain-tops of southern Thibet called Shangri-la, the most beautiful and refreshing of modern Utopias. The ideas of the story were provocative, the fantasy was appealing, the writing finely imaginative. But the sales of the book began very slowly. Its first printing was 2,500, and the distribution did not reach that figure for five or six months. Then *Mr. Chips* appeared in the *Atlantic* and Alexander Woollcott recommended it in the *New Yorker* and on the air. With prospects looking up, Morrow issued a new edition of *Lost Horizon* just a year after the first one, and the next week Woollcott announced over the radio that he had "gone quietly mad" about it. With this impetus, sales rose sharply, until the book was selling six thousand a week by Christmas. Following the usual system, the publishers poured on more advertising as the sales went up, spending some $12,000 on the campaign.

Among the hundreds of thousands who read *Lost Horizon* was Frank Capra, who made Columbia buy it for the screen because it "had bigness" and "held a mirror up to the thoughts of every human being on earth." The picture, starring Ronald Colman, was worthy, for once, of Hollywood's superlatives. Grosset & Dunlap issued a special motion picture edition of the book. Then in June, 1939, *Lost Horizon* became Number 1 of the Pocket Books series, where it has sold steadily ever since; the total is now over 1,300,000 in that form. And "Shangri-la" has taken its place in the language as a word for "Utopia."

We Are Not Alone was a 1937 best seller and popular on stage and screen, but it was not until four years later that a second Hilton book joined *Lost Horizon* in the top rank list. Though the scenes of *Random Harvest* were in England, the new book had the same Hilton charm and fascination—and in addition more of the mystery element so dear to the readers of romances. The experiences which Rainier, M.P. and successful businessman, had as he attempted to fill in his three blank years were full of pleasing adventure, humor, romance—and withal convincing. Published by Little, Brown & Company as an Atlantic Monthly Press book, *Random Harvest* had twenty-two printings in three years. Again there was a good advertising campaign. Again there was a G. & D. movie edition, and again a tremendous sale in the Pocket Books. It was becoming a familiar pattern—not only for Hilton books but for many best sellers.

Just a step ahead of *Random Harvest* on the best seller report for 1941 was another Little Brown book—A. J. Cronin's *Keys of the Kingdom*—which, with Book-of-the-Month Club help, eventually sold over 600,000 copies. Three years earlier, Dr. Cronin's *The Citadel* had ranked high in the lists, as did *The Green Years* in 1944; but neither has equaled *The Keys of the Kingdom* in total distribution.

In the *Publishers' Weekly* résumé for 1942, *The Robe,* by Lloyd C. Douglas, occupied seventh place, though it was eventually to be the only fiction book of that year to reach the top rank of best sellers.

This was the Rev. Dr. Douglas' ninth novel. His very first one had been a smashing success. Dr. Douglas had been a pastor, chiefly in university centers, for more than a quarter-century, and was more than fifty years of age, when he wrote his first novel, *The Magnificent Obsession.* It was the story of Bobby Merrick, brain specialist, who practiced a system of "personality investments" to help others and eventually benefited dramatically from his own service. It was frankly a purpose novel, but it was written with much skill and power and without direct preaching. Plotting and the succession of dramatic incidents were in the tradition of the older novel; some critics sniffed, especially at the mediocre writing, but vast numbers of people read with sincere enjoyment and deep feeling. The book was issued by Willett, Clark & Company, of Chicago, publishers of religious literature, in 1929. At first its popularity grew chiefly by word-of-mouth recommendation. Then Houghton Mifflin took it over, with advertising promotion, and printed more than fifty editions. A very successful screen version was produced. In 1943 it was issued by Pocket Books, which sold over 800,000 copies. Paper shortages forced Houghton Mifflin to turn it over to Grosset & Dunlap for a time in 1945, but the $2.75 price was maintained.

There was no other top-rank Douglas novel until *The Robe,* though *Green Light* led bookstores' best seller lists in 1935, and *Disputed Passage* ranked high in 1939.

The Robe is a long novel based on the life of the Roman soldier Marcellus, who was in charge of the crucifixion of Jesus and won his robe when his "garments were parted among them." Jesus is, of course, central in the story; and there is a fresh, if not new, attempt to show the relations of the discordant elements of Roman society in the first century of the Christian Era. It was the fourth novel of the times of Christ to reach our best seller list. The plot, as in most of the Douglas novels, is what is commonly called "absorbing." Published by Houghton Mifflin Company on October 16, 1942, at $2.75, it immediately became a best seller and kept its place among the top five in the bookstore reports for 95 weeks and in the top ten of the monthly summaries for more than two and a half years. With generous advertising campaigns, its sales increased in tempo in its second year. The People's Book Club made *The Robe* its first selection in 1943, selling 200,000 copies, while a cheap overseas edition sold a quarter of a million besides the free distribution of two printings in the Armed Services Editions. On its second birthday the book had passed the million mark. Paper shortages forced Houghton Mifflin first to change the format and later, in April, 1945, to turn the book over to Grosset & Dunlap; at that time about a million and a quarter of the regular edition had been sold, and the grand total was announced as 1,686,923. It "approached two million" at the end of 1945.

Another religio-historical novel published in 1942 was Franz Werfel's *The Song of Bernadette*. With the aid of the Book-of-the-Month Club, a Sun Dial reprint, and an excellent motion picture, this reverent story of the maid of Lourdes reached a total considerably in excess of a million copies; but it has not at this writing sold quite enough to reach the top rank of best sellers required for books published in the forties.

Among the novels published in 1943, the one sensational best seller was Betty Smith's *A Tree Grows in Brooklyn*. This story of a little girl growing up in Brooklyn slums was the first novel of a writer and producer of one-act plays at Chapel Hill, North Carolina. She had grown up in Brooklyn, and many of the incidents in her book are autobiographical. After an unsuccessful marriage, she took her two children and went first to the University of Michigan and then to Yale to study play-writing. With the aid of fellowships at North Carolina, she had written over seventy one-act plays (all published or produced or both) before she turned to long fiction. In the month that her novel was finished, she exchanged the name Smith for that of Jones, marrying a young Chapel Hill writer who had just entered the service for overseas duty.

Published by Harper & Brothers on August 18, at $2.75, adopted by the Literary Guild in September, and promoted by large advertising appropriations, *A Tree Grows in Brooklyn* got off to a flying start. Twentieth Century-Fox bought the motion picture rights before publication for $55,000; but the film, starring Joan Blondell, was not released until February, 1945. Before that time the book had become a runaway seller of the first magnitude. In August, 1944, paper shortages had forced Harpers to put the book in the hands of Doubleday & Company, who had recently purchased the Blakiston Company and thereby acquired a large paper supply. The advance sale in the reprint was nearly 800,000 at $1.49. By the end of 1944 the book's sales, in approximate round numbers, amounted to a half-million in the Harper edition, another half-million for the book club, and a million in the reprint, besides two printings in the Armed Services Editions. The interest in the motion picture later increased the grand total to somewhere near two and a half millions.

The year 1944 saw the publication of no less than four novels on our best seller list. Three were by English authors and one by a Canadian. One had its scenes set chiefly in Paris, one in the Channel Islands and New Zealand, one in London, and one in Montreal. Whether it is due to the new internationalism, or to a desire for novelty and escape, or to a superior skill in pleasing the American public on the part of foreign authors, or to all these things or something else, it is true that of the books published in the forties which have reached the top rank of best sellers very few deal with the American scene.

First in 1944 was Somerset Maugham's *The Razor's Edge*. Thirty years before, *Of Human Bondage* had won not only a *succès d'estime* but a very large sale in America. It has been one of the most popular titles in the Modern Library, and it may yet reach the over-all best seller list. *The Razor's Edge* was serialized in *Red Book,* published by Doubleday & Company, adopted by the Literary Guild, put into Blakiston and Dollar Book Club reprints, included in the Armed Services Editions, filmed by Twentieth Century-Fox, and issued in the Pocket Books series. In other words, it went through the entire publishing mill, accompanied, at all stages, by lavish advertising. As a literary work, it is undoubtedly inferior to the author's masterpiece, but the appeal of the central theme—the effect of an esoteric philosophy on the hero—is undeniable; and the portrait of Elliott, the elderly American snob, ranks with Maugham's best work. By the middle of 1946, sales of the original trade edition amounted to 233,000 at $2.75; of the book club edition, 532,000; of the reprints, 828,000. The Pocket Books edition was not yet out.

The winner of the Metro-Goldwyn-Mayer novel award of $125,000 in 1944 was Elizabeth Goudge (rhyme it with *rouge*). It was the first M-G-M award, and carried with it additional royalties of $50,000. Miss Goudge is an English novelist; her father was Regius Professor of Divinity at Oxford, and her mother's family live in the Channel Islands, where the scenes of much of her fiction are placed. The prize novel was *Green Dolphin Street,* a long historical romance, crowded with characters and incidents, and especially notable for its fresh and vivid pictures of Island life. "It is practically written in Technicolor," said *Time.* It was published by Coward-McCann in the fall of 1944, and selected as a Literary Guild book. It was reset in double columns the next spring to conserve paper, and the publishers were still trying to catch up with orders. It had sold about 1,200,000 copies by September, 1946, when a new dollar reprint was issued. Like all the other best sellers of this year, *Green Dolphin Street* was in the Armed Services Editions.

Another Englishwoman was the author of *Cluny Brown,* also a top best seller of 1944. Margery Sharp was already well known in America as the author of *The Nutmeg Tree* and stories in the *Saturday Evening Post* and *Harper's Magazine* when *Cluny* was serialized in the *Ladies' Home Journal,* published by Little, Brown & Company, and adopted by the Book-of-the-Month Club. This story is lighter than the other three which began their big careers in 1944; but it is not without significance, and most readers have found it delightful. The sprightly Cluny, who "doesn't know her place," became a general favorite. Her story sold half a million in the first six months, and over 1,100,000 before it went into a Pocket Books edition in September, 1946.

Gwethalyn Graham's *Earth and High Heaven* is a novel of "racial" problems, in which is incorporated a tender and moving love story. Besides the Jewish-Gentile prejudices involved, there are the differences which separate the French Catholics from the English Canadians. The story itself is realistic and compelling. The J. B. Lippincott Company published the book in October,

1944, and it became a Literary Guild selection. It passed the million post late in 1945, and went into the Sun Dial reprints.

Three of the four books on the top list of best sellers published the next year —1945—were big historical romances—*Forever Amber*, whose phenomenal record has been discussed in an earlier chapter; Samuel Shellabarger's *Captain From Castile*, and Thomas B. Costain's *Black Rose*.

The Shellabarger novel is a fast-moving story of the adventures of one Pedro de Vargas in the Age of the Inquisition, dealing with Cortes, the conquest of Mexico, and the downfall of the Aztec empire, with plenty of dramatic action, sword-play, and colorful description. It is reliable historically; its author is a scholar of some accomplishment. Dr. Shellabarger has written biographies of Chevalier Bayard and Lord Chesterfield. He is an accomplished linguist and speaks six languages, besides being well versed in Latin and Greek. He received his doctorate from Harvard, taught English at Princeton, and later became headmaster of a girls' school at Columbus, Ohio. While at Princeton, he became interested in popular literature and wrote nine adventure and mystery stories under the pen-names of John Esteven and Peter Loring. Little, Brown & Company published *Captain From Castile* in the first week of 1945 at three dollars, but had to resign it to the Blakiston Company in May in order to get paper to supply the tremendous demand. It was a Literary Guild book, and later a reprint best seller in the Sun Dial series. Twentieth Century-Fox bought the moving picture rights for $100,000. The book completed its first million in sales in the spring of 1946.

Canadian-born Thomas B. Costain was an associate editor of the *Saturday Evening Post* and later worked in Hollywood as a story editor for Twentieth Century-Fox. Then he became a member of the Doubleday organization. In view of his later success in the best seller field, all this may be regarded as apprenticeship. His historical romances, of which he has now written three, have been on an ascending scale of success. *The Black Rose* tells of the expedition of a young Saxon nobleman to Kublai Khan's country, his romantic adventures in the Orient, the perils and wonders of the return journey, and his triumph at home over those who had plotted against him. It is a long book—an *Anthony Adverse* turning eastward instead of to the West. Doubleday published it August 23, 1945, at three dollars, with a record first printing of 650,000, which included copies for the Literary Guild. It had sold over a million copies before it was issued in the "soft format" in the summer of 1946. It had reached a million and a half before the end of that year.

For the final 1945 best seller, we return to the United States of America and to Betty MacDonald's *The Egg and I*.

Mrs. MacDonald's story of her childhood and her adventures with the egg have made millions chuckle. Was ever autobiography more amusing? From the unconventional account of an unconventional birth to the story of the fire, it is all written with a gusto and verve—and often hilarity—hard to resist. It appeared serially in the *Atlantic Monthly* and was published on October 3, 1945, by the J. B. Lippincott Company, and was chosen as a Book-of-the-Month Club dividend. It gained steadily in weekly sales until it was at the top of most of the best seller lists by the end of the year—a position it kept through most of 1946. It reached its millionth copy in a little more than ten months after publication, with the aid of an advertising appropriation of $75,000; and at that time $15,000 more was appropriated to spread the anti-egg gospel. The book was then selling eight to ten thousand a week, and it is added to our list in the faith that the total will ultimately reach 1,300,000. The extra hundred thousand or so are necessary for the integrity of the list, whatever they may mean to the author or publishers. Mrs. MacDonald, by the way, after parting with her first husband and his chickens, had a tussle with tuberculosis, worked as publicity director for the National Youth Administration, married again in 1942, and is going on with the literary career so successfully begun.

And here we make an end, with Best Seller Number 324. Before this book is published, other books will have piled up 1,300,000 sales; but their triumphs are not for this record.

XLIII. IS THERE A BEST SELLER FORMULA?

Theories of best sellers from the point of view of their appeal always provide fascinating material for literary bull-sessions, but that kind of speculation is about as trustworthy as astrology.

George Stevens, in "Lincoln's Doctor's Dog"

WHAT makes a best seller? This is the sixty-four dollar question. It can be answered, though largely by guess and surmise, and never satisfactorily to the inquirer, who always wants a formula. There is no formula which may be depended upon to produce a best seller.

There are too many impalpable considerations, too many chances and accidents, too complex a combination of conditions affecting the writing, publication, and selling of a book to make the attainment of the top rank by even the most promising candidate a certainty. The creation of a best seller does not follow an exact pattern, or patterns, any more than does the making of a successful man; there are too many intangibles, too many unmeasurable human values, too many vicissitudes of fortune involved. Moreover, since there is not just one best seller audience, no single formula could be expected to provide books for a buying public which is, thank God, pretty heterogeneous after all.

But just as the biographer, the psychologist, or the sociologist may correlate cases in order to study the roots of human success, so may the student of best sellers analyze and classify his materials to learn more about what seems to have made books succeed. Many lines of investigation immediately present themselves, but only a few of the more obvious conclusions of such a study will be presented here. One cannot escape the almost constant appearance in all periods of our best seller history of certain elements of popular appeal—as religion, sensationalism, information and guidance, adventure, democracy, humor, characterization, juvenile suitability, timeliness, and so on.

The religious appeal is strong from one end of the list to the other. Of the first twenty best sellers, thirteen were definitely books of religious teaching, and that element was strong in four others. This was not remarkable in view of the prominence of religion in the life of early Colonial years; but it is more striking to find that of the 279 best sellers up to 1915,* eighty-seven (or almost one-third) contained a strong religious element. Though the average is much lower for the thirty years following 1915, the extraordinary records of *The Robe* and of other books which did not quite reach the top rank (like *The Song of Bernadette*) make us realize that religion is still a strong factor in popular reading. Many of the topmost best sellers have abounded in religious teaching, as *Uncle Tom's Cabin, The Wide, Wide World, Ben-Hur, In His Steps,* and the novels of E. P. Roe and Harold Bell Wright. Almost fifteen per cent of our best sellers have been written by clergymen.

Sensationalism, as the word is employed here, must not be understood to mean anything necessarily morbid, but rather an emotional excitement produced by extreme means, such as a definite emphasis on horrors, murder, extreme violence, irregular sex relations, or extraordinary adventures. Such things may be morbid and unwholesome in their effects, or they may stir one's deepest and finest feelings, according to the degree of art in presentation and the capabilities of the reader. They are inescapable in literature high and low; they are found in *Oedipus Rex* and *King Lear* and in Mrs. Southworth's *Ishmael.* They appear in remarkable quantity throughout the best seller list. Evaluation of such elements in a given book depends, of course, upon anyone's critical judgment; in that of the present writer, one or more of these sensational factors is strongly emphasized in just a little over half the books of our list. To give an idea of the range of this element in imaginative literature on the best seller level we need only mention *The History of Dr. Faustus* in the eighteenth century, the stories of Indian captivities, the devious intrigues of Quasimodo in Hugo's *Notre-Dame* or Sikes in Dickens' *Oliver Twist,* the whipping to death of Uncle Tom, the melodrama of Lippard and Southworth, the dime novels, the weird adventures of Rider Haggard's characters, the novels about courtesans, and the murder stories of the last period. This element is by no means limited to fiction: we find it in poetry, history, religion, and other categories. Indeed, it is very common in early religious books. The pictures of hell in *The Day of Doom* and *The Practice of Piety* and the tortures

* It is convenient to divide the history of American publishing into six periods, as follows: 1638-1775, 1776-1840, 1841-1870, 1871-1895, 1896-1915, and 1916-1945.

of Protestants in Fox's *Book of Martyrs* are extremely sensational, and Maria Monk's *Awful Disclosures* was part of a religious controversy.

The self-improvement motive may be founded on a desire for prestige, or a hope to get ahead, or simply upon the need for deeply personal satisfactions. But whatever its basis, its impulsions to education and training are about the same. The fields of literature into which it sends a reader are varied indeed. Such books on our list as Shakespeare's plays and Emerson's essays have been commonly read for the sake of self-improvement. An advertisement of the Classics Club recently contained this paragraph:

> It is not necessary to have a "higher education" to appreciate these books; and, after you have read and know them, you will have acquired a broader and more liberal education than most of your business and professional acquaintances. You will have lost any personal concern about an "inferiority complex" and any fear about not being the equal of others whose formal education is greater than your own.

Somewhat the same drive operates as soon as any book begins to lead the weekly best seller lists; the reader who wishes to be well informed feels that he must read it at once. But in the years before the world of readers was best-seller-conscious there was rather less reading for this by-product of vainglory; certainly in both earlier and later times a sincere desire for real self-improvement has been a major compelling force in readership. Not only the classics in *belles-lettres,* but history, biography, and all informative and personal-guidance books have been regarded as "improving."

Ten historical works appear on the best seller list, and eight biographies. Designation of historical novels is not easy, because there is no rule about how far back the "contemporary scene" reaches before it becomes history; but our count yields forty-nine historical romances, distributed rather evenly through the decades from *Thaddeus of Warsaw* to *The Black Rose.* Biographies make a poor showing in this list of the topmost best sellers. There is no life of Lincoln, though fiction introduces him more than once. A witticism in the book trade runs like this: Since books about Lincoln are always best sellers, and so are books about doctors and books about dogs, why doesn't someone write a sure-fire book about Lincoln's doctor's dog? The "gag" was not based on a list of over-all best sellers, but presumably upon such successes as Sandburg's *Lincoln,* Heiser's *An American Doctor's Odyssey,* and Eric Knight's *Lassie-Come-Home.*

But the self-improvement books devoted to personal precept and guidance make an impressive catalogue by themselves. They include most of the religious books, to begin with, and then there are ten or a dozen behavior books which emphasize rules of living; many novels, from *Pamela* to *Pollyanna,* which teach somewhat less by precept than by example; and books of advice from Chesterfield to Dale Carnegie. Nearly half the books on our list contain a large element of didacticism. Scores of guides in the Little Blue Books series told their readers *How to Improve Your Conversation, How to Play Golf,*

How to Write Advertising, and so on; and each sold in the hundreds of thousands.

Another important element in best sellers is that of personal adventure. We find it in the narratives of Indian captivity, in *Pilgrim's Progress,* and in *Robinson Crusoe,* for the Colonial Period; but it was not until Scott and Cooper showed what thrills the adventure story held that American readers made vicarious derring-do a favorite diversion. Since then tales of action and courage have been evenly distributed through the decades, whether in historical romance, dime novels, Zenda stories, "westerns," mysteries, or what-not.

Many readers think of adventure as being a chief ingredient in "a good story," and so it often is. Another factor is strong characterization; and though not a few novels on our best seller list get along with typed characters, a survey of the entire roll shows almost two-thirds of them placing strong emphasis on characters. That mythical person whom we adumbrate as "the general reader" likes people—and particularly strong, individualistic human beings. Dorothy Canfield Fisher, a member of the Book-of-the-Month Club board of selection, declares, "By and large, what readers seem to like to find in a book is contact with living, vital personalities."

The quality of vividness also ranks high. We find superior vividness—in portrayal of scenes, action, persons—in about half the books on our list. Force (to use the rhetoricians' old term) falls much lower in the scale. Sentiment, verging commonly into sentimentality, is hard to evaluate; but it seems to characterize about half the books between 1775 and 1915, while it is less apparent in the earlier and later periods.

So far as literary style in general is concerned, it would be absurd to generalize in the face of so much variety. There are, of course, those books which have become best sellers largely because they are classics; and there are others of much literary skill and power, from *The Practice of Piety* to *Mrs. Miniver.* On the other hand, there is much bad writing. In what we may call the lower third of the heap, it is easy to pick out nearly a hundred books that are ill-written and quite devoid of any of the literary graces. They make it clear that a vast reading public is not concerned with niceties of style. These are the books that critics often call "typical best sellers" simply because their immense popularity seems, to a reader sufficiently irked by sloppy writing, to be their only quality worth considering. But this is a double mistake. In the first place, there is no such thing as a "typical best seller"; and in the second place, it is not bad writing that has made them popular, and they all have their qualities. They usually have body and abundance of materials, they are commonly teeming with rather vital stuff, and more often than not they are well organized. Walter Hines Page published a discriminating essay in 1905 in which he pointed out "Why Bad Novels Succeed": he was convinced that "literary quality" made little difference in sales, but "substance" and construction met a popular demand.* Certainly a book does not have to be well written to become a best seller.

Democracy is another element of popular appeal that should not be neglected. The word is perhaps too big. What is intended to be designated is emphasis on the lives and aspirations of the common people, whether in fiction or non-fiction. It is in the very atmosphere and mood of *The Vicar of Wakefield,* the poems of Robert Burns, all the Dickens novels, *David Harum, The Egg and I;* and it marks four-tenths of all our best sellers.

Timeliness, or topical interest, has made many popular books, but few best sellers of the first rank. The thirty-nine which have some topical interest are an interesting group, however. *Common Sense* and *M'Fingal* belong to the Revolution, with *The Federalist* coming a little later. Hannah F. Lee's *Three Experiments of Living* was a hard-times story of 1837. *Uncle Tom's Cabin, Ten Nights in a Bar-Room, Progress and Poverty,* and *Black Beauty* reflect popular crusades. *Parson Brownlow's Book* was a Civil War product. *Coin's Financial School* and *In His Steps* were definitely topical and timely—and so on, down to best sellers like *The Grapes of Wrath* and *One World.* Timing a book is often important, and taking fortune at the flood has sometimes resulted in a first-class best seller, especially in these later years of quick sales. Philip Van Doren Stern has pointed out that if the publication dates of Margaret Halsey's anti-British *With Malice Toward Some* (1938) and Jan Struther's pro-British *Mrs. Miniver* (1940) had been exchanged, probably neither would have been very successful.

The element of humor is marked in a little less than one-fourth of the books, though only seventeen may be said to be primarily or very largely humorous. Of these only two—the Knickerbocker *History of New York* and the *Pickwick Papers*—were published before the 1870's, while seven of the seventeen belong to the last twenty-five years. Dickens did much to bring up the average of humor in the middle of the nineteenth century. He was the greatest of best sellers, and his popularity was built largely upon his humor: he could make his readers cry two or three times in a novel, but he made them laugh much oftener than that.

Fantasy is a notable characteristic of one-eighth of the best sellers. Fairy-tale motifs and sleight-of-hand with the semi-mystical have an appeal for many readers, though one finds such things chiefly in poetry and juveniles. Our judgment of this element of literary art as a lure to the general reader and a maker of best sellers is complicated by the fact that it is always closely integrated with other qualities and techniques which may have been more effective causes of popularity. To take a modern example of fantasy, Thorne Smith's *Topper* probably would not have been a winner without its sex appeal and the

* *A Publisher's Confession* (New York, 1905—anonymous until Page's death), chapter entitled "Why 'Bad' Novels Succeed and 'Good' Ones Fail."

picture of slightly adorned feminine pulchritude on the cover of the Pocket
Books edition.

Which suggests a word about pictures as a selling aid before we take up the
matter of sex appeal. Of course, pictures on covers and jackets are advertising
rather than contents, but many best sellers have owed much of their popularity
to pictures which were integral with the text. This is true of such older
books as *Pilgrim's Progress,* Fox's *Book of Martyrs,* and *Aesop's Fables,* and of
such diverse and more modern offerings as *Innocents Abroad, Trilby,* and
Ripley's *Believe It or Not.* Illustration was important in many of the editions
of Dickens and Thackeray, and of the *Rubáiyát,* James Whitcomb Riley's
poems, *The Virginian,* and many other books. Motion picture editions of
best sellers, adorned by "stills" from the films, have usually supplied a few
hundred thousand copies to movie-goers. And of course, juveniles have always
sold largely on the basis of their pictorial illustration.

As to the old S.A., which one writer of best sellers called "It," authors and
publishers have in this element of life and literature a two-edged sword.
Emphasis on sex may attract a large body of readers, and it may make the book
a kind of bawdy joke. Being banned in Boston has its desirable features from
the publishers' point of view, but it is probably not, on the whole, an experience to be invited. Though we find books of strong sex appeal scattered
through all periods of our publishing history (varying from a tenth to a fifth
of the best sellers), fashions in such things do change, and a big splurge by a
book like *The Sheik* is likely to be followed by imitators and then by a reaction. Not long after the publication of *Forever Amber,* which undoubtedly was
intended as a serious historical romance, a publisher advertised a new offering
to booksellers in the *Publishers' Weekly* as "the boldest and bawdiest" yet; some
months later *Amber's* publishers, presenting a new historical novel, were in-
sisting that there was not a bedroom scene in it.

About one-eighth of our best sellers employ exotic settings. By no means all
foreign settings are exotic, and perhaps we have to split hairs too much. The
Paris of *Trilby* was exotic to its readers, while that of *The Razor's Edge* was
not. At any rate, the exotic has had an appeal to the popular audiences from
the time of *The Oeconomy of Human Life* (1751) to *The Black Rose* (1945),
and about one-eighth of our best sellers have used it to a marked degree.

And finally, a word about juveniles. Since our best seller list is confined
to "general reading," juveniles would be excluded were it not for the fact that
it is quite impossible to draw a line between books for children and those for
adults. Most readers have agreed with what Theodore Roosevelt once wrote
in a *Bookman* article: "A thoroughly good book for young people is almost
invariably one of the best books that grown people can read." Probably half
of the best sellers which we classify as having juvenile appeal were actually
written mainly for adults, as *Robinson Crusoe, Gulliver's Travels,* and so on.
A little over a fifth of our books have that appeal. It was especially strong

in the Colonial Period, when ten out of the thirty best sellers were used for the instruction and entertainment of children, and in the one before the First World War, which included the stories of Gene Stratton-Porter and her compeers.

And so, after all, where are we with regard to the formula for best sellers? It is lost in the variety of forms, qualities, appeals, characteristics. The study of successful books may be rewarding to both writer and publisher, as well as to sociologists and historians, but it will not point out to anyone an easy way to produce a sure-fire best seller.

XLIV. WHAT MAKES A BEST SELLER SELL?

I returned and saw under the sun that the race is not to the swift . . . nor yet riches to men of understanding, nor yet favor to men of skill; but time and chance happeneth to them all.

Ecclesiastes 9:11

THE delightful and fascinating profession of book publishing seems to the outsider with bookish tendencies quite the most thrilling and stimulating occupation in the modern world. The publisher is a man who is on intimate terms with all the literary geniuses, is a part of the great hierarchy of opinion-formers, and contributes to the swiftest and deepest currents of modern thought. Occasionally he discovers in his mail some masterpiece from a young unknown who has written his inspired pages while starving in an attic; it is then the publisher's pleasure to touch the new author's shoulder with a sceptre of gold and make him famous and his book a best seller.

Five minutes' talk with a publisher in the flesh is likely to ruin this pretty picture, however. He is worried about paper and binder's cloth and the price of type composition. If sales are good just now, he thinks they are going to be bad next year. If he has a best seller on hand, he is frantic over his failure to keep up with orders. He knows he will lose money on a large part of his list and hopes against hope to recoup on a few big successes. And yet he is an optimist, or he would not be in this precarious business.

It is certainly a chancy game. Every book published is more or less a gamble —less, of course, for the man of experience and good judgment, but never free from a large element of luck. The first chance the publisher takes is in his acceptance of a book. Even a book by an established author is not wholly predictable, and one by an unknown often represents a speculation only a few degrees removed from crap-shooting. As a professional optimist, the publisher makes far more errors by accepting books that prove to be "duds" than he does by declining winners. Through the history of best sellers are scattered some stories of the manuscript repeatedly refused only to make a triumphant success when published (*Lorna Doone, Progress and Poverty,*

The Heavenly Twins, Mr. Barnes of New York, David Harum), but the phenomenon is really so infrequent as to make it a good story when it does happen.

When he once has the manuscript, the publisher may help it on its way toward success by suggestions for changes, as Ripley Hitchcock did with *David Harum,* and as many other publishers whose incidental collaboration with writers of best sellers has been less publicized have done. We know that Harold Bell Wright's publisher-friend advised him in regard to *The Shepherd of the Hills,* and we may surmise that he did so with later novels; but much of such help is, by a rule common among publishers, unacknowledged.

Titles are sometimes thought to have something to do with making best sellers. But it would be hard to draw any helpful conclusions from the array of titles on our over-all list. Is a short title—like *She* or *Trilby* or *Penrod*—preferred? But what about *Twenty Thousand Leagues Under the Sea, The Little Shepherd of Kingdom Come,* and *How to Win Friends and Influence People?* Is the hero's name—like *David Copperfield* or *Richard Carvel*—better than *The Count of Monte Cristo* or *Captain From Castile?* Is a concrete, objective title like *The Moonstone* or *The Robe* to be preferred to the more vague *Gone With the Wind* or *Earth and High Heaven?* Or perhaps you have a liking for homely titles, as *Mother, Laddie, Brave Men:* what then of the best sellers with names many have found difficult even to pronounce—*Quo Vadis, Les Misérables, The Rubáiyát of Omar Khayyám?* About all that can be said, in all this competition of titles, is that most of them are attractive and interesting.

How much influence the page-design and typography, the binding, and the jacket have on bookshop demand is hard to say; sometimes it may be considerable. Such admirable productions of the printer's art as the first editions of Irving's *Sketch Book* and Prescott's *Conquest of Mexico* delighted connoisseurs, but the mass circulation of these works and of most best sellers has come in cheaper editions. On the whole, nineteenth-century best sellers were badly printed in this country, in small type on cheap paper. And generally they were as poorly bound as printed. But binding was more important and effective in the years after 1900; the purple covers of *The Rosary* and the charming medallion on the cover of *Janice Meredith* were trademarks of the popularity of those books. Illustration has been important throughout best seller history, as was noted in the preceding chapter. The sales undoubtedly reacted to such "embellishments," to use the term Godey used to apply to his engraved plates. A late edition of *The Prisoner of Zenda* gave new life to the popularity of that romance by the addition of a set of Charles Dana Gibson illustrations, and pictures from the movies of more recent best sellers have helped the reprints.

Many things can happen before the actual publication of a book to make it a best seller—fortunate pre-natal influences, as it were. A good reception of a preceding serialization has often been a help, as it was with *Uncle Tom's*

Cabin, A Hoosier School-Master, and *Trilby.* An old device is to send out advance copies to booksellers and to prominent persons whose recommendation is desired. In this way Emerson's praise of *Leaves of Grass,* later used so conspicuously, was obtained. These recommendations are not necessarily for use in advertising "quotes," but to get influential people started talking about the book. Proofs are often sent out early, before advance copies are ready, to the leading booksellers. This was done in the case of *Anthony Adverse:* what a bundle of proof sheets it must have made! But many dealers sampled the first chapters—and then went on to the end. Also part of the prepublication campaign is the advertising in periodicals of the book trade, announcing the book, quoting advance readers, and often promising dealer helps and newspaper advertising after the book is published. For example, Little, Brown & Company announced *Captain From Castile* with a well designed display "ad" in *Publishers' Weekly* eight weeks before the publication date, using the following copy:

$10,000 initial advertising guaranteed for the first new Little, Brown best seller of 1945— CAPTAIN FROM CASTILE—Why all this furor? Just read the two sentences below: "I think that anyone who was once absorbed by *The Count of Monte Cristo* or *The Three Musketeers* will have the time of his life with this story."—From a reader's report. "Get ready for the finest adventure story since *Anthony Adverse.* Dr. Shellabarger has the Dumas touch."—Cosmopolitan preview.—The Literary Guild selection for January.— Coming January 3rd.—$3.

Nor should we forget the "travelers," who "call on the trade" in behalf of the publishing houses, with dummies and pictures and samples of dealer helps; they are the john-the-baptists of the coming messiahs.

Selection by a book club, commonly made from proofs, comes early enough to be announced in connection with the prepublication campaign. Not only does such a selection add its own hundreds of thousands to the total distribution of a best seller, but it stimulates the bookstore sales. A generation ago, a prominent publisher is said to have remarked that the best way to achieve a vast popular success with a good book would be to start it off with the free distribution of 100,000 copies: that would get it talked about. A similar result is obtained more practically today by a book club mailing, which is almost essential for a million-copy sale.

The influence of reviews on the early distribution of a book is important. They help to get it talked about. Probably all publishers, and certainly all authors, prefer favorable reviews; but unfavorable reviews of a controversial book may have a very favorable effect on sales. Gladstone's review of *Robert Elsmere* is a famous example. Attacks on *The Shepherd of the Hills* by church papers were answered by the publishers in advertisements. Duffield & Company ran adverse reviews in parallel columns with favorable ones in their advertisements of *Three Weeks.* Many controversial best sellers have been advertised by a considerable literature of counterblasts—Hervey's *Dialogues, The Age of Reason,* Maria Monk's *Awful Disclosures,* Dickens' *American*

Notes, Uncle Tom's Cabin, Leaves of Grass, Progress and Poverty, Looking Backward, Coin's Financial School, and so on.

Recommendations by famous personalities, designed for "quotes" in advertising, used as gratuitous "plugs" on the radio, or given out in interviews or in casual conversation, have often had an effect on the popularity of a book. Theodore Roosevelt's praise of *The Virginian,* Governor Flower's enthusiasm for *David Harum,* and Alexander Woollcott's radio talk about *Lost Horizon* may be mentioned, more or less at random. Lecture tours by authors have been good promotion for their books; among the most successful were those of Dickens, Thackeray, and Ian Maclaren.

Book advertising in America began with the first continuously published newspaper, the *Boston News-Letter.* In the eleventh issue of that paper on July 3, 1704, appeared the first publisher's "ad"—a notice of a pamphlet about the trial of a pirate, *The Tryal and Condemnation of Capt. John Quelch,* published by Nicholas Boone. Two years later Benjamin Eliot, bookseller, inserted the first advertisement of imported books; the short list included the best seller Russell's *Seven Sermons.* Advertising of books in Colonial papers was of those two types: announcements of new local publications, and lists of imported books. There was rarely any description of the book beyond title and author. By the middle of the eighteenth century book lists were becoming an important feature of newspaper advertising, and during the fifteen years just before the Revolution the papers of Boston, New York, Philadelphia, Hartford, and other cities occasionally carried lists containing over a hundred titles; in a few instances such lists occupied entire front pages of newspapers.

Book advertising shifted from importations to native production as the early publishing houses, such as Mathew Carey & Son, J. & J. Harper, and Wiley & Putnam, grew up in the first three decades of the new century. Came the forties, and the cheap-book campaign of the *New World* and *Brother Jonathan,* introducing more use of newspaper space by publishers of low-priced editions of Dickens, Bulwer, Sue, Dumas, and other romancers. Book advertising was very common in the fifties. Perhaps the most sensational campaign for any book in that decade was the one which young John P. Jewett, of Boston, put on for *Uncle Tom's Cabin,* in which he told of the mounting sales of that best seller in very much the modern manner. George W. Carleton, of New York, one of the most aggressive publishers of the mid-century, spent ten thousand dollars promoting his edition of *Les Misérables* in 1862.

Meantime magazines became somewhat more important as media for book advertising. The New York *Literary World* carried many book announcements, but not enough to make it prosperous. *Harper's Monthly* was begun in 1850 mainly to advertise Harper books, and for thirty years it admitted no other advertising. After the Civil War, publishers failed to keep pace with producers in other fields in the matter of advertising; their announcements were dignified, modest, even shy. Dodd, Mead & Company did well by E. P. Roe. J. B. Lippincott Company was active, promoting the novels of Ouida and others. The literary and book-trade periodicals filled lean advertising sections with announcements.

It was in the nineties that modern advertising began. The publishers lagged at first, though some bold experimenting was done, especially by some publishers who were not considered "regular": A. C. Gunter, for example, advertised his own books widely. There was some use of pictures, but titles were usually featured. Then in the first years of the new century came an unexampled flood of display advertising by publishers. It was led by Bobbs-Merrill, who boomed such books as *When Knighthood Was in Flower* and *Alice of Old Vincennes;* other publishers followed immediately with heavy advertising of the best sellers of the period, and of such sets as the *Harvard Classics,* Warner's *Library of the World's Best Literature,* encyclopedias, etc. Pictures were now common; for example, Appletons made Hall Caine's pointed beard almost as well known as T.R.'s teeth and eyeglasses. It was all very shocking to many persons both within and without the trade, and there was much bitter talk about selling literature like soap. But the results were evident in the first era of big-and-quick sales of new, first-run books in American publishing history.

In 1909 the Book Supply Company launched Harold Bell Wright's *The Calling of Dan Matthews* with an advertising appropriation announced as $48,000. What happened in the exploitation of the Wright novels has been told in detail in another chapter. Publishers' advertising doubtless would have increased steadily without the example of the Book Supply Company's $100,-000 campaigns, but the object lesson was important. Display space had proved its worth in selling books.

Publishers and book-clubs did their share in making the twenties a boom decade in advertising. Doubleday, Page & Company used large space in advertising Gene Stratton-Porter, Booth Tarkington, and other popular authors; and such firms as Little Brown and Bobbs-Merrill were not far behind. By 1929 the annual total of book advertising was estimated at six million dollars. The two big successes of the thirties, *Anthony Adverse* and *Gone With the Wind,* had the benefit of great advertising campaigns. *Anthony's* began modestly with small "ads" and increased with the sales; but *GWTW's* was more ambitious from the beginning, and three months after its publication Macmillans were "blanketing" the country with copy in papers in all cities of 100,000 population or over. At the end of the thirties book advertising was increasing by leaps and bounds. Doubleday, the leader, spent $198,699 in 1939, and the next year $290,732, according to *Printer's Ink.*

By the forties the system for advertising a major book in which the publisher has confidence had become more or less fixed. In such cases about ten per cent of the receipts expected from the sales of the advance printing (exclusive of book club orders) may be set apart as initial advertising expenditure. Announcements of $10,000 campaigns to launch a new book are fairly common for very promising ventures. But the larger campaigns are reserved for the books which have really "caught on" and are by way of becoming best sellers; then $50,000 to $75,000 for a single campaign is not unusual, nor $100,000 unheard of.

Publishers know that advertising alone never makes a best seller. Harold Bell Wright's books probably benefited as much by advertising as any best sellers ever published, but it was not until the first two Wright books had demonstrated remarkable vitality in their market that Book Supply poured on the advertising. Newspaper and magazine space is expensive, a new book is always a gamble, and publishers will not spend large sums without some indication that they are going to get it back in profits. But when a book shows signs of forging ahead, the shrewd publisher will give it a run for its money. Hence such announcements, to cite one example, as "another $10,000" for advertising *Earth and High Heaven,* Lippincott's best seller, in January, 1945, three months after publication.

Radio has become an important medium for book advertising in the last few years, though the response in sales seems less certain than for newspaper media. Digests are generally believed to benefit the sales of the complete book. Autographing parties and the personal appearances of authors are much used in early phases of a book's promotion. And window displays, postcard mailings, and other bookshop activities, in which the publisher cooperates, are of great and undoubted value.

Motion picture productions have played an important part in the making of best sellers. About thirty per cent of the best sellers published before 1914 have been adapted for the screen, and nearly all of the fiction, as well as some of the non-fiction, which has reached the top list since that date has gone into motion pictures. Old favorites like *The Count of Monte Cristo, David Copperfield, Gulliver's Travels,* and *The Hunchback of Notre Dame* have become new favorites by the grace of Hollywood. There are a few older novels on our best seller canon which would never have been put there without the help of a long-delayed popularity which came at last through the movies. Contemporary interest in *Wuthering Heights* is perhaps the most striking example of this tardy fame.

Screen rights of contemporary novels are often sold to producers before publication, with a provision for a bonus if they become best sellers. The production itself is commonly delayed until after the sales peak has passed. This is supposed to be an advantage, on the one hand, to the producer, who prefers that his audience should come to the theatre with little more than a remembrance that this was a great and successful story and small recollection of details; and, on the other hand, to the publisher, who hopes to rejuvenate the book's sales by means of a new low-priced edition, illustrated by stills from the movie.

Stage production of a best seller sometimes has a similar effect, though the stimulus to book sales seems more uncertain. Modern efforts to sell the dramatized book in the theatre lobby are not as successful as they were in the palmy days of Klaw & Erlanger's production of *Ben-Hur*—or, for that matter, in the years when Barnum's autobiography was sold by ushers at the circus. Yet many best sellers have undoubtedly made big gains in sales by reason of popular stage presentations—especially those that were exploited by touring troupes and stock companies.

But as we look over the entire list of best sellers and recall the publishing history of each, we must conclude that the chief factor in the production of big total sales (aside from the content itself) is the cheap reprint. Less than ten per cent of the entire list have become best sellers without this aid. Pirated editions, including those of American books in Colonial times and the floods of popular works by English, French, and Continental authors before the International Copyright Agreement of 1891, together with cheap reprints of expired American copyrights beginning in the seventies, have served to make the prosperity of most of the books on our list of best sellers. The cheap "extras" of the 1840's, the "libraries" of the twenty years beginning about 1875, and the modern Pocket Books have been of the first importance as best seller makers. The great reprint houses, such as Grosset & Dunlap and Doubleday's Dollar Books, have made many a best seller: the case of Gene Stratton-Porter's novels is outstanding. Finally, the new quarto "soft format" has made recent publishing history.

But finally, after recounting all that a publisher can do for a book, by way of employing all the old and proven methods and devising new and experimental techniques, we have to admit that his success in any given case is very uncertain. He must first have a winner in the book itself, and even the most experienced man in the game often picks the wrong horse. Nobody can be sure —neither the inspired author nor the inspired publisher—of the precise combination which will bring the tremendous response necessary to make a best seller. It is a tricky business, full of chances, timely and untimely strokes of fortune, lucky hits and unexplainable lapses. As the wise man of old observed, "the race is not to the swift . . . nor yet riches to men of understanding, nor yet favor to men of skill; but time and chance happeneth to them all."

XLV. A POSTSCRIPT ON BIBLES, SCHOOLBOOKS, ETC.

Jove and my stars be praised! Here is yet a postscript.
Shakespeare's "Twelfth Night"

IT IS probable that there was never a year in American history in which the Bible did not excel the next-best seller. Estimates of its total sales are complicated by the fact that figures usually given include not only complete Bibles but also testaments and parts of the Scriptures. Moreover, all English-language Bibles sold in Colonial times were imported * and thus more difficult to count; many Bibles are still imported. Then after the organization of the American societies for the distribution of the Scriptures early in the nineteenth century, many of the Bibles printed in this country were exported for the missionary efforts of the churches and must therefore be excluded from our totals.

However, some facts and figures emerge. The American Bible Society distributed 22,520,429 copies of the complete Bible from its founding in 1816 to the end of 1945. Its annual distribution in recent years appears to be about a tenth of the total distributed by publishers, booksellers, and societies. The World Publishing Company, leading producer of Bibles in America, has a yearly sale of over two million. The annual distribution of Bibles today appears to be about three millions, but this is several times what it was in the mid-thirties, if the Census Bureau's reports on manufactures are to be trusted. A conservative estimate of the grand total of whole Bibles distributed in the United States would place it at over two hundred million.

And if we take testaments and parts of the Bible into consideration, we should have to multiply such a figure several times. Of course a vast number of Bibles have been distributed free or below cost by the societies set up for that purpose. No book has been so much used for gifts, whether pious presents of relatives, or purposeful donations to the careless and unconverted. It has been issued in ninety-nine different languages and dialects in use in the United States, according to an American Bible Society report of a few years ago, and in many more for distribution abroad.

Surely no other book has been so minutely studied, so much discussed, so passionately loved. It cannot be placed on a level with works designed for general reading and thus included in our list of best sellers, because it is used chiefly for devotional purposes; and yet certain modern presentations in attractive typography and format have made the distinctively literary enjoyment of the Scriptures much easier.

Other devotional books have had very large sales. The *Bay Psalm Book* was the first American best seller, and hymnals have often had tremendous mass sales. Perhaps the best-selling song-book of modern times was Ira D. Sankey's *Sacred Songs,* for which the compiler claimed a distribution of fifty million copies the world over. In war times, not only testaments but books of daily devotions have sold heavily. Some Sunday school helps, such as George Adam Smith's *Bible Dictionary,* have enjoyed long popularity.

The *Book of Mormon* has circulated its millions, not only among church members but through missionary effort. Mary Baker Eddy's widely distributed *Science and Health* is published in a form suitable for use in church services.

* The first American edition was John Eliot's translation into the tongue of the Narragansett Indians in 1663; the second was Saur's German Bible (Germantown, Pa.) of 1743. First in English was Robert Aitken's edition (Philadelphia) of 1782.

Other books used by individual religious denominations have always been among the large sellers, such as *The Book of Common Prayer* of the Episcopal Church, and the various catechisms.

The first school-book best seller contained a catechism and was religious throughout. "In Adam's fall we sinned all" began the alphabet rhymes in the *New England Primer*. Published by Benjamin Harris in Boston about 1690, this was the chief reader and speller for a hundred years in New England and perhaps in the Middle Colonies (though the *Royal Primer* was also popular there); then for fifty years more it was often reprinted. P. L. Ford, the little book's bibliographer, thought three million a conservative estimate of its total sales.

In 1783 a book was published which came to supplant the *Primer* in the Middle States and in parts of New England itself. This was Part I of Noah Webster's *Grammatical Institute of the English Language,* called *The American Spelling Book* in many editions, but generally known for a hundred years as "Webster's blue-back speller." In the famous *Boston Post* list of best sellers before 1860 * the speller is credited with sales of thirty million copies. Appletons took the book over in 1855 and "one of the largest presses in the Appleton plant ran day after day, year after year, on this one book until it was completely worn out." So says Grant Overton in his little history of the Appleton house entitled *Portrait of a Publisher.* Here also is recorded the figure of thirty-five million as the book's sales from 1855 to 1890. If the two estimates are both correct, we have a grand total for the speller of sixty to sixty-five million. Much higher estimates have sometimes been made.

The great elementary Latin textbook in the eighteenth century, and long afterward, was *A Short Introduction to the Latin Tongue* (1737), commonly called "Cheever's Latin Accidence." Jedidiah Morse's *Geography Made Easy* (1784) was the leading text in that field until it was supplanted by *Peter Parley's Geography for Children* (1830), by S. G. Goodrich. "Two millions of copies of it were sold," stated Goodrich; "the publisher paid me three hundred dollars for the copyright, and made his fortune by it." † Another great best seller was Lindley Murray's grammar. Murray was a New York Quaker who made a fortune in business and then retired and lived near old York, in England. He wrote his *English Grammar* for a girls' school nearby; and it was an abridgment of this book, first published in 1797, which became so popular for many years in both English and American schools. Roswell C. Smith's *Productive Grammar* (1832) sold several million copies. It was first published by Spaulding & Storrs, of Hartford; it was promoted by Asher Smith, father of the Roswell Smith who was later publisher of *Scribner's Monthly* and the *Century.* J. C. Derby, in his *Fifty Years,* says that next to Webster's blue-back speller *Smith's Grammar* was the most successful school book ever published

* Reprinted in *Publishers' Weekly,* March 23, 1929, vol. CXV, p. 1500.
† Allibone's *Dictionary of English Literature* (Philadelphia, 1874), vol. I, p. 701.

in America. Wells' and Clark's grammars were immensely popular a little later.

Warren Colburn's *Intellectual Arithmetic* (1821) had a tremendous sale; it was later supplanted by such books as Davies' and Barnes' arithmetics, from the press of A. S. Barnes & Company, famous publishers of school books. Their *Barnes' United States History* and *McNally's Geography* were also best sellers in the textbook field.

Sanders' Pictorial Primer (1838) and the whole series of Charles W. Sanders' seven readers had a phenomenal sale, said to have amounted to thirteen million by 1860 and to have continued at the rate of two million a year through the sixties. They were published by Ivison & Phinney, of New York. *The American First Class Book*, compiled by the clergyman-poet John Pierpont and first issued in 1823, was long standard in many schools; it was followed by a series of readers for the grades. But the top best sellers among readers were those compiled and edited by the Rev. William H. McGuffey, president of Cincinnati College and later of Ohio University at Athens, with some assistance from his brother Alexander. The American Book Company, which in 1890 took over the publication of these books from Van Antwerp, Bragg & Company, of Cincinnati, the original publishers, state that the aggregate sale of McGuffey readers and spellers in all editions has amounted to 122,000,000 copies. McGuffey compiled his first and second readers in 1836 and his third and fourth the next year, and later added a primer, the fifth and sixth readers, and a speller. He received from his publishers a ten per cent royalty up to a thousand dollars, fees for later revisions, and, for the last several years of his life, a gratuitous annuity.*

It is impossible to present comparable figures of the sales of dictionaries. Revisions, abridgments, and publishers' reticences in a highly competitive field make even the shrewd guesser throw up his hands. Johnson's had a good sale in America for seventy-five years. Webster's has, of course, sold many millions in its long career. Worcester's, a bitter competitor of Webster's for many decades after its first appearance in 1830, and especially after its 1860 edition, had a multitude of partisans and doubtless sold millions in its various forms. Funk & Wagnalls report sales of about four and a half millions of dictionaries since the issue of their *Standard* in 1893. The *Winston Simplified Dictionary* has sold over two million, and the Winston *Pocket Dictionary* in the Pocket Books series is drawing near that mark. The World Publishing Company sells a million and a half low-priced dictionaries annually in normal times, though it went far above that figure in the war years.

Household manuals have also sold in large quantities. The first cookbook by an American was *American Cookery*, published in 1796 by Hudson & Goodwin, of Hartford, and much reprinted for more than twenty-five years. It was compiled by Amelia Summers, known as "The American Orphan." Eliza

* For McGuffey and his readers, see Mark Sullivan's *Our Times* (New York, 1927), vol. II, p. 10-48.

Leslie's 75 *Receipts* was the most popular of her several cookbooks. Lydia Maria Child's *Frugal Housewife,* first issued by Carter & Hendee, of Boston, in 1829, was a great success for many years, as was Mrs. Mary Cornelius' *The Young Housekeeper's Friend,* of 1845. Marion Harland's *Common Sense in the House-hold* and *National Cook Book* were great favorites in the seventies and eighties. Fannie M. Farmer's *Boston Cooking-School Book,* published in 1896, has made a respectable start on its third million copies. A more recent favorite in this field is the *Better Homes and Gardens Cook Book,* which has also sold over two million.

Some home "doctor-books" have made remarkable records. The most popular in the eighteenth century was Dr. John Tennent's *Every Man His Own Doctor* (1734). Dr. William Buchan's *Domestic Medicine,* an English work, eventually forged far ahead of the Tennent opus with its engaging title, and continued to be reprinted in America as late as the 1850's. The modern best seller in this field is Dr. R. V. Pierce's *People's Common Sense Medical Adviser,* which has sold over five million copies since it first appeared in 1875. The *American Red Cross First Aid Text Book,* which had sold 3,385,000 copies before the second World War, increased its distribution during war years to over sixteen millions.

And the *Boy Scout Manual* has sold over five million copies since it was first issued in 1919.

APPENDIX A. OVER-ALL BEST SELLERS
IN THE UNITED STATES

Each book in this list is believed to have had a total sale equal to one per cent of the population of continental United States (or the English Colonies in the years before the Revolution) for the decade in which it was published. These decade figures are given below. The list omits bibles, hymnals, text-books, almanacs, cookbooks, doctor-books, manuals, and reference works. Dates and publishers given are believed to be those of the first American editions, so far as ascertainable. When more than one publisher issued a book in the year named, and the compiler has been unable to learn which was first, the notation v.p. (various publishers) has been used. Asterisks follow disputed or conjectural dates, authors, or publishers.

Required Sale before 1690—1,000
1662 Wigglesworth, Michael. *The Day of Doom.* Cambridge: Samuel Green.
1664 Baxter, Richard. *A Call to the Unconverted.* Cambridge: Samuel Green.
1665 Bayly, Lewis. *The Practice of Piety.* Cambridge: Samuel Green.
1679 Hardy, Samuel. *A Guide to Heaven.* Boston: John Foster.
1681 Bunyan, John. *The Pilgrim's Progress.* Cambridge: Samuel Green.
1682 Rowlandson, Mary. *Captivity and Restoration.* Cambridge: Samuel Green.
1688 Bacon, Francis. *Essays.* Philadelphia: William Bradford.

Required Sale 1690-1699—2,000
1699 Dickinson, Jonathan. *God's Protecting Providence.* Philadelphia: Reinier Jansen.

Required Sale 1700-1709—3,000
1701 Russell, Robert. *Seven Sermons.* Boston: Bartholomew Green and John Allen.
1707 Williams, John. *The Redeemed Captive.* Boston: Bartholomew Green.
1709 Flavel, John. *Husbandry Spiritualized.* Boston: John Allen.

Required Sale 1710-1719—4,000
1719**Mother Goose's Melodies for Children.* Boston: Thomas Fleet.*
1719 Watts, Isaac. *Divine and Moral Songs for the Use of Children.* Boston: Samuel Gerrish.

Required Sale 1720-1729—5,000
1721 Josephus, Flavius. *Antiquities of the Jews.* Boston: publisher unknown.

Required Sale 1730-1739—7,000
1733 *History of Doctor Faustus.* Boston: Thomas Fleet.

Required Sale 1740-1749—10,000
1741 Penn, William. *No Cross, No Crown.* Boston: publisher unknown.
1741 Rede, Sarah. *A Token for Youth.* Boston: Hopestill Foster.
1741 Watts, Isaac. *Horae Lyricae.* Philadelphia: Benjamin Franklin.
1744 Richardson, Samuel. *Pamela.* v.p.
1745 *The History of the Holy Jesus.* Boston: Benjamin Gray.
1747 Pope, Alexander, *Essay on Man.* Philadelphia: William Bradford.

Required Sale 1750-1759—12,000
1750*Aesop's Fables.* Boston: Daniel Fowle.*
1750 Hervey, James. *Meditations and Contemplations.* Philadelphia: William
        Bradford.
1751 Dodsley, Robert.* *The Oeconomy of Human Life.* Boston: Daniel Fowle.

Required Sale 1760-1769—15,000
1768 Dickinson, John. *Letters from a Farmer in Pennsylvania.* v.p.

Required Sale 1770-1779—20,000
1772 Goldsmith, Oliver. *The Vicar of Wakefield.* Philadelphia: William
        Mentz.
1774 Sterne, Laurence. *The Life and Opinions of Tristram Shandy.* Philadel-
        phia: James Humphreys.
1775 Defoe, Daniel. *Robinson Crusoe.* New York: Hugh Gaine.
1775 Gregory, John. *A Father's Legacy to His Daughters.* Philadelphia: John
        Dunlap.
1775 Stanhope, Philip D. (Lord Chesterfield). *Letters to His Son.* New York:
        Rivington & Gaine.
1776 Paine, Thomas. *Common Sense.* Philadelphia: John Bell.
1777 Milton, John. *Paradise Lost.* Philadelphia: John Bell.
1777 Thomson, James. *The Seasons.* Philadelphia: John Bell.
1777 Young, Edward. *Night Thoughts.* Philadelphia: John Bell.

Required Sale 1780-1789—25,000
1782 Trumbull, John. *M'Fingal.* Philadelphia: William & Thomas Bradford.
1786 Richardson, Samuel. *Clarissa.* Philadelphia: William Spotswood.
1787 Cowper, William. *The Task.* Philadelphia: Thomas Dobson.
1788 Burns, Robert. *Poems.* v.p.
1788 Hamilton, Alexander, and others. *The Federalist.* New York: J. & A.
        M'Lean.

Required Sale 1790-1799—40,000

1793 Fox, John. *Book of Martyrs.* New York: William Durell.

1793 Swift, Jonathan. *Gulliver's Travels.* New York: William Durell.

1794 *Arabian Nights' Entertainment.* Philadelphia: H. & P. Rice.

1794 Franklin, Benjamin. *Autobiography.* v.p.

1794 Paine, Thomas. *The Age of Reason.* v.p.

1794 Rowson, Susanna. *Charlotte Temple.* Philadelphia: Mathew Carey.

1795 Hume, David. *History of Great Britain.* Philadelphia: S. H. Smith.

1795 Volney, Constantin François. *The Ruins.* Philadelphia: Author.

1796 Shakespeare, William. *Plays.* Philadelphia: Bioren & Madan.

1797 Foster, Hannah. *The Coquette.* Boston: Samuel Etheridge.

1798 Roche, Regina Marie. *Children of the Abbey.* Philadelphia: publisher unknown.

Required Sale 1800-1809—50,000

1800 Weems, Mason L. *Life of Washington.* Philadelphia: Carey & Lea.

1803 Addison, Joseph, and Steele, Richard. *The Spectator.* Philadelphia: publisher unknown.

1804*Porter, Jane. *Thaddeus of Warsaw.*

1808 Byron, George Gordon (Lord). *Poems.* Newark, N. J.: S. & J. Ridge.

1809 Irving, Washington. *History of New York.* New York: Innskeep & Bradford.

Required Sale 1810-1819—75,000

1810 Porter, Jane. *Scottish Chiefs.* New York: D. Longworth.

1811 Robertson, William. *History of Scotland.* Philadelphia: J. Bioren & T. L. Plowman.

1811 Scott, Walter. *Poems.* New York: Ezra Sargent.

1815 Scott, Walter. *Guy Mannering.* v.p.

1815 Scott, Walter. *Waverley.* Carey & Lea.*

1817 Moore, Thomas. *Lalla Rookh.* Philadelphia: Moses Thomas.

1818 Scott, Walter. *Rob Roy.* v.p.

1819 Irving, Washington. *Sketch Book.* New York: C. S. Van Winkle.

Required Sale 1820-1829—100,000

1820 Scott, Walter. *Ivanhoe.* Philadelphia: Carey & Son, and Boston: Wells & Lilly.

1821 Cooper, James Fenimore. *The Spy.* New York: Wiley & Halsted.

1821 Scott, Walter. *Kenilworth.* New York: J. & J. Harper.

1822 Cooper, James Fenimore. *The Pilot.* New York: Charles Wiley.

1823 Cooper, James Fenimore. *The Pioneers.* New York: Charles Wiley.

1824 Seaver, James E. *Life of Mrs. Mary Jemison.* Canandaigua, N. Y.: James D. Bemis.

1825 Swedenborg, Emanuel. *Heaven and Hell*. Boston: T. H. Carter.

1826 Cooper, James Fenimore. *The Last of the Mohicans*. Philadelphia: Carey & Lea.

1827 Cooper, James Fenimore. *The Prairie*. Philadelphia: Carey, Lea & Carey.

Required Sale 1830-1839—125,000

1832 Abbott, Jacob. *The Young Christian*. New York: John P. Haven.

1832 Austen, Jane. *Pride and Prejudice*. Philadelphia: Carey & Lea.

1832 Wyss, Johann R. *Swiss Family Robinson*. New York: J. & J. Harper.

1833 Abbott, John S. C. *The Mother at Home*. Boston: Crocker & Brewster.

1834 Bulwer-Lytton, Edward. *The Last Days of Pompeii*. New York: Harper & Brothers.

1834 Hugo, Victor. *The Hunchback of Notre-Dame*. Philadelphia: Carey, Lea & Blanchard.

1835 Bulwer-Lytton, Edward. *Rienzi*. Philadelphia: Carey & Hart.

1836 Monk, Maria. *Awful Disclosures*. New York: Howe & Bates.

1837 Bird, Robert Montgomery. *Nick of the Woods*. Philadelphia: Carey, Lea & Blanchard.

1837 Dickens, Charles. *Pickwick Papers*. Philadelphia: Carey, Lea & Blanchard.

1837 Hawthorne, Nathaniel. *Twice-Told Tales*. Boston: American Stationers Company.

1837 Lee, Hannah F. *Three Experiments of Living*. Boston: William S. Damrell.

1838 Dickens, Charles. *Oliver Twist*. Philadelphia: Carey, Lea & Blanchard.

1839 Dickens, Charles. *Nicholas Nickleby*. Philadelphia: Carey, Lea & Blanchard.

1839 Longfellow, Henry Wadsworth. *Poems*. (*Voices of the Night*. Cambridge: Samuel Coleman.)

1839 Sparks, Jared. *Life of Washington*. Boston: F. Andrews.

1839 Thompson, Daniel P. *The Green Mountain Boys*. Montpelier, Vt.: E. P. Walton & Sons.

Required Sale 1840-1849—175,000

1840 Cooper, James Fenimore. *The Pathfinder*. Philadelphia: Lea & Blanchard.

1840 Dana, Richard Henry, Jr. *Two Years Before the Mast*. New York: Harper & Brothers.

1840 Poe, Edgar Allan. *Tales*. Philadelphia: Lea & Blanchard.

1841 Cooper, James Fenimore. *Deerslayer*. Philadelphia: Lea & Blanchard.

1841 Dickens, Charles. *Barnaby Rudge*. Philadelphia: Lea & Blanchard.

1841 Dickens, Charles. *The Old Curiosity Shop*. Philadelphia: Lea & Blanchard.

1841 Emerson, Ralph Waldo. *Essays*. Boston: James Munroe & Company.

1842 Dickens, Charles. *American Notes*. New York: Wilson & Company.

1842 Griswold, Rufus W., ed. *Poets and Poetry of America*. Philadelphia: Carey & Hart.

1842 Sue, Eugène. *Mysteries of Paris*. New York: Wilson & Company.

1842 Tennyson, Alfred. *Poems*. Boston: W. D. Ticknor.

1843 Lippard, George. *The Quaker City*. New York: Harper & Brothers.

1843 Prescott, William Hickling. *Conquest of Mexico*. New York: Harper & Brothers.

1843 Sears, Robert. *The Wonders of the World*. New York: Author.

1844 Dickens, Charles. *A Christmas Carol*. Philadelphia: Carey & Hart.

1844 Dickens, Charles. *Martin Chuzzlewit*. New York: Harper & Brothers.

1844 Dumas, Alexandre. *The Three Musketeers*. v.p.

1845 Dumas, Alexandre. *The Count of Monte Cristo*. v.p.

1845 Poe, Edgar Allan. *The Raven and Other Poems*. New York: Wiley & Putnam.

1845 Sue, Eugene. *The Wandering Jew*. New York: E. Winchester.

1846 Headley, Joel T. *Napoleon and His Marshals*. New York: Baker & Scribner.

1847 Aguilar, Grace. *Home Influence*. New York: Harper & Brothers.

1848 Andersen, Hans Christian. *Fairy Tales*. (*Shoes of Fortune and Other Tales*. New York: John Wiley.)

1848 Brontë, Charlotte. *Jane Eyre*. Boston: Wilkins, Carter & Company.

1848 Brontë, Emily. *Wuthering Heights*. New York: Harper & Brothers.

1848 Dickens, Charles. *Dombey and Son*. v.p.

1848 Thackeray, William M. *Vanity Fair*. New York: Harper & Brothers.

1849 Macaulay, Thomas B. *History of England*. New York: Harper & Brothers.

1849 Whittier, John G. *Poems*. Boston: B. B. Mussey & Company.

Required Sale 1850-1859—225,000

1850 *Boccaccio, Giovanni. *The Decameron*. Philadelphia: Thomas Wardle.*

1850 Browning, Robert. *Poems*. Boston: Ticknor, Reed & Fields.

1850 Dickens, Charles. *David Copperfield*. v.p.

1850 Hawthorne, Nathaniel. *The Scarlet Letter*. Boston: Ticknor & Fields.

1850 Mitchell, Donald G. *Reveries of a Bachelor*. New York: Baker & Scribner.

1850 Thackeray, William M. *Pendennis*. New York: Harper & Brothers.

1850 Warner, Susan. *The Wide, Wide World*. New York: G. P. Putnam.

1851 Hawthorne, Nathaniel. *The House of the Seven Gables*. Boston: Ticknor & Fields.

1851 Melville, Herman. *Moby-Dick*. New York: Harper & Brothers.

1852 Dickens, Charles. *Bleak House*. New York: Harper & Brothers.

1852 Southworth, Mrs. E. D. E. N. *The Curse of Clifton*. Philadelphia: Carey & Hart.

1852 Stowe, Harriet Beecher. *Uncle Tom's Cabin*. Boston: John P. Jewett & Company.

1854 Barnum, Phineas T. *Struggles and Triumphs*. New York: J. S. Redfield.

1854 Cummins, Maria S. *The Lamplighter*. Boston: John P. Jewett & Company.

1854 Dickens, Charles. *Hard Times*. New York: Harper & Brothers.

1854 Holmes, Mary Jane. *Tempest and Sunshine*. New York: D. Appleton & Company.

1854 Thoreau, Henry D. *Walden*. Boston: Ticknor & Fields.

1855 Arthur, T. S. *Ten Nights in a Bar-Room*. Philadelphia: J. B. Lippincott Company.

1855 Bulfinch, Thomas. *The Age of Fable*. Boston: Sanborn, Carter & Bazin.

1855 Ingraham, J. H. *The Prince of the House of David*. New York: Pudney & Russell.

1855 Reade, Charles. *The Cloister and the Hearth*. New York: Harper & Brothers.

1855 Thackeray, William M. *The Newcomes*. New York: Harper & Brothers.

1855 Whitman, Walt. *Leaves of Grass*. Brooklyn: A. & J. Rome.

1856 Holmes, Mary Jane. *Lena Rivers*. New York: Miller, Orton & Company.

1856 Mulock, Dinah Maria. *John Halifax, Gentleman*. New York: Harper & Brothers.

1857 Dickens, Charles. *Little Dorrit*. New York: Harper & Brothers.

1857 Hughes, Thomas. *Tom Brown's School Days*. New York: Harper & Brothers.

1859 Dickens, Charles. *A Tale of Two Cities*. Philadelphia: T. B. Peterson & Company.

1859 Eliot, George. *Adam Bede*. New York: Harper & Brothers.

1859 Evans, Augusta J. *Beulah*. New York: Derby & Jackson.

1859 Southworth, Mrs. E. D. E. N. *The Hidden Hand*. Philadelphia: Peterson & Brothers.

1859 Thackeray, William M. *The Virginians*. New York: Harper & Brothers.

Required Sale 1860-1869—300,000

1860 Ellis, Edward S. *Seth Jones*. New York: Beadle & Adams.

1860 Harris, Miriam Coles. *Rutledge*. New York: Derby & Jackson.

1860 Meredith, Owen. *Lucile*. Boston: Ticknor & Fields.

1860 Stephens, Mrs. Ann S. *Malaeska*. New York: Beadle & Adams.

1861 Dickens, Charles. *Great Expectations*. New York: Harper & Brothers.

1861 Eliot, George. *Silas Marner*. New York: Harper & Brothers.

1861 Grimm, Jacob and Wilhelm. *Household Tales*. Boston: Crosby, Nichols, Lee & Company.

1861 Wood, Mrs. Henry. *East Lynne*. New York: Dick & Fitzgerald.

1862 Brownlow, William G. *Parson Brownlow's Book*. Philadelphia: George W. Childs.

1862 Hugo, Victor. *Les Misèrables*. New York: George W. Carleton.

1862*Trollope, Anthony. *Barchester Towers*. New York: Dick & Fitzgerald.*

1863 Braddon, Mary E. *Lady Audley's Secret*. New York: Dick & Fitzgerald.

1863 Southworth, Mrs. E. D. E. N. *The Fatal Marriage*. Philadelphia: T. B. Peterson & Brothers.

1863 Whitney, Mrs. A. D. T. *Faith Gartney's Girlhood*. Boston: A. K. Loring & Company.

1864 Southworth, Mrs. E. D. E. N. *Ishmael*. Philadelphia: T. B. Peterson & Brothers.

1864 Southworth, Mrs. E. D. E. N. *Self-Raised*. Philadelphia. T. B. Peterson & Brothers.

1865 Dickens, Charles. *Our Mutual Friend*. New York: Harper & Brothers.

1865 Dodge, Mary Mapes. *Hans Brinker and His Silver Skates*. New York: James O'Kane.

1866 Carroll, Lewis. *Alice's Adventures in Wonderland*. New York: D. Appleton & Company.

1866 Reade, Charles. *Griffith Gaunt*. Boston: Ticknor & Fields.

1867 Alger, Horatio, Jr. *Ragged Dick*. Boston: A. K. Loring & Company.

1867 Evans, Augusta J. *St. Elmo*. New York: George W. Carleton.

1867 Ouida. *Under Two Flags*. Philadelphia: J. B. Lippincott Company.

1868 Alcott, Louisa M. *Little Women*. Boston: Roberts Brothers.

1868 Collins, Wilkie. *The Moonstone*. New York: Harper & Brothers.

1869 Twain, Mark. *Innocents Abroad*. Hartford: American Publishing Company.

Required Sale 1870-1879—375,000

1870 Fitzgerald, Edward. *The Rubáiyát of Omar Khayyám*. Columbus, Ohio: no publisher.

1870 Harte, Bret. *The Luck of Roaring Camp and Other Stories*. Boston: Fields, Osgood & Company.

1871 Alcott, Louisa M. *Little Men*. Boston: Roberts Brothers.

1871 Eggleston, Edward. *The Hoosier School-Master*. New York: Orange Judd & Company.

1871 Reade, Charles. *A Terrible Temptation*. Boston: Osgood & Company.

1872 Roc, E. P. *Barriers Burned Away*. New York: Dodd, Mead & Company.

1873*Verne, Jules. *Around the World in Eighty Days*. Philadelphia: Porter & Coates.*

1873*Verne, Jules. *Twenty Thousand Leagues Under the Sea*. Boston: G. M. Smith & Company.*

1874 Blackmore, R. D. *Lorna Doone*. New York: Harper & Brothers.

1874 Roe, E. P. *Opening A Chestnut Burr*. New York: Dodd, Mead & Company.

1875 Green, John Richard. *A Short History of the English People*. New York: Harper & Brothers.

1876 Habberton, John. *Helen's Babies*. Boston: A. K. Loring & Company.

1876 Haines, Thomas L., and Yaggy, Levi. *The Royal Path of Life*. Cincinnati: Western Publishing Company.*

1876 Twain, Mark. *Tom Sawyer*. Hartford: American Publishing Company.

1878 Green, Anna Katharine. *The Leavenworth Case*. New York: G. P. Putnam's Sons.

1879 George, Henry. *Progress and Poverty*. New York: Author.

Required Sale 1880-1889—500,000

1880 Harris, Joel Chandler. *Uncle Remus*. New York: D. Appleton & Company.

1880 Sidney, Margaret. *Five Little Peppers and How They Grew*. Boston: D. Lothrop & Company.

1880 Wallace, Lew. *Ben-Hur*. New York: Harper & Brothers.

1880 Zola, Emile. *Nana*. Philadelphia: T. B. Peterson & Brothers.

1881 Flaubert, Gustave. *Madame Bovary*. Philadelphia: T. B. Peterson & Brothers.

1882 Halévy, Ludovic. *L'Abbé Constantin*. v.p.

1883 Riley, James Whitcomb. *The Old Swimmin' Hole and 'Leven More Poems*. Indianapolis: Merrill, Meigs & Company.

1883 Smith, Hannah Whitall. *The Christian's Secret of a Happy Life*. New York: Fleming H. Revell Company.

1883 Twain, Mark. *Life on the Mississippi*. Boston: J. R. Osgood & Company.

1884 Spyri, Johanna. *Heidi*. Boston: Cupples, Upham & Company.

1884 Stevenson, Robert Louis. *Treasure Island*. Boston: Roberts Brothers.

1885 Stevenson, Robert Louis. *A Child's Garden of Verses*. New York: Charles Scribner's Sons.

1885 Twain, Mark. *Huckleberry Finn*. New York: Charles L. Webster & Company.

1886 Burnett, Frances Hodgson. *Little Lord Fauntleroy*. New York: Charles Scribner's Sons.

1886 Haggard, H. Rider. *King Solomon's Mines*. New York: Harper & Brothers.

1886 Tolstoi, Lyof. *War and Peace*. New York: William S. Gottsberger.

1887 Corelli, Marie. *Thelma*. New York: M. J. Ivers & Company.

1887 Haggard, H. Rider. *She*. New York: Harper & Brothers.

1888 Bellamy, Edward. *Looking Backward*. Boston: Ticknor & Company.

1888 Caine, Hall. *The Deemster*. New York: D. Appleton & Company.

1888 Corelli, Marie. *A Romance of Two Worlds.* New York: M. J. Ivers & Company.

1888 Gunter, A. C. *Mr. Barnes of New York.* New York: Deshler, Welch & Company.

1888 Ward, Mrs. Humphry. *Robert Elsmere.* New York: Macmillan Company.

1889 Maupassant, Guy de. *Stories.* (*The Odd Number.* New York: Harper & Brothers.)

Required Sale 1890-1899—625,000

1890 Doyle, Arthur Conan. *The Sign of the Four.* Philadelphia: J. B. Lippincott Company.

1890 Doyle, Arthur Conan. *A Study in Scarlet.* Philadelphia: J. B. Lippincott Company.

1890 Kipling, Rudyard. *Barrack-Room Ballads.* New York: United States Book Company.

1890 Kipling, Rudyard. *Plain Tales From the Hills.* New York: United States Book Company.

1890 Sewell, Anna. *Black Beauty.* Boston: American Humane Education Society.

1891 Barrie, James M. *The Little Minister.* New York: United States Book Company.

1891 Kipling, Rudyard. *The Light That Failed.* New York: United States Book Company.

1891 Kipling, Rudyard. *Mine Own People.* New York: United States Book Company.

1892 Barrie, James M. *A Window in Thrums.* New York: United States Book Company.

1892 Doyle, Arthur Conan. *The Adventures of Sherlock Holmes.* New York: Harper & Brothers.

1893 Grand, Sarah. *The Heavenly Twins.* New York: Cassell & Company.

1893 Stevenson, Robert Louis. *Dr. Jekyll and Mr. Hyde.* New York: Charles Scribner's Sons.

1894 du Maurier, George. *Trilby.* New York: Harper & Brothers.

1894 Harvey, William H. *Coin's Financial School.* Chicago: Coin Publishing Company.

1894 Hope, Anthony. *The Prisoner of Zenda.* New York: Henry Holt & Company.

1894 Maclaren, Ian. *Beside the Bonnie Brier Bush.* New York: Dodd, Mead & Company.

1894 Saunders, Marshall. *Beautiful Joe.* Philadelphia: Judson Press.

1895 Crane, Stephen. *The Red Badge of Courage.* New York: D. Appleton & Company.

1895 Read, Opie. *The Jucklins*. Chicago: Laird & Lee.

1896 Sienkiewicz, Henryk. *Quo Vadis*. Boston: Little, Brown & Company.

1897 Sheldon, Charles M. *In His Steps*. Chicago: Advance Publishing Company.

1898 Connor, Ralph. *Black Rock*. New York: Fleming H. Revell Company.

1898 Westcott, Edward Noyes. *David Harum*. New York: D. Appleton & Company.

1899 Churchill, Winston. *Richard Carvel*. New York: Macmillan Company.

1899 Ford, Paul Leicester. *Janice Meredith*. New York: Dodd, Mead & Company.

Required Sale 1900-1909—750,000

1900 Bacheller, Irving. *Eben Holden*. Boston: Lothrop Publishing Company.

1900 Churchill, Winston. *The Crisis*. New York: Macmillan Company.

1901 McCutcheon, George Barr. *Graustark*. Chicago: H. S. Stone & Company.

1901 Rice, Alice Hegan. *Mrs. Wiggs of the Cabbage Patch*. New York: Century Company.

1902 Wister, Owen. *The Virginian*. New York: Macmillan Company.

1903 Fox, John, Jr. *The Little Shepherd of Kingdom Come*. New York: Charles Scribner's Sons.

1903 London, Jack. *The Call of the Wild*. New York: Macmillan Company.

1903 Wiggin, Kate Douglas. *Rebecca of Sunnybrook Farm*. Boston: Houghton, Mifflin & Company.

1904 Hurlbut, Jesse Lyman. *The Story of the Bible*. Philadelphia: John C. Winston Company.

1904 London, Jack. *The Sea Wolf*. New York: Macmillan Company.

1904 Porter, Gene Stratton. *Freckles*. New York: Doubleday, Page & Company.

1906 Grey, Zane. *The Spirit of the Border*. New York: A. L. Burt & Company.

1907 Glyn, Elinor. *Three Weeks*. New York: Duffield & Company.

1907 Haddock, Frank C. *Power of Will*. Meriden, Conn.: Pelton Publishing Company.

1907 Service, Robert W. *The Spell of the Yukon and Other Verses*. New York: Barse & Hopkins.

1907 Wright, Harold Bell. *The Shepherd of the Hills*. Chicago: Book Supply Company.

1908 Fox, John, Jr. *The Trail of the Lonesome Pine*. New York: Charles Scribner's Sons.

1908 Montgomery, Lucy M. *Anne of Green Gables*. Boston: L. C. Page & Company.

1908 Rinehart, Mary Roberts. *The Circular Staircase*. Indianapolis: Bobbs-Merrill Company.

1909 Porter, Gene Stratton. *A Girl of the Limberlost*. New York: Doubleday, Page & Company.

1909 Wright, Harold Bell. *The Calling of Dan Matthews*. Chicago: Book Supply Company.

Required Sale 1910-1919—900,000

1910 Barclay, Florence L. *The Rosary*. New York: G. P. Putnam's Sons.

1911 Norris, Kathleen. *Mother*. New York: Macmillan Company.

1911 Porter, Gene Stratton. *The Harvester*. New York: Doubleday, Page & Company.

1911 Wright, Harold Bell. *The Winning of Barbara Worth*. Chicago: Book Supply Company.

1912 Grey, Zane. *The Riders of the Purple Sage*. New York: Harper & Brothers.

1913 Porter, Eleanor H. *Pollyanna*. Boston: L. C. Page & Company.

1913 Porter, Gene Stratton. *Laddie*. New York: Doubleday, Page & Company.

1914 Burroughs, Edgar Rice. *Tarzan of the Apes*. Chicago: A. C. McClurg & Company.

1914 Tarkington, Booth. *Penrod*. New York: Doubleday, Page & Company.

1914 Wright, Harold Bell. *The Eyes of the World*. Chicago: Book Supply Company.

1915 Porter, Gene Stratton. *Michael O'Halloran*. New York: Doubleday, Page & Company.

1916 Guest, Edgar A. *A Heap o' Livin'*. Chicago: Reilly & Lee Company.

1916 Wright, Harold Bell. *When a Man's a Man*. Chicago: Book Supply Company.

Required Sale 1920-1929—1,000,000

1920 Oppenheim, E. Phillips. *The Great Impersonation*. Boston: Little, Brown & Company.

1920 Wells, H. G. *Outline of History*. New York: Macmillan Company.

1921 Hull, Edith M. *The Sheik*. Boston: Small, Maynard & Company.

1924 Wodehouse, P. G. *Jeeves*. New York: George H. Doran Company.

1926 Durant, Will. *The Story of Philosophy*. New York: Simon & Schuster.

1926 Smith, Thorne. *Topper*. New York: Doubleday, Doran & Company.

1929 Douglas, Lloyd C. *The Magnificent Obsession*. Chicago: Willett, Clark & Company.

1929 Ripley, Robert L. *Believe It or Not*. New York: Simon & Schuster.

Required Sale 1930-1939—1,200,000

1931 Buck, Pearl. *The Good Earth*. New York: John Day.

1931 Queen, Ellery. *The Dutch Shoe Mystery*. New York: F. A. Stokes Company.

1932 Queen, Ellery. *The Egyptian Cross Mystery*. New York: F. A. Stokes Company.

1933 Allen, Hervey. *Anthony Adverse*. New York: Farrar & Rinehart.

1933 Gardner, Erle Stanley. *The Case of the Sulky Girl*. New York: William Morrow & Company.

1933 Hilton, James. *Lost Horizon*. New York: William Morrow & Company.

1934 Gardner, Erle Stanley. *The Case of the Curious Bride*. New York: William Morrow & Company.

1934 Queen, Ellery. *The Chinese Orange Mystery*. New York: F. A. Stokes Company.

1935 Gardner, Erle Stanley. *The Case of the Counterfeit Eye*. New York: William Morrow & Company.

1936 Carnegie, Dale. *How to Win Friends and Influence People*. New York: Simon & Schuster.

1936 Gardner, Erle Stanley. *The Case of the Stuttering Bishop*. New York: William Morrow & Company.

1936 Mitchell, Margaret. *Gone With the Wind*. New York: Macmillan Company.

1937 Gardner, Erle Stanley. *The Case of the Dangerous Dowager*. William Morrow & Company.

1937 Gardner, Erle Stanley. *The Case of the Lame Canary*. New York: William Morrow & Company.

1938 Brand, Max. *Singing Guns*. New York: Dodd, Mead & Company.

1938 Gardner, Erle Stanley. *The Case of the Substitute Face*. New York: William Morrow & Company.

1938 Page, Marco. *Fast Company*. New York: Dodd, Mead & Company.

1938 Runyon, Damon. *The Best of Damon Runyon*. New York: F. A. Stokes Company.

1939 Steinbeck, John. *The Grapes of Wrath*. Viking Press.

Required Sale 1940-1945—1,300,000

1940 Queen, Ellery. *New Adventures of Ellery Queen*. New York: F. A. Stokes Company.

1940 Speare, M. E., ed. *Pocket Book of Verse*. New York: Pocket Books, Inc.

1940 Struther, Jan. *Mrs. Miniver*. New York: Harcourt, Brace & Company.

1941 Hilton, James. *Random Harvest*. Boston: Little, Brown & Company.

1941 *Pocket Book of Boners*. New York: Pocket Books, Inc.

1941 Speare, M. E., ed. *Pocket Book of Short Stories*. New York: Pocket Books, Inc.

1942 Douglas, Lloyd C. *The Robe*. Boston: Houghton Mifflin Company.

1942 Hargrove, Marion. *See Here, Private Hargrove*. New York: Henry Holt & Company.

1943 Cerf, Bennett, ed. *Pocket Book of War Humor*. New York: Pocket Books, Inc.

1943 Pyle, Ernie. *Here Is Your War*. New York: Henry Holt & Company.

1943 Smith, Betty. *A Tree Grows in Brooklyn*. New York: Harper & Brothers.

1943 Willkie, Wendell. *One World*. New York: Simon & Schuster.

1944 Goudge, Elizabeth. *Green Dolphin Street*. New York: Coward-McCann Company.

1944 Graham, Gwethalyn. *Earth and High Heaven*. Philadelphia: J. B. Lippincott Company.

1944 Hope, Bob. *I Never Left Home*. New York: Simon & Schuster.

1944 Maugham, Somerset. *The Razor's Edge*. New York: Doubleday & Company.

1944 Pyle, Ernie. *Brave Men*. New York: Henry Holt & Company.

1944 Sharp, Margery. *Cluny Brown*. Boston: Little, Brown & Company.

1945 Costain, Thomas B. *The Black Rose*. New York: Doubleday & Company.

1945 MacDonald, Betty. *The Egg and I*. Philadelphia: J. B. Lippincott Company.

1945 Shellabarger, Samuel. *Captain From Castile*. Boston: Little, Brown & Company.

1945 Winsor, Kathleen. *Forever Amber*. New York: Macmillan Company.

APPENDIX B. BETTER SELLERS

These are the runners-up believed not to have reached the total sales required for the over-all best sellers. Limitations are the same as in the No. 1 list.

1670 Wigglesworth, Michael. *Meat Out of the Eater*.

1700 Willard, Samuel. *The Fountain Opened*.

1700 Janeway, James. *A Token for Children*.

1700 Doolittle, Thomas. *Treatise on the Lord's Supper*.

1722 Vincent, Nathaniel. *The Day of Grace*.

1727 Penn, William. *Fruits of a Father's Love*.

1729 Bunyan, John. *Grace Abounding*.

1729 Defoe, Daniel. *Religious Courtship*.

1740 Erskine, Ralph. *Gospel Sonnets*.

1742 Rowe, Elizabeth S. *Devout Exercises of Heart, and Letters*.

1744 *The French Convert*.

1745 Tillotson, John. *Sermons*.

1745 Erskine, Ebenezer. *Sermons*.

1748 Eliot, Jared. *Essays Upon Husbandry in New England*.

1749 Doddridge, Philip. *Lectures*.

1750 Addison, Joseph. *Cato: A Tragedy*.

1751 Pomfret, John. *Poems.*

1751 Elwood, Thomas. *Davideis.*

1753 Young, Edward. *The Last Day.*

1760 Law, William. *Spirit of Prayer.*

1760 Anson, George. *Voyage Round the World.*

1762 Sandeman, Robert. *Letters on Theron and Aspasio.*

1766 Montagu, Lady Mary Wortley. *Letters.*

1766 Ogilvie, John. *Providence: A Poem.*

1768 Johnson, Samuel. *Rasselas.*

1770 Penn, William. *A Brief Account of the People Called Quakers.*

1774 Cook, Capt. James. *Three Voyages to the Pacific.*

*   Thornton, Bennel, and Colman, George. *The Connoisseur.*

*   Johnstone, Charles. *Chrysal; or, The Adventures of a Guinea.*

*   Gordon, Thomas, and Trenchard, John. *Cato's Letters.*

*   Cervantes, Miguel. *Don Quixote.*

*   Hawkesworth, John. *The Adventurer.*

*   Johnson, Samuel. *The Rambler.*

*   More, Edward. *The World.*

*   Steele, Richard. *The Tatler.*

*   Steele, Richard. *The Guardian.*

*   Montesquieu, Baron de. *The Spirit of the Laws.*

*   Neal, Daniel. *History of the Puritans.*

*   Pope, Alexander. *Iliad* and *Odyssey.*

*   Salmon, Thomas. *The Universal Traveller.*

1775 Burke, Edmund. *Conciliation With America.*

1779 Allen, Ethan. *A Narrative of Col. Ethan Allen's Captivity.*

1784 Goethe, Johann Wolfgang von. *Sorrows of Young Werther.*

1786 Richardson, Samuel. *Sir Charles Grandison.*

1786 Fielding, Henry. *Tom Jones.*

1790 Macgowan, John. *Life of Joseph.*

1790 Le Sage, Alain R. *Gil Blas.*

1791 Webster, Noah. *The Prompter.*

1791 Paine, Thomas. *The Rights of Man.*

1792 Brackenridge, H. H. *Modern Chivalry.*

1792 Belknap, Jeremy. *The Foresters.*

1794 Locke, John. *Essay on Human Understanding.*

1794 Smollett, Tobias. *Roderick Random.*

1794 Hervey, James. *A Dialogue Between Theron and Aspasio.*

1794 Rowson, Susanna. *The Fille de Chambre.*

1794 Radcliffe, Mrs. Ann. *The Mysteries of Udolpho.*

* No dates are assigned to the books starred because, though they were not published in the Colonies in the eighteenth century, large sales of imported editions before 1775 make it desirable to include them here.

1796 Day, Thomas. *History of Sandford and Merton.*
1796 Smollett, Tobias. *History of England.*
1796 Rollin, Charles. *Ancient History.*
1796 Rousseau, J. J. *The New Eloisa.*
1796 Watson, Richard. *Apology for the Bible.*
1797 Lyttleton, Lord. *Dialogues of the Dead.*
1797 Radcliffe, Mrs. Ann. *The Italian.*
1798 Brown, Charles Brockden. *Wieland.*
1799 Brown, Charles Brockden. *Edgar Huntly.*
1799 Lewis, M. G. *The Monk.*
1801 Tenney, Mrs. Tabitha. *Female Quixotism.*
1801 Edgeworth, Maria. *Moral Tales.*
1801 Opie, Mrs. Amelia. *Father and Daughter.*
1803 Wirt, William. *Letters of a British Spy.*
1807 Manvill, Mrs. P. D. *Lucinda.*
1807 Jones, Paul. *Life and Adventures.*
1809 Cottin, Marie Restaud. *Elizabeth; or, The Exiles of Siberia.*
1810 Trumbull, Henry. *History of the Discovery of America.*
1810 Horry, Peter, and Weems, M. L. *Life of General Francis Marion.*
1811 Mitchell, Isaac. *Alonzo and Melissa.*
1815 Scott, Walter. *The Antiquary.*
1817 Wirt, William. *Life of Patrick Henry.*
1817 Robbins, Archibald. *The Loss of the Brig Commerce.*
1818 Scott, Walter. *The Heart of Midlothian.*
1820 Scott, Walter. *The Monastery.*
1820 Scott, Walter. *The Abbot.*
1822 Scott, Walter. *The Pirate.*
1822 Irving, Washington. *Bracebridge Hall.*
1823 Scott, Walter. *Peveril of the Peak.*
1824 Edgeworth, Maria. *Harry and Lucy.*
1824 Irving, Washington. *Tales of a Traveller.*
1824 Scott, Walter. *Redgauntlet.*
1824 Cooper, J. Fenimore. *Lionel Lincoln.*
1825 Scott, Walter. *The Talisman.*
1827 Sigourney, Mrs. Lydia H. *Poems.*
1827 Sedgwick, Catharine M. *Hope Leslie.*
1828 Croly, George. *Salathiel.*
1828 Bulwer-Lytton, Edward. *Pelham.*
1829 Irving, Washington. *The Conquest of Granada.*
1829 Hale, Sarah Josepha. *Sketches of American Character.*
1830 James, G. P. R. *Richelieu.*
1830 Bulwer-Lytton, Edward. *Paul Clifford.*
1831 Paulding, James Kirke. *The Dutchman's Fireside.*

1832 Bulwer-Lytton, Edward. *Eugene Aram.*

1832 Thatcher, Benjamin Bussey. *Indian Biography.*

1833 Sigourney, Mrs. Lydia H. *Letters to Young Ladies.*

1833 Crockett, David. *Autobiography.*

1833 Bourne, George. *Lorette.*

1833 James, G. P. R. *Mary of Burgundy.*

1833 Flint, Timothy. *Daniel Boone.*

1833 Smith, Seba. *Life and Writings of Major Jack Downing.*

1834 Bancroft, George. *History of the United States.*

1834 Davis, Charles Augustus. *Letters of J. Downing, Major.*

1834 Sigourney, Mrs. Lydia H. *Sketches.*

1835 Crockett, David. *Life of Martin Van Buren.*

1835 Wordsworth, William. *Poems.*

1835 Fay, Theodore S. *Norman Leslie.*

1835 Scott, Michael. *Tom Cringle's Log.*

1835 Kennedy, Joseph P. *Horse-Shoe Robinson.*

1835 Longstreet, Augustus B. *Georgia Scenes.*

1835 Sedgwick, Catharine M. *Home.*

1835 Simms, William Gilmore. *The Yemassee.*

1836 Ingraham, J. H. *Lafitte: or The Pirate of the Gulf.*

1836 Hildreth, Richard. *The Slave.*

1836 Sedgwick, Catharine M. *The Poor Rich Man.*

1836 Marryat, Frederick. *Mr. Midshipman Easy.*

1837 Prescott, William H. *Ferdinand and Isabella.*

1837 Lover, Samuel. *Rory O'More.*

1837 Lee, Mrs. Hannah F. *Elinor Fulton.*

1837 Pardoe, Julia. *The City of the Sultan.*

1837 Hawthorne, Nathaniel. *Twice-Told Tales.*

1837 Marryat, Frederick. *Peter Simple.*

1837 Ware, William. *Zenobia.*

1838 Drake, Benjamin. *Life and Adventures of Black Hawk.*

1838 Neal, Joseph Clay. *Charcoal Sketches.*

1839 Lever, Charles. *Harry Lorrequer.*

1839 Longfellow, Henry W. *Hyperion.*

1839 Pardoe, Julia. *A Romance of the Harem.*

1840 Hoffman, Charles Fenno. *Greyslaer.*

1840 James, G. P. R. *King's Highway.*

1841 Gore, Mrs. Catherine. *Cecil, or the Adventures of a Coxcomb.*

1841 Lever, Charles. *Charles O'Malley.*

1841 Ainsworth, W. Harrison. *Old St. Paul's.*

1841 De Quincey, Thomas. *Confessions of an English Opium Eater.*

1841 Channing, William E. *Works.*

1842 Bulwer-Lytton, Edward. *Zanoni.*

1842 Arthur, T. S. *Temperance Tales; or, Six Nights With the Washingtonians.*

1842 Lover, Samuel. *Handy Andy.*

1842 Marryat, Frederick. *Masterman Ready.*

1842 Ainsworth, W. Harrison. *The Miser's Daughter.*

1843 Bulwer-Lytton, Edward. *The Last of the Barons.*

1843 Child, Lydia M. *Letters From New York.*

1843 Lever, Charles. *Jack Hinton.*

1843 Bryant, William Cullen. *Poetical Works.*

1843 Balzac, Honoré de. *Père Goriot.*

1843 Bremer, Fredrika. *The Neighbors.*

1844 Disraeli, Benjamin. *Coningsby.*

1844 Kendall, G. W. *Narrative of the Texan Santa Fé Expedition.*

1844 Simms, William Gilmore. *Life of Francis Marion.*

1845 Willis, Nathaniel P. *Dashes at Life.*

1846 Hawthorne, Nathaniel. *Mosses from an Old Manse.*

1846 Melville, Herman. *Typee.*

1847 Melville, Herman. *Omoo.*

1847 Headley, Joel T. *The Sacred Mountains.*

1847 Prescott, W. H. *Conquest of Peru.*

1847 Montgomery, H. *Life of Zachary Taylor.*

1848 Judson, Mrs. Emily. *Alderbrook.*

1848 Bulwer-Lytton, Edward. *Harold.*

1848 Lowell, James Russell. *The Biglow Papers.*

1848 Lowell, James Russell. *The Vision of Sir Launfal.*

1848 Taylor, Bayard. *Views Afoot.*

1849 Kingsley, Charles. *Alton Locke.*

1849 Mayo, William S. *Kaloolah.*

1849 Mulock, Dinah Maria. *The Ogilvies.*

1849 Parkman, Francis. *The Oregon Trail.*

1849 Dumas, Alexandre. *The Man in the Iron Mask.*

1850 Mayo, William S. *The Berber.*

1850 Hentz, Caroline Lee. *Linda.*

1850 Bulwer-Lytton, Edward. *The Caxtons.*

1850 Kimball, Richard B. *St. Leger.*

1850 Browning, Elizabeth Barrett. *Poems.*

1850 Foster, G. G. *New York by Gas-Light.*

1851 Mitchell, Donald G. *Dream-Life.*

1852 Thackeray, William M. *Henry Esmond.*

1852 Warner, Susan. *Queechy.*

1852 Reade, Charles. *Peg Woffington.*

1852 Bailey, Philip James. *Festus.*

1853 Kingsley, Charles. *Hypatia.*

1853 Creasy, E. S. *Fifteen Decisive Battles of the World.*
1853 Baldwin, Joseph G. *Flush Times in Alabama.*
1853 Gaskell, Mrs. Elizabeth. *Cranford.*
1853 Parton, Sarah P. Willis. *Fern Leaves.*
1853 Harland, Marion. *Alone.*
1853 Yonge, Charlotte. *The Heir of Redcliffe.*
1854 James, G. P. R. *Ticonderoga.*
1854 Robinson, Solon. *Hot Corn.*
1854 Dickens, Charles. *A Child's History of England.*
1854 Stephens, Mrs. Ann S. *Fashion and Famine.*
1854 Southworth, Mrs. E. D. E. N. *The Missing Bride.*
1855 Whitcher, Miriam Berry. *The Widow Bedott Papers.*
1855 Derby, George H. *Phoenixiana.*
1855 Stephens, Mrs. Ann S. *The Old Homestead.*
1855-59 Irving, Washington. *Life of Washington.*
1855 Kingsley, Charles. *Westward Ho!*
1856 Cobb, Sylvanus, Jr. *The Gun-Maker of Moscow.*
1856 Kane, Elisha Kent. *Arctic Explorations.*
1856 Curtis, George William. *Prue and I.*
1856 Reade, Charles. *Never Too Late to Mend.*
1856 McIntosh, Maria J. *Violet.*
1857 Headley, Joel T. *Washington and His Generals.*
1857 Holmes, Mary J. *Meadowbrook.*
1857 Lawrence, George A. *Guy Livingstone.*
1857 Helper, H. R. *The Impending Crisis.*
1858 Holland, Josiah G. *Timothy Titcomb's Letters to Young People.*
1858 Holland, Josiah G. *Bitter Sweet.*
1858 Holmes, Oliver Wendell. *The Autocrat of the Breakfast Table.*
1859 Michelet, Jules. *L'Amour.*
1860 Eliot, George. *The Mill on the Floss.*
1860 Smiles, Samuel. *Self-Help.*
1860 Ingraham, J. H. *The Throne of David.*
1860 Darwin, Charles. *Origin of Species.*
1860 Michelet, Jules. *La Femme.*
1860 Southworth, Mrs. E. D. E. N. *The Haunted Homestead.*
1860 Holmes, Oliver Wendell. *Elsie Venner.*
1860 Collins, Wilkie. *The Woman in White.*
1860 Dickens, Charles. *The Uncommercial Traveller.*
1861 du Chaillu, Paul B. *Explorations and Adventures in Equatorial Africa.*
1861 Palgrave, F. T. *Golden Treasury.*
1861 Holmes, O. W. *Poems.*
1861 Victor, Metta V. *Maum Guinea.*
1861 Hughes, Thomas. *Tom Brown at Oxford.*

1861 Moore, Frank. *The Rebellion Record.*
1862 Thackeray, William M. *The Adventures of Philip.*
1862 Le Fanu, J. Sheridan. *Uncle Silas.*
1862 Browne, Charles F. *Artemus Ward: His Book.*
1862 Saunders, John. *Abel Drake's Wife.*
1862 Gilmore, James R. *Among the Pines.*
1862 Collins, Wilkie. *No Name.*
1863 Eliot, George. *Romola.*
1863 Reade, Charles. *Hard Cash.*
1863-64 Headley, Joel T. *The Great Rebellion.*
1863-65 Oliphant, Mrs. M. O. W. *The Chronicles of Carlingford.*
1863-66 Abbott, J. S. C. *The Civil War in America.*
1863 Holmes, Mary J. *Marian Grey.*
1863 Charles, Elizabeth R. *Chronicles of the Schönberg-Cotta Family.*
1864 Edwards, Amelia B. *Barbara's History.*
1864 Holmes, Mary J. *Ethelyn's Mistake.*
1864 Trowbridge, John T. *Cudjo's Cave.*
1864 Yates, Edmund. *Broken to Harness.*
1864 Locke, David Ross. *The Nasby Papers.*
1865 Ebers, Georg. *The Egyptian Princess.*
1865 Shaw, Henry Wheeler. *Josh Billings: His Sayings.*
1865 Sophie May. *Dottie Dimple.*
1865 Thomas, Annie. *Denis Donne.*
1865 Nichols, George Ward. *The Story of the Great March.*
1865 Ingelow, Jean. *Poems.*
1865 *Harper's Pictorial History of the Civil War.*
1865 Seeley, John Robert. *Ecce Homo.*
1866 Greeley, Horace. *The American Conflict.*
1866 Collins, Wilkie. *Armadale.*
1866 Eliot, George. *Felix Holt.*
1866 Hugo, Victor. *Toilers of the Sea.*
1867 Trollope, Anthony. *The Last Chronicle of Barset.*
1867 Richardson, A. D. *Beyond the Mississippi.*
1867 Farjeon, B. L. *Grif.*
1867 Gaboriau, Emile. *File No. 113.*
1867 Finley, Martha. *Elsie Dinsmore.*
1867 Holland, Josiah G. *Kathrina.*
1868 Beecher, Henry Ward. *Norwood.*
1868 Ward, Elizabeth Stuart Phelps. *The Gates Ajar.*
1868 Yates, Edmund. *The Black Sheep.*
1868 Smith, Matthew Hale. *Sunshine and Shadow in New York.*
1869 Alger, Horatio, Jr. *Fame and Fortune.*
1869 Holmes, Mary J. *Darkness and Daylight.*

1869 Southworth, Mrs. E. D. E. N. *Tried for Her Life.*

1869 Reade, Charles. *Foul Play.*

1869 Aldrich, Thomas Bailey. *The Story of a Bad Boy.*

1869 Hugo, Victor. *The Man Who Laughs.*

1869 Trollope, Anthony. *Phineas Finn.*

1869 Gaboriau, Emile. *M. Lecocq.*

1870 Alger, Horatio, Jr. *Luck and Pluck.*

1870 Disraeli, Benjamin. *Lothair.*

1870 Collins, Wilkie. *Man and Wife.*

1870 Reade, Charles. *Put Yourself in His Place.*

1870 Dickens, Charles. *The Mystery of Edwin Drood.*

1870 Verne, Jules. *The Mysterious Island.*

1870 Broughton, Rhoda. *Red As a Rose Is She.*

1871 Alger, Horatio, Jr. *Tattered Tom.*

1871 Smiles, Samuel. *Character.*

1871 Jenkins, Edward. *Ginx's Baby.*

1871 Black, William. *A Daughter of Heth.*

1871 Trowbridge, John T. *Jack Hazard and His Fortunes.*

1871 Bryant, William Cullen, ed. *Library of Poetry and Song.*

1872 Twain, Mark. *Roughing It.*

1872 Eliot, George. *Middlemarch.*

1872-74 Forster, John. *Life of Dickens.*

1873 Seward, William H. *Travels Around the World.*

1873 Guizot, F. G. P. *History of France.*

1873 Hemans, Mrs. Felicia D. *Poetical Works.*

1873 Trollope, Anthony. *The Eustace Diamonds.*

1873 Carleton, Will. *Farm Ballads.*

1874 Black, William. *A Princess of Thule.*

1874 Farrar, F. W. *Life of Christ.*

1874 Hardy, Thomas. *Far From the Madding Crowd.*

1875 Alcott, Louisa M. *Eight Cousins.*

1875 Holland, Josiah G. *Sevenoaks.*

1875 M'Carthy, Justin. *Dear Lady Disdain.*

1875 Reid, Christian. *Land of the Sky.*

1875 Roe, E. P. *From Jest to Earnest.*

1875 Smiles, Samuel. *Thrift.*

1876 Eliot, George. *Daniel Deronda.*

1876 Verne, Jules. *Michael Strogoff.*

1876 Young, Ann Eliza. *Wife No. 19.*

1877 Geikie, J. Cunningham. *Life and Words of Christ.*

1878 Fothergill, Jessie. *First Violin.*

1878 Hardy, Thomas. *The Return of the Native.*

1878 Stanley, Henry M. *In Darkest Africa.*

1879 Duchess, The. *Airy, Fairy Lilian.*
1879 Sprague, Mary A. *An Earnest Trifler.*
1880 M'Carthy, Justin. *History of Our Own Times.*
1880 Ouida. *Moths.*
1880 Smiles, Samuel. *Duty.*
1880 Tourgée, Albion W. *A Fool's Errand.*
1881 Greene, Sarah Pratt. *Cape Cod Folks.*
1882 Crawford, F. Marion. *Mr. Isaacs.*
1882 Howells, William Dean. *A Modern Instance.*
1882 Wilcox, Ella Wheeler. *Maurine.*
1883 Wilcox, Ella Wheeler. *Poems of Passion.*
1883 Peck, George W. *Peck's Bad Boy and His Pa.*
1883 Crawford, F. Marion. *Dr. Claudius.*
1883 Broughton, Rhoda. *Belinda.*
1884 Jackson, Helen Hunt. *Ramona.*
1884 Hay, John. *The Breadwinners.*
1884 Conway, Hugh. *Called Back.*
1885 Howells, William Dean. *The Rise of Silas Lapham.*
1885 Roe, E. P. *Driven Back to Eden.*
1885 Strong, Josiah. *Our Country.*
1886 Stevenson, R. L. *Kidnapped.*
1886 Barr, Amelia E. *A Bow of Orange Ribbon.*
1886 Alcott, Louisa M. *Jo's Boys.*
1886 Smith, Uriah. *The Marvel of Nations.*
1886 Tuttiet, Mary G. *The Silence of Dean Maitland.*
1887 Holley, Marietta. *Samantha at Saratoga.*
1887 Cox, Palmer. *The Brownies, Their Book.*
1888 Deland, Margaret. *John Ward, Preacher.*
1888 Rives, Amélie. *The Quick or the Dead?*
1889 Gunter, A. C. *Mr. Potter of Texas.*
1889 Corelli, Marie. *Ardath.*
1889 Kipling, Rudyard. *Soldiers Three.*
1889 Lyall, Edna. *A Hardy Norseman.*
1889 Twain, Mark. *A Connecticut Yankee in King Arthur's Court.*
1889 Marx, Karl. *Capital.*
1890 Caine, Hall. *The Bondman.*
1890 Jerome, Jerome K. *Three Men in a Boat.*
1891 du Maurier, George. *Peter Ibbetson.*
1892 Crawford, F. Marion. *Don Orsino.*
1892 Hardy, Thomas. *Tess of the D'Urbervilles.*
1892 Ward, Mrs. Humphry. *The History of David Grieve.*
1893 Crockett, S. R. *The Stickit Minister.*
1893 Wallace, Lew. *The Prince of India.*

1894 Caine, Hall. *The Manxman.*

1894 Weyman, Stanley J. *Under the Red Robe.*

1894 Ford, Paul Leicester. *The Honorable Peter Sterling.*

1894-95 Kipling, Rudyard. *The Jungle Books.*

1894 Harraden, Beatrice. *Ships That Pass in the Night.*

1895 Nordau, Max. *Degeneration.*

1895 Corelli, Marie. *The Sorrows of Satan.*

1896 Parker, Gilbert. *The Seats of the Mighty.*

1896 Weyman, Stanley J. *The Red Cockade.*

1896 Johnston, Annie Fellows. *The Little Colonel.*

1897 Trine, Ralph Waldo. *In Tune With the Infinite.*

1897 Allen, James Lane. *The Choir Invisible.*

1897 Caine, Hall. *The Christian.*

1897 Davis, Richard Harding. *Soldiers of Fortune.*

1897 Kipling, Rudyard. *Captains Courageous.*

1898 Mitchell, S. Weir. *Hugh Wynne, Free Quaker.*

1898 Smith, F. Hopkinson. *Caleb West.*

1898 Ollivant, Alfred. *Bob, Son of Battle.*

1898 Major, Charles. *When Knighthood Was in Flower.*

1898 von Arnim, Countess. *Elizabeth and Her German Garden.*

1899 Kipling, Rudyard. *The Day's Work.*

1899 Tarkington, Booth. *The Gentleman from Indiana.*

1900 Baum, L. Frank. *The Wonderful Wizard of Oz.*

1900 Corelli, Marie. *The Master Christian.*

1900 Crawford, F. Marion. *In the Palace of the King.*

1900 Johnston, Mary. *To Have and to Hold.*

1901 Parker, Gilbert. *The Right of Way.*

1901 Thompson, Maurice. *Alice of Old Vincennes.*

1901 Wagner, Charles. *The Simple Life.*

1902 Atherton, Gertrude. *The Conqueror.*

1902 Kipling, Rudyard. *Just-So Stories.*

1902 Major, Charles. *Dorothy Vernon.*

1902 Reed, Myrtle. *Lavender and Old Lace.*

1903 McCutcheon, George Barr. *Brewster's Millions.*

1903 Ward, Mrs. Humphry. *Lady Rose's Daughter.*

1903 Wright, Harold Bell. *That Printer of Udell's.*

1904 Churchill, Winston. *The Crossing.*

1904 Gordon, S. D. *Quiet Talks on Power.*

1904 Henry, O. *Cabbages and Kings.*

1904 McCutcheon, George Barr. *Beverly of Graustark.*

1905 Beach, Rex. *The Spoilers.*

1905 Hichens, Robert. *The Garden of Allah.*

1905 Ward, Mrs. Humphry. *The Marriage of William Ashe.*

1906 Churchill, Winston. *Coniston.*
1906 Henry, O. *The Four Million.*
1906 Little, Frances. *The Lady of the Decoration.*
1906 Sinclair, Upton. *The Jungle.*
1907 Henry, O. *The Trimmed Lamp.*
1907 Parker, Gilbert. *The Weavers.*
1908 Beach, Rex. *The Barrier.*
1908 Churchill, Winston. *Mr. Crewe's Career.*
1908 Grey, Zane. *The Last of the Plainsmen.*
1909 Henry, O. *Options.*
1909 King, Basil. *The Inner Shrine.*
1910 Churchill, Winston. *A Modern Chronicle.*
1910 Henry, O. *Whirligigs.*
1911 Farnol, Jeffery. *The Broad Highway.*
1911 Harrison, Henry Sydnor. *Queed.*
1911 Kester, Vaughan. *The Prodigal Judge.*
1912 King, Basil. *The Street Called Straight.*
1912 Webster, Jean. *Daddy-Long-Legs.*
1912 Wright, Harold Bell. *Their Yesterdays.*
1913 Churchill, Winston. *The Inside of the Cup.*
1913 Harrison, Henry Sydnor. *V. V.'s Eyes.*
1915 Maugham, Somerset. *Of Human Bondage.*
1915 Porter, Eleanor H. *Pollyanna Grows Up.*
1915 Rinehart, Mary Roberts. *"K".*
1915 Tarkington, Booth. *The Turmoil.*
1916 Porter, Eleanor H. *Just David.*
1916 Tarkington, Booth. *Seventeen.*
1916 Wells, H. G. *Mr. Britling Sees It Through.*
1917 Empey, Arthur Guy. *Over the Top.*
1918 Adams, Henry. *The Education of Henry Adams.*
1918 Blasco Ibáñez, Vicente. *The Four Horsemen of the Apocalypse.*
1918 Streeter, Edward. *Dere Mable.*
1919 O'Brien, Frederick. *White Shadows in the South Seas.*
1919 Wright, Harold Bell. *The Re-Creation of Brian Kent.*
1920 Bok, E. W. *The Americanization of Edward Bok.*
1920 Gibbs, Philip. *Now It Can Be Told.*
1920 Grey, Zane. *The Man of the Forest.*
1920 Lewis, Sinclair. *Main Street.*
1921 Canfield, Dorothy. *The Brimming Cup.*
1921 Grey, Zane. *The Mysterious Rider.*
1921 Hutchinson, A. S. M. *If Winter Comes.*
1921 Sabatini, Rafael. *Scaramouche.*
1921 van Loon, Hendrik Willem. *The Story of Mankind.*

1921 Wharton, Edith. *The Age of Innocence.*

1922 Ford, Henry. *My Life and Work.*

1922 Hough, Emerson. *The Covered Wagon.*

1922 Lewis, Sinclair. *Babbitt.*

1922 Robinson, James Harvey. *The Mind in the Making.*

1923 Atherton, Gertrude. *Black Oxen.*

1923 Papini, Giovanni. *Life of Christ.*

1923 Sabatini, Rafael. *The Sea Hawk.*

1924 Ferber, Edna. *So Big.*

1924 Ludwig, Emil. *Napoleon.*

1924 Milne, A. A. *When We Were Very Young.*

1924 Sedgwick, Anne Douglas. *The Little French Girl.*

1925 Barton, Bruce. *The Man Nobody Knows.*

1925 Erskine, John. *The Private Life of Helen of Troy.*

1925 Halliburton, Richard. *The Royal Road to Romance.*

1925 Jones, E. Stanley. *Christ of the Indian Road.*

1925 Kennedy, Margaret. *The Constant Nymph.*

1925 Loos, Anita. *Gentlemen Prefer Blondes.*

1925 Wren, Christopher. *Beau Geste.*

1926 Biggers, Earl Derr. *The Chinese Parrot.*

1926 Christie, Agatha. *The Murder of Roger Ackroyd.*

1926 Deeping, Warwick. *Sorrell & Son.*

1926 de Kruif, Paul. *Microbe Hunters.*

1927 Hart, Frances Noyes. *The Bellamy Trial.*

1927 Horn, A. A., and Lewis, Ethelreda. *Trader Horn.*

1927 Lewis, Sinclair. *Elmer Gantry.*

1927 Lindbergh, Charles. *We.*

1927 Wilder, Thornton. *The Bridge of San Luis Rey.*

1927 VanDine, S. S. *The Canary Murder Case.*

1928 Biggers, Earl Derr. *Behind That Curtain.*

1928 Delmar, Viña. *Bad Girl.*

1928 Dimnet, Ernest. *The Art of Thinking.*

1929 Hammett, Dashiell. *Red Harvest.*

1929 Munthe, Axel. *The Story of San Michele.*

1929 Remarque, Erich Maria. *All Quiet on the Western Front.*

1929 VanDine, S. S. *The Bishop Murder Case.*

1930 Bentley, E. C. *Trent's Last Case.*

1930 Biggers, Earl Derr. *Charlie Chan Carries On.*

1930 Brand, Max. *Destry Rides Again.*

1930 Ferber, Edna. *Cimarron.*

1930 Hammett, Dashiell. *The Maltese Falcon.*

1930 Means, Gaston, and Thacker, M. D. *The Strange Death of President Harding.*

1930 Queen, Ellery. *The French Powder Mystery.*
1931 Charteris, Leslie. *Enter the Saint.*
1931 Hammett, Dashiell. *The Glass Key.*
1932 Christie, Agatha. *Peril at End House.*
1932 Pitkin, W. B. *Life Begins at Forty.*
1933 Caldwell, Erskine. *God's Little Acre.*
1933 Gardner, Erle Stanley. *The Case of the Velvet Claws.*
1933 Gardner, Erle Stanley. *The Case of the Lucky Legs.*
1934 Dickens, Charles. *The Life of Our Lord.*
1934 Hilton, James. *Goodbye, Mr. Chips.*
1934 Queen, Ellery. *The Adventures of Ellery Queen.*
1934 Woollcott, Alexander. *While Rome Burns.*
1935 Day, Clarence. *Life With Father.*
1935 Douglas, Lloyd C. *Green Light.*
1935 Gardner, Erle Stanley. *The Case of the Caretaker's Cat.*
1935 Kains, Maurice G. *Five Acres and Independence.*
1935 Lindbergh, Anne. *North to the Orient.*
1935 O'Brien, Patrick J. *Will Rogers.*
1935 Queen, Ellery. *The Spanish Cape Mystery.*
1936 Edmonds, W. D. *Drums Along the Mohawk.*
1936 Heiser, Victor. *An American Doctor's Odyssey.*
1936 Latimer, Jonathan. *Lady in the Morgue.*
1936 Stout, Rex. *The Rubber Band.*
1937 Cronin, A. J. *The Citadel.*
1937 Curie, Eve. *Madame Curie.*
1937 Roberts, Kenneth. *Northwest Passage.*
1937 van Loon, Hendrik Willem. *The Arts.*
1938 du Maurier, Daphne. *Rebecca.*
1938 Field, Rachel. *All This, and Heaven Too.*
1938 Halsey, Margaret. *With Malice Toward Some.*
1938 Hertzler, A. E. *The Horse and Buggy Doctor.*
1938 Lin Yutang. *The Importance of Living.*
1938 McKenney, Ruth. *My Sister Eileen.*
1938 Rawlings, Marjorie Kinnan. *The Yearling.*
1939 Ambler, Eric. *Coffin for Dimitrios.*
1939 Asch, Sholem. *The Nazarene.*
1939 Charteris, Leslie. *The Happy Highwayman.*
1939 Christie, Agatha. *Easy to Kill.*
1939 Morley, Christopher. *Kitty Foyle.*
1939 Vance, Ethel. *Escape.*
1939 van Paassen, Pierre. *Days of Our Years.*
1940 Ambler, Eric. *Journey Into Fear.*
1940 Chandler, Raymond. *Farewell My Lovely.*

1940 Christie, Agatha. *And Then There Were None.*
1940 Hemingway, Ernest. *For Whom the Bell Tolls.*
1940 Knight, Eric. *Lassie-Come-Home.*
1940 Johnson, Osa. *I Married Adventure.*
1940 Llewellyn, Richard. *How Green Was My Valley.*
1940 Roberts, Kenneth. *Oliver Wiswell.*
1941 Christie, Agatha. *The Patriotic Murders.*
1941 Cronin, A. J. *The Keys of the Kingdom.*
1941 Gunther, John. *Inside Latin America.*
1941 Hilton, James. *Random Harvest.*
1941 MacInnes, Helen. *Above Suspicion.*
1941 Miller, Alice Duer. *The White Cliffs of Dover.*
1941 Miller, Douglas. *You Can't Do Business With Hitler.*
1941 O'Hara, Mary. *My Friend Flicka.*
1941 Shirer, William L. *Berlin Diary.*
1941 Valtin, Jan. *Out of the Night.*
1941 Williams, Ben Ames. *Strange Woman.*
1942 *Bedside Esquire.*
1942 Buck, Pearl S. *Dragon Seed.*
1942 Davenport, Marcia. *The Valley of Decision.*
1942 Runyon, Damon. *Damon Runyon Favorites.*
1942 Skinner, Cornelia Otis, and Kimbrough, Emily. *Our Hearts Were Young and Gay.*
1942 Steen, Marguerite. *The Sun Is My Undoing.*
1942 Steinbeck, John. *The Moon Is Down.*
1942 Werfel, Franz. *The Song of Bernadette.*
1943 Asch, Sholem. *The Apostle.*
1943 Carlson, John Roy. *Under Cover.*
1943 Franken, Rose. *Claudia.*
1943 Lippmann, Walter. *U. S. Foreign Policy.*
1943 Marquand, John P. *So Little Time.*
1943 Marshall, Rosamond. *Kitty.*
1943 Saroyan, William. *The Human Comedy.*
1943 Tregaskis, Richard. *Guadalcanal Diary.*
1944 Bowen, Catherine Drinker. *A Yankee From Olympus.*
1944 Cronin, A. J. *The Green Years.*
1944 Hersey, John. *A Bell for Adano.*
1944 Seton, Anya. *Dragonwyck.*
1944 Smith, Lillian. *Strange Fruit.*
1944 Welles, Sumner. *The Time for Decision.*
1944 Williams, Ben Ames. *Leave Her to Heaven.*
1945 Cerf, Bennett, ed. *Try and Stop Me.*
1945 Hilton, James. *So Well Remembered.*

1945 Langley, Adria Locke. *A Lion Is in the Streets.*
1945 Lewis, Sinclair. *Cass Timberlane.*
1945 Ullman, James Ramsey. *The White Tower.*
1945 Wright, Richard. *Black Boy.*

APPENDIX C. ANNUAL BEST SELLERS IN THE BOOK STORES

Alice Payne Hackett's *Fifty Years of Best Sellers, 1895-1945,* presents a list of the ten top books based on compilations of the monthly *Bookman* lists and *Publishers' Weekly's* résumés, from 1895 to 1945, with a brief and concise comment for each year.

Based on "Bookman" Records

1895 Maclaren, Ian. *Beside the Bonnie Brier Bush.*
1896 Parker, Gilbert. *The Seats of the Mighty.*
1897 Sienkiewicz, Henryk. *Quo Vadis.*
1898 Smith, F. Hopkinson. *Caleb West.*
1899 Westcott, Edward N. *David Harum.*
1900 Johnston, Mary. *To Have and to Hold.*
1901 Churchill, Winston. *The Crisis.*
1902 Wister, Owen. *The Virginian.*
1903 Ward, Mrs. Humphry. *Lady Rose's Daughter.*
1904 Churchill, Winston. *The Crossing.*
1905 Ward, Mrs. Humphry. *The Marriage of William Ashe.*
1906 Churchill, Winston. *Coniston.*
1907 Little, Frances. *The Lady of the Decoration.*
1908 Churchill, Winston. *Mr. Crewe's Career.*
1909 King, Basil. *The Inner Shrine.*
1910 Barclay, Florence. *The Rosary.*
1911 Farnol, Jeffery. *The Broad Highway.*
1912 Porter, Gene Stratton. *The Harvester.*
1913 Churchill, Winston. *The Inside of the Cup.*
1914 Wright, Harold Bell. *The Eyes of the World.*
1915 Tarkington, Booth. *The Turmoil.*
1916 Tarkington, Booth. *Seventeen.*
1917 Wells, H. G. *Mr. Britling Sees It Through.*

Based on "Books of the Month" Records

1918 Fiction: Grey, Zane. *The U. P. Trail.*
       Non-fiction: Service, Robert W. *Rhymes of a Red Cross Man.*
1919 Fiction: Blasco Ibáñez, V. *The Four Horsemen of the Apocalypse.*
       Non-fiction: Adams, Henry. *The Education of Henry Adams.*

1920 Fiction: Grey, Zane. *The Man of the Forest*.
Non-fiction: Gibbs, Philip. *Now It Can Be Told*.

1921 Fiction: Lewis, Sinclair. *Main Street*.
Non-fiction: Wells, H. G. *The Outline of History*.

1922 Fiction: Hutchinson, A. S. M. *If Winter Comes*.
Non-fiction: Wells, H. G. *The Outline of History*.

1923 Fiction: Atherton, Gertrude. *Black Oxen*.
Non-fiction: Post, Emily. *Etiquette*.

1924 Fiction: Ferber, Edna. *So Big*.
Non-fiction: Peters, Lulu Hunt. *Diet and Health*.

1925 Fiction: Gibbs, A. Hamilton. *Soundings*.
Non-fiction: Peters, Lulu Hunt. *Diet and Health*.

1926 Fiction: Erskine, John. *The Private Life of Helen of Troy*.
Non-fiction: Barton, Bruce. *The Man Nobody Knows*.

1927 Fiction: Lewis, Sinclair. *Elmer Gantry*.
Non-fiction: Durant, William. *The Story of Philosophy*.

1928 Fiction: Wilder, Thornton. *The Bridge of San Luis Rey*.
Non-fiction: Maurois, André. *Disraeli*.

1929 Fiction: Remarque, Erich Maria. *All Quiet on the Western Front*.
Non-fiction: Dimnet, Ernest. *The Art of Thinking*.

1930 Fiction: Ferber, Edna. *Cimarron*.
Non-fiction: Munthe, Axel. *The Story of San Michele*.

1931 Fiction: Buck, Pearl S. *The Good Earth*.
Non-fiction: Grand Duchess Marie. *The Education of a Princess*.

1932 Fiction: Buck, Pearl S. *The Good Earth*.
Non-fiction: Adams, James Truslow. *The Epic of America*.

Based on "Publishers' Weekly" Records

1933 Fiction: Allen, Hervey. *Anthony Adverse*.
Non-fiction: Pitkin, W. B. *Life Begins at Forty*.

1934 Fiction: Allen, Hervey. *Anthony Adverse*.
Non-fiction: Woollcott, Alexander. *While Rome Burns*.

1935 Fiction: Douglas, Lloyd C. *Green Light*.
Non-fiction: Lindbergh, Anne. *North to the Orient*.

1936 Fiction: Mitchell, Margaret. *Gone With the Wind*.
Non-fiction: Carrel, Alexis. *Man, the Unknown*.

1937 Fiction: Mitchell, Margaret. *Gone With the Wind*.
Non-fiction: Carnegie, Dale. *How to Win Friends and Influence People*.

1938 Fiction: Rawlings, Marjorie Kinnan. *The Yearling*.
Non-fiction: Lin Yutang. *The Importance of Living*.

1939 Fiction: Steinbeck, John. *The Grapes of Wrath*.
Non-fiction: van Paassen, Pierre. *Days of Our Years*.

1940 Fiction: Llewellyn, Richard. *How Green Was My Valley*.
      Non-fiction: Johnson, Osa. *I Married Adventure*.
1941 Fiction: Cronin, A. J. *The Keys of the Kingdom*.
      Non-fiction: Shirer, William L. *Berlin Diary*.
1942 Fiction: Werfel, Franz. *The Song of Bernadette*.
      Non-fiction: Hargrove, Marion. *See Here, Private Hargrove*.
1943 Fiction: Douglas, Lloyd C. *The Robe*.
      Non-fiction: Willkie, Wendell L. *One World*.
1944 Fiction: Smith, Lillian. *Strange Fruit*.
      Non-fiction: Hope, Bob. *I Never Left Home*.
1945 Fiction: Winsor, Kathleen. *Forever Amber*.
      Non-fiction: Pyle, Ernie. *Brave Men*.

INDEX